Sea Kayaker's
MORE
DEEP TROUBLE

INTERNATIONAL MARINE / McGRAW-HILL EDUCATION
Camden, Maine ▪ New York ▪ Chicago ▪ San Francisco
Lisbon ▪ London ▪ Madrid ▪ Mexico City ▪ Milan ▪ New Delhi
San Juan ▪ Seoul ▪ Singapore ▪ Sydney ▪ Toronto

Mc
Graw
Hill
Education

Sea Kayaker's MORE DEEP TROUBLE

More True Stories and Their Lessons from *Sea Kayaker* Magazine

Edited by

CHRISTOPHER CUNNINGHAM

Sea Kayaker Magazine

1 2 3 4 5 6 7 8 9 10 11 12 13 14 15 FGR/FGR 1 9 8 7 6 5 4 3
ISBN 978-0-07-177009-5
MHID 0-07-177009-7
Also available as a full-color ebook: E ISBN 0-07-177985-X.

Library of Congress Cataloging-in-Publication Data is available from the Library of Congress.

McGraw-Hill Education books are available at special quantity discounts to use as premiums and sales promotions or for use in corporate training programs. To contact a representative, please e-mail us at bulksales@mcgraw-hill.com.

Questions regarding the content of this book should be addressed to
www.internationalmarine.com

Questions regarding the ordering of this book should be addressed to
McGraw-Hill Education
Customer Service Department
P.O. Box 547
Blacklick, OH 43004
Retail customers: 1-800-262-4729
Bookstores: 1-800-722-4726

If you enjoyed this title, you might also enjoy *Deep Trouble*/Gronseth. Contact your favorite bookstore.

Contents

Acknowledgments

I am especially grateful to all of those kayakers whose mishaps brought them first to *Sea Kayaker* magazine and then again to these pages. It is as easy for them as it is for us to look back and see what they could have done differently to avoid the trouble they found themselves in. These stories aren't news reports. Most come from the people who suffered the consequences of their mistakes, yet they still have the compassion for the rest of us to share their stories as cautionary tales for the benefit of other kayakers. Like you and me, they didn't intend or expect to come to grief. While it is easy to avoid shortcomings in equipment or lapses in judgment, it is not so easy to escape being human. We all make mistakes.

Thanks to Molly Mulhern of International Marine for patience and persistence through the years between her suggesting we do this book and my delivering it to her. A special thanks also goes to Kat Wertzler, the assistant editor at *Sea Kayaker*. She was instrumental in gathering and formatting materials for the book and keeping track of all of the contributors. Without her considerable skills and cheerful can-do attitude, this book would not have happened.

Preface

Christopher Cunningham

Following the publication of *Deep Trouble* in 1997 I heard from many kayakers who had read the book and said it put them on a path to safer paddling practices. Several of those who found the book valuable bought five or six copies at a time and handed them out to friends and acquaintances who were just getting into kayaking. *Deep Trouble* also had a profound effect on my own approach to kayaking. I was familiar with all of the stories in the book, having read them as articles in *Sea Kayaker*, and I took to heart much of the advice offered in the Lessons Learned. I credit those articles with many of the improvements I made to my skills and additional gear I now carry. Individually, those twenty-two stories put my focus on technique and equipment, but taken collectively in *Deep Trouble*, they revealed something more to me: insight into human nature. In *More Deep Trouble* we present twenty-nine more stories of incidents that have occurred since 1997.

When reading these stories, please keep in mind that they reflect the technology that was available at the time they were written. Electronic devices evolve rapidly, adding new capabilities and becoming more readily available with each passing year. In the years encompassed by *Deep Trouble*, handheld VHF radios went from being bulky, heavy, expensive, and easily damaged to now being compact enough to fit in a PFD pocket, submersible, and costing less than an average paddle. Satellite-linked distress-signal and messaging devices are also now practical and affordable. GPS, of course, has transformed navigation. While modern electronics have vastly improved our ability to communicate and convey information, the kayaking skills we acquire through education and practice remain central to paddling safely and the responsibility of every paddler.

Lapses in safe practices, shortcomings in equipment, and gaps in knowledge are often easily corrected. It's not as easy to escape being human. It may be natural for us to distance ourselves from those who've suffered misfortune. That's particularly easy to do when the kayakers in these stories have skills and training that fall short of our own. The last chapter in this book, however, comes to us from one of the strongest, most capable kayakers I know. Even the best of us can make mistakes that will seem, in retrospect, painfully evident and avoidable. I've added one of my own fiascos also to that last chapter. Recognizing my own lapses in judgment makes it much easier for me to be sympathetic to the kayakers—no matter what their abilities— whose mishaps appear in these pages and in *Sea Kayaker*.

The aim of *More Deep Trouble* is not to make kayakers more anxious. It is to make kayakers more aware. While the book's title may seem to emphasize trouble, what you'll come away with after reading these stories will make you not only a safer kayaker but also one more in touch with the land, sea, and sky. Be fully present, be safe, and enjoy the time you spend on the water.

Introduction
Ten Essentials for Sea Kayakers

Roger Schumann

For us air-breathing, warm-blooded, terrestrial mammals, taking to the water is inherently dangerous, and anytime we put out to sea—or lake or even local pond—we are out of our element and put our lives at risk. And while the odds may be small, some people even come to grief in backyard swimming pools or bathtubs.

Whether you're paddling a mighty ocean or a local lily pond, however, you can stack the odds in your favor. A few basic precautions can greatly increase your safety at sea. For sea kayakers, safety involves much more than simply gathering together a pile of the proper gear, although that is certainly important. So before discussing essential safety gear, let's start with a look at some of the essential knowledge—the "mental provisioning"—you need to be as safe as possible when kayaking.

While hypothermia may be the single greatest threat to paddlers' lives, the two main *causes* of most kayaking accidents are ignorance—not knowing what the dangers are or how to avoid them—and its close cousin, arrogance: knowing the risks but choosing to ignore them. So before you pack your boat, pack your mind with the following basic safety concepts.

1. Mental Provisioning for Safety

One of the best things to take kayaking with you is knowledge of common risks. You'll stand a better chance of avoiding trouble if you know what forms it usually takes. Because hypothermia is far and away the main ingredient in most kayaking fatalities, it makes sense that much of the safety gear listed in the following sections is intended to keep you warm when you fall in the water or provide you a way to quickly get out of the water and back into your boat.

1

Whatever the water temperature, offshore winds and currents can sweep you far from shore or into wave-pounded cliffs, shipping lanes, or lightning storms. Of course, you can simply paddle yourself into any of these hazards, as well.

It's important to have a thorough knowledge of established norms and safety protocols. For good reasons, certain safety standards, such as wearing a PFD (life vest) and dressing for immersion, are considered standard. The paddlers who get into trouble are generally those who are unaware of or ignore established standards. Hedge your bets by learning the standards and following them.

2. Capsize-Recovery Techniques

It's important to have a thorough knowledge of and ability to perform capsize-recovery techniques. Most instructors speak of "when" you capsize, not "if." Regular practice of basic recoveries such as the paddle-float reentry and the T-rescue will keep your skills sharp and increase your likelihood of being able to get back into your boat after an accidental capsize. However, swimming-pool practice is less likely to prepare you adequately for a real-life event. Find a safe shore (one with a sandy beach and an onshore wind) and a partner, and take the time to practice in rough water as well. As you master the basics, you further broaden your safety net by adding a few of the more advanced recovery techniques, such as rolling and the "cowboy scramble" reentry (see Chapter 4).

3. Gear Essentials

Now we're ready to talk about the gear and a few tips on its use.

Kayak with adequate flotation: The term "adequate flotation," as it pertains to sea kayaks, refers to having enough flotation in the bow and stern to float the kayak high enough for the paddler to climb back aboard in open water and bail it out. Generally, this flotation is provided in most modern kayaks by bulkheads and hatches. Float bags are sometimes used as well and, more rarely, sea socks. Open-top kayaks typically have integral flotation provided by the hull itself, which is hollow and can't be swamped unless there is a crack or other breach in the hull or if the hatches leak.

Whatever provides the flotation, it must be secure. A few ounces of leaked water in so-called "watertight" hatches is acceptable, but a few gallons is not; that much water moving around in the hull can significantly reduce the kayak's stability. If you use float bags—essential in kayaks without bulkheads—they must be fitted snugly enough to minimize how much water can enter the boat, and they must also be secured so they don't come floating out of the cockpit after a capsize. Some kayakers even like to back up their bulkhead compartments with float bags for a "belt and suspenders" approach to reliable flotation.

Some short recreational kayaks have watertight compartments in the ends, and while the flotation they provide might keep the empty boat afloat when swamped, it may not be enough to support a cockpit full of water *and* the paddler. Such a kayak is fine if all you intend to do is poke around near shore in an area where you'd feel comfortable swimming. But you're really pushing your luck if you take it onto open water. The only way to be sure if your kayak has adequate flotation to support you and a swamped cockpit is to practice recoveries—very close to shore at first—in order to find out. After a wet exit, your kayak should float high enough for you to reenter the cockpit and bail it out.

Paddle and a spare: In addition to using a primary paddle sturdy enough for my planned activity, I always take a spare. Well, I do now. I stopped carrying a spare after my first three years of paddling because I'd never used it. Then I snapped off a blade landing in surf. The 3-mile walk dragging my kayak down the beach back to my car gave me plenty of time to think about carrying a spare again.

There should be at least one spare paddle per group, but since paddlers in groups can become separated, carrying several spares per group makes good sense. Because I seem to have a special talent for breaking paddles (one every other year or so), I like to carry my own spare, a two-piece, take-apart paddle, securely fastened on deck.

Type III PFD or life vest: Not only is a personal flotation device (PFD) one of the most important pieces of safety gear, but the law requires having one aboard. However, while U.S. federal law requires all kayakers to *carry* a Coast Guard–approved PFD, it doesn't go so far as to require us to actually *wear* one (some state and local laws do). Accident reports are full of accounts of paddlers who thought that they would simply put on their PFD when the seas got rough. In reality—and as you will discover in several of these stories—many ended up in the water with the PFD still lashed securely under the deck bungees only to discover that it's very difficult if not impossible to don a PFD while you're in the drink. In addition to keeping you afloat, wearing a PFD keeps you warmer in cold water, not only from the extra insulation it provides but also by reducing the cooling that occurs when you tread water to stay afloat.

Modern, short-waist Type III PFDs with large armholes are very comfortable to paddle in, and PFDs with pockets are handy for providing easy access to everything from snack bars to sunblock and keep rescue flares and radios where you need them—on you.

Spray skirt: For closed-cockpit kayaks, spray skirts help keep your lower body warmer and keep water out of the cockpit. Novices may feel more comfortable with a nylon skirt that releases easily to help assure trouble-free wet exits during practice or an accidental capsize. In rougher conditions or surf, however, a snug-fitting neoprene skirt will stay on your cockpit much better than nylon. Whatever skirt you use, make sure you can release it with one hand. .

Paddle float: A paddle float attaches to one of the blades of your paddle to create an outrigger to stabilize your kayak as you climb back in. Some paddle floats use foam for buoyancy, while others are inflatable. The better inflatables have two large chambers: If you get a hole in one, you still have useful buoyancy in the other. Paddle floats are often stowed on deck, but UV rays can easily damage such gear. I stash mine in the cockpit behind my seat.

Your paddle float must be securely attached so that it doesn't float away after a capsize. I keep my paddle float tethered on a length of bungee cord just long enough to let me perform the reentry without there being so much slack that it gets tangled up. Some paddlers don't like leashing their paddle floats, but I've found that with a little practice, most of my students can quickly learn to use a leashed paddle float without getting tangled in it.

Pump: Once you're back in your boat after a capsize and wet exit, you need an efficient way to get the water out. The handheld pumps in common use seem to work fine, especially if you're rafted up with a partner. I stash mine under the front deck bungees with the handle end toward me, with a twist of the bungee wrapped around the handle in a "surf wrap" for extra security in rough seas. Some paddlers put their pump under the back deck bungees, but it is almost impossible to access it there except in the calmest conditions. Other paddlers like to attach their pumps inside the cockpit against the underside of the deck between their knees. This works well for keeping the pump out of the way, but it means that you have to open your spray skirt and expose yourself to swamping if you want to pump out a partner's boat in rough seas.

Another good option is to custom-fit your kayak with a built-in, hands-free pump (foot or electrical) or a deck-mounted pump system that you can operate with one hand. These are easier to use when you're on your own in rough seas. Any electric pump should be backed up with a manual pump in case the batteries fail.

4. Immersion Apparel

Dress for the water temperature, not the air. If the air is warm, you may get hot, but you can always splash yourself or practice a roll or a reentry to cool off. Standard issue for many kayakers in temperate water (approximately 50°F to 65°F) is a 3 mm Farmer John wetsuit, under a waterproof or waterproof/breathable paddling jacket. Depending on personal preference and water temperature, varying insulating layers under the jacket may be used. These layer garments are generally made of some type of wicking, synthetic fabric—fleece or neoprene—but never cotton. In cold water, you've probably heard it said: Cotton kills.

In warmer climates and water, neoprene wetsuits can be thinner and shorter. In Baja, Mexico, I often wear only 2 mm neoprene shorts and a lightweight, long-sleeve top, more for protection from the sun than for warmth. In chillier latitudes, when the water temperature is in the fifties or below, dry suits are the more common choice of experienced paddlers.

5. Spare Warm Clothes

In case you do end up in the water, carry a set of dry clothes to change into when you get to shore, either to be more comfortable or perhaps to prevent hypothermia. Even if you don't get wet, it's nice to have some extra dry clothes along. I find that most of my students become chilled not during recovery practice but later during lunch, sitting around in damp neoprene on a windy beach. During breaks on shore I peel my wetsuit down to my waist and put on a dry fleece top, windbreaker, and fleece hat and stay toasty on all but the chilliest days. When it's a bit colder, I put on a pair of wind pants over my wetsuit, which stops evaporative cooling. All of my extra clothing is stowed in a dry bag belowdecks to ensure it stays dry even if the hatch leaks.

6. Food and Water

Staying fed and hydrated not only keeps you warmer and happier but also keeps you safer. Food is fuel for the body, and water is essential to keep the body functioning efficiently and effectively. It often turns out that hypothermia victims are also dehydrated. Easy access to water and food is the key. I use a hydration pack on my PFD for hands-free drinking, which I find much easier in heavy seas, and I always stash several energy bars in the pockets of my PFD.

7. Towline and Knife

Among the most overlooked pieces of safety gear, a towline gives you options when you or another paddler becomes tired or hurt. Without one, if an offshore wind comes up and your paddling partner can't make it back to land, you either have to leave that paddler behind or stay and also get blown out to sea. There are a plethora of systems available, but I find that 30 feet of quarter-inch line on a waist belt works best for me, because it's easy to take the belt off and let another paddler take the load to let me recover. Longer or thicker line tends to be more difficult to repack. If it's shorter than 30 feet, you may risk having the towed kayak surf into your back in following seas.

A quick-release buckle on the waist belt is standard for safety, as is a knife (or trauma scissors) to cut the line in an emergency. The knife must be easily accessed, usually kept somewhere on your PFD. Sheath knives have the advantage of not needing to be opened for use. I use a folding knife designed to be opened with one hand so I don't have to let go of my paddle with my other hand.

8. Signaling Devices

The U.S. Coast Guard requires us to carry an audible signaling device. I keep a plastic whistle in a chest pocket on my PFD, on a lanyard just long enough to reach my mouth easily but short enough (less than 6 inches) to minimize the chance of entanglement. Even a footlong line dangling from a PFD can get tangled up in your deck rigging, spare paddle, or body parts during rescues.

Depending on where you're paddling, it is common to carry three types of signaling devices, all of which should be stored where they are accessible. Common devices include signal mirrors, handheld pencil flares, flare pistols, and smoke flares. Other valuable communication devices include an immersion-proof VHF marine radio for calling other boats, assuming you are within a line-of-sight range of about 2 to 5 miles, or the U.S. Coast Guard within 20 miles of the Rescue 21 communications system; a cell phone, assuming you have coverage in the area; or, for more remote locations, a satellite phone. DSC-equipped VHF radios will transmit identifying information and location coordinates with a push of a button. A personal locator beacon (PLB), emergency position-indicating radio beacon (EPIRB), or satellite messenger can send a distress signal and your location to rescue agencies via satellite (see the sidebar "EPIRB and PLB Recommendations" in Chapter 17).

9. First Aid, Repair, and Emergency Kits

When a paddler is injured or gear is damaged, it's important to have the means to take care of common problems. On day trips, in addition to a standard first-aid kit, I keep a small "ouch pouch" handy with bandages, tape, and ibuprofen to take care of common minor injuries. Of course, some first-aid training is very valuable, and a weekend-long Wilderness First Aid class is good minimum training for most kayakers to consider.

A few basic tools for boat repair, such as a multitool, also come in handy. And for emergency bivouacs, some fire starters and a space blanket can help you survive the night.

Depending on your paddling destination, any or all of the following miscellaneous items may be necessary as well: up-to-date weather report, tide and current tables, chart, map, compass, GPS, and bear rifle.

10. A Healthy Respect for the Sea

For me, showing respect for the sea means arriving at the shoreline prepared with my essential safety gear, even on those days when I'm certain that I won't need it. And most of the time, I don't. If you use common sense, odds are that you'll rarely, if ever, use any of it. But that doesn't mean you don't need to take it with you.

Think of the hundreds of times you've driven a car without needing a spare tire, safety belts, or air bags. You can certainly get around fine most of the time without these things. But on those rare occasions when you do need them, you really, really need them. It doesn't make any sense to tempt fate and the sea unnecessarily. Covering your bets with a little respect is so easy, and stacking the odds in your favor can be very simple.

1

Trust Your Skills, Not Your Kayak

George Gronseth

This story should serve as a wake-up call for individuals who believe they can sea kayak safely without practicing rescues or testing their skills and equipment. As these paddlers learned the hard way, a stable kayak can create a dangerous false sense of security. No matter how stable a kayak feels in calm water, when conditions are rough only the paddler's skill can keep a kayak from capsizing. And getting back into a swamped kayak that is rolling in waves is not as easy as the uninitiated may think.

It was a partly cloudy but otherwise nice spring day when Ralph and his friend Chris began paddling. The air temperature was around 60°F, unusually warm for the U.S. Northwest in early April. They planned to do a short day trip from Greenbank, on Washington's Whidbey Island, to Baby Island and back. The wind was blowing out of the south at about 10 to 15 knots. Saratoga Passage, which was just east of their route, looked a bit rough, but inside the entrance to Holmes Harbor, the south wind had a shorter fetch so the waves were somewhat smaller. "We were a little concerned about the conditions," Ralph said later, "but we thought we'd go out a ways and see how things were. If it was too rough, we'd turn around."

The two men were using Ralph's Eddyline San Juan (a three-cockpit kayak that is often used as a double, with cargo stowed in the center cockpit). The kayak was equipped with front and rear bulkheads for buoyancy. A cut-off plastic bleach bottle served as a bailing device, but they had no bilge pumps or other emergency gear. Ralph had been sea kayaking for about a year; his friend had some canoeing experience but had done only a little kayaking. Neither of them had taken lessons or practiced reentries.

Around noon they launched from a beach a little north of Greenbank. They angled their kayak into the wind and paddled for an hour to reach Baby Island. The waves were about 2 feet high, but since they were angling into them, the crossing went well. They then rested for a half hour before heading back, during which time conditions became a bit rougher. Even worse, if they headed straight back to where they started, the waves would be hitting them nearly broadside, so they decided to zigzag in order to minimize the time spent sideways to the waves. In retrospect, Ralph said, "Neither of us was really too worried. I think I had a false sense of how stable my boat was. I never had any concept that the thing could ever tip over. It just felt like such a solid boat."

For the first part of the return crossing, they angled upwind and did OK, but on the downwind leg the kayak began to surf in the quartering seas. Ralph remembered, "Some of the waves lifted us up so much that the rudder wasn't totally in the water." Near the middle of the crossing, the kayak broached (turned sideways to a wave) and started to capsize. "It tipped us over very slowly," Ralph said, "like it happened in slow motion."

Both men exited the kayak and held onto it and their paddles. In Ralph's words, "Neither of us was too panicky. I mean, we went about things in a very calm way, partly because we didn't think we were that far offshore—even though it was actually about a mile to shore in either direction. We thought we could just tip the boat up and get in it. We didn't realize how difficult it was going to be." Fortunately, both men were in good shape. Ralph was a former competitive swimmer with experience in ocean swim races.

The two paddlers used teamwork to push the kayak up and right it, similar to how that is done with an open canoe. Next, Chris steadied the kayak while Ralph climbed back into the rear cockpit. This went well, but when Chris attempted to climb in, the kayak flipped again. Over the next 15 minutes, they capsized about ten times while trying to reenter the kayak. Getting the first person in was easy, but because they lacked bracing skills, neither was able to steady the kayak enough for the second person to get in. Ralph said, "In calm conditions we may have been able to accomplish it, but substantial waves kept breaking all around the boat, making it very unstable. We never could get the second person in."

By this time, Ralph's hands and feet were becoming numb from the cold, and he wasn't feeling well. The water temperature was in the low fifties. Ralph was wearing pile pants, a cotton shirt, and a Gore-Tex windbreaker. Chris had on a shorty wetsuit and was doing much better than Ralph. Both were wearing PFDs. They decided to have Chris stay in the water and hold onto the bow while Ralph paddled them both to shore. Ralph hoped that paddling would help him warm up, but he stayed cold the whole time.

There was a lot of water in the kayak from the repeated capsizes, and this made the otherwise-stable kayak quite tippy. Nonetheless, Ralph got in and immediately started paddling, rather than taking the time to bail the water out. He paddled in a kneeling position, which makes a kayak less stable and eventually becomes very uncomfortable, because he felt the kayak was too unstable for him to lift himself up in to get properly seated. Apparently he didn't know the technique for reentering a kayak feet first while lying facedown on the rear deck. Meanwhile, the kayak continued to fill with water as waves came over its sides.

Luckily, the wind and waves were now helping push them toward the beach where they had launched. Ralph said, "I just paddled like crazy. We went like that for a long time and made it within about a quarter mile from shore." From that distance they could see activity on the beach. (A woman who lived there had seen them struggling and called the fire department.) By this time Chris's condition was getting serious. Hypothermia was slurring his speech and sapping his strength. When they were a couple hundred yards from shore, Chris told Ralph he was having difficulty holding on. Ralph thought to himself, "We're going to make it, but what happens if Chris can't hold onto the bow anymore?"

When they were within a hundred yards of shore, Ralph decided that the kayak was so full of water that it wasn't worth continuing to paddle it. He got out of the kayak and pulled it from the bow while swimming toward shore. Fire department personnel were coming to help, but their rescue boat launched about the same time the two paddlers made it to shallow water where they could stand up. As they were getting out of the water, Chris momentarily lost consciousness and Ralph began shivering uncontrollably.

They were taken to the hospital and treated for hypothermia. Ralph's core temperature was 92°F, and Chris's was 90. Upon rewarming, Chris's heart developed an arrhythmia, so he was kept in the hospital overnight. Both soon fully recovered.

LESSONS LEARNED BY RALPH

"I now have more respect for the conditions. I'm trying to get into some lessons, and I've bought a couple of self-rescue paddle floats to help stabilize the kayak during reentry."

ANALYSIS AND LESSONS LEARNED

When conditions get rough, unprepared sea kayakers may pay for their carelessness with their lives. Their lack of safety equipment (no bilge pumps, paddle floats, flares, whistles, or other distress signals), as well as their faith in the kayak's stability, speaks for itself about these paddlers' inexperience and lack of knowledge—an unfortunately common element in many, if not most, sea kayak accidents. These two were lucky to have survived.

Even wide, "stable," double kayaks (and in this case, a triple) can capsize when the waves get steep. And reentry is often harder to perform with a two-person kayak than with a single because most double kayaks have higher decks than singles. The higher the deck, the harder it is to climb onto and the less stable the kayak is with the person's weight on the deck. Further, two people paddling an unaccompanied two-person kayak are taking most of the same risks as a solo paddler.

Those who rely on their kayak's stability to prevent capsizing need to understand that this works only in relatively flat conditions. When the kayak is sideways to a wave, the same design features that keep a kayak upright in calm water (static stability) become a lever by which the wave capsizes the kayak. Until you have confidence in your ability to lean into waves and brace with the paddle for balance, venturing farther from shore than you can swim (a distance greatly reduced in cold water) is risky unless you are accompanied by someone more skilled and whom you really trust.

Even for skilled paddlers, knowingly heading out in rough conditions or on long crossings when conditions may change is not to be taken lightly. Question your preparedness before going out. Do you have the appropriate safety equipment (PFD, towrope, spare paddle, paddle float, etc.) and survival gear (distress signals, handheld VHF radio, extra clothes, etc.)? Have you tested your kayak's buoyancy when it is fully swamped? Are you dressed for immersion? Are there more-experienced paddlers in your group who are confident they could rescue you in the worst-case scenario? Then, if you choose to go out, look for ways to test yourself in the conditions without taking great risks. For example, while near shore, try turning all the way around, rafting up, and going a short distance upwind, downwind, and across the wind. If all goes well, consider practicing some reentries and Eskimo rolls. Consider also whether it is likely that conditions will worsen. For example, will the current speed up or switch directions and oppose the wind, does the forecast range of wind speed exceed what you are currently observing, does the forecast mention squalls in the area or are squalls visible in the distance, etc.?

With cold water, dressing for immersion means wearing a dry suit or Farmer John wetsuit, preferably made of 5 mm or thicker neoprene, rather than the 3 mm suits commonly marketed to kayakers, to slow heat loss and the onset of hypothermia. When the weather is windy, rainy, or cold and the water is too cold for you to enjoy swimming, it is very unlikely that anyone would feel too warm wearing a dry suit or Farmer John wetsuit. In fact, in these conditions, a dry suit or wetsuit may be necessary for comfort and to prevent hypothermia even if you don't capsize.

When a two- or three-person fiberglass kayak swamps, the amount of water that enters the cockpit area can be so immense that it is exhausting to pump out. Worse yet, the buoyancy from the end compartments of some double kayaks is insufficient to keep the cockpit above water once the kayak is swamped. In this case, it may not be possible to empty the kayak while you are in it, at least not in rough conditions. It pays to know and test your equipment.

To solve the flotation problems unique to doubles, some two-person kayaks are built with a center flotation compartment. Another solution is to add a pair of sea socks. Sea socks are waterproof nylon bags that line the cockpit and seal around the coaming; they greatly reduce the amount of water that can enter the kayak. Another gadget that is especially beneficial for a two-person kayak is a submersible, battery-powered bilge pump. A battery-powered pump can be used simultaneously with hand pumps or left running while the kayakers paddle to shore.

If you own a kayak, test it fully swamped. Pump water in if necessary, with and without camping gear, to see if the coaming stays above the water after you reenter the kayak. Also try paddling while the kayak is swamped; this will build and test your bracing skills. Afterwards, check the kayak's flotation chambers to see if the bulkheads leak. If your kayak lacks sufficient buoyancy, consider adding a sea sock or a pair of sea socks for a two-person kayak.

2

Trial and Error
A Novice Capsizes off Victoria, British Columbia

Doug Lloyd

On his fiftieth birthday, Bob Gauthier was probably pining for a bright red Porsche. What his wife gave him on that June day in 1997 was a sporty Solstice GTS by Current Designs. It even came with a well-written owner's manual and dealer-equipped compass, but no glove box.

At a height of 5 feet and 8 inches and weighing 195 pounds, Bob was a physically fit 50-year-old. He had recently retired from 27 years with the Canadian Armed Forces. As a consequence of his military experience, Bob was able to stay calm and collected during times of physical and psychological stress. Although he had undergone years of land-based wilderness training, Bob, by his own admission, did not understand the complexities of water settings and, like many men at the half-century decade of life, he was not in the habit of seeking formal instruction.

Bob did rent a sea kayaking instructional video. After watching a couple shows about sea kayaking on the Outdoor Life Network, he quickly understood that he needed to practice rescue techniques. He worked on wet exits, paddle-float self-recoveries, and assisted rescues prior to departing on a week-and-a-half trip along the British Columbia mainland coastline with his son. After the trip he continued to practice and became proficient at self-rescues in calm water.

On the morning of November 22, 1997, Bob's plan was to go paddling with his daughter on a local lake. Behind in her homework, she decided to stay home. Bob made a quick decision to go solo, following a saltwater route he had done once before in the summer. He would start at Ten Mile Point, which would leave an approximately 6-mile paddle to Clover Point. Bob expected to arrive at his take-out point by five o'clock at the latest. He left instructions with his daughter to call the authorities if he did not report in via cell phone for pick up by seven o'clock. (In retrospect, Bob realized that this was far too late in the day for a fall trip.) He then checked the morning weather on a local radio station, which gave an anecdotal version of the marine forecast issued by Environment Canada. A Small Craft Warning had been downgraded, despite an approaching front and high winds forecast for the north coast. After a hearty breakfast, Bob was ready to paddle.

Bob's daughter drove him to Ten Mile Point. From the road's high vantage point, the sea looked calm. Launching, he surveyed the scene once again. The surface of the sea was as calm as glass. The air was cool, the temperature in the fifties. There was no indication of poor weather coming, and his tide book showed a helpful ebb current all the way to Clover Point. He launched and paddled southeast along the shoreline, then rounded Cadboro Point and headed southwest, crossing Cadboro Bay and Oak Bay. Once out of the relative protection of the Discovery Islands, Bob noticed the seas starting to build from the now-apparent easterly wind. He stayed close to shore and pressed on.

Rounding Gonzales Point, Bob turned west. With the only possible take-out point at Willows Beach far behind, all he could do was continue to stay close to shore and paddle with the tide through Enterprise Channel and into the shelter of McNeil Bay, where the wind shadow of the Trial Islands obscured the true extent of conditions in Juan De Fuca Strait. Bob had no knowledge of the hazards posed by currents and was unaware of the real jeopardy he could have placed himself in if a big spring tide had been running.

Then he made a serious error in judgment: To avoid the wash of small, alongshore breakers, he left his nearshore route and veered away, setting course for Clover Point. He did not realize how much rougher it would become once he was out of the security of the lee of the islands. He could have paddled into McNeil Bay or to the somewhat rougher beach of Ross Bay, but he was unfamiliar with ferry gliding and did not realize that he could have made the crossing by angling his bow into the 2-knot current.

As he had not checked a marine weather broadcast before leaving, Bob was unaware of the localized, 20-knot easterly breeze and developing swell off the Trial Islands. Partially beam-on to the seas, Bob nervously watched the rushing waves growing higher. He had negligible bracing skills and did not know how to lean into breaking waves, even though the 22-inch-wide GTS fit him well enough to do secure braces. Lacking the ability to lean into and brace against a beam sea, Bob was eventually unable to negotiate the whitecaps and capsized.

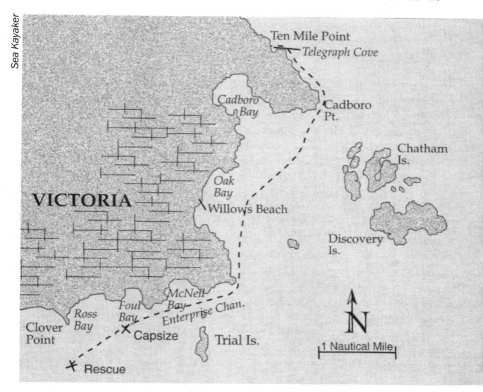

As he wet-exited, the shock of the 50°F water took his breath away. He was clad only in deck shoes, nylon shorts, a cotton sweatshirt with arms removed, a hiker's Gore-Tex jacket, a fedora, and his PFD. For blister prevention, Bob was wearing half-finger gloves. Although he had brought along dry fleece clothing and rain pants, they were stored in the inaccessible bow compartment. He did not have any immersion apparel, and the cold reality of his situation sank in instantly.

Far from shore and immersed in relatively rough water is the last place a novice wants to be. Bob had never practiced rough-water self-rescues. He surfaced on the downwind side of the kayak. Several items, including his water bottle, snack bag with food, and sponge, started to drift away. Letting the nonessentials go, Bob kept his nerve. He concentrated on retrieving his paddle, then struggled to grab his boat as it bounced up and down in the waves. He bashed the ends of his fingers badly, and a few of his fingernails were bent backward. Bob worked his way around to the windward side of the kayak and deployed the paddle float on the left-hand paddle blade. He tried to push the free blade under the doubled paddle-float rescue bungees that ran parallel to the port gunwale on the rear deck just behind the cockpit through to the other doubled bungee on the starboard side, but the curvature of the deck, the rolling motion of the boat, and his cold fingers frustrated the attempt. Opting for an easier procedure, Bob then slid the blade under the looser X-pattern bungees crisscrossing atop the square-rigged rescue arrangement, keeping the float end of the paddle extended to windward (toward the waves). Bob hooked his right leg over the paddle shaft and got his left leg into the cockpit, but a cresting wave caused him to lose balance while corkscrewing back into the cockpit. With the float arcing through the air, Bob catapulted back into the cold water on the opposite side.

Bob figured that removing the water from the flooded cockpit first would make the kayak less susceptible to rolling during reentry. Showing resourcefulness, he placed the paddle float under his arm and, with the added buoyancy of his PFD, was able to lift the bow and drain at least a portion of the water from the cockpit. With the kayak's stability increased, it was much less difficult for him to perform the float self-rescue. His hand pump, stowed on the aft deck, was reasonably accessible, but with the odd wave washing into the cockpit, Bob felt it imperative to secure the neoprene spray skirt first, planning to leave a small gap for the 15-inch pump. While he was sitting in the cockpit reattaching his spray skirt, another wave rolled him over to the lee side.

Surfacing again, Bob was becoming really cold. His legs had turned lobster red. Though stiff and sore from the cold and a bruised torso, adrenaline helped keep him mobile. Bob gave up attempting to remove water prior to his next reentry attempt. As he struggled to perform one more paddle-float rescue, he found that his sense of balance had been diminished by the cold, and it was increasingly difficult to push himself up onto the rear deck. Finally seated in his kayak, his boat was now riding low in the sea with waves breaking regularly into the cockpit. Getting colder by the minute, Bob gave up reattaching the skirt for a moment while he launched a flare.

He normally carried only one flare from the three-pack set he owned, but on the way out that morning he had taken the two remaining ones from his wife's PFD. He had taken the time to familiarize himself with the flares' firing instructions when he had bought them in the summer. With the float still secured, Bob held the paddle shaft with his right hand to maintain stability and used his free left hand to hold the flare. Using his teeth, he twisted the cap off the flare and pulled the chain, being careful to tilt the device away from his face. Though it didn't rise very high in the sky, Bob thought the distress signal would attract attention.

After firing the flare, Bob once again attempted to reattach the spray cover. In the process, he took his eyes off the horizon, looking down at the spray skirt briefly. This compromised his sense of balance just as another big wave rolled along. Bob once more found himself in the cold ocean. His muscles now started cramping. Initiating his fourth paddle-float self-rescue, Bob again struggled but managed to reenter his swamped vessel. He removed the paddle from the bungees aft of the cockpit but left the paddle float in place on the blade. Bob had now been in and out of the water for 20 minutes or more. Realizing that his first distress signal hadn't been sighted, at 3:40 he set off his next-to-last flare, again using one hand and his teeth.

His shivering had grown so intense that Bob figured that if he went over again, it would be the end of him. Given the difficulty of reattaching the skirt around the cockpit rim, Bob decided to leave the spray skirt undone and not even attempt to retrieve the pump from the rear-deck bungees. He simply hunkered down low in the flooded cockpit in an attempt to reduce the wind-chill factor and to achieve a lower center of gravity. Paddling with the float still on the windward paddle blade, he turned the boat to keep the wind and waves at his back, then gave it every effort to use the float to keep the boat balanced as each wave passed by.

Then Bob saw a car due west, about a quarter mile away on the turnaround of Clover Point, flashing its headlights. He felt sure that he had been seen and that rescue personnel were on the way. By 4:15 in the afternoon, the current had swept Bob about a quarter mile farther southwest off Clover Point. He was distressed to see the car with flashing headlights leave. Despondent, Bob began to think that he hadn't been seen after all. He contemplated how furious his wife would be if he didn't make it. He had no other rescue or safety gear, with the exception of his cell phone and chemical light sticks—both inaccessible in the front hatch.

About 40 minutes had elapsed since his first capsize, and he had one flare left. Should he fire it? Save it? Wait a while? Bob trembled in the cold, flooded cockpit. It was becoming progressively more difficult to balance the boat as it rode even lower in the choppy seas. Bob did his best to scan the seas on each wave crest for any sign of a rescue operation, while bracing with the paddle and paddle float. He remained patient and kept faith that he would be rescued.

Now almost an hour had gone by. The overcast sky had darkened the area quickly. Bob was bouncing up and down in his kayak in the blustery swells, violently shivering and shaking. Suddenly he saw green and red lights coming toward him from the direction of Enterprise Channel. When Bob ascended from the depths of the next trough, he saw only a port-side red light over his right shoulder, which meant that the boat was turning away. Unknown to Bob, the Coast Guard Auxiliary Zodiac had been directed based on position information from an onshore sighting of his flare. Bob was now a quarter mile south of Clover Point and drifting out toward open water. He knew that the moment he was waiting for had arrived. The partial warmth of his half-finger gloves had left him just enough dexterity, and he fired his last flare, again using his one free hand and teeth.

Bob quickly lost sight of the vessel, but he remained hopeful. A few minutes later, the bright orange Zodiac pulled alongside. His tension dissipated rapidly as warm waves of relief washed over Bob. A crewman asked Bob to raise his arms. Utterly rigid, Bob was unable to comply. Reaching down, two men grabbed Bob's wrists and manhandled him up out of the kayak.

The rescue volunteers replaced Bob's fedora with a warm toque. They placed heat packs on his neck, groin, and armpits. Bob trembled so violently that they could not measure his pulse. The helmsman opened the throttle, and they had a rough ride to the base at Ogden Point, leaving Bob's kayak behind. To provide more warmth, two rescuers lay beside Bob, one partially on top of him. With the world whirling about him, Bob was whisked away to a waiting ambulance, which transported him to a hospital. Even after being warmed up in the Zodiac and ambulance, Bob's core body temperature upon arrival at the hospital was about 90°F.

Three hours later, safely home again, Bob still felt very cold. He spent the night with hot water bottles. When he awoke the next morning, he felt like he had been badly beaten up and was black and blue from his knees down, over his upper torso and hips, and on the ends of his fingers.

Late the next afternoon, Bob went to a storage site near the rescue headquarters to get his kayak, which had been retrieved by the rescue crew. Unable to lift it, he opened the molded ABS plastic stern hatch and was surprised to find it half full of sea water.

Bob returned to the kayak retailer and purchased a paddling jacket, a wetsuit, pogies, a spare paddle, a paddle leash, current tables, and more flares. Bob reflected that gear may seem expensive when you're in the store, but the cost would seem inconsequential when you were out in rough water and would then pay absolutely anything to have it.

He subsequently took a sea kayaking course through Scouts Canada. Bob now knew to avoid locations like the Trial Islands during adverse conditions and that there are many more marine hazards awaiting the unwary paddler. He said his main errors were paddling alone, not having the proper gear, and heading too far out. He also realized that, in addition to having the right gear, he needed to develop better boat-handling skills and a greater understanding of marine weather. Bob only recently became aware that free, continuous marine broadcast weather reports and recorded marine broadcast numbers are listed in the phone book, and that a VHF marine-weather radio is inexpensive and essential. Bob now is planning to purchase either a submersible VHF radio or a touch-pad VHF that can be placed in a see-through waterproof pouch.

To his credit, Bob had taken the time to modify his paddle float with a homemade retainer strap, which was the only reason he didn't lose the float and very likely his life.

LESSONS LEARNED

Cold water kills. The only difference between survival in 60, 50, and 40°F water temperatures is one of time. You are not dressed to paddle if you are not dressed to swim, and being dressed to swim only buys you more time. It is also important to avoid situations that might place you in cold water.

It is critical to avoid panic and to keep focused if you do capsize in cold water. Take stock of the situation, and move quickly and methodically to minimize your immersion time. It is best to paddle with a partner, who can assist with a rescue in the case of a capsize or other emergency.

Many paddlers are able to perform the first stage of a solo recovery rescue with great proficiency, but, not having experimented in rough water, they may be unaware of extreme second-stage difficulties. Spray skirt reattachment in rough water is a commonly overlooked skill. Make sure you know the exact sequence for attaching your particular spray skirt. Practice reattachment in rough water with a friend close at hand. Try it with and without gloves—and without looking down. It will require two hands. You may need to point the bow into the waves and time the sequence between crests.

After a capsize, once you are back in the cockpit, leave the paddle-float system in place while you attend to the spray skirt and pump out the boat, keeping your weight shifted toward the paddle to maximize your stability.

Pumping or bailing procedures are always difficult. Electric or foot-operated pumps are the only hands-free options. Deck-mounted pumps still require one hand to operate, leaving the other hand to hold the paddle for bracing. Bob's choice of a handheld pump is the norm for many paddlers, but using a handheld pump in a self-rescue can be very difficult. Handheld pumps are most effective in assisted rescues, where another boat provides stability for the swamped kayak while leaving the paddler with both hands free to operate the pump.

If using only one hand, you can hold the pump against the cockpit rim with your knee. Bob could have placed it between his body and the spray skirt opening; his tight neoprene skirt would have held the pump close to his body for pumping. If a temporarily open spray skirt doesn't matter, a solo paddler would be better off with one hand on the paddle and the other working with a sponge or a simple, one-hand bailer cup. After his accident, Bob installed some bungees in the cockpit to hold the pump underneath the foredeck. That will make it easier for him to get to the pump when he needs it.

Even fully inflated, a paddle float may fail to pinch securely on certain blade designs, allowing the float to slip off. Novices should consider using a foam float, which usually provides secure attachment, sweeps more easily, can't leak, and won't blow away in the wind as easily. Unfortunately, paddle floats may give paddlers a false sense of security and promote novice solo paddling.

You can modify your paddle-float rescue bungee cords by running them through 1-inch wooden balls available from a bead store. They allow the paddle blade to slip under the bungees much more easily. Some manufacturers use nylon webbing and quick-release buckle straps to hold the blade in place. Using an offset cleat arrangement and a rope tie-down also works well. Whatever attachment is used, a critical point occurs when the paddler has to reach behind and undo the quick release or pull the blade free. At this point the paddler loses the stability provided by the outrigger and has to get both hands on the paddle in order to brace with it. Bob may have been able to complete his skirt reattachment and bailing procedures much more readily if the paddle float had been securely attached to the back deck.

Keeping water out of your boat is one of the first rules of good seamanship. Bob had read his owner's manual and knew the importance of proper hatch-cover placement and tension. His reentry struggles on the back deck may have loosened the cover, however, making it prone to leakage. Most new bulkheads don't leak, but it's a good idea to test them. Bob had previously sometimes backed up his boat's buoyancy with empty 2-liter bottles, but that morning he had not used them in his rush to go paddling. Float bags or gear bags that fill most of the space in the compartment can prevent the kayak from sinking in the event of leaky hatches or bulkheads.

How a novice like Bob should make the transition from novice to a proficient paddler is a legitimate question. New paddlers are told to avoid paddling alone, strong tidal currents, windswept shorelines, crossings, remote areas, long distances, trips with difficult navigation, and winter paddling—or even the shoulder seasons. The skills needed to paddle safely cannot be simply pulled from thin air. Skills require a period of development and knowledge gained through experience. Much of this knowledge is accessible through courses and training schools. Seek qualified instruction or guidance, and safely gain confidence alongside competent friends or by joining a club or paddler's network while learning.

The two types of paddlers most at risk are the novice and the expert: the novice because of a lack of experience, the expert because experience can lead to taking on greater levels of risk. My own difficulties in the same area—capsizing and being rescued near the Trial Islands—demonstrated the latter. Bob's experience demonstrated the former, highlighting how difficult it is for a novice to realistically appraise his own abilities in order to stay within them. In both of our cases, we were paddling alone. In both cases, we failed to pay heed to early indicators of impending trouble. We have also both been given another chance.

3

Lone Madsen's Last Journey

Tore Sivertsen

The rain was drumming on our tent. It was early in the morning on September 30, 1998, by Danell Fjord, near Iluileq, in southeast Greenland. "Another day of bad weather," I thought, and crawled deeper into my cozy sleeping bag. I could hear Lone Madsen, my friend and expedition partner, sleeping heavily. There were still a few hours until the alarm clock would sound. After a while, I heard the alarm, but I didn't want to get up as long as it was still raining. The previous day we had paddled hard in the last 43 kilometers down toward Iluileq and Danell Fjord, and we had stayed up late into the night as Lone told stories about old Greenlandic kayak hunters.

I drifted back to sleep, only to be awakened by a friendly pat on the shoulder. "Get up, Tore! It's time to paddle, before winter brings the fjord ice," Lone said. In the next moment she served me a steaming cup of hot chocolate and a big, tasty piece of marzipan. Lone was fresh and ready to go. "I hope we get real snowy weather at our next camp," she said. "It would make for some exciting pictures."

"If it's up to me," I answered, "the winter can just wait until the dog sled season starts in January."

By eight o'clock it was completely quiet outside and I could see from the shining red color on the nylon of the tent that the sun was back again. We stuck our heads outside and breathed in the fresh, clear air of fall. High up on the mountain peaks I could see the first snow of the year. Winter was on its way. By the campfire site our little stove was underwater. Pans and cups were sloshing around in a little pond of rainwater from the night's deluge. We ate breakfast in a hurry, then climbed up a hill close to our camping spot to get a better view of the horizon and the conditions out in the mouth of the fjord. I told Lone I felt a little insecure about the weather because of last night's heavy rain and the look of the gray horizon out over the

22

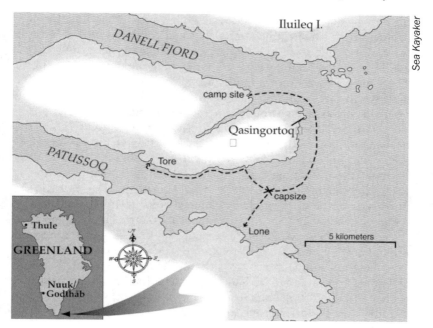

Atlantic Ocean. It looked like a low-pressure system was somewhere out there. We both had handheld VHF radios, but at our position it was not possible to reach the coastal station in Ammassalik for a weather report. We had a satellite telephone in my kayak, but we intended to use that only for emergencies.

With the binoculars we studied the horizon and the movement of the sea. The air pressure had been stable at 1018 millibars (30.06 inches of mercury) for the last 8 hours. Danell Fjord was like a mirror, without wind or waves. Out by Iluileq's southern islands we saw only calm and glossy waves. We looked at the map and discussed a reasonable route for the day. We decided to paddle out to the mouth of Danell Fjord, then make a stop on the Qasingortoq headland. Once there, we would make a final decision on whether to paddle farther south or stay, depending on the weather conditions. We gathered our gear and packed in a hurry. We put on our Gore-Tex dry suits, launched our kayaks, and pushed away from the shore. To keep our hands warm, we put on our neoprene pogies. The air and the water temperature were both rather chilly at 1° to 2°C, so it was pleasant to warm up with these on.

At about eleven thirty in the morning we paddled out of our little Arctic lagoon and into Danell Fjord. As usual, Lone was paddling with energy and enthusiasm from the very start, and soon she was a short distance away from me. I always spent the first 15 to 20 minutes of the day on a slow warm-up. After a while we were paddling through passages with small chunks of ice that had come out farther into the fjord on the tide from Innlandice's cobalt-blue glacier arms. After a good hour of paddling, we were approaching the mouth of the fjord. The 1-meter waves were smooth and reflected the light. By now Lone was two to three hundred meters ahead of me, and we were getting pretty close to Qasingortoq, our agreed-upon meeting spot.

All of a sudden, I could see and hear a wind coming out of the north at about 5 to 10 knots. The surface of the water in the mouth of the fjord changed from glossy to gray. I sensed that bad weather was on its way, and I stopped paddling. I stayed there, drifting with the waves and looking out over the sea to the northeast. The water on the north side of the fjord suddenly changed color from gray to black— a sign of strong wind. Shortly after, the waves started building up from the north, tumbling whitecaps toward us. It was definitely time to turn around and get away from there, and to seek shelter back in the fjord.

I held my paddle in the air with both hands and shouted as loud as I could to Lone that we had to turn around. She didn't hear me. (In her childhood Lone had lost hearing in one ear.) Our VHF radios did not have hands-free operation and were carried in the cockpit, turned off.

We had agreed not to continue paddling if we encountered whitecaps anywhere along our route. From a distance, it looked like she was busy studying the ocean and the horizon toward the south, where we were actually heading. I started paddling and raced to warn her about the change in weather and the danger approaching from the north and northeast. I wanted us to turn around and seek refuge as fast as possible. Now Lone also noticed the drastic change in weather. She stopped, looked toward the north, then looked back toward me. I stopped again and held my paddle in my right hand and signaled with my left hand that we should turn around.

The high winds were suddenly on us. I had to lean forward and brace with all my strength to keep from capsizing. I could see that Lone too was paddling very forcefully to keep from being blown into the breakers and cliffs along Qasingortoq's shoreline to the south of us. I paddled as hard as I could and went after her. I could tell from the motion of my kayak that we were in an area of very strong currents. The waves were breaking all around us. I judged the wind speed to be around 25 knots with gusts up to 50 knots.

Due to the extreme weather, we could not get our kayaks turned around quickly. (Lone's Valley Canoe Products Skerry had a skeg and my Prijon Seayak had a rudder.) We had to focus our strength on getting away from the breakers and the waves reflecting back off the cliffs at the shoreline. I couldn't see any landing site anywhere nearby—only vertical black cliffs.

The waves grew to 4 to 5 meters high and were breaking forcefully around us. We were now about a kilometer beyond Qasingortoq and struggling in the unprotected ocean a kilometer offshore. Along the shore to the south, I could see a gigantic surf building and the waves slamming against the cliffs, sending water flying 15 to 20 meters into the air. We had been completely surprised by a full-force northeasterly storm, combined with powerful fall winds from the Innlandice plateau near Iluileq. Our situation was becoming critical.

I worked feverishly to keep control of my kayak and my wits. Several times I shouted to myself both to push myself mentally and to stay calm. I was in a life-threatening situation that had come on surprisingly quickly. I realized that if I were to lose my focus and concentration and stop paddling, everything would be lost. We were pushed south and rapidly found ourselves 2 kilometers from shore. It seemed a little less noisy offshore, but the waves were gigantic: 6 to 7 meters high. I felt at first oddly like a passenger in the middle of all of this and was thinking that this was pure madness—how the hell did everything get so far out of hand? I felt like a complete idiot for getting into this situation, but I had to fight the waves. I had by now lost sight of Lone and was becoming worried about her.

I focused intensely on how the ocean was behaving around me. The wind and waves were now coming from behind and to the right. Big chunks of glacier ice sometimes popped up ahead of me, and I had to work hard to steer clear of them. Often I found myself surfing on big waves. It was difficult to balance on the crests of waves 6 to 7 meters high where the wind pushed strongly against me, threatening to capsize the kayak. I felt my life was hanging by a thread. "Tore, you can handle this—now you just have to play with the ocean," I said to myself and felt a great rush of self-confidence, self-control, and power. I followed the movements of the waves and shifted constantly between paddling and bracing. In the chaos I somehow managed to find a comfortable paddling rhythm, which gave me a feeling of calmness and inner strength.

In the sky above me there were now a lot of mallemuks, or storm petrels. Fifteen to twenty of them stayed with me and flew around me for a long time. I felt safer seeing other living creatures. I thought about my son and my girlfriend, about my Greenlandic husky dogs, and my family in northern Norway.

The wind stayed very strong, and it pushed the big waves with enormous power. Their wavelength was increasing, and I was now gaining speed and accelerating down from the crests with almost too much speed. Many times I had to try to brake and slow down when I was about to fly into the air while on top, and often I would land ahead of the wave with a big splash. Frequently I was engulfed in foam and water up to my head.

I tried to read the map in front of me to find a possible landing site in the area. The only commonsense alternative seemed to be in the next fjord to the south, Patussoq Fjord. I hoped that the high mountainside on the north side of the fjord would slow the wind and waves and give me some shelter against the storm.

All of a sudden, I caught sight of Lone three or four hundred meters ahead of me to the right. I tried to catch up with her. After what seemed like an unusually short time, I was only ten to fifteen meters behind her. I shouted over to her with a somehow relaxed voice: "Hi, Lone, how are you doing?"

She looked surprised and answered, "My God, Tore, I thought you were lost!" I could see from the look on her face that she was very tense, probably feeling the same way I was. "Don't get too close to me—we could collide!" she shouted.

I shouted back, "This is nasty weather. We have to get away from here before we get carried too far south. Let's go into Patussoq Fjord up close to the mountains on the north side and get away from these waves!" As I spoke, I saw that it had started to rain and snow, and the visibility toward land was only 3 to 5 kilometers.

I paddled into the lead. I noticed that Lone was paddling more slowly than usual. In smaller waves she would normally have been paddling a lot faster than I. I was riding high on a big wave about 50 meters ahead of her when I heard a loud scream. Quickly turning my head, I saw that she had capsized. Lone had worked on rolling but hadn't become proficient or practiced it for a long time.

Just as she capsized, the wind grew even stronger and I was again bracing, coasting at high speed over the top of the wave ahead. I glanced over my shoulder to see what was happening to Lone. In short glimpses I saw her heavily loaded red kayak upside down with Lone 3 to 4 meters behind it, swimming toward it. Her paddle was 6 to 7 meters ahead of the kayak, and her red fleece cap was floating on the water. We both had paddle floats, but we had not practiced assisted rescues together.

An icy cold feeling of horror swept through me. I tried to stop, but the strong wind and big waves continuously drove me farther away from Lone. I made several attempts to turn around, but I nearly capsized every time the waves and wind slammed into the side of the kayak. Lone's screams for my assistance were continuous: "Tore, Tore, you must help me! You cannot paddle away from me!" I knew she was in a life-or-death situation if she couldn't get out of the cold water soon enough.

I thought about how cold the water must be. During the winter two years previous, I had tested a Gore-Tex dry suit similar to the ones we were wearing. I had jumped into the ocean in Nuuk (Godthåb) to find out how cold the water felt and to see how long I could function normally. I was wearing a fleece suit, neoprene head cap, life vest, and neoprene gloves. Even in calm water I stayed in only 15 minutes before I couldn't take it anymore. I shook violently from the cold and spent about an hour on land before I felt myself again. I knew that Lone was in terrible circumstances.

Terror, shock, and grief flooded my consciousness as I realized that I was unable to do anything for her. I believed, however, that I was doing everything that was humanly possible in the conditions. Lone and I had on several occasions discussed our expeditions. We knew the risks and we both took responsibility for our own lives—and, until now, we had been living life to the fullest.

The wind and waves pushed me farther and farther away from Lone. Each time I was on top of a wave, I could hear Lone shout my name, her voice growing more and more faint. I tried to fight my way into the lee of the mountains on the north side of the fjord as quickly as possible so I could turn around and get out to her again. I fought with unpredictable stormy winds and breaking waves for over 45 minutes while I struggled to turn the kayak in a big half circle. I finally got turned around but was about 4 kilometers from where Lone had capsized. I loosened my cramped grip from the paddle shaft and for a brief moment tried to thaw my frozen, white fingertips by putting them into my mouth. The snow and rain were whipping into my eyes. I realized it was impossible to paddle back out against the wind and waves, and I had to abandon hope of assisting Lone.

Reaching the cliffs at the north side of Patussoq Fjord, I was overwhelmed by a painful sadness. Tears ran down my cheeks. I knew that by now Lone would be losing consciousness. After a few moments I experienced a strange feeling, as if I could actually sense the energy on its way out of her body as she sent me her last thought.

For about an hour, absorbed in grief, I drifted in a somewhat stable position among waves around 3 meters high. I kept trying to see what was going on out there, to see if she would somehow turn up after all. But the storm raged as strongly as ever, and I could see that the bad weather was hitting the cliffs on the south side of the fjord with enormous power. I had to regain my composure and get ashore to use our satellite phone to initiate a search and rescue.

I paddled into the fjord to find a place where I could land. I could see that the water was calm far inside the fjord. I found a landing site and went ashore, pulled out the necessary equipment, erected the tent, and got the satellite phone warmed. I called emergency headquarters, Grønlands Kommando, located in Grønnedal, in southwest Greenland. They were very surprised when I called. "Are you guys still alive?" they asked. I gave them the essential details of our situation and my position. They had already picked up Lone's 406 personal locator beacon (PLB) distress signal shortly after she capsized. Since it had been such a long time since the PLB started transmitting, they had assumed that the worst had happened to both of us. Our "Kayak '98 Expedition" had been officially filed with the Danish Polar Center (DPC) in Denmark, so Grønlands Kommando knew that the distress signal was coming from us.

I walked up to a high point on top of a hill and fired a series of green flares with my signal pistol, just in case Lone somehow had survived and was close by. I then made a call on my handheld marine VHF radio on emergency Channel 16, in the hope that Lone might answer on her radio. I wanted to believe that she might still show up, as she had always done before. I couldn't accept that my friend and traveling companion was gone.

After a while, I heard the sound of an airplane in the clouds overhead. It was Greenlandair's Twin Otter airplane searching for us. They were at an altitude of 21,000 feet, above the clouds. It was impossible for them to get down between the mountains to conduct a visual search for Lone. I briefed them over the marine VHF radio, but neither they nor I managed to contact Lone. They finally had to return to Narsarsuaq Airport. The last transmission I heard was, "Let's hope for the best."

It grew dark, and the darkness and bad weather prevented a rescue helicopter from coming right away. Grønlands Kommando informed me later on the satellite phone that all available resources would be dispatched for search and rescue the next day. During the night I asked Grønnedal for an update on the position of Lone's PLB signal. I entered the coordinates into my GPS unit to see where she could be. According to the GPS, the distress beacon was coming from a position in the mouth of the fjord toward the southeast, about 7 kilometers from my camp.

During the night, 15 centimeters of fresh snow fell on my lonely campsite. Thinking of Lone out in the ocean somewhere, I could not sleep. At eight thirty the next morning I was picked up by a Greenlandair S-61 Sikorsky helicopter from Narsarsuaq.

We spotted Lone in about 15 minutes. She was floating in the area reported by her 406 PLB, a hundred meters from her kayak, surrounded by a lot of glacial ice. A nylon tether line around her waist was frayed through by the ice. After her capsize she had apparently managed to reach her kayak and tied the line from her waist to her kayak. She had put her neoprene gloves on and had activated her PLB. Eventually she had succumbed to the cold and the awesome power of the North Atlantic storm. When we approached her kayak, we could see that its bottom had been torn open from being tossed against the rocky shoreline and the glacier ice.

I was relieved that we had found her body and that I could take her home to her family and friends in Denmark. On the way back to Nanortalik, due to bad weather with strong winds and rain, we had to fly around Kap Farvel. In this way Lone and I came around the big Kap of Greenland, around which we had planned to paddle on our expedition. I sat beside her in the helicopter on the way home. I thought about all of the good and happy moments we had had together during the last month, about sharing our thoughts, ideas, and experiences, about her generosity and friendly open-mindedness toward the people of Greenland and Denmark, and about all of the unconditional understanding, respect, and helpfulness that she had given me. The flight around Kap Farvel was the most difficult and sad journey of my lifetime.

When the accident happened, we were only about three kayaking days, or 100 kilometers, from Prins Christian Sund. Because our planned expedition deadline, the first of October, was so close, we had planned to use the satellite phone from the next campsite to call our contact persons to inform them that we were a bit delayed but would soon show up.

Neither Lone nor I were experts in doing Eskimo rolls with our kayaks. We had had several discussions about rolls during our journey. Lone doubted that we could manage to do Eskimo rolls under demanding conditions with high seas and a heavy load aboard. Personally, I believed then, as I still do today, that an Eskimo roll might be your only hope. I had told her that my first goal, after rounding Kap Farvel and reaching Nanortalik, would be to perfect my Eskimo roll. We had agreed to take an intensive course in rolling after our expedition. We planned to practice rolling with and without cargo, and in rough water with a rescue boat standing by. We had also discussed looking into one-person life rafts such as are used on military aircraft. I have since found some that weigh only around 3 kilograms and measure 36 by 36 by 18 centimeters.

Next time I undertake a paddling expedition, I will do so earlier in the summer. Earlier in the summer there is still a lot of sea ice in southeast Greenland. While it is important not to get too far offshore or to get trapped and crushed in moving ice masses, the ice dampens the waves a lot and was of great comfort to us during the first part of this expedition.

After I become competent at rolling, I will eventually return to Patussoq Fjord to complete that expedition and to pay my respects to Lone, a woman of uncommon courage, strength, and human warmth. I had promised her I would build a memorial from rocks if she should happen to lose her life somewhere along that rough coast of southeast Greenland.

4

A Very Near Miss off the Coast of Maine

David Boyle

I t was whitewater I always worried about—I didn't think sea kayaking would almost kill me. Although I have been a whitewater paddler for 15 years, sea kayaking had come later, at the urging of my wife, Audrey. Together we explored Nova Scotia, Newfoundland, and Grand Manan Island in the Bay of Fundy. As the appeal of kayaking on the ocean took hold, many trips would follow. Paddling with friends, I would reach some of the islands far off the Maine coast, often during late-season overnight trips. It is somewhat ironic, but somehow not surprising, that when I finally came to grief it was so close to home.

Health problems now prevent Audrey from paddling with me, and solo outings have proven to be an excellent way to escape and think about things. On June 12, 1999, I set out to paddle my Naiad (a 17 ft. 1.5 in. by 20.5 in. Derek Hutchinson design manufactured by Southern Exposure Sea Kayaks) to Seguin Island, about 2 miles out from the mouth of the Kennebec River in the midcoast region of Maine. The Seguin trip starts only 12 miles from our home and offers an intriguing destination: a lighthouse and museum operated by volunteer caretakers during the summer. The Maine Island Trail Association guidebook lists the region as a "danger area . . . deserving of extreme caution" because of the strong river currents and ocean swells. I had visited Seguin on five previous outings, including three solo trips.

This time I set out about 2 hours before low tide to ride the ebb out of the river. I planned to wait on the island and return on the incoming flood tide. The weather radio reported seas of 2 to 4 feet, with winds at 11 mph. As I departed from the river mouth on this sunny, 73°F afternoon, I told Audrey not to worry if I was late getting back.

Once beyond Pond Island, the last island in the mouth of the river, conditions were rougher than I expected, with 4- to 5-foot waves coming in from the southeast. Waves were creating ugly breakers over a shallow bar extending from the island well out to sea. I considered turning back, but I didn't want to paddle against the strong current in the river. I continued on a course parallel to the breakers until clear of Wood Island to my right, then turned west to paddle away from the breakers on a course parallel to shore. This would offer me a chance to bail out by heading to shore at Popham Beach State Park, to the west. Following this new course, I saw what appeared to be a safe route leading to Seguin—another 2 miles offshore—and I headed out, paddling directly into the oncoming waves.

I made good progress as I passed between a line of breakers on the left and a smaller area of breaking waves off to the right. During

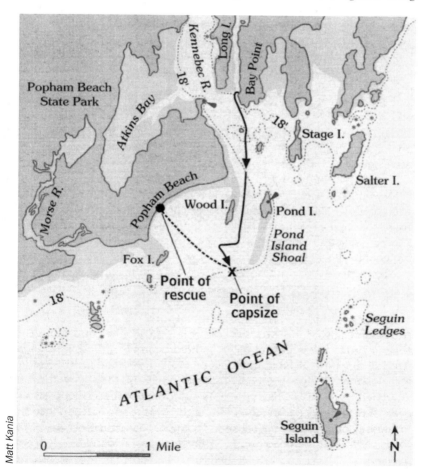

the entire time of my approach I hadn't seen any waves in the section I was paddling in. With only a short distance remaining to reach clear water beyond the area of breakers, a particularly large wave—maybe 8 feet—approached and steepened, then broke just ahead of the boat. I sped up to punch through the oncoming foam crest, but my kayak was stopped and then surfed backward down the face of the wave. In an instant the stern dove under and the boat pitchpoled end-for-end over backward, landing upside down. The impact wasn't violent, however, and I prepared to right the boat with an Eskimo roll. I probably rushed through my first attempt and failed to roll up. On the second try, I told myself to take my time and concentrate on setting up. I knew very well how important it was not to fail. I was somewhat shocked when the second attempt also failed. I was running out of air and had to make a quick escape from the overturned boat, but I couldn't find the grab loop on the spray skirt. Finally, I grabbed the neoprene of the skirt itself and yanked it free.

As I surfaced, another breaking wave came rushing forward, and I knew that I had to keep my grip on the boat and the paddle at all costs if I were to have any chance of saving myself. I barely managed to do this as the wave swept over. A third breaking wave advanced and again I hung on. These waves pushed me back into calmer water, where I was able to rest while hanging onto the cockpit rim of the overturned kayak. I was OK, except that I was choking and coughing up sea water that I must have swallowed while getting thrashed in the waves or while bailing out of the boat.

I was wearing polypropylene underwear (long-sleeve shirt and pants) under a sleeveless shorty Thermal Stretch wetsuit. Over that I was wearing a paddle jacket with neoprene cuffs and a Velcro-closure collar that had a tear at the back of the neck. The neoprene spray skirt and life jacket also helped insulate my torso, so initially I didn't feel too cold in the water.

By now my prescription sunglasses were gone and it was hard to judge distance, but I estimated that I was about a half mile from the tip of Wood Island, the nearest land.

I ducked under water and climbed into the overturned boat. Although I have done a reentry and roll in favorable conditions, the water I had swallowed kept me from holding my breath long enough. After sliding into the boat, I was out of air before I could get the paddle into position and managed only to get partway up. I took my PFD off and tried unsuccessfully to use it as a paddle float to do an assisted roll. With it off, I felt much colder, and I was terribly frightened of losing it. I quickly put it back on. Hoping to make the boat easier to roll, I discarded the bilge pump on the deck and a water bottle from the cockpit. In all, I tried to reenter and roll eight *(continued page 36)*

MAKING ROUGH-WATER RESCUES WORK

Roger Schumann

It's a wet slog into a south wind across Princeton Harbor near Half Moon Bay, California. The wind is at 25 knots with occasional gusts into the 30s. Paddling hard, I'm able to make little over a knot of headway against the steady staccato of whitecaps smacking the hull and spraying my face. The sea conditions include 8- to 10-foot swells at close intervals, steep breaking seas with 2 to 3 feet of confused chop, and rain heavy at times. It is a typical winter storm front on the Pacific Coast. With no rocks downwind to wash into, I capsize and pop my skirt, careful to hold tight to my kayak in the sloshing seas. For this exercise I've limited my rescue options: The demo kayak I've borrowed from the nearby shop has no rear-deck rigging to secure my paddle for a paddle-float self-rescue. But that's not much of a problem since I have no paddle float, pump, or paddle leash. No rescue gear at all. The boat is equipped, however, with bulkheads fore and aft and has a large cockpit, which make a good combination for the rescue I want to practice: the cowboy scramble.

I make my way to the front of the boat and grab hold of the bow and time the swells. As I bob to the crest, I give a hard scissors kick with my legs and punch the bow skyward with my outstretched right arm; as the stern drops into the trough, most of the water in the cockpit drains to the aft bulkhead and dumps back into the sea; then with one quick motion, I spin the kayak back upright just before it drops back onto the water.

I scramble across the stern and straddle it like a cowboy on a bronco. I use my paddle to brace. Keeping my weight low, I slither up the kayak on my stomach, and when my face is even with the front deck bungees and my butt is hovering over the cockpit, I wait to let a wave crest splash past, then quickly drop my butt onto the seat and slap a high-brace on my right (strong) side. I scull for support as another wave passes by. I lift my right leg into the cockpit and find the foot brace with my toes. In the lull of the next trough, I bring my left foot in. I've drifted sideways to the swell by now, so I spin my bow back to face the waves before attempting to reseal the skirt. This can be tricky. I let a crest pass, set the paddle across my lap, attach the skirt in back, grab the paddle and brace against the next swell, set the paddle down, finish attaching the skirt in front, and grab the paddle and brace again. Waves have sloshed a few inches of water back into the cockpit, but not *(continued next page)* so much that the kayak becomes unstable. Skirt in place, I turn and paddle toward the harbor and slip back into the lee of the jetty.

I have to say I broke at least three cardinal rules of safe kayaking: I went out alone, ignored gale warnings, and failed to carry even the most basic rescue gear. But it's important to practice a variety of rescues in rough conditions. Although deliberately underequipped, I had practiced this self-bailing cowboy scramble rescue enough times to have faith in its success. I'm not recommending that you rush out in rough water to try this self-rescue. My height and long arms make it possible for me to raise the bow high enough to drain the cockpit. The scramble onto the aft deck may be difficult for some even in calm water. For this rescue to work at all, the cockpit must be large enough (or your legs short enough) to get your legs back in the boat after you've planted your butt in the seat. The best rescue for you in rough water may well be different.

It's not that I don't believe in rescue gear. I routinely carry a paddle float and a pump. And I have no bones to pick with those who take the trouble to rig elaborate self-rescue lashings on their back decks and customize their boats with electric pumps. But gear can fail. Deck rigging can break or become tangled; paddle floats can leak or blow away. In cold water, when it's important to get out of the water quickly, equipment takes time to rig. In rough conditions, where you have to work in the brief lulls between wave crests, speed is of the essence. Having only self-rescue methods that depend on your own custom-outfitted kayak can leave you unable to safely paddle any other boat; heaven help a gear junkie who rents or borrows a kayak that lacks the rigging needed for self-rescue. If you practice self-rescues without using deck rigging or even a paddle float, you may be surprised to discover what you can accomplish without them. Practicing without gear will make using it that much easier by comparison. I'm not advocating gearless rescues. The point is to develop a variety of rescues for use in a range of conditions: The more rescue options you have, the safer you'll be.

Practice is the Key

Although I've learned ways to climb back into my boat without using sponsons or a paddle float even in fairly rough seas, my success is much less a matter of talent than of persistence. During my first year of paddling, I practiced self-rescues nearly religiously, every time I went out, until they became second nature, even boring. Then I worked on variations. I still practice regularly. Practice is the only way first to discover which rescues will (or won't) work for you in rough water and then to keep those skills sharp.

It's especially important to practice in the kinds of conditions that are likely to cause a capsize in the first place, in order to discover the many ways rough water can complicate the standard rescues you may have previously practiced only on flatwater. Everything gets a little harder. Boats, paddles, rescue floats, water bottles, and other gear can quickly wash out of reach, and even if you manage to hang onto all your stuff, you can drift into a surf zone or shipping channel before finishing the rescue. Your boat can fill with water faster than you can pump; balancing is tricky. A lot of little things can go wrong.

Rough-Water Simulator

Although it makes an excellent training ground, rough water is not always convenient to come by, and the catch-22 is that if it's not safe to paddle in rough water before you've practiced rescues in it, how are you supposed to get rough-water practice in the first place? Before you have to use the following rescues in a gale, practice them first. You don't need to find rough water. Just create some of your own.

Take turns playing "virtual ocean" with your rescue partner as the "ocean": standing in waist-deep water, bouncing and twisting the bow of your capsized boat while you attempt to reenter. The idea is for the "ocean" to make it slightly challenging at first. Later, as your skills improve, let all hell break loose.

When you can get back into your boat regardless of the worst the ocean can throw at you, and you can do it in well under 2 minutes, you're ready to test yourself in the actual sea. In addition to being effective, a good rough-water reentry is also quick, so you don't end up drifting from bad conditions to worse with hypothermia creeping in to complicate matters. It's good if you can reenter your kayak in under 2 minutes; the closer to 1 minute the better, and anything under a minute is excellent.

Rough-Water Practice

Location is crucial for rough-water training sessions. When it's windy, make sure to choose a site with onshore winds and a soft, sandy beach to wash into if you don't finish reentering fast enough. A tide rip can be another handy practice area, assuming it will sweep you around into an eddy and not out into a shipping lane. A gale is not necessary, or even recommended, as a training ground.

Start gradually in whatever conditions are "rough" for you; if you regularly paddle flatwater, then the foot of chop kicked up by the 15-knot afternoon winds you typically paddle home in would be a good place to start. Ideally, you'll have a seasoned rough-water paddler with you to keep an eye on things. The *(continued next page)* rougher the water you eventually practice in, the more you'll expand your margin of safety as well as your confidence and your comfort zone. But besides being good for you, rough-water rescue practice is also fun.

The idea of practicing in rough water is to discover which re-entries work best for you in which situations. Each rough-water situation is a little different. With practice you'll learn to anticipate problems, and you'll probably develop a few twists and tricks of your own, which is the whole point. Practice to fine-tune your favorite reentries and develop a few backups, and you'll be that much safer on the water.

or ten times, needing longer and longer to rest each time before trying again. Ducking under the cold water was uncomfortable.

After coming to the surface on my tenth or so try, the boat seemed to be spinning in the water, then the whole ocean appeared to be spinning. I knew that I had to fight the disorientation or it would kill me. I had stowed my neoprene hood in the front hatch of my boat. It would have slowed the significant amount of heat I was losing from my head and would have been especially helpful when I was ducking under water to try self-rescue rolls. Unfortunately, I could not get to it now without the risk of flooding the forward compartment of the boat. Realizing that I needed help, I activated the strobe light on my PFD.

I spotted a sailboat that seemed to be headed directly for me. I waved my paddle vertically overhead in an attempt to be more visible above the wave chop, and yelled as they came closer. I had a set of flares that I could have used to attract their notice, but these were also in the forward compartment of the kayak. I had a compressed-gas foghorn in the pocket of my PFD, but I didn't think to use it. The sailboat passed maybe 200 yards off, without noticing me.

I turned the kayak upright and tried to lie across the cockpit, but it took too much energy to balance in this position. Given the kayak's narrow beam and small cockpit, any attempt to reenter the boat by sliding over the stern was out of the question. With the boat capsized, there was no way to get a grip to climb onto the slippery hull. It seemed absurd that I couldn't find some way to get back into the boat.

The cold water was becoming decidedly more uncomfortable. At times I felt as though I had become a second person, passively observing myself. As I drifted with the boat, I had a sense of moving in the direction of Popham Beach. Since earlier I had paddled west well beyond Wood Island, which is connected by a sand bar at low tide to the eastern end of Popham Beach, I had probably escaped the outflow of the river. This could have been the only reason I was drifting in toward shore rather than out to sea.

The last conscious thought I remember was that the waves seemed to be getting short and choppy, as they do in shallow water. After that, I have no memory of anything until I woke up in the emergency room of Mid Coast Hospital.

I later learned that I drifted in to shore at Popham Beach. My empty kayak was seen adrift, and a beachgoer saw me in the water with my strobe light flashing and pulled me ashore. I was unconscious and had swallowed a lot of water. The 3 hours I had been in the 58°F water had left me in a serious state of hypothermia. Park ranger Matt Guilfoil did an excellent job of responding and, in the short time before the ambulance came, was able to get me into dry clothing with the help of items lent by bystanders.

When I reached the hospital, my core temperature was down to 83°F; it had probably been slightly lower on the beach. This is about as low as you can get without permanent damage, and very close to not surviving at all. One of my doctors estimated that another half hour in the water would have finished me off. I remained on oxygen that night and the following day before my lungs could maintain the proper blood oxygen level. After the trauma of water in my lungs, pneumonia set in.

I remained coated in sand until I could finally manage a shower. When I mentioned that I had a sore throat, my ICU nurse slyly suggested that I gargle with salt water.

Four days later I was home, and a month later I was back to normal, at least physically. I continue to think a lot about the incident. I was extremely lucky to come ashore and in a populated area where immediate help was available. I am very glad to be alive.

EPILOGUE

Right after the capsize, I hadn't felt that I was in any immediate danger. I felt at peace with my surroundings. I think that the adrenaline from the emergency initially overrode any sensation of being cold. Ducking my head underwater during my reentry-and-roll attempts made my head spin and accelerated the hypothermia process. I became apathetic about trying to judge how far from shore I was. It seemed too far to hope I could drift in, so I didn't want to think about it. Eventually, the cold became painful, and I was terrified that there was no escaping it. Dying by hypothermia is not a pleasant way to go, as people sometimes think. Later, the sensation of being an outside observer watching myself became distressing because this alter ego was telling me, "It really doesn't matter." I wrestled to overcome this feeling. I am still surprised by how suddenly I lost consciousness and by how I have absolutely no memory of anything until I woke up in the hospital. There was no life flashing before my eyes, no light at the end of the tunnel—just nothing. I remain grateful to everyone involved in my rescue, including the Popham Beach State Park staff, the people on the beach who assisted, the Phippsburg volunteer ambulance crew, and the Mid Coast Hospital staff.

AN ANALYSIS
Christopher Cunningham

Although David, 54, had made the crossing to Seguin a number of times, both alone and with partners, on this trip he happened to be at the wrong place—crossing a shallow river bar—at the wrong time—the moment an exceptional set of waves arrived.

Exceptional waves may be infrequent, but they are a common factor in emergencies. David had been diligent in watching the water along the path he intended to take, but unfortunately he didn't see any water breaking there until it was too late to avoid it. David attacked the wave, hoping to punch through, but he hadn't gained enough momentum by the time the falling crest hit him. He might have avoided pitchpoling if he had capsized just before impact, but that wouldn't have changed his situation much: He would still have had to roll up.

It is commendable that David knew how to roll and that he tried a second roll when his first failed. In pool practice the previous winter he could roll without fail on either side. David had paddled whitewater, which kept his reflexes sharp and his bracing skills tuned. While he had rolled a number of times in whitewater this summer, his rolling was not as reliable in moving water as it was in the pool, so he avoided stretches of whitewater that might go beyond his skills and force him to roll.

Rolling before you set out from the beach is a useful exercise. If you are not dressed for the water, you'll get a reality check on what it means to be in the water. You'll see if your gear is properly secured and if you can count on your roll with the load you have in the boat and the gear you are wearing.

Since the waters along the Maine coast are cold, David didn't practice rolling while he was out sea kayaking. A number of his friends had had surgery to remove bony growths (osteomata) from their ears, the result of repeated exposure to cold water. Earplugs are now available for watersports to protect your ears from cold. A neoprene hood can offer some protection, at least to keep water that is slapping the side of your head from being driven into the ear canal. While osteomata are a hazard of long-term exposure, the vertigo that David experienced can happen quickly when the cold reaches the inner ear and your sense of balance deteriorates. Feeling like the world is spinning makes it difficult to get your bearings while rolling and impairs your ability to balance and brace effectively as you try to paddle. David had brought a neoprene hood with him, but he had packed it in the forward compartment.

There may be several reasons that David's efforts to roll failed. He jettisoned his bilge pump from the deck and a water bottle from the cockpit. He had both a 2-liter and a 1-liter bottle aboard. The weight of the water could have been an advantage for his roll if it had been secured against the bottom of the hull. I have a strap just forward of the seat in my kayak that holds a 2-liter bottle. The weight of it, low in the boat, increases the boat's stability and helps to right the boat when I roll. David also thought that he may have lost some flexibility due to aging—a good reason to stretch regularly—and because of the many layers of clothing he was wearing. Whatever the case, he may have discovered that his roll was not reliable had he practiced before setting out, and he might have chosen a route closer to shore because of it.

After his roll failed, David's next option was to wet-exit. This is a fairly common practice, although a number of options are available to the capsized paddler. You can use the paddle to scull up for air, or use your hands to swim up for air. If you have a foam paddle float, a partially inflated paddle float, or a self-inflating float, a float roll can be an option—if not to right the kayak, at least to get some air. It is possible to attach the float to the end of the paddle as an aid to rolling. David tried this float-assisted roll using his PFD—a good improvisation—but, as he realized, it posed the risk of losing his PFD. David's wife had an inflatable paddle float, but he had not practiced with it. A paddle float is not just a tool for a kayaker who can't roll: It is a backup for a paddler whose roll fails.

David showed good composure in getting his spray skirt off when he couldn't find the grab loop. He was using a whitewater spray skirt with a small grab loop. A grab loop that is easy to use while you are right side up might not be so easy to use in an emergency. A loop of webbing might not be enough. You might need to add something to the loop, such as a small plastic ball, that you can easily find and grip while you are upside down with your eyes shut and with gloves on.

Once he was out of the kayak, he still felt in control of the situation, but his options were limited. As a solo paddler, he could not count on the assistance of another paddler. Since groups of paddlers are often scattered by adverse conditions and may be unable to help each other, every paddler should have several ways to recover from a wet exit. Since an assisted rescue was not a possibility, David moved to a reentry and roll, a quick and effective self-rescue for a roller. Unfortunately, the water he had inhaled made it impossible to hold his breath long enough to position himself securely in the cockpit and to set up properly for a roll. While a reentry and roll is a useful technique, it isn't going to do you much good if you have no remedy for the reason you might have failed to roll in the first place. And, as David found out, dunking his head underwater in each attempt had debilitating consequences.

With the exception of a cowboy scramble rescue (which is practical only in kayaks with cockpits long enough so that you can straddle the kayak, drop your rear end into the seat, and then swing your legs into the cockpit), effective reentry techniques rely on various kinds of equipment to stabilize the kayak: a paddle float and deck rigging to secure it as an outrigger, or a device like inflatable sponsons. David's boat did not have outrigger deck rigging for a paddle float. He had taken along a webbing sling that he could have used to rig a stirrup and hold the paddle on deck, but the sling drifted away after the capsize. Without the extra stability this gear provides, David found it impossible to get back aboard. He was too far from shore, and his clothing didn't provide enough insulation from the cold water for him to survive a swim. His options for recovery from the capsize had run out. He needed to be rescued.

Getting out of the water and on top of the boat would have extended his survival time. He tried to get on top of the boat while it was right side up, but he had to work too hard to keep the boat from capsizing. If the boat had been more stable while upside down, David might have been able to get onto the upturned hull by crawling up over the bow or stern and wrapping his arms around the kayak, then pulling himself toward the middle of the hull by grabbing the deck lines underwater.

David had flares, but they were stowed in the forward compartment. Since he was in rough water, he couldn't risk opening the hatch and flooding the compartment to get the flares. Anything that you might need while on the water should be in your PFD, secured under your deck lines, or in a deck bag—somewhere that you can get to it when you need it. As long as you are afloat, a watertight compartment's essential function is to keep the kayak afloat. If he had had access to flares, they might have caught the attention of the sailboat. However, a flare will be noticed only if someone is looking in your direction. The aerial flares that paddlers usually carry are visible for only a few seconds. A set of three is a bare minimum. Parachute flares, smoke flares, and signal mirrors are useful additions to a signaling kit. David had an air horn on his PFD that he didn't think of using. He found out later that it didn't work anyway when wet. A distress whistle is easy to carry on a PFD, and the sound of a whistle carries farther than a voice. While visual and audible signals could have attracted the attention of people in the area, a VHF radio could have reached the Coast Guard or other vessels in the area. Submersible VHF radios are now quite economical and require no license to operate. The latest PLBs are small enough to fit in a PFD pocket and can transmit a distress signal and location.

With his prescription glasses gone, David found it difficult to gauge the distance to the nearest land, but he was able to see a sailboat at 200 yards and discern that it was coming his way. Although the loss of his glasses didn't have a significant impact on David's situation, if your vision without contact lenses or glasses would prevent you from using a VHF radio or signaling devices or from seeing potential rescuers in the distance, you should secure your eyeglasses against loss and carry a backup pair.

David did many things to make himself a safe paddler. He had at least one layer of clothing designed to keep him warm in the water, he knew how to roll, he had whitewater paddling skills, he had some emergency equipment, and he had been keeping an eye on the route he intended to take. He might have had another successful crossing to Seguin under his belt if not for one unexpected wave. Many of the things he discovered after capsizing would have made themselves evident if he had practiced capsizing, rolling, and performing self-rescues closer to shore. The place to find out what can go wrong is on a lee shore where the consequences of a failure of technique or equipment are not so severe.

5

Lost and Stranded on a Columbia River Island

Andrew Emlen

The Lewis and Clark National Wildlife Refuge, in the lower Columbia River, is a network of low islands intersected by a maze of sloughs. The solitude and wildlife among these islands in the 35,000-acre refuge is attracting an increasing number of sea kayakers, but that same inviting tangle can make navigation difficult when things go wrong. As a kayak guide, I know this area well.

On Saturday, March 4, 2000, two kayakers set out from Skamokawa, Washington, where the Columbia River is 3 miles wide, and headed toward Welch Island, which lies a little over a mile away to the southwest across the shipping channel. Jeff and Tom (not their real names) were both in their early fifties. Jeff had 14 years of kayaking experience, most of it in Puget Sound. He and his wife, Linda, had taken three kayaking courses at a highly regarded kayak school in Seattle, including a weekend campout to practice navigation. Tom had taken a one-day introductory kayak course and had gone out with Jeff once before.

Jeff had planned a nice, leisurely afternoon complete with a big picnic lunch, in hopes of enticing Tom to be his partner in future kayaking adventures. The day looked promising: sunny with a temperature in the low fifties, with winds from 2 to 10 mph.

Before setting out, the two men stopped to eat at the Skamokawa Kayak Center's café; then they launched from Skamokawa, paddling toward Welch Island. They paddled Jeff's 22-foot Current Designs Libra double kayak. They carried a small cooler of food, a camp stove, a coffeepot, duct tape, a mini first-aid kit, two towropes, and a plastic jar holding matches, toilet paper, a gauze bandage, and sunscreen. They also had a nautical chart, a handheld compass, and a storm whistle, and each carried a water bottle. Tom wore a shorty 2 mm wetsuit over CoolMax polyester long underwear. Jeff wore a dry suit over CoolMax underwear, a heavy fleece vest, and neoprene gloves. Both wore Type III PFDs. Jeff had intended to take a second dry bag containing flares, first-aid supplies, and extra fleece clothing, but forgot and left it in the truck. Tom left his cell phone in the truck because he had not received a strong enough signal in Long Beach, 30 miles away, and figured he wouldn't be able to use it.

They probably reached the northwest end of Welch Island by 12:30 or so, 30 minutes before the day's high tide of 8.4 feet. They thought that they were rounding the northwest tip of Fitzpatrick, the next island downstream—a mistake they made because most of Fitzpatrick is underwater at that tide. The part of Fitzpatrick that is never submerged is over half a mile from Welch Island and is easily visually lost against the far shoreline.

They intended to return through the passage between Welch and Fitzpatrick, the passage they had, in fact, just gone through. As they headed upstream along the Oregon side (southwest) of Welch Island, they bypassed the pair of sloughs at its downstream end (including the one that bisects the island), mistaking them for the dead-end marsh in the center of Fitzpatrick. They then headed up the next slough, assuming it was the one that provides a clear passage between Fitzpatrick and Welch. In fact, however, that slough was a dead-end to the center of Welch. As they continued, the slough got narrower, until they were pushing aside branches in water just wide and deep enough for their boat.

Still believing that they were on narrow Fitzpatrick Island, they pressed on, convinced that they must be close to the far side. But as the tide receded, they became stranded. Trying to walk through this slough is difficult, as it is full of waist-deep sinkholes, soft mud, logs, and brush. They decided to wait for the next high tide at 2:06 A.M. and then paddle out by starlight.

The early morning tide, however, was only 7.8 feet, and there wasn't enough water to fill the slough. Jeff and Tom were crestfallen as they concluded that it would be impossible to pull the boat back through the mud to open water. The night was clear and about 28°F. They stayed warm by walking around all night and building a short-lived fire with dead grasses. They were thankful for the warmth of their life vests. All night they were surrounded by the shrieks of coyotes and unidentified noises emanating from the thicket around them. Even in that situation, Jeff said he found himself torn between the concern for being lost and cold and being enthralled by "how cool it was!"

In the morning they used the stove to heat up a pot of tea mixed with generous amounts of cream and sugar. They dragged the boat north through the mud and brush for 100 yards or so, then decided to abandon it. They headed north, reckoning that if they were on

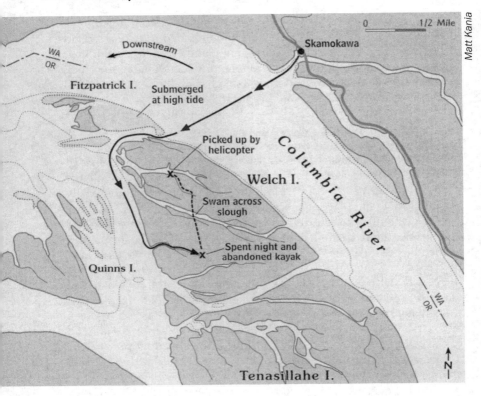

Fitzpatrick Island, a northerly course would soon bring them close to the main river channel where they could flag down help. They packed two dry bags with most of their food and their matches and used their paddles as walking staffs.

Meanwhile, I walked into the Skamokawa Center café at 8:15 Sunday morning after an early-morning walk in the Julia Butler Hansen Refuge with my kayak tour guests. Michaela, who had served and talked to Jeff and Tom as they ate on Saturday, saw their truck still in the parking lot and was sure that yesterday they had said they were out only for the day to visit Tenasillahe Island.

I called the Wahkiakum County sheriff's office. They tracked down Jeff's home number from his license plate and tried to verify with his wife that they were indeed missing. Meanwhile, my tour guests declined the second day of our tour so I could search. I called Dave Christenson, another guide. Jan Miller, the Skamokawa Center manager, stood on the dock and flagged down every boat going out to fish, asking them to watch for the missing kayakers. A kayaking group from Lane Community College also volunteered, and soon more than 15 boats were searching the area.

Jeff and Tom, meanwhile, were slogging through dense willow and dogwood, clambering over fallen cottonwood trees, and sinking into waist-deep mud holes. Every once in a while, Tom blew a set of three blasts on the storm whistle as Jeff yelled for help. They eventually reached the slough that bisects Welch Island at a point where the slough is about 200 feet wide. They used grass to light an abandoned tire on fire and attempted to warm up. The fire didn't produce enough heat to warm them or enough smoke for signaling. As the fire dwindled, they decided that their best option was to swim the slough and press on toward what they hoped would be the north side of Fitzpatrick, where they might attract the attention of a boat. Tom plunged into the 43°F water and immediately climbed out again, insisting, "I'd only get halfway across and I'm going to die!"

"Just let your wetsuit do its job," Jeff urged. "In two minutes your body will warm up the water against your skin. I'll take the gear." Tom plunged in again and Jeff swam after him with both paddles and the two dry bags. They clambered onto the far shore and continued walking north.

As I paddled in a loop around Welch and then upriver to Tenasillahe Island in search of Jeff and Tom, I called in to Skamokawa Center every hour. Each time I called, I was told that the sheriff's office would launch a search once they had verified with Jeff's wife, Linda, that the men were missing. The Coast Guard, whom Jan had called from Skamokawa Center, was also waiting for verification before sending a helicopter. When I called at 1:00 P.M., I was told that the search had been called off. The sheriff's office had reached Linda and reported that she said the men had spent the night at a house in Long Beach. The sheriff's office subsequently called off the search.

What Linda had actually said was that the men had *intended* to spend the day paddling in the Skamokawa area and then drive to Long Beach to stay at a friend's vacation home because they weren't equipped for camping. She had no idea that the sheriff's office had understood that to mean that they had, in fact, spent the night in Long Beach and weren't missing.

Linda decided to drive down from Seattle to be nearby during the search for her husband. When she arrived at Skamokawa Center, Linda introduced herself to Lori, a staff member, and was surprised by Lori's nonchalance. When Linda brought up the subject of her husband and his friend, Lori happily asked, "Oh, how are they?"

"I don't know," Linda replied. When Lori informed Linda that everyone thought the men were safe in Long Beach and that the search had been called off hours earlier, Linda was stunned. "How could they get that so wrong?" she wailed. It was now just after 4:00 P.M.

About the same time, Jeff and Tom had gotten as far as they

could walk. They were still on the shore of a slough within Welch Island, but they could see out to the shipping channel to the west and hoped they could flag someone down. In fact, due to shallows at the mouth of the slough, it was unlikely that any motorized boat would pass within half a mile. Since it was late in the day and evening was approaching, they built a platform of sticks where they could spend the night if they had to, and they continued to blow the whistle and call for help periodically.

At 4:30, Linda filled out a missing person's report at the sheriff's office, and the Coast Guard was notified. A Coast Guard helicopter that was out on another mission was asked to respond. By the time they would begin searching, little over an hour of daylight would remain.

TAKING COMFORT
Christopher Cunningham

An adventure is interesting enough in retrospect, especially to the person who didn't have it; at the time it happens, it usually constitutes an exceedingly disagreeable experience.
—Vilhjalmur Stefansson, Arctic explorer

I grew up believing that camping entailed a fair bit of discomfort. When my father first took me backpacking, I was often cold and wet, and my shoulders and hips ached from sleeping on hard ground. He never bought a tent for backpacking, so our only shelter was a large sheet of black plastic. Hung from trees, it provided some protection from the rain, but it was hot during the day, cold at night, and in the morning dripping with condensation.

Since then, I have changed my approach to the outdoors. I now measure the success of my camps by the degree of comfort I can achieve. My greatest challenge was a 2,400-mile solo river trip in the middle of winter. The weather was either cold, wet ,or both, but I was able to carry on for two and a half months by steering well clear of discomfort. I always ate well, and with only two exceptions I slept well. There was no shortage of hardships, and I might end one day with my parka and PFD skinned in ice and start another by trudging through knee-deep, boot-sucking mud to the water's edge. In foul weather, I counted getting warm and dry as a significant achievement.

One of the worst nights I've ever had was during what was supposed to be a summer day trip. My kayaking partner and I were unexpectedly stranded on an island, quite unprepared to spend the night. We had cell phone coverage and could let folks at home know that we were safe, but we were stuck for the night. At dusk hoards of mosquitoes grew fat and happy at our expense. A thunderstorm blew them away but brought cold wind and rain. We lay down on the ground wishing for sleep, but there was only a long miserable night of waiting for dawn. I had plenty of time to think about all of the bivouac gear I'd carry next time, not just to be comfortable on an unexpected night out but to be able to face the morning well rested and rational. At first light we were hell bent on escaping our island prison, wind and waves be damned.

Whether you are ashore or afloat, the comfort you're able to create for yourself in a harsh environment is a good measure of your skill, preparedness, and adaptability. Discomfort consumes energy; comfort renews it. But it's more than a practical matter of energy management. Just as your blood is shunted away from your extremities when your warmth dissipates into cold, the sphere of your awareness shrinks around discomfort. The world around you dims whether the sun has set or not. Comfort is often the buffer between you and Stefansson's brand of "adventure." Eating and sleeping well prepare you for paddling safely.

Feeling the need to do something, Linda went to the Elochoman Slough Marina in Cathlamet to see if she could hire someone to take her out in a boat to look. She asked a group of fishermen coming in to the marina if they would do so, but they refused, explaining that their boat was not equipped for running at night. Seeing how desperate she was to find her husband, one of them mentioned that he had heard whistles and someone shouting while they were motoring toward the marina. "I thought it was someone training their dog."

"Where?" asked Linda.

"At that island across from the park," he said, indicating Welch Island.

Linda rushed back to the sheriff's office, insisting she knew where the missing men were. The Coast Guard helicopter crew were acting on a report of a kayaker six miles downriver and agreed to check Welch when they were finished.

When Lori told me that Jeff and Tom were still out there, I launched my kayak and began checking under the overhanging trees along the north shore of the river. At sunset I saw a helicopter descending over Welch Island and heard on the VHF that they had recovered the missing kayakers. The Coast Guard dropped them off at Vista Park, a quarter mile from the Center, where Linda was waiting.

Back at Skamokawa Center, Jeff and Tom told me their story before going to Long Beach for a hot bath. I should have given them a warm beverage and put them in a tub right there. Although they were perfectly lucid and coordinated, had been checked and released by the Coast Guard, and told me they weren't hypothermic, an acute stress reaction no doubt had been masking the effects of their ordeal. Jeff told me later that after an hour in a heated car, fatigue, soreness, and chills set in, and he literally had to crawl to the bathtub. Another day would pass before he felt his body was producing enough heat to keep warm.

The next day, Dave and I found the men's paddles on a slough in the interior of Welch Island. A water bottle Dave spotted hanging on a willow was the only giveaway, as the tide had covered the ground with a foot of water. Their stick platform, paddles, and a spray skirt were all floating in the brush. I shuddered to think of the 30°F night they would have had in store, standing calf deep in 43° water. Jeff later said that, considering all they had endured up to that point, he didn't think they would have survived another night out there.

Their food container, surprisingly, still contained some smoked salmon and sliced meat and cheese, as they had saved food for another day. Jeff said that he had never been hungry during the time they were lost and that when they ran out of water they resorted to drinking from the river.

Knowing their story and the exact location where they had been picked up, I surmised which slough they had entered. When I went to retrieve their boat the following Tuesday, there was an 8.5-foot tide at about 3:00 P.M. Even knowing where I was and knowing how much time I had (unlike Jeff and Tom, who had not brought or checked a tide guide when they left), it was still a little hairy. Encouraged by the sight of a few broken branches, I pushed under trees and through willow thickets until I could go no farther. The slough dissolved into a swamp of intersecting passages, beaver meadows, and thickets.

I got out and walked a little to find a better vantage point, but saw nothing and returned to my boat, figuring I had blown my chance. Then I saw two sets of footprints, one with a wetsuit bootie tread. Assuming that at this point they would have already ventured out on foot, I calculated the boat must be to the south, so I doubled back and took another fork, which proved impassable. With less than half an hour before the turn of the tide, I returned to the first site and blundered through another passage where previously there hadn't been enough water for me to get through. I broke into another beaver meadow and saw the boat.

My enthusiasm was tempered by the fact that I now had to tow it out through the tangle. Clipping a towline to their boat, I turned around and began to paddle back out. Their kayak kept veering to the side, and I continually had to back up, redirect the bow, and pull it again. When I emerged into the open slough, I called in to the Center. My cell phone worked fine from within Welch Island. When I returned to the main river, I covered the cockpits with skirts I had brought along and began the slow tow back to Skamokawa. With a curious sea lion following, we made an interesting parade back across the shipping channel.

LESSONS LEARNED

Jeff and Tom would not have fared so well if they hadn't done some things right. The dry suit and wetsuit helped keep them warm enough to survive, as did the large amount of food that they took and the means to heat it. The storm whistle ultimately proved to be a valuable signaling device, even though the fisherman who heard it did not realize that the three blasts were a distress signal. They also kept a good attitude throughout and focused on taking action instead of panicking. That said, both men recognized that they had made some mistakes, and they were pretty contrite upon their return. "This has taken me down a couple notches," conceded Jeff.

Their story is a good example of the importance of a float plan, even for a short afternoon paddle. Jeff and Tom should have left a detailed float plan with Linda, including instructions for her to initiate a search if they did not call in by a specified time to report that they were safely ashore. With such a float plan in effect, the search for them would have been launched the first night.

Jeff and Tom's informal conversation with Michaela Miller and the fact that she recognized their truck among the others in a full parking lot turned out to be a stroke of luck that eventually led to a search long before they would have been missed Sunday night when they didn't return to Seattle. Both the sheriff and the Coast Guard still needed to have verification from a responsible party before undertaking the risk and cost of a search. That meant they needed to get in touch with a relative. Not only would a float plan have initiated the search quickly, but it would also have provided the searchers with a better idea of what to look for and where to search. (You can find a float plan form on the *Sea Kayaker* website at www.seakayakermag. com/PDFs/Float_Plan_cs3_0909.pdf.)

A float plan would have sped up the search, but another simple item might have prevented the mishap altogether. A tide guide would have let Jeff and Tom know that they were starting just before high tide, so they would have expected Fitzpatrick Island to be largely submerged. On the chart Fitzpatrick appears mostly dark green, indicating land that is inundated at high tides. Uplands appear as a yellowish-brown.

Moreover, had they realized that it was almost high tide, they might well have headed in the opposite direction to begin with: upstream, to avoid fighting the ebb tide upon their return.

Most importantly, they might not have attempted to enter a shallow slough if they had known that the tide was ebbing. The islands of the Lewis and Clark Refuge are full of sloughs that need varying amounts of water to be navigable. In many sloughs, low tide leaves nothing but waist-deep mud, providing no practical alternative to waiting for the water to return. A good rule would be never to enter an unknown slough on an ebb tide unless the chart clearly shows a deep channel.

Finally, a tide guide would have shown that Sunday afternoon would provide a tide just higher than the one they went in on, offering a chance to return the way they came, paddling.

Of all the decisions made in their misadventure, each is understandable in some way. Most of us have forgotten equipment, gotten disoriented, or left on short trips without leaving a detailed float plan. However, abandoning a boat is a pretty serious action.

If, as they believed, Jeff and Tom had been on Fitzpatrick Island, they would have had to travel no more than a couple of hundred yards to reach the channel to the north, particularly after having gone in so far via water. Once they had gone farther to the north than would have been possible on Fitzpatrick, it would have been a good time to reassess their assumption about their whereabouts and return to the boat. If you get there by water, chances are you can return by water. The high tide on any given day is rarely significantly higher or lower than the same tide on the next day.

Moreover, a boat can have functions other than the obvious. If it has a bright color, it can enhance your chances of being spotted by rescuers. In an emergency, it can serve as a shelter, especially if one can get inside and place a skirt over the cockpit. A kayak hull can retain a lot of heat, and even more if it is filled or covered with dead grasses and leaves. They might have been able to pierce the bulkheads to provide themselves with room to lie down in their boat. As they carried duct tape, they may have been able to resecure the bulkheads temporarily before paddling.

Furthermore, they were carrying a pair of items that might have prevented their misadventure: a chart and an orienteering compass. Entire books are devoted to kayak navigation, but even basic position finding with a map and compass would have saved Jeff and Tom a good deal of misery.

Many people assume that it is nearly impossible to get lost on a river, but that's not the case. A minimal precaution when making a crossing in any unfamiliar waters is to find your position on the chart, sight on a landmark at your heading if possible, and, as you paddle on that heading, make sure that what you see corroborates your expectations. A deck compass makes this easier. A GPS with the charts loaded will also show you at a glance where you are.

When unsure where you are, you can sight on two landmarks and use those bearings to triangulate to find your location. All kayakers should learn this skill. Jeff and Tom, until they were in the midst of the thicket, were always within sight of two or more landmarks that appeared on their chart, including channel markers and prominent hills along the shore. Had they taken a couple of sightings before entering the dead-end slough, they would have realized that they were not where they thought they were. It's worth practicing these skills in a setting in which they aren't needed, so that you can use them quickly and confidently when you do need them.

Once Jeff and Tom were mired, there were a number of things they wished they had brought. It must have pained them to realize that some items they needed were right there in the truck. Had Tom tested his cell phone at the launch site, he would have known that it could indeed work on the river. It is definitely worth testing cell phones and radios at the launch site to make sure they are functioning properly.

A handheld VHF radio is a valuable piece of equipment in the marine environment, and it may be your best, if not your only, communication device in areas where cell phone reception is poor or nonexistent. Every paddling group should carry one. A PLB or a satellite messenger can be a life saver in an emergency.

As for their forgotten bag with flares and extra clothes, I also forget things. I've found that I need a written list of gear and supplies that I should take. I make an effort to read it every time I go out, and more than once it has sent me back to get my water bottle or even a VHF radio I'd left inside to recharge. That list should include signaling devices. In addition to the forgotten flares, smoke canisters, a signal mirror, or an air horn might have served Jeff and Tom well during the day. Air horns designed for use with personal watercraft are appropriately sized for use aboard kayaks.

When I asked Jeff and Tom what they most would have liked to have taken that they did not, the immediate response was "More warm clothes!" Jeff's dry suit and Tom's wetsuit made them better dressed for the elements than plenty of other people I've seen undertaking similar trips. But this was still less than ideal for long-term exposure.

In particular, it nearly wasn't enough for the 200-foot swim that they undertook. Tom made the swim relatively quickly, but Jeff, dragging the paddles and their dry bags full of food and equipment, said that his muscles had begun to seize up with cold by the time he neared the far shore. He felt lucky to reach shore, and indeed he was.

A dry suit keeps the water out, but its insulating value is only as good as the clothing underneath it. Only with clothing with some loft to it, such as wool or pile, does it preserve much warmth—and Jeff had only his thin polyester. When I wore a single thin layer under a dry suit during practice in cold water, I at first thought my dry suit had a leak, such was the shock of the cold through the thin layers. Moreover, swimming in cold water causes the body to lose heat faster than merely floating in it. Being on a slough in the center of an island where they had little hope of encountering rescuers, they felt as if they had no option other than swimming. On foot in the center of Welch Island, they had no pleasant options, but Jeff's description of his swim illustrates that a cold-water swim should be done only as a last resort.

It is essential to pack a dry bag filled with extra wool, pile, or polypropylene clothing. I've pulled out my extra clothing on plenty of days in which I never expected to use it. It's a good idea to supplement this with bivouac gear. A space blanket is small enough to fit in a vest pocket or bailout pack. More elaborate gear can make an unexpected night out almost comfortable. Bivy bags range from a simple, water-resistant sack to something resembling a small tent, complete with a set of poles, a rain fly, and mesh for the opening. An Ensolite closed-cell foam pad is a lightweight item that can provide valuable insulation from the cold ground and that can easily be stuffed into a bow or stern. In cold weather on an extended day trip, I carry a sleeping bag.

I recommend backing up bivy equipment with some solid shelter-building and fire-building skills. Any kayak trip that goes out among islands or along a remote shoreline has the potential to turn into a trip in which wilderness survival skills are as necessary as paddling skills. Just like paddling techniques, the ability to build a good shelter improves dramatically with expert advice and hours of practice. Tom Brown's *Field Guide to Wilderness Survival* is an excellent source to take into the woods to work on skills. A well-built debris hut is considerably warmer than a tent, and the materials to build one can be found in any forested environment. Likewise, though Jeff maintains they could not find dry wood to burn in the thickets of Welch Island, with a stove at their disposal, even damp wood should have sufficed to make a fire for heat and signaling.

It should be noted that Jeff and Tom probably would not have been found the night of March 5 if they had not been signaling.

Indeed, had the boaters who heard the whistles recognized the sets of three whistles as a distress signal, the rescue would have occurred sooner. I talked later to others who had heard the whistles from Vista Park, across the shipping channel, but had not recognized them as a distress call at the time. Three whistles, or three of any signal—fires, gunshots, ground markings—is a standard distress signal. Keeping Jeff and Tom in mind, however, if I ever need to whistle for help, I'll stick to Morse code for SOS: dot-dot-dot-dash-dash-dash-dot-dot-dot, with each dash lasting about three times as long as each dot. At the very least, it won't be confused with dog training. I'll also use a storm whistle, as they did. I resisted having such a bulky thing tied to my PFD until testing one side by side with the Fox 40 whistle I carried. The storm whistle won hands down. The extra bulk isn't noticeable.

Jeff and Tom's misadventure did not stop them from continuing to kayak. When I next saw them months later, they handed me a float plan and took off on a trip loaded with every recommended piece of safety equipment. When talking to them the night of their rescue, even as I recognized their mistakes, I was struck by their intelligence and humor. I couldn't help thinking that I was not only glad they were alive but also that they would be good company on a kayak camping trip, given better circumstances. It was touching to see Jeff's wife, Linda, repeatedly interrupt him with an embrace as he recounted his part of the story. It was all the reminder anyone could ask for of what is at stake every time you pack a boat to go out. Someone loves you! Make sure you leave a float plan and have the skills and equipment you need.

6

Attacked by a Bear in the Middle of Nowhere

Susan Jewell

As a special education teacher in Juneau, Alaska, Steve Byers loved having summers off. He enjoyed spending his free time canoeing or kayaking. His first trip in the summer of 2000 was a two-week canoe trip in southeast coastal Alaska, guiding a school group. A week after returning, Steve was off again, canoeing a 225-mile stretch of the Teslin and Upper Yukon Rivers in the Yukon Territory with me. And a week after that, he departed once more, this time by kayak, to scout an area near Sitka for a potential location to take a canoeing group. He was alone on this particular trip, and his sea kayak was the perfect vessel to explore with. He had planned a week for the exploration.

Steve was a veteran outdoorsman and a conscientious no-impact camper. He was also a volunteer fireman in Juneau and an emergency medical technician. For half of his 40 years, he had canoed and kayaked the rivers and coasts of the United States and Canada. As an interpretive and backcountry ranger in such U.S. national parks as Yellowstone, Everglades, and North Cascades, he explored their waters regularly. Instructing at Hurricane Island Outward Bound, Ranger Rick's Wildlife Camp, and other outdoor schools had been his natural occupation, with his education degree, bachelor's degree in parks and recreation, and associate degree in forestry.

His destination for this week in July was Mitchell Bay on Admiralty Island, the third largest island in southeast Alaska. Most of Admiralty Island is unpopulated. The largest community is Angoon, with a population of 450. The ferry stops at Angoon four times a week. East of the village is the scenic and island-studded inlet of Mitchell Bay, which offers many sheltered places to explore. Steve had never been there, but he had heard a lot about it. Because of the cold water, strong currents, extreme tides, rocky shallow water, often poor visibility, and remoteness, the trip required his careful planning.

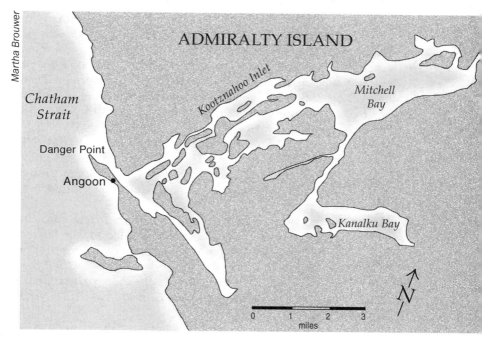

Martha Brouwer

ADMIRALTY ISLAND

Kootznahoo Inlet

Chatham
Strait

Mitchell
Bay

Danger Point

Angoon

Kanalku Bay

N

0   1   2   3
miles

The island is part of the 937,400-acre Admiralty Island National Monument in Tongass National Forest. The area is also known as Kootznoowoo Wilderness, from the native Tlingit word for "Fortress of the Bears." Admiralty Island is known for the density of its brown bear population, the highest in the world.

Around 2:00 P.M. on Friday, July 21, Steve headed to the Alaska Marine Highway ferry station at Auke Bay, just north of Juneau. It was a misty day, about the same as it is every other day of the year; when it's sunny in Juneau, the townsfolk call it a holiday. Steve carried his 18-foot kayak onto the car deck of the ferry, and at 4:15 P.M. the ferry *Le Conte* threw its moorings and departed. Eleven rainy hours after leaving Juneau, the ferry arrived at Steve's destination, Angoon.

After carrying the kayak to the run-down terminal, Steve assessed his options. It was 3:30 in the morning, dark and rainy, and he was tired. Should he start his journey now? No, it wasn't a good idea to be paddling in the dark, he concluded. After stashing his gear in a quiet corner of the terminal, he curled up in his sleeping bag under an overhang and slept.

At sunrise, the din of people loading boats to go fishing roused Steve out of slumber. The tide was receding, so Steve lugged his gear down to the water and quickly loaded his boat. He loaded his kayak the same way he had practiced in his garage so he would remember where he put everything. The day hatch contained his medical kit, wool hat, flashlight, handgun, bear spray, VHF radio, and lunch. He secured his hydration system with bungees behind the cockpit, next to the paddle float. On the foredeck he had a Tongass National Forest Recreation Guide chart in a waterproof bag and a bilge pump. Then he donned his sky-blue Kokatat dry suit, stretching his arms and legs first to erase the soreness from sleeping awkwardly, then put on his booties with the treaded soles.

Steve paddled for 2 hours along the coast by Angoon, hugging the shore until he felt comfortable. Then he rounded Danger Point Reef and headed to Stillwater Anchorage. Two bald eagles measured his progress along the point, and a dozen harlequin ducks rafted near him on the rising tide.

He noticed the racing water from the incoming current, and not wanting to be pulled onto the rocks he was headed for, he ferried across quickly. Hitting calm water again, he relaxed at the feel of the boat skimming along. It was too late to head into Mitchell Bay that afternoon, so he opted to explore some of the nearby islands. He ventured deep into the islands until he reached a peaceful cove at which to end the day.

He chose a campsite on the end of a point, under the dripping Sitka spruces and western hemlocks. The first order was to check for bear signs. There was digging around a tree and droppings, which looked about four days old because they were dried. The lack of a bear trail seemed to be a good sign.

Steve set up the tent and cooking area apart from each other, to keep the food smells away from him at night. Dinner was a feast of fresh crab and boiled 4-inch-long black leather chitons that a native fisherman he passed along the way had given him. Chitons have long been a staple of the diets of coastal natives from the Aleutians to California.

Steve washed his dishes below the tide line, then hung the food bag about 25 feet high in a conifer. After years of camping in bear country, he had perfected the technique of tying a rock to a rope and hurling it over a high branch to hoist his food up out of reach of bears.

Heavy rain in the night awakened Steve. By morning it was still raining, and Steve's tent had puddles in it. Everything was wet: the ground, his gear, the trees. In the fog and drizzle, Steve lowered the food bags and breakfasted on dried mangos, granola bars, and soy nuts. Around 8:00 A.M., Steve packed the soggy tent and loaded the kayak. The only things left at the campsite that he still had to pick up were his PFD and paddle.

Last on his checklist was to put on his dry suit. He remembered a convenient "seat" by the cooking area, so he carried his dry suit there and sat down. He took off his Xtratuff rubber boots (standard wet-weather boots in Juneau) and rain pants. He pushed his feet through the dry suit gaskets and put on his booties with treaded soles. He was about to pull on the top of the dry suit, but as he raised the dry suit with the neck gasket poised over his head, he felt a presence nearby. He lowered the suit to look and scanned the woods.

A bear was 35 feet away and barely visible through the dense vegetation and thick fog. It must have been upwind of Steve, because it didn't see him. "I need to make my presence known," Steve thought. Before he could act, however, the bear turned and faced him, then lowered its nose, flattened its ears, raised its head, and charged without hesitating. All Steve could focus on was a big head with ears laid back, black gums outlining white teeth. He could see its brown shoulders, muscles rippling beneath the fur. "I don't want him to hit me head on and knock me over the logs," he reasoned. "That would kill me for sure!"

Feeling that he had a better chance in the water, and knowing that his gun and bear spray were in the day hatch, Steve turned and ran toward the boat, but the dry suit, sleeves flapping at his sides, slowed him down. Desperate to get to the beach 50 yards away, he sprinted awkwardly. Behind him came the sound of breaking branches. He turned to see the brown form gaining on him.

Then something smacked his right side harder than he'd ever felt. The impact knocked his 6-foot, 230-pound frame to the ground. The bear was biting him, encasing his side within its massive jaws. Gripping his hip with its teeth, the bear dragged Steve several feet and then dropped him. Steve curled into a fetal position, protecting his head with his arms. The bear stepped over him and stopped.

Steve could see fur out of the corner of his eye, but he didn't dare look up. He lay as still as he could. Piercing his mind was the terrifying thought: I am no longer at the top of the food chain! He had heard only weeks earlier that a 41-year-old man was killed and partially eaten by a 300-pound brown bear in Hyder, southeast of Juneau. This was the same kind of bear, only larger. "Will I be next?" he wondered.

As he lay there, every noise in the woods became the focus of his universe. Branches were breaking, but the sounds were getting fainter. Was the bear leaving? Steve could feel his head and heart pounding. He felt something on his side, but it wasn't exactly a pain. He needed a strategy to calm himself. He tried to be still, but it was tough. Adrenaline was surging through him.

When all was quiet, he pushed himself up and felt a pain shoot through his right side. Then he saw blood on his dry suit. He limped the 20 feet to his boat, glancing frantically over his shoulder as he went, and retrieved the handgun from the day hatch. Quickly, he cocked the gun, ready with a finger on the trigger. "The bear will be back," he thought, "and I've got to be ready." Armed with gun and bear spray, he turned toward the woods and scanned the trees, waiting for the bear to charge again.

Thirty dreadful seconds later, it was still quiet. Steve thought, "I have to get out of here! I'll be safe in my boat." But his paddle and life jacket were back at the campsite. Fetching the second ammunition clip from the boat, he worked his way back to the campsite, dragging his aching leg and yelling, "Here bear, here bear!" to advertise his presence. He grabbed the paddle and PFD. There was no sign of the bear. Keeping his back to the water, he retraced his steps to the kayak.

Steve slipped into his dry suit faster than he ever had and pushed his boat offshore. His side was starting to throb. He could feel warm blood trickling down his leg. Paddling desperately, he found deep water. With no bears in sight he stopped to assess his situation. With the dry suit on, he couldn't tell how bad his side was. And a hatch was askew on the kayak, so he'd have to land somewhere to fix it.

He started to paddle again, but angry energy was welling up inside. In that remote corner of the bay, with no one around for miles, his piercing "Ahhhh!" echoed across the water. Rounding the point, he felt more energy and yelled again: "I did nothing to you, bear! You had no right to do this! No right!"

With his anger spent, Steve steered toward the west side of the islets to find the channel that led back toward Angoon. It was a complicated maze, and his attention was waning. He grew tired and rested, then paddled, rested, paddled . . . Then he saw what he was looking for—an island devoid of trees and clearly without bears—and he pulled ashore. Finally feeling safe, Steve crawled out of the cockpit, peeled off the top of his dry suit, and saw the blood and lacerations for the first time. Worried that a kidney was punctured, Steve realized that he needed to get to Angoon fast.

Now his true personality revealed itself. Despite his pain and worry over unknown injuries, he wanted to get to Angoon himself, and not subject anyone to the risks of coming to get him. "I am supposed to be the *rescuer*. People have died doing rescues," he thought. "I should get as close to Angoon as I can."

By now, the cloud ceiling had lifted to 500 feet. The water was calm, and a group of seals graced the nearby rocks. He whistled to a pair of common loons, and they answered. It raised his spirits. He rounded the island and headed south. Whenever he stopped to rest, he would feel his side with his hand; it was very tender.

He paddled for 2 hours to the Narrows, a place known for its high waves and fast currents. He listened to the waves and watched the water flow increasing on the outgoing tide. He knew that there could be 3- to 5-foot standing waves. The water was just too fast; it could flip the boat if he continued. He ferried across the water to the left bank, then climbed out and tied the boat off. He'd wait for slack tide—but when would that be?

Taking out his VHF radio, which had been working only sporadically in the steep terrain, he called for any station in Angoon to tell him when the tide was changing. George Golden, the mechanic for Whaler's Cove Sport Fishing Lodge in Angoon, answered his call. After asking about the tides, Steve added, "I was nailed by a bear." Taken aback by the casual statement, George offered, "Why don't I come and get you? I have a boat of my own." Now weak and succumbing to shock, Steve agreed. It took George almost a half hour to motor the 4 miles in the treacherous waters.

George arrived with a youth named Jim Perkins. As Steve was too weak to climb onto the motorboat, Jim had to pull him onboard. At Steve's request, the men pulled his kayak onto the stern of George's 20-foot boat. George headed through Stillwater Anchorage to the float plane dock. At the dock, Sharon Powers from Whaler's Cove Lodge was waiting to drive Steve to the clinic.

The modest Angoon Clinic didn't have a doctor, so Lena, an EMT and nurse practitioner, called the Juneau hospital to consult with one. It was 12:10 P.M., 4 hours after the attack. She gave Steve injections for infection and tetanus. The doctor in Juneau was worried about infection. The wounds were full of grit from being dragged over the ground, not to mention the rather unsanitary conditions of the bear's mouth. Steve needed a hospital, but no planes could fly to Juneau or Sitka because of the low clouds. The nurse practitioner called the Coast Guard. They couldn't fly over land either, but their helicopter could fly low over the water.

By the time the Coast Guard arrived, Steve had lapsed deeper into shock and was doing whatever people told him to do, but as he climbed into the helicopter, he recognized one of the medics. They had been partners on a mock emergency scenario in Juneau ten months earlier. The medic also recognized Steve and joked, "Now we're doing the real thing!"

At the emergency room at Sitka Community Hospital, Steve was rushed to be x-rayed and then into surgery. His veins had collapsed from the cold, and administering the IV proved a real challenge, but ultimately the cold likely reduced his blood loss. He had a 4- to 5-inch-deep puncture wound in his side from one of the bear's canines. In addition, the bear's three other canines had torn equally deep gashes in Steve's skin, with the longest gash 5 inches long. The surgeon cleaned the wounds, straightened and stitched the lacerations, and inserted a drain in the half-inch-wide puncture. Fortunately, no organs, arteries, or bones were damaged.

Steve awoke in a hospital bed, very groggy, with an IV in his arm and a sore side. The next day he was flown back to Juneau. He recovered well and will suffer no permanent injuries. He was one of the lucky ones.

LESSONS LEARNED

Brown bears and grizzlies belong to the same species, *Ursus arctos.* Browns are larger than grizzlies and, along with polar bears, are the largest bears in the world. Males are known to tip the scales at 1,500 pounds. Most mature males weigh between 600 and 1000 pounds, females between 250 and 600 pounds. Steve thinks his attacker weighed about 500 pounds and was a young male.

The bears along the coast of Alaska and British Columbia are brown bears. They attain huge sizes by feeding on a super-high-protein diet of salmon and other fish. The Kodiak brown bear is the best known. In the lower 48 states and interior Alaska, *Ursus arctos* is known as the grizzly. Another species, the black bear, is smaller and usually coexists with browns and grizzlies, except on Admiralty Island where only the browns exist. While grizzlies are listed by the U.S. Fish and Wildlife Service as threatened in the lower 48 states, the Alaskan grizzlies and browns have healthy populations.

Why did the bear attack Steve? Many factors likely contributed to this situation. One is that the density of brown bears on Admiralty Island is about one per square mile; that makes a bear encounter a high probability. Another factor is the dense vegetation of spruces and hemlocks, which along with the fog effectively camouflaged the bear and Steve from each other. Also, Steve was alone and very quiet. Being solo reduced the options a competent partner can provide, and the sound of voices in conversation alert bears to the presence of people. Furthermore, brown bears are at the top of the food chain and are so large that they rarely worry about what is on the trail ahead. Sometimes they just stumble onto people.

Most likely, the heavy rainfall had erased the smell of human presence, and the bear was ambling along searching for food when it stumbled upon Steve at close range. Bears often treat humans as they would another bear, which they try to chase off with a warning nip. That the bear bit Steve only once suggests that it was just a warning to leave. The bear could easily have killed him, but it was not being aggressive.

Camping alone on an island with the highest density of brown bears in the world (equal to that of Kodiak Island) was a mistake that could have cost Steve his life. People later asked Steve if he would go back to wilderness camping and kayaking. "Absolutely!" Steve said, "but I have a new respect for my place in the food chain." What lessons did he learn? He'd prepared by taking a gun and bear spray with him, but, minutes away from pushing off in the kayak for the day's exploring, those safety items were already stowed. As he said later, "If you don't have them on you, you don't have them." From now on, he planned to carry them with him whenever he was in bear country. He was grateful that he had a VHF radio and had filed a float plan, and he encouraged all boaters to do so.

7

Tragedy in Wisconsin's Door County

John Andrew

Erik and Kris Schuman had lived in Wisconsin's Door County area for years. The Schumans had moved to Grand Blanc, Michigan, for work the previous year and now returned to Wisconsin for a holiday, visiting Erik's mother and friends. They enjoyed being back in the area they both knew and loved. They planned to spend a few days paddling and camping before Erik was to take a business trip to Germany the following week.

On Wednesday, June 21, 2000, they drove across the isthmus that connects Cana Island to the east coast of the Door Peninsula. They parked at the lighthouse parking lot and got ready to paddle in Lake Michigan.

Erik and Kris had met and started dating in 1995. Erik was the more experienced paddler; he had about eight years of kayaking experience, and Kris had two to three years of experience. They were not strangers to the cold waters of Lake Michigan and Lake Superior. According to their friends and fellow paddlers, both were considered proficient paddlers. Erik was 35 years old, 6 feet tall and 185 pounds. Kris was 28 years old, 5 foot, 8 inches tall and 165 pounds. Erik knew how to roll and could even do a hand roll in the swimming pool. Kris was not able to roll, but she was able to perform a paddle-float self-rescue.

They often paddled their Valley Canoe Products (VCP) Aleut Sea II tandem in the Apostle Islands National Lakeshore, around Isle Royale National Park, and at various places around the Door County peninsula. On this occasion they chose to paddle their VCP singles. Erik paddled a yellow-and-white fiberglass Skerry with a tight-fitting, "ocean-size" cockpit. Kris paddled a yellow-and-white fiberglass Selkie with a smaller "ocean-size" cockpit. They wore Type III personal flotation devices with whistles attached. Erik wore a red,

62

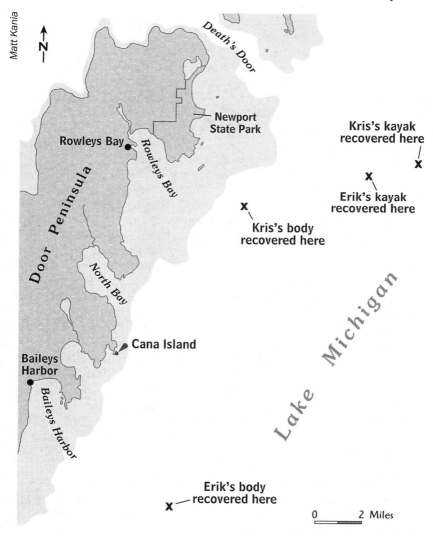

Matt Kania

short-sleeve paddling jacket, tan shorts, neoprene booties, gloves, and a blue PFD. Kris wore a green PFD, a blue, short-sleeve paddling jacket, a green one-piece swimsuit, neoprene booties, and gloves.

On the previous day, Tuesday, the winds had been out of the southwest at an average of 12.7 mph with peak gusts at 36 mph. The air temperature had reached 81°F degrees with a low of 62°. Visibility was 5.6 miles. By Wednesday, the wind had picked up. Sturgeon Bay, 22 miles to the southwest, reported clear with 10 miles of visibility and winds out of the west at 23 knots with gusts to

31 knots. (Average wind speed for the day was 13.8 mph with gusts at 38 mph. The high temperature for the day was 77° with a low of 62°, and the barometric pressure was on the rise.)

In addition to the wind, there were a lot of hazards in the area. There are quite a few submerged fishing net stakes and shoals in the vicinity of the Cana Island Lighthouse. The submerged net stakes are mentioned in the *U.S. Coast Pilot* #6 for the Great Lakes and are noted as a warning on nautical chart #14909. According to a local resident, the water levels for the lake were "three to five feet lower [this] year, the lowest [he had seen] in the past 25 years."

Other kayakers in the area decided not to paddle that day. Craig Charles, one of the owners of Life Tools in Green Bay, Wisconsin, stated, "We called off all of our instructional programs in both Green Bay [on the west side of the Door Peninsula] and Fox River [at the south end of Green Bay] for the day, due to the strong winds." An outfitter operating in the Sister Bay area (on the west side of the Door Peninsula) had a group out on the water and found that the conditions that day were too windy for them, so he kept his group in the bay. A group of paddlers in North Bay, 3 miles north of Cana Island, also decided to stay in the bay because of the strong westerly winds.

Erik and Kris paddled out from Cana Island. (The exact time is unknown.) A photographer snapped several photos of the two while they were on the beach and as they paddled out into the lake.

Two days later, on Friday evening, Erik's mother, Mrs. McCullin, became concerned when they didn't show up for dinner. Before their outing, Erik and Kris had made plans to have dinner with Mrs. McCullin. She contacted the sheriff's department at 7:42 P.M. to report her son and daughter-in-law overdue. Erik and Kris had not left a float plan with Mrs. McCullin, so she did not know where they intended to paddle.

In her report to the Coast Guard, Mrs. McCullin stated, "Erik and Kris have made numerous kayak trips along this same route of Door County." She also went on to say, "Erik and Kris were known to take extended kayaking trips."

That evening, an extensive land and water search was initiated. The search team included three Coast Guard search-and-rescue boats, four Coast Guard search-and-rescue helicopters, two Coast Guard auxiliary fixed-winged aircraft, one Department of Natural Resources (DNR) vessel, the Door County Sheriff's department, and volunteer fire departments in the area. In addition, friends and volunteers helped with the land search, and an ultralight aircraft searched the coastline for the two missing kayakers. According to Door County Deputy Sheriff Paul Mickelson, this was one of the largest search-and-rescue efforts that he had seen and participated in.

The Coast Guard sent out multiple Notice to Mariners broadcasts about the two missing paddlers on Friday night and all day Saturday. According to Wisconsin DNR Game Warden Mike Neil, there may have been as many as a hundred fishing vessels in the area throughout the weekend. Friday night, a fishing boat recovered Kris's kayak approximately 12 miles east of Rowleys Bay (around 15 miles northwest of their launch site.)

On Saturday, June 24, search efforts were hampered by poor weather conditions. Strong thunderstorms were reported approaching the rescue area. The marine forecast warned: "Mariners can expect wind gusts as high as 30 knots, along with locally high waves, heavy rain, and dangerous cloud-to-water lightning. Boaters near the coast should move into safe harbor immediately, and boaters over open waters should move below deck to avoid being thrown overboard."

A Coast Guard helicopter spotted Erik's overturned kayak on Saturday at 45°12.1'N, 86°49.7'W. The next day, although heavy fog hampered visibility, the Coast Guard spotted and recovered Kris's body in Green Bay off Rowleys Bay at 45°10.9'N, 86°56.2'W. The Coast Guard called off its search for Erik because of the heavy fog and the length of time that had elapsed since his disappearance. Erik's body was recovered the following Saturday, June 30, 6 miles east and 5 miles south of Baileys Harbor by the Wisconsin Department of Natural Resources game warden.

Without eyewitness accounts, it is impossible to piece together exactly what occurred to the two paddlers; we can only speculate about what went wrong. As is often the case in an incident where there are no survivors, we are left with more questions than answers. For example, why did they decide to go for a paddle when the winds were blowing offshore and were so strong? Why did they decide not to wear their wetsuits when they were paddling in 51°F water? Water colder than 70°F requires paddlers to wear clothing designed to protect them from the cold. Erik had a wetsuit stowed in his kayak; Kris did not have a wetsuit with her. Why did they decide to take the single kayaks on this trip instead of the tandem, the kayak they usually paddled on extended trips?

All of their camping equipment was found in their car, including three bags of clothing packed in dry bags, a water filter, and a first-aid kit, so we can assume that their Cana Island paddle was intended as a day trip. Recovered with Erik's kayak were a deck-style dry bag on his foredeck containing three chemical light sticks, a headlamp, a GPS, parachute cord, an empty chart case, a towline, and a paddle float. The paddle float was rolled up, suggesting that it had not been used.

An equipment list also was found in the car. Many of the items found with the kayaks were checked off the list. A listing for pyrotechnic aerial flares was checked, suggesting that they had carried flares, though none were found in the Schumans' kayaks, dry bags, or pockets. It is not known which type of flares they had or how many. It is possible that they fired the flares and discarded the spent cartridges, but there were no reports of sightings of aerial flares in the area. They did not have a handheld VHF marine radio.

What happened after they got on the water involves another set of questions. Did they paddle south toward Whitefish Dunes or north to Newport State Park? (Each direction presents its own set of hazards to negotiate.) Did they overextend themselves or run into some unforeseeable problems? Were the conditions that day beyond their skill and fitness levels? With the water levels so low, did the submerged fishing net stakes produce problems, or did the shoals produce larger-than-expected waves?

Were there no emergency take-outs where they could land and seek shelter? Did the wind's direction and velocity make them decide to change their route once they were on the water? Had one of them capsized first and possibly lost one of the kayaks in the windy conditions? Were they separated and capsized due to strong winds? We will never know the answers to these questions.

The deputy sheriff and the game warden speculated that Erik and Kris made a judgment call to go out for a day paddle in cold water with very windy conditions while they were not dressed for immersion. One of them may have capsized and lost his or her kayak due to the strong winds. The other paddler may then have either capsized while performing an assisted rescue or not been able to come to the aid of the first and then later capsized.

With the water temperature at 51°F, it would not have taken very long for Erik and Kris to succumb to the effects of the cold water and to lose their ability to perform a self-rescue or to hold onto their kayaks. With advanced hypothermia, the victim eventually loses consciousness. Since a Type III flotation device (the type most commonly worn by sea kayakers) does not necessarily keep the wearer's face out of the water, unconsciousness is soon followed by drowning.

LESSONS LEARNED

If you don't already own one, consider purchasing a submersible, handheld VHF marine radio. A VHF marine radio can both transmit to and receive communications from other vessels and the Coast Guard. VHF radios also can be used to listen to marine weather reports and forecasts. When you transmit with a VHF, the Coast Guard can use a radio direction finder to locate you in an emergency. The cost of submersible VHF radios has dropped significantly in recent years, and there is no longer a licensing requirement to use one. PLBs and VHFs eqiupped with DSC/GPS also alert rescue services to your emergency and location.

Before you leave on any kayak outing, whether a day trip or an extended cruise, leave a detailed float plan with a friend or relative. Note exactly where you are going to paddle and when. List put-ins and take-outs, campsites, where you are going to park your vehicle, and when you plan to return. If your plans change, call the person holding your float plan on either a cell phone or a VHF and provide an update. If you are overdue but safe and can't get in touch with the person holding your float plan, you can notify the Coast Guard or other authorities of your status to avoid having an unnecessary search initiated.

Have weather forecast equipment with you to help make an informed decision on whether to paddle. Use a weather radio or your VHF to listen to marine forecasts. Pay particular attention to the nearshore forecasts, which are for waters within 5 nautical miles of shore. These forecasts include predicted wave heights, wind, and weather up to 36 hours in advance. Inexpensive handheld weather instruments can measure wind speed, maximum wind speed, temperature, wind chill, and dew point. Waterproof watches with a built-in barometer are becoming more affordable and accurate. Quick changes in barometric pressure can help you predict and prepare for strong winds. Exercise extreme caution in offshore breezes. If there isn't a sufficient lee to paddle in, stay off the water.

Dress for immersion. Although the Schumans were paddling on a warm summer's day, they could ill afford to paddle without immersion clothing. A dry suit with appropriate insulating layers or a wetsuit will buy you more time to work out recoveries and rescues if you wind up in the water. If you get hot while paddling, an Eskimo roll or a thorough splashing of water is a good way to cool down.

When paddling on open water, have more than two paddlers in your group. There is a saying for paddlers on open water: "When at sea, no fewer than three." This increases the number of resources out on the water if any one paddler has difficulty.

Carry pyrotechnic aerial flares. Get permission from your local Coast Guard station and practice firing your aerial flares so that you learn their height, burn time, and range. Twelve- or 25-gauge flares can shoot higher and burn longer and brighter than the pencil-type aerial flares, so they're a better choice when paddling on open water.

Acquire as much information as you can about the area in which you are going to paddle from sources like *Coast Pilots,* nautical charts, and local knowledge.

8

A Kite-Sailing Mishap

Doug Lloyd

Around noon on Sunday, April 30, 2000, Eric Dunalo and his daughter Marina were crossing the short channel that separates Marina Island from Manson's Landing on Cortes Island, located at the northern end of the Strait of Georgia in British Columbia, Canada. Marina noticed a gray sea kayak moving northward toward them at about 1 knot, pulled by a bright parafoil kite. Eric was somewhat perplexed, as there didn't appear to be a paddler in the kayak.

He maneuvered his 16-foot outboard skiff alongside the kayak. The kayak was right side up, but the cockpit was almost completely swamped. The kite was flying at the end of about 40 feet of line tied to the foredeck. Additional kite line was wrapped around a board tucked under the deck rigging. The rudder was in the down position. Some dry bags were in the water alongside the kayak, tethered to the deck rigging. A paddle was sticking out of the cockpit, also tethered. The Dunalos scanned the waters around the kayak but saw no sign of a paddler.

Eric returned to drop Marina off at the landing and then went back out to recover the kayak. He tied a line to the errant kayak and towed it to his dock at Marina Island. The kite remained aloft and subsequently was tangled in the treetops at the island's shoreline. After Eric got the kayak to the dock, he searched it for anything that would identify its owner. He found no name or address in the kayak or on any of the gear. Eric called the authorities. The Royal Canadian Mounted Police (RCMP) came to the dock and took the kayak to their station on Quadra Island. The Mounties thoroughly inspected the contents of the kayak, hoping to find some kind of identification that would lead to or provide clues about the kayaker's name or route. The Victoria Rescue Coordination Center (RCC)—now known as Joint Rescue Co-ordination Centre Victoria (JRCC)—was notified of a possible person in the water.

By 2:30 P.M. the Canadian Coast Guard vessel *Point Race* had taken on fuel and headed out to lead the search operation. Various private and commercial vessels including BC Ferries provided assistance with the extensive search. Military aircraft from the 422nd Squadron operating out of Comox searched the area from the air, joined by a number of small civilian planes.

It had been a weekend of very blustery weather. On Saturday a sudden noontime squall racing northward had leveled the display area at the Paddlefest at Ladysmith on Vancouver Island, far to the south of where the kayak was recovered. A group of sea kayakers attending the Paddlefest on Sunday watched the Coast Guard Auxiliary's waterfront safety patrol craft race away to join the effort as the search area expanded to the south.

The kayak, a Kyook manufactured by Necky Kayaks, had three hatches and was equipped with a compass, tethered bailer, and stern and bow painters. There was a folded marine chart under the front deck elastics. The contents of the dry bags and the bulkhead-enclosed compartments included bulk food supplies like rice and beans, partially full water containers, camp kitchen supplies and pots, light cotton clothing and a jean jacket, rain gear, and a sleeping bag, pad, tent, fly, and tarp. In the day hatch were assorted lines, a sea anchor, drawing supplies, and other personal items. A laptop computer was stowed in the kayak, along with a bag of library books and a notepad filled with what at first was thought to be Arabic handwriting (it turned out to be German shorthand). The notepad bore a name the RCMP read as "Art Way." No signaling devices or any self-rescue devices were among the gear found with the kayak.

Search efforts continued through the afternoon and early evening. Bulletins about the missing kayaker were widely broadcast on VHF radio and local AM and FM radio stations. Reports filtered back to the RCC. A couple who had been walking along the southern end of Cortes Island said they had seen an unoccupied kayak sailing behind a kite early Sunday morning but did not report it until much later that day. Another couple aboard a sailboat reported seeing something black with straps floating in the waters off Comox, but they said they were unable to retrieve it during a few passes in the choppy seas.

The RCMP checked with the library on Vancouver Island looking for some positive identification of a "Mr. Art Way." They learned that there was someone using the name "Artway" living on Jenkins Island, a small islet off the west coast of Lasqueti Island, located in the middle of the Strait of Georgia. The RCMP was on its way to Jenkins

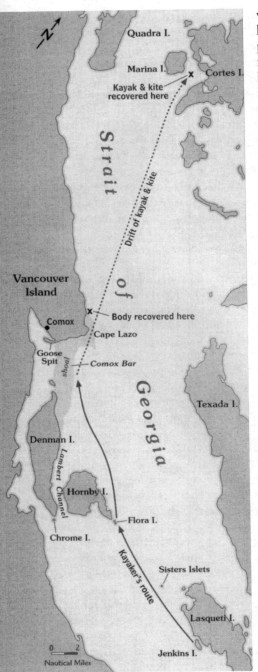

Matt Kania

when somebody contacted them late in the day to report an overdue paddler, an artist friend who had failed to arrive with a package he had promised to deliver at Goose Spit, near the town of Comox. The overdue kayaker was Werner Szyleyko, a resident of Jenkins Island. Werner used "ArtWay" as a nickname.

The search rapidly broadened to include all coastal waters between Lasqueti and Cortes Islands, a distance of over 50 miles, while the Coast Guard used computer-generated drift-analysis plotting to try to narrow the search grid. The search was called off at dusk and resumed at daylight.

On Monday, May 1, shortly before midday, the RCC received news from the Military Police in Comox that a body had been recovered floating 200 feet off Air Force Beach. The coroner serving the communities of Courtenay and Comox was called in, and the body was identified as that of 56-year-old Werner Szyleyko. The search was called off. It was left to the coroner to figure out exactly what misfortune had befallen the kayaker.

Werner's body was recovered dressed in a red, full-length, buoyant Mustang Survival cruiser suit. This foam-insulated suit was rated by the Coast Guard as a flotation device. Although it provided some thermal protection, the knit cuffs at the wrists, ankles, and neck weren't designed to keep water out. Underneath the cruiser suit Werner wore a gray cotton athletic suit and cotton socks. He was wearing rubber boots. A wool cap dangled from a Velcro tab on his cruiser suit. He was not wearing an additional PFD, nor did he wear neoprene gloves or hood.

The pathology exam noted that the 150-pound, 5-foot 8-inch paddler had been in excellent, even enviable health. Injuries to Werner's face and knuckles were identified as postmortem abrasions likely caused by the rocky shoals in the water where the body was recovered. No other injuries or medical problems were noted. Death was listed as accidental as the result of hypothermia and salt water drowning. The presence of extensive goose bumps was indicative of immersion hypothermia.

The research conducted by the coroner led him to believe that Werner left his island home on Thursday or Friday and crossed the 10 miles to Flora Islet at the southern tip of Hornby Island. The partially empty freshwater containers along with the salt water deposits found on his cooking gear suggested he most likely spent a day or two camping there. Friends on Jenkins Island said Werner always left with clean gear and often camped on Flora for a day or more, painting and relaxing, before making the 15-mile passage to Comox.

Fellow islanders knew him to be a cautious individual who was comfortable traveling on the water alone. He had been kayaking for 10 years, and his kayak was his preferred method of transportation. An early riser who generally avoided paddling in rough water that was beyond his skill level, Werner likely departed Flora Islet early Saturday morning under kite power. The last entry in his laptop journal was written late Friday night while on Flora. His route lay almost parallel to the northwest-southeast orientation of Vancouver Island and Georgia Strait. His direction of travel would have been perfect for downwind sailing on light southerly winds. Low tide was at 9:00 A.M. The flood tide would bring a favorable current shortly thereafter.

The area is known for strong southeasterlies that come up suddenly in advance of a weather system. Beyond the limited lee of Hornby Island, boaters are exposed to the full effect of the southeasterly wind moving up the Strait. Wind funneling between Denman Island and Hornby Island intensifies along Lambert Channel. There is some limited protection from the wind along the eastern shoreline of Denman Island, especially in the lee of the Komas Bluffs. The region is subject to confused, breaking seas where the tidal currents flow over a broad area of shoals extending from the north end of Hornby Island, along the east side of Denman, and almost all the way to Comox. On a very low tide it is possible to wade from the north end of Denman across to the Sandy Islands, just off the north end of the island, and then halfway to Comox. The shallow waters of the Comox bar extend far offshore from Goose Spit. Local boaters avoid the area and keep well away from the shoreline, seeking shelter quickly when the weather turns rough.

Werner did not own a VHF or marine weather radio, so he would not have heard the Small Craft Warning issued for the weekend. The marine reports, issued every 3 hours from Chrome Island at the south end of Denman, provide some indication of the conditions Werner would have encountered from the time of his departure from Flora Island. Winds were southerly at 15 knots at 7:40 A.M., with a 1-foot chop. By 10:40, winds had shifted a bit to the southeast at 15 knots with a 2-foot chop. By 1:40 P.M., winds had increased to the southeast at 25 knots with a 4-foot chop and low easterly swell off Chrome Island. Werner probably left Flora Islet with an easily manageable 10-knot breeze.

If he had taken the straight-line course farther offshore, the conditions would have been less benign. The marine report from Sisters Islets, north of Lasqueti Island, would be more indicative of what conditions were like away from land. The hourly reports from Sisters indicated southeast winds of 13 knots at 9:00 A.M., 20 knots at 10:00, then increasing to 25 knots by 2:00 P.M., with winds gusting regularly to 29 knots between 3:00 and 6:00 P.M.

It is possible that Werner began using the kite (a 7.5-square-foot vented parafoil that he had owned for 2 years) early in the day when the winds were mild. With the kite aloft as the wind strengthened, he would have been white-knuckle surfing down growing wind waves. Whether he capsized while trying to bring in the kite or as a result of broaching, we will never know. No knife was found on Werner's person or on his kayak. It is unclear whether he may have had one close at hand but lost it while attempting to cut the kite loose in the squirrelly conditions. It was reported that Werner was having problems with his kayak's rudder system and had replaced the control lines with fishing line. A friend had tried out the boat with his refit and felt it was way too spongy and would not allow proper bracing or rudder control in rough seas.

It is likely that sometime on Saturday afternoon, Werner got into serious trouble. The evidence suggests he may have spent time in the water alongside his kayak. His paddle was tethered and firmly wedged in beside the seat. The coroner speculated that after several attempts to reenter the kayak after a capsize Werner could have been in the water holding on to the kayak in an attempt to be towed, kayak and all, toward shore.

That possibility could be supported by Werner's statement to a friend that he thought if he ever did capsize, he could right the kayak with the kite line. Launching the kite after a capsize seemed unlikely, however, since vented parafoil kites can be difficult to launch under the best of conditions, let alone from water level in rough, very windy conditions. It seems safe to assume that the kite was flying when Werner capsized.

Werner's black nylon spray skirt was never recovered. It may have been the object sighted by the sailors off Comox. He may have either removed it while attempting to reenter or discarded it for some other reason. If he had indeed tried to reenter his boat, *(continued page 74)*

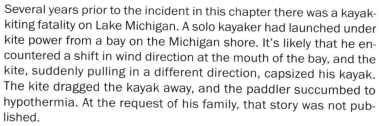

KAYAK KITING

Christopher Cunningham

Several years prior to the incident in this chapter there was a kayak-kiting fatality on Lake Michigan. A solo kayaker had launched under kite power from a bay on the Michigan shore. It's likely that he encountered a shift in wind direction at the mouth of the bay, and the kite, suddenly pulling in a different direction, capsized his kayak. The kite dragged the kayak away, and the paddler succumbed to hypothermia. At the request of his family, that story was not published.

Prior to that Lake Michigan incident I was drawn to using a kite for power by a photograph of a double kayak making about 12 knots behind a parafoil kite. I tried on several occasions to get a parafoil launched from my kayak but never succeeded: I just didn't have enough hands to hold the kite up, hang on to the kite line, manage my paddle, and keep my bow pointed downwind. Inevitably my kite wound up in the water, and once it was wet it was useless. Launching a kite while on land is child's play; aboard a kayak, the task is complex.

Modern traction kites, the sort used by kiteboarders, are designed with inflatable spars that make the kites easy to launch from the water. Jean Phillipe Soule and Luke Shullenberger planned to use traction kites for a sea-kayaking expedition from northern Mexico to Panama, and while their sea trials proved that a kite could pull fully loaded kayaks at a brisk pace, they discovered it would be of limited use. A kayak moving straight downwind behind a kite may not create enough drag to maintain the line tension that keeps a kite aloft, and going across the wind or upwind would have required outfitting their kayaks with leeboards. They concluded that "kite kayaking certainly has the potential to *(continued next page)* become a big water sport but it may not be practical for covering long distances on long expedition paddles, at least not when most of the paddling is against headwinds or irregular crosswinds."

As Doug Lloyd points out, once a kite is aloft, it continues to pull as long as the wind is blowing and there is tension on the kite line, so in an emergency, the best option may be to cut the line. If you're lucky, you'll find the kite in the water, but in rough water it would be all too easy to lose it. While sails can add risk and complexity to a kayak, they have an important advantage over kites: In the event of a capsize, they cease to drive the kayak. With a sail you have more control while you're underway than you do with a kite. If you want to slow down, you can ease the sheets and let the wind spill out of the sails; if you want to stop, you can cast them off entirely or turn the bow into the wind. I've cast my lot with sailing. My kites stay ashore.

the weight of his rubber boots surely would have hampered his efforts to clamber back aboard (or swim), yet he had not removed his boots. Werner was known to carry three Skyblazer-type flares in his cruiser suit. Whether he had carried or fired these on the day of the accident is not known. The shoreline is well populated, and there were no reports of distress signals being sighted that weekend.

LESSONS LEARNED

One of Werner's close friends said that Werner was a very well-seasoned kayaker, having done two trips up the Inside Passage to Alaska and a full circumnavigation of Vancouver Island in stages. He had done the crossing to Comox only once or twice as far as she knew, usually in the summer. She said Werner had told her a number of times never to wear gum boots while paddling; they were for shore duty only. It was uncharacteristic of him to wear them while paddling. He might have been in a hurry, trying to outrun the weather with an early start. He often would leave at the crack of dawn to beat the weather. She said Werner was prudent but would not let the weather deter him from reaching his destination. She indicated he could handle his kayak very well, but that the kite was relatively new to him.

Werner's kayak was found about 35 miles from Flora Islet. His body was recovered just north of Cape Lazo, a headland near the town of Comox. The coroner's estimate put his death between 8:00 and 10:00 P.M. The cruiser suit would have allowed Werner to survive between 3 and 5 hours in the water. His lack of neoprene gloves and hood would have contributed to the onset of hypothermia. Given the downwind line of travel of the unmanned kayak, Werner may have gotten into trouble either in the deeper water south of Comox or in the agitated waters between Denman and Hornby Islands around 3:00 P.M. Once he was immersed in the cold 50°F water, his options were severely limited. Given the lack of adequate immersion apparel, he may have lost the strength and dexterity in his hands—and therefore his ability to execute a self-rescue—within an hour. By 7:40 P.M., Chrome Island was reporting southeast winds at 22 knots with a moderate sea running. If he was still in the water alongside his kayak in the evening, he may have lost the strength or the will to hold onto the kayak. In its advanced stages, hypothermia often brings on a warm euphoria, and one simply slips away peacefully.

Solo sailing in a kayak, whether by rigged sail or kite, adds a significant risk factor to sea kayaking. As long as a kite remains airborne, it will tow the kayak downwind. In the event of a capsize and wet exit, the pull of the kite poses the distinct possibility of separating the kayak from the paddler. A boat-to-person tether would address this problem. If the wind builds while the kite is in the air, it may be very difficult—if not impossible—to reel it in, especially if the water gets rough enough to require the paddler to have both hands on the paddle to brace. A tethered knife with a blunt point and serrated edge should always be readily available so that the kite line can be cut at the first hint of trouble or if reeling in by hand isn't possible. Once cut free, a kite will fall into the water and the paddler may be able to retrieve it.

Adding to Werner's difficulties were improper footwear and negligible self-rescue skills and equipment. A set of three Skyblazer flares, if he had them, would have been a bare minimum supply of marine distress signals. The lack of identification in his kayak and gear also meant that the authorities could not quickly track down a float plan or other information that would help narrow the search area.

Werner was regarded as a good paddler with ample local knowledge from years living on a weather-bound island, but he set off with inadequate forecast information. While the light wind in the morning may have been ideal for kite sailing, the forecast for increasing winds would have put a kite-drawn kayaker at increased risk. After his wet exit Werner did not have the option of doing a reentry and roll because he did not know how to roll. His only option was to right the kayak and reenter it, but that would require the additional stability usually provided by inflatable devices like sponsons or a paddle float. Werner did not own a paddle float but had told a friend that if he ever did capsize, he would tie a dry bag to his paddle blade in lieu of a paddle float. It is not known if he had tried this in practice. It is essential for a kayaker travelling solo to have a wide range of self-rescue skills and equipment. Werner had told friends on a number of occasions that he didn't want to learn any self-rescue techniques, including the roll recovery, because if he did, he would then need to use them one day. While his intent may have been to maintain a cautious approach to kayaking and paddle only in reasonable conditions, the more time one spends at sea, the more one ought to expect trouble someday—and so prepare for it.

9

Life and Death off Baffin Island

Doug Lloyd

Mark Seltzer, a 40-year-old computer consultant, and Marilyn Chan, a 43-year-old management specialist, were both passionate globetrotters. Savvy and cautious, the Canadian couple had traveled to nearly every corner of the planet. Mark had a vast collection of travel literature and had transformed his love for travel into an Internet business. Both shared a fascination for aboriginal culture, which had led them north to the Canadian Eastern Arctic a number of times. They wanted their longtime friends and travel companions, Phil King and Rosemary Waterston, to accompany them to a particularly special place in the new Canadian territory of Nunavut.

The two Toronto couples flew from Ontario during mid-July of 1998 and arrived at Pond Inlet, a town of 1,100 residents on the rugged northern tip of Baffin Island (72°41'N, 77°58'W), 644 kilometers above the Arctic Circle. With its seasonal profusion of flora and fauna, spectacular scenery, and affordable accessibility, the town of Pond Inlet had become a popular summertime destination for paddlers and hikers alike. The ice had broken up by the time they had arrived, so the four, deliberating whether they should hike or paddle, decided that kayaking was the easier option to get from Pond Inlet to Mt. Herodier close by.

Mark knew the local outfitter from a similar previous trip to Pond Inlet in the summer of 1996. They had kept up a friendship from a distance and had made arrangements for this trip to borrow either two double kayaks or trekking gear. Mark, the driving force for the trip, was a little disappointed when the outfitter went off leading an expedition prior to making final lending arrangements, and the employee left in charge of the outfitter's operation informed Mark the next day that only single kayaks were available. Mark was reluctant to discuss his concerns with the employee, so he settled for borrowing four single kayaks, all of them Solstice models made by Current Designs.

The other three paddlers also had been looking forward to double kayaks, according to Phil. It was an important consideration given the imbalance of strength between the women and the men. Rosemary and Phil in particular had understood they were supposed to be in a double if they opted to go kayaking instead of hiking, and they had even rented a double only a few weeks prior in order to train in Toronto Harbour.

The group also borrowed four one-piece exposure suits, the standard apparel used by many boaters in the north. The suits offer flotation, warmth, and protection from salt spray or light rain but are not designed as immersion apparel for cold water. Other than paddles and skirts, no other rescue gear or electronic communication equipment was requested or offered. No one felt that the trip was of a level that required charts for navigation, as their destination, Mt. Herodier, was within easy walking distance. According to Phil, for anything more difficult, they would have hired licensed guides or simply opted not to kayak. The paddlers didn't ask to be apprised of any relevant weather information at this time, and no forecast details were discussed or sought as the group took the kayaks. Mark and Marilyn had paddled the exact same route without incident on their previous trip, and they would have shared with the other couple any route concerns they were aware of.

Mark was an advanced-level scuba diver, water wise, and had always demonstrated good awareness and leadership in the outdoors. He had been paddling with Marilyn for 2 to 3 years. Phil and Rosemary's only wilderness paddling had been one previous camping trip in an Ontario provincial park, but the two new paddlers had no illusions about their experience level. Nevertheless, everyone was satisfied at departure time that the trip was to be a safe, self-guided paddle in fairly sheltered waters during the brief window of prime paddling weather for Pond Inlet. The four paddlers anticipated dealing with deteriorating weather simply by getting off the water and staying ashore until conditions improved. None of the paddlers thought their plan was foolhardy or would put them at risk.

With enough gear loaded into the single kayaks for one or two nights of camping, the four paddlers slipped away at about 11:00 on Thursday morning, July 16, from the pebble beach fronting the town of Pond Inlet. The waters were oily calm. The day was quite clear and relatively warm (10°C). Only a small amount of fog obscured Bylot Island across Eclipse Sound. The route to Mt. Herodier was completely clear. Mark estimated that the 10-kilometer distance would take 5 hours at a slow pace with a rest stop. Everyone looked forward to reaching Mt. Herodier. Marilyn was an avid gardener and loved to see the fragile wildflower blossoms fighting the harsh elements in the valleys below Mt. Herodier. Kayaking for her, as well as the others, was merely a means to an end.

The waters in the area are subject to a tidal range of approximately 6 feet, ruling out difficulties with strong currents until they reached the Mt. Herodier headland. Beyond the headland, the inlet was still blocked by pack ice. The group progressed at a leisurely pace, keeping 100 to 200 meters offshore and passing car-sized icebergs and increasing amounts of nearshore sheet ice. They had a great morning admiring the beauty around them and were getting used to the gentle swell and being in the Arctic. At 1:30 they stopped along the western shore just past James Creek for a late lunch. They discussed setting up camp there but decided to take advantage of the ample traveling time provided by the continuous high Arctic daylight.

By 2:30 that afternoon the kayaks were back in the water. Marilyn and Rosemary both were experiencing some lower back discomfort, so they improvised backrests using sweatshirts wrapped in plastic bags. They were looking forward to reaching Mt. Herodier and resting.

A French couple, Elizabeth Mitchell (originally from Canada) and Pascal Ertlé, had left Pond Inlet in a double kayak at 2:00 that day headed for the same camping area (as a jump-off point to Bylot Island). They had spoken with the four Canadians back in town and had watched them load their gear down at the beach. It didn't take long for this experienced duo to overtake the group, and they had the impression that the four Canadians might not be adequately prepared for Arctic paddling. Only Elizabeth spoke English. Although she wanted to express her concern that the four kayakers were paddling too far from shore, because of the idyllic conditions and not wanting to stick her nose into other people's business she just bid them farewell as they parted company.

Sometime in the late afternoon Mark, Marilyn, Phil, and Rosemary approached the changing topography near the large bay formed by the elbow south of Mt. Herodier's 765-meter peak. Rosemary felt she should keep well away from the nearshore ice, which she had read could roll over without warning and cause a sudden surge. The group did not come together to discuss concerns or form a consensus at this juncture. It wasn't long before a strong offshore wind sprang up. Rosemary later described their initial positioning: "The coastline was rather scalloped [the map is not at a scale that can show this] with

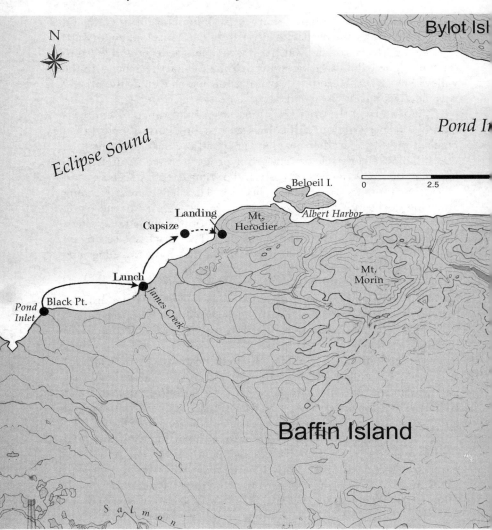

Martha Brouwer

points of land between pebbled beaches. I could see where we were going, and rather than staying close to the shore and having a longer route, I cut across the last bay to make a straight line to the last point before landing. Once I got past that point of land I stopped paddling and took out the camera to take a picture ahead. I waited for Marilyn and Phil, who were closer to shore, to paddle into the shot. I asked Mark to move in closer to shore so I could take his picture too, but he joked that, no, he had paddled out to take a video of me taking a photo of Marilyn and Phil."

At that time a large weather system out at sea was moving rapidly over Baffin's northern tip. The wind accelerated through gaps in the mountainous topography and over ice fields in the interior. After crossing the land, the wind rushed out into Eclipse Sound. Rosemary continued: "As soon as I put the camera away I became aware that I was being blown away from the shore at a fast rate. The waves had also changed. Rather than facing the kayak, they were now parallel to it and getting higher. I tried to turn my kayak to point into the waves and toward shore but wasn't able to at all. Phil was yelling at us to come on and get in closer, and I was shouting back that I was trying and I couldn't; but he couldn't hear me because the wind was carrying our voices, and us, away from shore. I was feeling very anxious and yelled to Mark that I was really uncomfortable because I couldn't make the kayak go in the direction of shore."

Within 5 minutes of the time that Rosemary was taking pictures, conditions on the water deteriorated dramatically, and it didn't take long for things to unravel. Mark came right over, calmly instructing Rosemary not to panic and to keep paddling parallel to shore past the next point of land, where they might have more success turning the kayaks shoreward. But within only a few strokes a big wave from the direction of shore caused Rosemary to capsize. It all happened quickly. Her blade may have caught a gust, or a beam wave may have pushed her kayak sideways, tripping her over the paddle as she set the blade on the downwind side.

Rosemary had never practiced wet exits but knew to pull the grab loop and exit forward. She described the next moments: "I remember the water being very green as I came up for air. Mark was right there beside me when I surfaced, and I assured him I was OK as he held my hands and got me to hold onto the side of his kayak. Both of our kayaks were now parallel to the waves, which were pushing us farther from shore. He asked if I could climb up onto his kayak and I said I thought so. The next thing I remember is Mark coming up out of the water after his kayak capsized. His hat was gone, though his glasses were still on. He looked so surprised."

At this point, Phil remembered being a few meters from Marilyn and not much more than 50 meters from Mark and Rosemary. He didn't remember leaving his position closer to shore with Marilyn until she alerted him that both Mark and Rosemary were in the water. Marilyn had been keeping a close eye on the other two. Rosemary remembered Phil being right beside them as Mark surfaced but concluded that she and Mark must have been in the water for a while: "I guess Mark and I must have bobbed around for a while, holding onto our kayaks. I remember Mark fumbling with his video camera case, getting out his air horn and using it, but it was waterlogged and didn't make any sound. I think we had been blown about a quarter mile from shore at this time."

The frigid Arctic waters were 1° to 2°C. Rosemary, like the others in her group, had worn ski gear under her exposure suit, gloves on her hands, and a baseball cap. Their exposure suits got their insulation and flotation capacity from an inner core of closed-cell foam. They fit like a pair of coveralls with cinch straps at the open cuffs and provide protection only for a brief immersion. Ice-cold water inundated Rosemary's suit, making her susceptible to rapid hypothermia. Although her extra clothing may have prevented cold shock, she was still in a serious situation. Survival time in the Arctic is often measured in minutes. When Phil arrived, the two kayaks and paddlers were beside each other. Mark and Phil quickly instructed Rosemary to get onto the back of Phil's kayak. Rosemary was afraid that she would cause Phil to flip. Mark had already righted Rosemary's kayak, and he then draped himself over it and reiterated instructions to Rosemary to go to the stern of Phil's kayak and crawl up on the end of it. Without Mark's instructions, Phil would not have known what to do.

Rosemary explained what happened next: "As I moved over to Phil's kayak, I realized that my foot was wrapped up in the ropes attached to the kayak [the deck lines] that Mark was on—the kayak I had been paddling. I explained the problem, and when I dunked backward under the water to bring my foot up, Mark turned around to untangle my foot while still lying on the kayak. Then I swam to Phil's kayak and crawled onto it lengthwise so I was lying facedown and holding onto the edge of the central hole [cockpit]. Phil was holding onto the empty capsized kayak, and Mark told him that in this circumstance the book said we should let the empty kayak go."

Mark and Rosemary's kayaks, only moderately loaded with gear but swamped, were too heavy for them to drag one boat over the other to drain the water from it. There were no pumps aboard. Mark and Phil's main concern was getting Rosemary out of the water and back to shore. Perhaps due to his haste or lack of assisted rescue practice or knowledge of standard rescue procedures, Mark failed to suggest that they try to get him into the other righted kayak, and ultimately he had Phil release the capsized kayak. With every second the situation was getting more desperate as the wind, despite what would seem to be a limited fetch, gained strength and the seas grew much worse.

Unfortunately, during the time it took to get Rosemary onto Phil's back deck, Marilyn, who had been closer to shore, was blown farther out to sea and had now drifted past the three other paddlers. She had somehow spun herself 180 degrees. Her kayak was perpendicular to the wind, as were the others, but facing opposite the direction the group had been paddling. As Rosemary recalled the scene, Marilyn turned her head and "shouted back to the three of us that she didn't know what to do. Mark told her to stay calm. Marilyn replied that she was calm but didn't know what to do. Mark told her to just stay upright."

Phil was under great psychological duress at this juncture. With Rosemary shivering and precariously balanced on his rear deck, Phil had no other option in his mind than to head for shore with her. Mark agreed. Phil took one last look at his friends. Mark was clinging to the upright kayak by himself, and Marilyn was drifting quickly farther offshore, fighting to keep her kayak upright.

Phil found the wind extraordinarily difficult to paddle against. Rosemary described the difficulties: "Phil paddled to shore, cutting diagonally through the waves when he could. Because of the wind and the need to be careful, he had to go a long way east from where we had the accident, eventually landing on a little cove three beaches over. On the way waves kept breaking over me as I lay on the back of the kayak. I lifted my legs up out of the water to try to reduce the drag on the boat, but I was very afraid of making the kayak unstable. I kept my head down and just kept saying 'I'm OK' over and over again so that Phil wouldn't have to turn around to ensure I was all right. We almost tipped many times during the trip to shore. As we approached shore, Phil yelled to the French couple on the beach that there had been an accident so they knew to get ready to help."

Phil had spotted Elizabeth and Pascal on the beach. It took a few minutes before Elizabeth and Pascal could hear him shouting. As they hit the beach, Phil rushed to seek the couple's assistance and advice, while Rosemary dragged the kayak up the shore and stumbled to empty needed gear, including a change of clothing. She then resecured the hatches and tightened the straps, readying the kayak for Phil. The French couple did not hesitate to take to the water. Phil told Rosemary to get warm, and then at great risk he returned to his kayak, paddling out into the rough seas following behind the double.

Rosemary quickly dragged Phil's gear bag to a dilapidated hunter's shed nearby and changed into dry clothes. She checked her watch. It was 5:00 P.M. Phil eventually returned. The three had not been successful finding any sign of Mark or Marilyn where the incident had taken place. At significant risk, Elizabeth and Pascal had left the accident scene for Pond Inlet to get help, safely negotiating the beam seas. They arrived exhausted and sore and immediately alerted authorities. From the beach back at the cove, Phil spotted something rolling around in the waves and went out one more time, alone, into virtually unmanageable seas. But what looked like the white hull of a kayak turned out to be just more ice. After his return, conditions became so bad that he dared not go out again.

Under the circumstances, Rosemary took the liberty to look through the French couple's gear, looking for anything that might help her get outside assistance or establish visual contact with the two missing friends. She found a pair of binoculars. Scrambling up an escarpment for a better view, Phil and Rosemary searched in vain for signs of their companions. Walking west along the beach, the couple had difficulty even staying upright in the powerful wind funneling through the valley. Rosemary was knocked down by the wind a few times and occasionally had to sit down just to catch her breath. Phil, increasingly anxious about the fate of the French couple as well as their friends, set out on foot for Pond Inlet later that evening. Less than an hour into the hike, he spotted two motorboats heading toward the bay and ran back to the campsite. It was almost 9:00. Rosemary told the boat drivers where she had last seen Marilyn and Mark. The two boats went out to search, but one returned after 10 minutes with engine trouble. The driver, Norman, quickly radioed town for a replacement boat. He said that they couldn't see anything in the accident area and that the waves downwind in the open channel were 5 meters high. Fog was also forming out in the channel, and visibility would deteriorate further.

Phil and Rosemary remained on the wind-blown shore waiting in an extremely stressful state. Around 11:30 P.M. another boat arrived. Despite Rosemary and Phil's desire to assist with the search, the boat driver determined he had to avoid the rough seas, so despite the couple's protests, he would not venture out to the accident scene or, more importantly, downwind in deeper water. The boat motored carefully back to town close to shore, dropping the couple off near the nursing station, where Rosemary was treated for mild hypothermia. Phil and Rosemary heard a helicopter leave town around 1:00 in the morning to join the boats in the search. In the high wind, waves, and cold mist that blanketed the sound, the searchers found no trace of Mark and Marilyn.

In the days following the disappearance of Mark and Marilyn, a number of aircraft—including a military Hercules from Trenton, Ontario—participated in an extensive search. Days of poor visibility made the search difficult and eventually impossible. When the search resumed, flat ice sheets had moved into Eclipse Sound from the ice-choked entrance. Mark's brother flew to Pond Inlet as soon as he could, contracted a helicopter, and then combed the 884-square-kilometer search area in the Twin Otter he'd also hired. All three of the missing kayaks had white hulls, making it difficult for low-flight spotters to spot them among the ice.

The Hercules was recalled Monday morning. By Wednesday the family called off their search efforts after a complete inspection of the coast perimeter. There was no hope that Mark or Marilyn had survived the frigid Arctic water or made it to landfall. Locals eventually found all three kayaks. Two weeks after the accident, Mark's body was found in the Sound. His bright orange exposure suit was still intact. Because the suit would have been easy for the searchers to spot, it is likely that Mark may have been pulled under the ice during the search.

LESSONS LEARNED

A dry suit with proper insulation worn underneath it is the only apparel that realistically provides an adequate amount of survival time in Arctic waters for rescue and post-rescue complications. Wetsuits will work but can be a bit restrictive to paddling in the thickness usually required for protection in near-freezing waters. Marine survival suits, often used by marine workers in Alaska in the event they have to abandon ship, are watertight but too cumbersome for kayakers.

Exposure suits like those used by the paddlers in this chapter do not provide enough protection after immersion in near-freezing water. These suits lack cuff and neck seals and permit water to enter and make quick and direct contact with the paddler's skin. Only a sealed dry suit, combined with insulating undergarments, maintains a layer of air between the fabric and the paddler's skin, which acts as a barrier to heat loss. Although exposure suits do add to total survival time in near-freezing water, actual functional survival time is severely diminished by the ready infiltration of water. Nursing staff at the First Aid Station assured Rosemary that Mark would have a good chance of being found alive in the water during the night as he was wearing his suit. This is a common misconception about the ability of exposure suits in very cold water, although improved models do now incorporate neoprene wrist cuffs, ankle and thigh cinch straps, and stowaway hoods, which add somewhat to functional survival time.

Given the paddlers' proximity to Pond Inlet, distress signals may have brought quicker aid to the group once they encountered problems. Aerial flares would be less effective in the continuous Arctic daylight, and an EPIRB-type device likely would have brought help but far too late. A radio may have proven useful. High frequency (HF) and VHF radio were a common way to summon help in many areas of northern Canada. In Pond Inlet, however, there were no repeater stations, and the locals did not monitor VHF. There, HF and CB radio were the norm. The telephone remained the most common way to summon specific help, so hunters often carried satellite phones. There was an airport located near the town, which could coordinate weather-dependent aircraft evacuations, and a small RCMP detachment for emergencies and for updating float or travel plans. The ability to call for emergency assistance is an important consideration not to be ignored in the Arctic, even for short trips.

Even the experienced couple in the tandem kayak had no way of quickly securing outside help. It is only prudent to ask what the communication implications are for the area you are about to go paddling in: ranges, the frequencies locally monitored, and important telephone numbers where applicable. Some Arctic outfitters later expanded their rental options to include items like HF radios and satellite phones. PLBs and satellite messengers are now compact and effective distress signals for the region. It is also important to have contingency plans in place. Help in the Arctic can be costly and slow to arrive, delayed by weather, so even if you can make a call for help you need to be prepared to take care of your group until aid arrives. Usually paddlers research an intended area of travel to find out if a small weather radio or handheld VHF radio can pick up marine weather broadcasts or warnings; however, in this case, the closest active forecasting facility was 550 kilometers away in Resolute, leaving the paddlers more or less on their own.

One item often excluded by outfitters—and by self-organized paddlers themselves—is a towline. An easily deployable towline would have given Phil the option to hook onto Marilyn's kayak and provide the assistance she needed before conditions worsened. Carrying some form of basic towline is always a good idea. Neither Marilyn nor Rosemary would have had the strength, unaided, to regain shore in single kayaks. If the two stronger paddlers had hooked onto the weaker paddlers at the first hint of changing conditions, this also may have helped Marilyn and Rosemary to get their bows turned into the wind. Of course, if the two couples had been in tandem doubles, there is little doubt in Phil's mind that the two men could have powered both boats to shore safely.

Experience and environment both weighed heavily in this incident. Constable Burton, representing the RCMP detachment in Pond Inlet, indicated that the waters around Mt. Herodier are known for rough conditions. Severe winds from Greenland divert around Mt. Herodier and grow more intense in the vicinity around the mountain. The strong, sudden winds can catch even experienced kayakers off guard. Burton admitted that Pond Inlet is popular with kayakers precisely because the winds are infrequent and usually from the east such that the water in the lee of the land is calm. It is not unusual for paddlers visiting Pond Inlet to forego hiring professional guides.

The paddlers lacked the experience and knowledge to understand the risks of paddling in the Arctic and of approaching a headland like Mt. Herodier. Offshore winds rank high as one of the greatest threats to a paddler. Whether it is a katabatic gravity wind or (as in this group's case) wind that results from a weather-related pressure gradient, the farther out you are pushed, the worse it gets. A minute or two of inattention can mean the difference between getting to safety in the lee of the land and fighting a losing battle while being blown out to sea. It is best to avoid exposure to offshore winds by keeping close to shore and being especially wary of winds funneling through low spots in the shoreline topography. The difference in wind speed between land and offshore can be as high as 50 percent. With an offshore wind it also can be very difficult to recognize how rough it is farther away from shore, as you see only the backs of the waves. They may appear smooth while hiding the churning white foam on their downwind faces.

Although the group was given no warnings before leaving Pond Inlet, they also failed to do their homework and to ask pertinent questions. Moreover, a team of experienced paddlers would normally keep a tight formation approaching a significant topographical feature, having already anticipated the possibility of associated wind compression, and headed much closer to shore at the slightest hint of an offshore wind. The four friends, while seasoned travelers, were not experienced sea kayakers. In this situation the outfitter had not acted in his professional role as guide or equipment provider. He had just done a favor for a friend by lending him some kayaks. His employee had also made the four kayaks available outside the standard rental process. Both may have assumed the group was more experienced than they actually were.

If the four paddlers had had more experience, a number of things might have occurred differently once trouble started. Rosemary would have known to be wary of presenting the flat of her blade on the upwind side to the gusts of wind and also to lean into the waves as each one hit, taking advantage of the upward movement of water on the wave face. Turning a sea kayak into a strong wind and waves is never an easy task. Mark could have paddled slightly ahead of Rosemary on her windward side, shielding her bow while she tried to turn her boat into the wind. Rosemary could have raised her rudder onto the rear deck. With a rudder deployed, the stern of a kayak will not slip downwind, making it more difficult, if not impossible, to get the bow turned into the wind. If she had raised the rudder and paddled hard and fast straight across the wind, she could have taken advantage of a kayak's tendency to weathercock: With more boat speed the turbulence at the stern would allow it to slip downwind, letting the kayak turn with less effort into the wind. She could have taken advantage of the weathercocking by using sweep strokes on the downwind side.

Rosemary also could have shifted her hands along the paddle shaft toward the upwind blade, thereby providing greater leverage for wide, downwind sweep strokes, and paddled only on the downwind side. Performing this kind of a turn with a strong lean that places the kayak further on edge makes for an even tighter turn. These are all skills learned with time and training.

It is rarely a good idea to let a kayak go. Well-practiced assisted rescues may have allowed Rosemary and Mark to get back into their kayaks after their capsizes. Bailers could have been improvised from anything close at hand, including items such as saucepans, rain hats, a day bag, etc.

This group was overwhelmed by sudden and severe winds that, although they may be uncommon, should be expected in the waters near Pond Inlet. It is always the responsibility of paddlers to be fully prepared, to avoid problems before they become insurmountable, and to be prepared and able to accomplish their own rescues. In the final analysis it is the paddler who needs to research the intended area of travel, possess the boat-handling and rescue skills to deal with the environment, and have backup equipment and plans in place. This group of paddlers thought their short outing would be easy, no more difficult than a paddle in less extreme latitudes. Phil related his feelings this way: "I just wish someone had tapped us all on our shoulders and said, 'Hey, this is the Arctic, you need to be ten times as careful up here.'"

The deaths of Mark and Marilyn were a terrible tragedy. The story is compelling because it could have happened to anyone, as suddenly changing conditions can catch paddlers of all experience levels off guard. Even experts would have been hard pressed to perform some rescues in these conditions or turn their kayaks into the fierce wind that hit the group. Both Phil and Rosemary were extremely lucky to survive—Phil doubly so.

Nicholas Mark Seltzer was awarded the Governor General of Canada's Medal of Bravery posthumously in 1999 for his "act of bravery in hazardous circumstances." Phillip King, Elizabeth Mitchell, and Pascal Ertlé each received a commendation from the Governor General for "an act of great merit in providing assistance to others in a selfless manner."

Marilyn Chan's body was never recovered. She remains somewhere near her favored wildflowers, high in the Canadian Arctic Archipelago where the struggle for life and death is never very far away.

Doug would like to thank Gail Ferris for technical help and expresses appreciation to Phil and Rosemary for opening the incident to review and sharing a difficult story for publication. In memory of Mark and Marilyn, the Seltzer-Chan Pond Inlet Foundation exists to provide assistance to local Inuit communities. Details can be found at http:// pondinletfoundation.org.

10

The Fifth Paddler
Kayaking Tragedy in Baja

Melesa (Hamer) Rennak

The sun had just dropped below the horizon in a brilliant shower of red and gold, and the sky was growing dusky purple as we paddled into the cove near Punta Don Juan off the coast of Baja, Mexico. This is the last cove to the south in the expansive Bahia de Los Angeles, or L.A. Bay, a paddling paradise known for its great snorkeling, fishing, and diving. My partner Dave and I were happy to reach shelter before dark after setting out from the town of Bahia de Los Angeles so late in the afternoon.

As we coasted around the point, pelicans dived for their dinner, dropping vertically through hundreds of feet of air to pierce the water and strike fish swimming several feet beneath the surface. Just after rounding the point, we encountered a small group of paddlers heading out toward L.A. Bay from the mouth of the cove. We were practically on a collision course, and as we drew close, all of us stopped.

"What are you doing heading out in the dark?" I asked the five college-age paddlers in a somewhat joking tone but with underlying curiosity. "We've been trying hard to get in before it gets dark," I added.

They laughed and shrugged and told us about some great clamming they'd found on the beach they had just left. Dave asked again what they were up to. They said they felt like they just needed to get back to town. They said goodbye and set out across the quickly darkening L.A. Bay, singing songs and joking about clams, boats, and bugs. It was going to be a moonless night, and they had a 4-mile crossing ahead of them.

"Boys," I sighed to Dave. "Only boys would set out in the dark like that."

Just after we landed, the wind started picking up—and up, and up. It was coming off the land, driving the hot, dry air of the desert toward the cooling water and out to sea. Soon we were staking out the tent's guylines and huddling together in our windbreakers as we cooked dinner.

"I hope they're OK," Dave said as we ate.

"I hope they stick together," I added.

"I wonder if they made it to town yet with this wind. They've got to be going nowhere fast if they're paddling against it. Maybe they'll turn around and come back here," Dave said.

"Do you think they have headlamps or wetsuits?" I asked.

The next morning, I was clamming in the area that the boys had told us about, scooping them up by handfuls, when a boat pulled up. Miguel, who owns the campground where the boys were staying and had rented them kayaks, was out looking for one of the boys. Only four of the five had made it across the bay the previous night. Miguel had received a call that morning from a friend who had recognized one of the rental kayaks sitting on shore on the other side of the bay.

"Really? Oh no," Miguel had said, then headed out in his panga, a local style of motorboat, to see what was going on. He followed the shore of the bay and soon spotted a paddle, a kayak, and the paddler who had left them on the beach. The young man was one of the five paddlers. He had just started walking back toward camp when Miguel pulled his panga alongshore and asked if he was OK. He said he had just reached shore and was exhausted after spending a grueling night on the water.

"Where's everyone else?" asked Miguel.

"I don't know," the young man replied. "We got split up."

Miguel continued along the beach and found two of the other kayakers walking down the shore toward camp and another one walking along a different spot on the beach. One kayaker was still missing. The four young men on the beach had not yet caught up with each other and didn't realize that one of them hadn't made it ashore yet.

There was no sign of the fifth kayak on the beach. Miguel scanned the bay with his binoculars and saw a red kayak floating in the middle of the bay, but no one was with it. He was hoping that the fifth paddler had reached shore and had left the kayak where the rising tide had floated the boat and carried it out from shore. If that was the case, he might find the missing boy walking down the beach like the others.

The four kayakers who had reached shore were utterly exhausted and were not only too tired but also too inexperienced to take part in the search. They stayed at the campground, answered questions from the authorities, and called the missing boy's mother.

After listening to Miguel's story, Dave and I spent the better part of the day paddling the bay, looking for the missing kayaker. Miguel, Dave, and I skirted the coastline, searching everywhere for the telltale

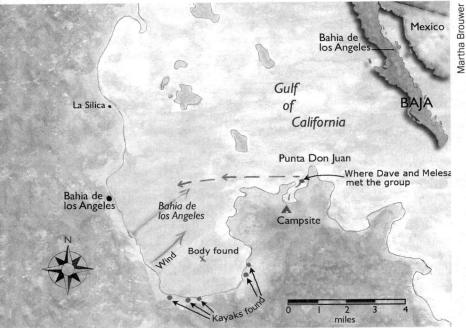

La Silica •

Mexico

Bahia de
los Angeles

Gulf
of
California

BAJA

Punta Don Juan

Where Dave and Melesa
met the group

Bahia de
los Angeles

Bahia de
los Angeles

Campsite

N

Wind

Body found
X

Kayaks found

0   1   2   3   4
miles

Martha Brouwer

flash of yellow or orange that might be a lifejacket. We were hoping
we would see the young man—tired, wet, and scared but very much
alive—washed up on shore. We spent the day monitoring the VHF radio and paddling up to fishing boats to ask if they had seen anything.

We radioed out on Channel 16, the VHF emergency channel, to
see if anyone knew what happened to the lost kayaker.

"Anyone, anyone. Come in, anyone. Does anyone have any information on the missing kayaker from last night?" I spoke hesitantly
into the radio.

A minute or two later a female voice answered. "Did someone
out there call about the kayaker?"

"Yes," I said.

"Who is this?" the voice on the other end asked.

"We saw his group set out last night and have been looking for
him today," I said.

"Well, they found his body over at Punta Rincon. They're waiting
for the authorities."

There was nothing but silence for a while as Dave and I digested
this.

"Thank you," I finally said weakly, forgetting to say "over" in
the protocol of radio transmission.

Dave still held out hope, prodding me to ask the final question. Yes, they found the body but. . . .

"So he's not alive then," I asked, already knowing what I was going to hear.

"That's an affirmative."

Later we learned that Miguel, after combing all the points and islands, had searched the bay one more time and found the missing kayaker's body floating far from shore. Dave was wracked with guilt. "I should have stopped them," he kept saying. "I should have told them they were being dumb and they shouldn't go."

"Who could have known the wind was going to pick up like that?" I asked him. "And you said just yesterday you wouldn't mind paddling in the dark, but how could we know how much experience they had?"

At the time the group left, the conditions weren't anything we wouldn't have gone out in ourselves, but the rising wind quickly created conditions that they were not prepared to handle.

The group hadn't been scheduled to return the kayaks to Miguel's Campground until the day after we saw them heading across the bay. For some reason, they decided to head back to the campground early and make the passage across the water that night instead of waiting until morning.

Miguel told us that he'd asked why they tried to come back early instead of camping the last night and waiting for daylight to cross the bay. "They said they had been thinking about fish tacos and drinking tequila. And when they rented the kayaks, they said they had experience, but now I've learned only one of them had any experience, and he's the one who died!"

The account from the four survivors was that they had stayed together for the first hour or so but then the wind split them up, three one way and two another. Then the two got separated, and only one of them made it back to shore. The coroner who examined the body of the fifth kayaker listed hypothermia as the cause of death.

I thought about everything we could have told the group, and how all the information in the world is useless if it isn't shared. I felt so deeply and painfully sorry for the boy's mother who would just now be hearing she would never see her son again. I thought about a cold, dark, and lonely death.

This incident raised a lot of questions for Dave and me. Should we have asked the group if everyone had a headlamp so they could keep track of each other in the dark? Should we have checked to see if they were wearing wetsuits? As the more experienced kayakers, did we have an obligation to do something?

We had questioned what they were doing but hadn't asked them specific questions about their gear or level of skill. *(continued page 99)*

ECONOMICS OF DECISION MAKING

Aras Kriauciunas

In most discussions of the mistakes kayakers make, the focus is on understanding the risks the paddlers faced on the water and their ability to correctly evaluate and/or overcome them. This line of inquiry is incomplete because it does not account for how people perceive risks and because it fails to take into account how we actually make the decision to launch.

Most paddlers would agree that the efforts that go into getting ready for a trip are, in economic terms, an investment, and that the pleasure of paddling is a return on that investment. If you've spent a week getting ready for a big trip and then drive 5 hours to the launch site, you're going to be very eager to get on the water: Paddling is the return on your investment.

If being out on the water seems the best use of our time, we launch. Since every kayaking incident starts with the decision to launch, it follows that our safety on the water is influenced by the alternatives that are available to us at launch time.

While reading reports of kayaking incidents over the past few years, I became convinced that something fundamental was missing in how kayakers made decisions to launch in marginal circumstances. Having recently completed my MBA, it occurred to me that concepts from economics and consumer behavior could be applied to better understand how we make our decision to launch. I realized that things we consider to be optional when preparing for a trip should actually be considered as an important aspect of safety. It also became clear why many attempts at discouraging kayakers from launching into deteriorating conditions are unsuccessful—and how that can be improved.

Following are some economic terms that can be applied to decision making at the start of a paddling day:

Potential value: The amount of enjoyment you might have or the goals that you'll achieve by paddling today.

Perceived risk: The downsides of paddling today, the things you will not enjoy or that might harm you.

Perceived value = potential value minus perceived risk: Is the payoff worth the risk or effort you take on? If the potential value clearly outweighs the perceived risk, the perceived value is high.

Opportunity cost: What else could you be doing if you chose not to paddle today? Could a day ashore be time well spent?

Incremental value = perceived value minus opportunity cost: How much more will you enjoy paddling over whatever else you could be doing? This is the difference between perceived value and opportunity cost.

Potential Value

The potential value is what we typically focus on when deciding whether to launch. This includes both the experience of being out on the water as well as what might be gained from achieving the day's objective: getting to the campsite or completing the trip on time.

Economic theory says that the effort we put into getting ready for a trip should have no bearing on the launch decision. It is referred to as a "sunk cost," meaning that we have already spent our time and resources in such a manner that it cannot be undone. As paddlers, we often view the work of packing and getting to the put-in as an investment, which puts additional pressure on us to "protect" that investment when we arrive at the launch. This is a dangerous perspective. No matter how much we've invested in getting to the water, a bad launch decision is still a bad launch decision; it is in no way excused because we worked hard to make it possible.

Perceived Risk

When evaluating conditions, the skill level of the paddler is important because of our heavy reliance on previous experiences. Thus, risk assessment is subjective in nature because it is the perception of risk that drives our decision. Numerous factors affect how we perceive risk. Two of them are described below.

First, we are much more willing to accept a risk when it is voluntary. Voluntary risk is why people believe they are safer driving cars versus flying in an airplane, even though the airplane is statistically much safer. We feel comfortable with significantly higher risks when we feel in control of our fate. This is important, since it distorts how we evaluate risk. I have happily launched in conditions when I felt it was my decision to make, but I have been opposed to launching in similar conditions when someone else was pressuring me to do so.

Next, we evaluate risk by comparing it to something we know or by extrapolating when it lies beyond the boundaries of what we have already experienced. Unfortunately, we tend to significantly underestimate the additional risk that lies *(continued next page)* outside of our experience. Experienced paddlers know that key variables for paddling difficulty are wave height, wind speed, and the paddling direction relative to the wind and waves. We listen to the weather forecast and try to extrapolate the conditions based on what we have already experienced. The smaller the gap between what we have experienced and what we are considering, the more likely we are to correctly evaluate the new situation.

Novices are especially bad at assessing the risk associated with adverse conditions they encounter for the first time. Evaluating the additional risk when moving from paddling in calm conditions to making a 2-mile crossing with 15-knot winds is a jump beginners simply cannot make. As a result, the weather forecast may have limited value because new paddlers cannot comprehend the associated risk. Making matters worse, they may not be aware of their limitations, which can make it very difficult, at best, for a concerned paddler to have a conversation with them about the risks associated with launching in challenging conditions. The result may be an "I know what I am doing" response, since they may not even be aware of the fact that they can't fully understand the situation. The perceived risk associated is low for new paddlers, since they lack the knowledge needed to correctly interpret what it will feel like on the water once they launch.

"Perceived risk" here signifies possible negatives. Large waves may not be a negative for everyone, but the possibility of having to call for a rescue certainly is.

Perceived Value

Perceived value starts with how much we *might* enjoy paddling today and accounts for the associated risk. The result is how much we reasonably *expect* to enjoy paddling today. Bringing the components—potential value and perceived risk—into play makes it easier to bring our traditional kayak-focused discussion of risk into this economic framework.

Opportunity Cost

Although an accurate assessment of risk is a key step when deciding to launch, the opportunity cost is always considered, either explicitly or implicitly. This explicit discussion is often missing when discussing the launch decision at the beach. As mentioned above, the opportunity cost is what the alternative use of our time will be if we don't go paddling now. The higher the opportunity cost, the higher the requirements are for a fulfilling time paddling. Staying on the beach has some level of value, and the better prepared you are to enjoy the time you spend ashore, the higher that value is. Giving up something that has a high value implies a high cost for the activity you choose. Good alternatives to paddling have a high opportunity cost.

If the opportunity cost of staying ashore (warm and happy) exceeds a low value in launching in marginal conditions (high degree of anxiety), it is easy to opt to stay on land for the day.

Incremental Value

Understanding perceived value and opportunity cost brings us to the idea of incremental value. A decision to launch should go through these steps:

1. How much are you going to enjoy or gain from going paddling?
2. Weigh the negatives associated with paddling (e.g., potential for strong winds and large waves or the chance of rain).
3. Compare your experience if you go paddling to what else you might do instead.
4. The gain you might realize by going paddling versus doing something else is your incremental value. The larger the incremental value, the more likely you are to launch.

Consider when launching whether the incremental value is high for the right reasons. Is it high because the paddling conditions are great, or because your current situation is miserable and almost anything would be better than staying where you are? The incremental value should be high because the expected value is high—anything else should be a red flag.

The opportunity cost is important to keep in mind when planning a trip. Think of good food, an interesting book, and comfortable accommodations as your insurance policy. These "luxuries" will help protect you from being forced into unsafe decisions by a positive incremental value for paddling that is elevated simply by discomfort and/or boredom in camp.

Influencing the Launch Decision for Others

It's one thing to make better decisions as a group, but what can you do when you come across other paddlers (especially those you don't know) getting ready to launch in questionable conditions? You might try to initiate a discussion that focuses solely on the risks involved. This is generally ineffective with new paddlers because they lack the personal experiences required to assess risk correctly. A better approach is to influence the *perception* of risk and the opportunity cost associated with launching. *(continued next page)*

My friend Dave came across a paddler getting ready to launch near Meyers Beach in the Apostle Islands. Conditions were windy, and Dave knew that several paddlers had died exploring the sea caves in that area when their boats flipped and they found themselves in the water. Dave tried to explain that capsizing in Lake Superior without at least a wetsuit is a bad idea, because the 45°F water quickly leads to hypothermia, making it nearly impossible to get back into the boat. The paddler was not convinced. Dave asked him to stand in water up to his knees while they continued their conversation. After a minute, Dave asked if he could still feel his legs and was told "no." Dave then asked him how effectively he would be able to get back into his boat if his whole body felt as numb.

The paddler now had a new personal experience that made his knowledge gap much smaller, allowing him to assess the risk more effectively. His potential value remained the same—the sea caves are cool—but his perceived risk just increased, resulting in a reduced perceived value.

The paddler was new to the area and had no idea what else he might spend the afternoon doing, so his opportunity cost was pretty low; just sitting on the beach was of little interest to him. The incremental value was still positive but had become marginally so. Dave next addressed the opportunity cost. He suggested checking out a slough that's sheltered from the wind and an interesting place to explore via kayak. This sounded pretty interesting, so the opportunity cost provided by the alternate destination went up. The incremental value of exploring the caves became negative, and not launching to go there made the best sense. The alternative destination was now the better choice.

Conclusions

The decision to launch is the last decision in a chain that starts with trip planning at home and continues on to the environment at the time of the launch. By focusing on each step along the way to ensure we always have an enjoyable backup plan, we are more likely to avoid launching in marginal conditions.

Understanding the components of this process also enables us to be more effective at helping others understand the implications of launching in poor conditions. Discussing risk is a good starting point, but the incremental value will be decreased more effectively by suggesting interesting alternatives. It is the awareness of those alternatives that may persuade both new and experienced kayakers to come back and paddle on a better day.

We chatted about superficial things in spite of our feeling that the circumstances they were setting out under were strange. Had we talked with the group about their preparedness instead of just the best place to camp in the cove, maybe we could have been more certain about their capabilities and things would have played out differently.

"It was pretty obvious right away that they didn't have any experience," said Dennis, a college-level outdoors professor who was camped next to the group the night before they left on their trip. "I asked them, 'Do you have tide tables?' They said, 'Do we need them?' I asked, 'Do you have any maps?' They said, 'Do we need those, too?'" Dennis dropped his shoulders, shaking his head as he recalled the conversation. He too must have felt great sadness and regret that in his brief encounter with the five, he could not have found a way to get them to understand the risks they failed to see.

"The westerlies pick up so fast around here," Dennis said. "I've paddled up and down this coast in different sections, and this is the most dynamic area there is. The wind can pick up in 15 minutes and be blowing 40 miles an hour."

The wind is always a concern for kayakers paddling in Baja in the spring. Dave and I had just finished sitting through a windstorm for three days, and it continued to be windy off and on all week. While the kind of land breeze that overtook the five is not a daily occurrence, it happens often enough to be a consideration for anyone boating in the area.

In years past, kayakers seldom crossed paths with each other, and the novelty of seeing other paddlers was reason enough to go talk with them and find out where they came from and where they were going. Now, tour groups pass each other going back and forth along the same well-used strips of coastline. They don't want their outdoor experience interrupted by seeing other people, so they don't approach them in the first place. Groups of kayakers may camp on the same beach within a few yards of each other but remain as distant as two strangers sitting next to each other on a bus. Most groups we encounter in the wilderness don't even make eye contact with us. And it's not just while paddling: This can be a part of any wilderness experience.

Sharing information used to give us the benefit of other paddlers' experience. But now with kayaking becoming ever more popular, people may take to the water with little or no knowledge of safe paddling practices. How do you approach people when you think they may be heading into a situation beyond their abilities? How do you find out what their experience level is? How can you make sure they are prepared to deal with situations that arise without offending them? Does it matter if you offend someone if you are trying to pass along important information about risks they may not be aware of?

I decided that from that point on, I wouldn't worry about offending kayakers if I felt their abilities were a poor match for the risks they were taking on.

The next morning, the water started out as perfect glass. It was the kind of day made for kayaking. Our route took us past tiny islets covered in saguaro cactus. As the sun blazed, a man with no hat, sunglasses, or shirt paddled a bright red sit-on-top kayak across the bay.

"He's going to turn the same color as his boat," I joked to Dave. Even with such hot weather, sunburn wouldn't be the only risk he'd face. Hypothermia from an unexpected swim could also pose a threat.

Our boats were packed and we were doing a last check before shoving off when a group of three kayakers approached the beach—more college-age boys. They steered away from us and landed on the other end of the beach. They looked very much like the five paddlers who had been scattered by the wind. They were young and energetic, ready to take on the world, and free from worry. I couldn't stop thinking about everything we could have said to the first group and decided not to make the same mistake again. I took a deep breath and walked over to introduce myself. I asked if they had heard about the incident.

Only one of them had heard of the accident, but he had decided not to tell his friends about it. He said he didn't want to start their trip off on a down note. I thought it was absurd not to talk beforehand about the dangers you might face on a trip like this, especially in light of what had happened last night.

"Yeah, but that guy wasn't wearing his life jacket," he said in an offhand sort of way.

"Yes, he was," I said. "He didn't drown. He died of hypothermia." The two other boys were amazed someone could die of hypothermia here where it was so warm. "Yeah, but try swimming," I said. "In the water, you can get really cold after about 15 or 20 minutes. It's almost unbearable after an hour. The time for clear thinking and good strength and dexterity starts ticking away from the moment you hit the water. You need to be prepared for the water temperature, not the air temperature. Do you guys have wetsuits?" They didn't.

"Yeah, but I guess if you fell out of your boat you could swim to shore," said the same one who was so sure of himself. "That would keep you warm."

I just said, "Have you ever tried swimming five miles against a headwind?" This was just the kind of "downer" conversation he didn't want to be involved in, so he excused himself to go fishing.

I was frustrated. Here I was, making an effort to communicate with obviously less-experienced kayakers, trying to get the seriousness of what they were attempting across to them, and I was getting the big blow-off. But the other two seemed genuinely interested in what I had to say. "If it gets windy out, head for a cove immediately. And no matter what, stick together," I said.

We asked them if they had maps and showed them where the little bailout cove was on their mediocre chart. We talked to them about how to steady someone's boat after a capsize so the paddler can crawl back in from the other side.

It was easy to see that this was their first time out in kayaks. They didn't have any idea what to do if the wind picked up or how to plan for other emergencies. After imparting a few more words of wisdom, Dave and I wished the two boys (who didn't mind hearing the downer information) a good journey. We told them about the excellent clamming spot and emphasized again to keep a close eye on the weather and each other, then Dave and I headed out on the water.

It had been easy to open up a dialogue with the second group of kayakers because of what had happened the *(continued page 103)*

TO SAY NOTHING

Christopher Cunningham

I can often spot novices at quite a distance. A paddle held upside down is one of the more obvious signs of an inexperienced kayaker, but there are many more: lack of proper equipment, inadequate clothing, poor route selection, or, as Melesa Rennak describes in this chapter, setting out onto the water when prudent paddlers would be packing it in.

On a calm summer's day a few years ago, my friend John and I were paddling around the south end of Washington's Lopez Island along a steep rocky shore that offered little protection from southerly winds. Coming toward us were two single kayaks. I noticed that both paddlers had their paddles flipped, so I changed course to meet them. They stopped paddling when I approached. I said hello, and we talked about how beautiful the day was. I asked where they were headed and learned they had only a few hundred yards to go to return to the cove they had launched from. They mentioned that they had borrowed kayaks for the day and had never been paddling before. They wore clothes that would have been fine for wandering on the land side of the coast but not for paddling in the 50°F water. I knew that the weather would remain calm *(continued next page)* for the rest of the day and that they'd easily get back to shore, so I didn't explain to them why I was wearing a wetsuit. Before I said goodbye, I told them they'd find paddling a bit more comfortable if they flipped their paddles over. They happily made the correction and pulled away. There was a lot more I could have offered them, but regrettably I let them carry on without doing more to increase their understanding of safe kayaking practices.

A few years earlier, and a few miles from that Lopez Island shore, a lone kayaker was seen paddling along Lime Kiln Point, the southernmost tip of nearby San Juan Island. He had crossed paths on the water with an experienced paddler that evening. They had spoken, and the experienced paddler saw one of the other signs of a novice: a PFD tucked under the bungees on the foredeck. The novice was last seen paddling away from shore shortly before sunset. His rented kayak was found the next morning several miles from shore, upside down, with the PFD still on deck. He was never found.

Do experienced kayakers have an obligation to speak up when they encounter poorly outfitted paddlers? It would seem that when a life is at stake, the answer is obvious. It is easy to see that novice kayakers are in need of help when their lack of preparedness is made evident by conditions that have overwhelmed them. At that point, I'm sure anyone would make an effort to help. On a calm summer day, however, there may not be any immediate danger. If that happens to be the time experienced paddlers cross paths with novices, making an effort to ensure their safety can still be of great value—if not at the moment, then at some time in the future.

But, as Melesa writes, "People generally don't want their inexperience pointed out to them." Her attempt to impart some of her kayaking knowledge to a second group of kayakers, shortly after she'd heard of the fatality suffered by the first group, was not well received. I have to confess that I sometimes still hold my tongue when I see paddlers out for a summer paddle wearing shorts and T-shirts. It's easy to take the least awkward option of saying nothing, but that can leave the innocent to suffer serious consequences for their ignorance. If we are to learn anything from Melesa's story, it's that the anguish felt by the people who have lost someone will be shared by those who could have foreseen and perhaps prevented the loss. I believe we have an obligation to give novices we happen upon the benefit of our experience. There's always a chance that the advice may not be well received, but speaking up will, in the long run, be easier to live with than saying nothing.

day before, but sometimes it's not so easy. People generally don't want their inexperience pointed out to them.

As we left L.A. Bay, a sheet of glass covered the ocean, rippled only by the drops falling from our paddles and the slight turbulence of our wakes. I watched Dave's reflection on the water as he paddled alongside me. Our early start that morning let us take advantage of the tendency of Baja weather to be better in the morning. It also let us catch a free ride on the current making its way out of the Sea of Cortez, rushing past the islands on its way to the Pacific.

It was hard to imagine tragedy on a day like that. The sea was calm and clear, and you could see through 50 to 60 feet of water to the white sand and kelp-covered rocks and coral below. Another day simply made for paddling, and after all the wind and rough seas lately, I appreciated the calm that much more.

Note: By request, some names in this chapter have been changed.

11

The Loss of a Novice
The Tragic Consequences of an Unexpected Capsize

Charles A. Sutherland

On Saturday, May 26, 2001, 51-year-old Robert Beauvais participated in a sea kayaking course for beginning paddlers, a 6-hour class listed as Essential Skills I, run by a New England kayak school. The participants included four students and Carla, a British Canoe Union–trained Four Star instructor. (Names of the staff and other students have been changed.) Paul, an unpaid volunteer, helped with instruction during the morning session. Class started at about 10:15 A.M. The kayak school provided boats and equipment for the students, including a wetsuit, spray skirt, paddling jacket, and PFD for Robert, who was 5 foot 11 inches and of average build.

The day was partly sunny with a light southeast wind at approximately 5 knots, which strengthened later in the day. The air temperature was 75°F, and water temperature was about 58°F. The water in the area was well protected from the southeast wind and waves.

The initial instruction was carried out on shore. Instructor Carla showed the students how to get in and out of their boats and how to get the spray skirts on and off the cockpit rims of their boats. Under her direction, the students each went through this exercise twice on shore before launching. Carla asked the students if they understood the maneuver and confirmed that they all felt comfortable with their ability to perform it. She told the students they would do wet-exit training in the water at the end of the day, as she didn't want them to start the session by getting wet and risk having them become hypothermic during the course of the outing. Before launching, the students also were instructed on how to hold the paddle, perform various paddling strokes, and do a deepwater rescue. They launched their boats at about 10:45 A.M.

Once on the water, Carla taught forward, reverse, and turning strokes. Shortly after launching, while working on a forward sweep stroke, Leslie, one of the students, capsized. Initially, she tried to struggle to the surface while still in the boat but then remembered she had to first remove her spray skirt from the rim of the cockpit. As she reported later, her first attempt to get it off failed, and in spite of the wetsuit she was wearing, the cold water made her want to gasp for air. She continued to hold her breath and made a second effort to free the spray skirt. Simply pulling on the grab loop failed to remove it from the cockpit rim, but then she remembered to punch it forward and up. The skirt came free of the cockpit rim, and Leslie bailed out successfully. She estimated that it took her about 5 seconds to get out of the kayak.

Carla then pulled Leslie's boat across her own boat to dump out the water (a T-X rescue) and helped her reenter it from the water. Carla used the capsize as an opportunity to review the wet-exit procedure and to demonstrate a deepwater rescue.

The students continued working on strokes, and Carla spoke about other marine subjects while they paddled south along the shore. George, Mary, and Leslie stayed up front with Carla, while Robert moved a bit slower in the company of the assistant, Paul.

About noon, Paul headed back to the launch site. Carla kept the group together, and they usually stayed within 10 to 15 yards of each other. They crossed the boating channel to have lunch on a small

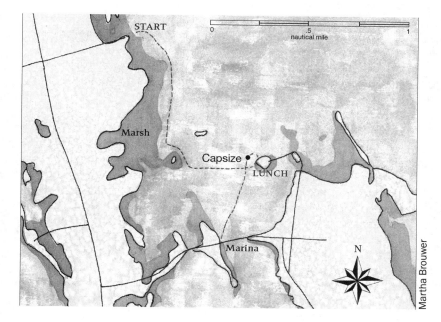

island. During the lunch break ashore, Carla assisted Robert in adjusting the position of his foot braces.

They launched again at about 12:45 and paddled around to the lee side of the island to work on more paddling skills. These included the draw stroke and more paddling forward (continued page 110)

ENTRAPMENT AND EXITS
Doug Lloyd

An intense westerly winter wind had kicked up a mean chop off the Victoria, British Columbia, waterfront, and I was taking advantage of the churning water to refine my rough-water paddling technique. I was riding in to shore on the back of a 4-foot wind wave when the stern of my kayak was suddenly and steeply lifted by an unusually large wave. Before I could lean back, the bow buried deep into the trough and hit the rocky bottom. The force of the impact broke the foot bar and drove my legs and hips deep into the cockpit. Hanging upside down, I discovered that being twisted in the cockpit threw off my set-up for rolling. Out of air, I released the spray skirt and attempted a wet exit but was unable to extricate myself from the cockpit. I was both surprised and annoyed that I couldn't push out of the cockpit. The waves pushed me into a narrow, shallow surge channel where I didn't have enough space to try to roll or scull to the surface for air. Panicking and starting to suck in water, I was on the verge of blacking out. Fortunately, two good Samaritans watching the storm from the road above the beach rushed down to the shoreline to help me. That was almost 20 years ago, but I can still recall the sense of helplessness and despair I felt the moment I realized I was trapped in my kayak.

Entrapment

A number of situations can prevent a quick and safe wet exit. A capsized paddler stuck in the cockpit and unable to roll or get to the surface for air is at serious risk of drowning. There are a variety of causes of entrapment in sea kayaks: forces of nature, medical or disability complications, ignorance of technique, spray skirts that can't be released, inexperience, and entanglement with gear. Entrapment can also be caused by equipment failure, forgotten procedures, simple panic, or lack of preparation. Even experienced paddlers have to be wary of circumstances that might lead to risk of entrapment.

Entrapment often catches paddlers by surprise. For some, the substantial stress of an entrapment has led to abandoning sea kayaking. In a few cases, there have been fatalities. Entrapment may not be common, but it is a matter worthy of our awareness and preparedness.

Entry-level paddlers are particularly vulnerable to the untoward aftermath of capsizing. Unfortunately, an unreasonable fear of suddenly submerging and subsequently getting stuck in a kayak may prevent new paddlers from even practicing wet exits. Other novices—most often those who have had no training in kayaking—may head out without even thinking about the consequences of capsizing or the procedure necessary to exit safely while inverted.

The initial stages of a capsize can be very disconcerting. Cold water can cause a painful "ice-cream headache" or, even worse, induce a gasp reflex that draws water into the lungs. Dizziness, disorientation, darkness, stinging eyes, and cold, numb hands can make it difficult to go through the routine of releasing the spray skirt and curling out of the cockpit. Experienced paddlers learn to exhale slowly through their noses to prevent water from going up their nostrils while inverted. By keeping water out of their sinuses, they can typically remain upside down and relaxed significantly longer.

It is important that new paddlers practice wet exits in a safe, stress-free environment with experienced and reliable help ready to assist. The basics can initially be demonstrated and practiced in kayaks on shore but must be followed up with doing wet exits in the water. Some individuals can lose their composure with something as simple as placing their face in the water, so it is essential to progress to the in-water exit with someone standing alongside to assist. The first wet-exit practice sessions can be done without a spray skirt or paddle. Nose clips and face masks are useful aids, although they should ultimately be put aside in the interest of practicing more realistic scenarios. The wet exit is a basic skill that must be mastered both physically and psychologically in order to effectively cope with the problems associated with entrapment.

The improper fit of a spray skirt can lead to entrapment. Given the variety of cockpit configurations, sizes, rim widths, and boat materials, the chance for a mismatch is high. Spray skirts designed for use on plastic kayaks present a dangerous hazard when used on a fiberglass rim where they grip tenaciously. Whenever you try a new or different combination of spray skirt and kayak, make sure you can release your spray skirt with one hand. To release a tight-fitting spray skirt, you must push the grab loop forward toward the bow of the kayak until the bungee clears the coaming flange, then away from the deck and back to release the spray skirt. If the bungee is under a lot of tension, this maneuver *(continued next page)* can require a lot of strength. Novice paddlers can use a loose-fitting nylon skirt for their initial year. It will make wet exits easier.

Frank, a proficient paddler, was trying out a friend's new boat one winter. He was alone in shallow water wearing neoprene gloves and a cap and had decided to use his own neoprene skirt, which provided a tight but manageable fit on the borrowed boat. He capsized to try a wet exit. He was unable to locate the grab loop, which was located much farther forward than it would have been on his own boat. Running out of air, Frank was rather dismayed at the prospect of dying so close to shore. He managed to keep from panicking, let go of his paddle, and swam his head to the surface to get a gulp of air. He released the skirt by grabbing a fold of material near the edge of the coaming on one side, where the flatter curve of the coaming makes it easier to pull the bungee from the coaming flange.

If you have a skirt that uses an adjustable bungee—usually protruding from the rear of the skirt—you should be able to reach back and use this as an alternative grab loop. You may also be able to reach down through the waist tube of the spray skirt to release the skirt. If you wear your PFD on the outside of your spray skirt, you will need to slip your hand under the bottom edge of the PFD, reach up over the top of the skirt's tube, and then slip your hand downward through the tunnel. Then lift the spray deck's underside and push it out beyond the lip. You may need your other hand to help peel it from the coaming.

It may also be possible to slip out of the spray skirt's waist tube, leaving the spray skirt attached to the kayak. This can be very easy to do with zippered models: Just unzip and slip out. If the spray skirt has suspenders, you have to release them. A rescue knife can be employed to cut an opening in the spray skirt's deck to provide something to grasp, but most paddlers would probably be at the point of incapacitation by the time they would resort to a knife.

Wearing paddling gloves during the off-season or in cold climates can pose challenges with locating the spray skirt's grab loop. The layer of neoprene robs the wearer of the tactile sensitivity required to find the thin webbing release found on many spray skirts. Hands cold to the point of being numb can create the same problem. A grab loop fitted with a carabiner makes it easier to locate the loop by touch and makes the loop hang away from the coaming where it is easier to find. A locking carabiner is recommended because it is less likely to inadvertently snag anything.

One paddler I know uses electrical ties to attach a Whiffle ball to the end of his grab loop to serve as a locator device.

A very common problem is unintentionally securing the spray skirt with its grab loop tucked inside the cockpit. A trapped grab loop is an accident waiting to happen. Ensuring your spray skirt grab loop is fully exposed and free from entanglement should be part of everyone's prelaunch ritual. Grab loops weakened by age, sunlight, or chlorine in pool water can fail or tear away. All paddlers should practice alternative methods for releasing their spray skirts without using the grab loop.

Footwear

Shoelaces and sandal straps both have the potential to snag foot braces. Some footwear designed specifically for paddlesports have addressed this problem by covering or eliminating straps and laces. Think through your choice of footwear and test it in the kayak while on dry land for entanglement dangers. If you find yourself snagged by your footwear, try slipping back into the cockpit to release the tension on the snag and coax it free. If that doesn't work, try to pry off the snagged shoe by using your other foot to push the heel off and free yourself. Don't take it for granted that gravity alone will provide for a graceful exit.

Backup Methods

It's not a bad idea to have at least one or two backup methods to get your head to the surface where you can get some air. Rolling, of course, is a good solution to a capsize, but if you are doing a wet exit, it is usually because you are unable to roll. If you carry an inflated paddle float or, better yet, a rigid paddle float under the bungees on the back deck within easy reach, you can pull it out and use it to roll up or at least get your face above the water. Developing the ability to scull your way to the surface with your paddle, even if only partially, is an invaluable skill. By extending your paddle and sweeping out sideways and back to the stern, you can gain tremendous leverage and perhaps a breath of air while you evaluate possible solutions to your entrapment situation. Developing the ability to swim to the surface on either side of the kayak provides a skill that you can add to your survival strategies, and it doesn't rely on having extra equipment.

Entrapment is a serious situation. It takes only a small amount of preventive maintenance, prior training, and a little ongoing practice to make sea kayaking a safe sport for almost everyone. Common sense and an awareness of potential hazards should help you avoid life-and-death situations if a wet exit doesn't go as well as you expect. When and if you encounter an entrapment problem, maintaining your composure and having a number of well-practiced backup plans may save your life.

and backward. The students also worked on paddle bracing. They were to lean to one side until starting to fall, then recover by slapping the surface of the water with the paddle blade in the low brace position.

To avoid the wind, Carla lined the students up near shore for more practice doing the low brace, but the wind carried the group about 100 yards away from shore as they practiced. Leslie's boat was parallel to Robert's and about 25 feet to his left. At about 1:45 P.M., Robert capsized toward Leslie while trying to practice the low brace. According to Leslie, "When he tipped, he almost immediately began splashing the water on his left side facing me. He was flailing his arms, and I think he was trying to yell for help."

Carla started paddling toward him, noting that Robert hadn't exited the kayak. George called out that Robert wasn't getting out of his boat. Carla paddled to the right side of Robert's boat and reached across it to pull him upright. Robert clutched at Carla and tried to pull himself up. She noticed that Robert's hips were apparently outside the cockpit but his spray skirt was still attached to the rim of the cockpit coaming.

Carla got to Robert's kayak in about 5 seconds (according to Leslie's estimate) and was able to get Robert partially upright after he had been underwater for 10 to 15 seconds (according to estimates later provided by her and the students). Mary got out of her boat, released Robert's spray skirt, and got him out of his boat. She then held Robert's head out of the water while holding onto his boat. Carla attached her towline to Robert's boat, and both she and George blew their emergency whistles in an effort to attract the attention of passing boat traffic. At this point, both Robert and Mary were still in the water, with Mary holding Robert's head out of the water while still holding onto Robert's boat.

During the first 5 minutes after being brought to the surface, Robert was conscious but had difficulty breathing. Mary said he was able to talk a little bit. In another 3 to 4 minutes, he lost consciousness. Mary, a professional nurse, began rescue breathing, while Carla towed them (both still in the water) to shore. One powerboat passed them without stopping.

Leslie started paddling toward a marina about 0.4 mile distant, where she saw a sailboat maneuvering near the docks. She repeatedly yelled out the boat's name and waved her paddle in the air. In the course of this effort, she capsized. This time she remembered the proper technique for a wet exit and immediately bailed out. Momentarily, two men in a powerboat arrived and offered her their assistance. She told them she would be fine and directed them to Carla, Mary, and Robert.

The boat's owner, Thomas Guard, took Robert and Mary aboard. Mary and passenger Gregory Haley immediately began CPR on Robert. At the marina, police officer Macy Joseph (also an EMT) assisted Mary with the CPR effort. Off-duty police officer Bouvier arrived and provided 100% oxygen and a defibrillator, but they were not successful in reviving Robert. CPR was continued during transport to the emergency room at a hospital about 7 miles away.

In the course of his capsize, Robert had inhaled water to an extent that compromised lung function even after Carla and Mary got him up and out of his boat. He was declared dead at 2:51 that afternoon. An autopsy carried out the next day determined that he died from asphyxia due to drowning and that the manner of death was accidental.

LESSONS LEARNED

Robert capsized unintentionally in cold water. He was not mentally prepared for the unexpected capsize, and he *(continued page 112)*

OVERCOMING INSTINCT

Christopher Cunningham

Many paddlers speak of the freedom they feel in a sea kayak, but in the fraction of a second that it takes to capsize, they may suddenly feel quite the opposite: trapped. Few people have any previous experience to prepare them for hanging upside down from the cockpit of an inverted kayak, and for some inexperienced paddlers, a capsize can be completely unnerving.

Chuck Sutherland's account of the kayak student's death is a disturbing story. The incident led to a lawsuit that was eventually settled out of court. It is the only fatality of its kind that I know of, and yet it's chillingly close to an incident I experienced 3 years ago when I took a friend of mine out paddling.

Tom (fictional name) was eager to give kayaking a try, so I took him paddling with two of my more experienced friends. I lent him some paddling clothes, a PFD, and a nylon spray skirt and got him into a kayak. I followed closely behind him as we paddled about 100 yards to a sandy beach tucked into a small cove. I put my kayak ashore, then waded back out into waist-deep water to run Tom through some wet-exit drills. To get him used to capsizing, I had him set his paddle aside and take both my hands and lower himself into the water, stay submerged as long as he felt comfortable, and then pull himself back up. From there *(continued next page)* we progressed to having him tuck forward, reach around the hull, and capsize. Each time I'd have him count to 10 and tap on the hull before I'd roll him back up. I had Tom finish up with some wet exits. The first were with the spray skirt detached from the coaming, and the last few were with it in place, requiring him to pop it free before he pushed himself out of the cockpit. After each wet exit, I coached him through reentries while I stabilized the kayak.

After the session, I gave back his paddle and told him to stay put while I got back into my kayak. I backed away from him so I could keep an eye on him, and when I was about 10 feet away he put his hands on the sides of the kayak to shift himself in the seat. Before I could finish shouting "Get your hands back on the paddle!" Tom capsized. I rushed toward him as he flailed the water white with his arms. He managed to keep from going completely under for the few seconds it took me to get to him and pull him upright.

Tom had just gone through several capsize drills, but when he accidentally capsized it was as if none of the training we'd just done had ever happened. He had just practiced two options—wet exiting or banging on the hull and waiting for me to assist him—but then he instinctively tried to fight going underwater.

Over the years, I've watched a lot of people get into kayaks and capsize, but I'd never seen anyone react as Tom did. As long as he frantically dog-paddled to keep his head out of the water, his hands weren't free to push himself out of the cockpit. Fortunately, Tom managed to avoid inhaling any water while he thrashed in the water. The student in Sutherland's account wasn't so lucky. For some there can be a big difference between an anticipated capsize they know is coming and one that catches them by surprise. Practicing under close supervision is a good first step for learning to take a capsize in stride. As with many skills that you may need under duress, the goal is to turn your training into your reflex.

panicked. At the moment he capsized, about 3 hours after doing the wet-exit drill on shore, he was unable to compose himself, release his spray skirt, and exit his boat. When he went over, no one was near enough to his boat to lift him up immediately. In his panic, he inhaled water to a degree that could not be reversed by subsequent rescue efforts.

Leslie capsized at about 11:00 A.M., some 15 to 20 minutes after launching. Although she had just reviewed the wet-exit drill on shore, Leslie did not immediately remember what to do. The cold water on her head and up her nose made her want to gasp. She composed herself after two false starts and finally succeeded in getting the spray skirt off and herself out of the boat. After doing an actual wet exit, the lesson stuck with her: When she capsized later in the day, she had no further difficulty bailing out of her boat.

The fiberglass kayaks provided to Leslie and Robert had keyhole cockpits that required them to follow a specific routine to exit their boats if they capsized. Once over, they had to tuck forward, grab the spray skirt grab loop, and push it forward, up, and away from the deck to get it off the cockpit coaming. Then, with legs straight, they had to push off the cockpit rim at their hips and somersault forward out of their boats.

The British Canoe Union's *Canoeing Handbook*, second edition, which was current at the time of the accident, had various recommendations for wet-exit practice but conceded the following: "To capsize your group, especially at the beginning of the session, puts people off and creates other problems. We therefore have to content ourselves with an explanation, or perhaps a dry land demonstration, and then be prepared to come quickly to the assistance of a capsized person." At later points in this book, the BCU authors recommend the use of large-cockpit boats without spray skirts to assure an easy exit in the event of capsize.

Although the spray skirts used by Robert and Leslie had plastic balls attached to the grab loops and were one size larger than recommended for the boats, their capsizes demonstrated that these skirts would not slip off the coaming if the paddlers just came out of their seats. The abrupt edge of the cockpit rim on these composite boats combined with the design of the neoprene spray skirts prevents them from coming off the rim by accident. This can provide a measure of safety by keeping the skirt in place in rough sea conditions. The consequence, however, is that the paddler must be trained to remove the skirt in order to do a wet exit. The mastery of this skill requires practice in the water.

The British Canoe Union's third edition handbook, retitled *Canoe and Kayak Handbook,* published after this incident, addresses the issue of novices doing their first wet-exit drills with a more consistent recommendation that the drills be carried out in a swimming pool with an instructor or informed friend standing in the pool adjacent to the boat. The first try should be carried out without the spray skirt in place on the cockpit rim. For comfort, the student should use nose clips. They even recommend that students practice somersaulting into and out of the cockpit of the capsized boat several times before trying the drill with a loose-fitting nylon spray skirt in place.

The student's first wet exit is discussed in this more recent edition as follows: "When people are practicing [the] capsize drill for the first time, particularly if it is the first time with the spray deck, they should be closely supervised. Stand next to the kayak and when they go upside down watch the boater carefully. Problems are rare but to be on the safe side you are looking for: 1.) Signs of panic (undirected, futile movements), or 2.) Signs of counter panic (no movement), i.e., the paddler freezing." In such cases, the instructor is told to immediately turn the capsized boat upright.

Those who teach novice kayakers know that many students are afraid of their first wet exit. Protestations to the contrary ("I'll be fine!"), we cannot predict who will panic the first time they go over! Thus we must stand next to them in the water, ready to pick them up immediately if they panic.

In the case presented here one student panicked, inhaled water, and drowned, and one was able to think what to do and bail out on her third try while upside down. I believe this truth about panic explains the large number of annual drownings among all boaters who suddenly enter the water by accident and drown within a few feet of shore or other safety regardless of water temperature! The ability to swim has nothing to do with this phenomenon.

Many of the introductory paddling courses I have taught for the American Canoe Association or private groups have been in situations not satisfactory for working on wet exits. These included insufficient time for the specific program, cold water, high river levels, and dirty water. In such situations, I have given the students or guests stable, large-cockpit boats without spray skirts. It is the practice of other instructors I know not to provide spray skirts to students who haven't demonstrated skill at doing the wet-exit drill. Students or guests were always required to wear PFDs. Although I instructed them on how to get out if they capsized and how to do a deepwater assisted rescue, I had a high level of confidence that they would not be trapped in their boats even if they panicked after capsizing.

On one occasion, a student in one of my classes was attempting a low brace for the first time, threw all his weight onto the paddle, and instantly capsized. He leaped from the boat even as it was going over and ran for the shoreline through the waist-deep water. After a few minutes, he agreed that he had totally panicked. He was more cautious after that, but his momentary panic was something that can happen to any novice.

In the lowest level BCU assessment for paddlers, the One Star Performance test, candidates must successfully perform the capsize and wet-exit drill along with other paddling skills. Even though candidates are supposed to be well practiced and entirely comfortable doing the wet exit before taking the performance test, they are allowed to release the spray skirt from the cockpit coaming before capsizing.

What alternatives are available to sea kayaking instructors? If it is impossible to start a class with wet-exit drills, *(continued page 118)*

WAITING TO INHALE
Breath-holding Drills for Kayakers

Roger Schumann

Most paddlers tend to bail out after only one or two roll attempts. In small part, this is due to running out of air, but mostly it's psychological: People simply panic. Your body can do without air for a lot longer than your panicky mind may think, however. Whether you're just learning to roll, or your roll is basically bombproof, or you're a nonroller just hoping to become more comfortable after a capsize, developing breath-holding drills can help you learn to be more relaxed and more successful rolling or bailing out after you've found yourself upside down in the drink.

These drills will train you to take deeper breaths and to relax so you don't burn that breath of air so quickly. I've modified several of them from practice drills used by competitive free divers who are able to remain underwater for several minutes at a time. My own meager training in free diving enabled me to double my breath-holding time after only a week of practicing the on-land drills, then nearly double that again when diving and enjoying 1- to 2-minute bottom times. I could push it to 3 minutes with some effort. I quickly saw the relevance for kayakers to train to relax and hang out underwater.

The ability to take a quick, deep breath is a cornerstone skill for these drills. While you sit reading this, with each breath you are likely exchanging in the neighborhood of a mere 15 percent of your total lung volume. A 90-percent exchange is common among most marine mammals. If you've ever heard orca whales breathe, you have a sense of how much air they move in and out of their lungs. There is this sudden, huge *whoosh* of exhalation, followed immediately by a giant, equally sudden but less obvious in-rush of breath. Then they dive. The exchange takes barely a second.

To practice what I call orca breathing, start slowly increasing your exchange of air. If you've done any yoga breathing, you're probably already familiar with this. The difference is learning to do it quickly. Take a couple of slow deep breaths. See how much air you can exhale. Try bending over and even pressing on your stomach to squeeze out as much air as you can. Then breathe in slowly. Fill your lungs from the bottom up by pushing your belly out first, then filling your chest. Finally, "pack" your upper chest by raising your chin and extending your neck and "sipping" in more air through pursed lips, as if sipping up the last few *(continued next page)* drops of a milkshake through a straw. Take as many sips as you can, then hold for a few seconds. Repeat several times until you have a good sense of what a deep lungful of air feels like. *Never take more than three deep breaths in succession.* Any more can cause you to hyperventilate and pass out, which would be especially dangerous in the water. Completely purging the carbon dioxide from your lungs will eliminate your impulse to breathe. In other words, with too little carbon dioxide in your lungs you'll feel you can remain underwater indefinitely and lose consciousness before you feel the need to surface for air. While practicing, take a few normal breaths between each deep breath.

In the context of capsizing and rolling, we don't have time for a full, slow, yoga breath. So imagine rolling up enough to get your head above water but missing your roll and having to do orca breathing: quickly taking a big gulp of air in the second or two before your head plunges back underwater. Think about trying to exhale on your way up, and take a big gulp as you stall, so that you don't breathe in water on your way down. Start slower at first, taking 2 seconds or so for both exhaling and inhaling. Then speed up to 1 second for the full cycle. To see how effectively you are filling your lungs, hold your breath and then pack to see how much more air you can get in. With practice, you'll soon find you can gulp from 60 to 90 percent of your lung volume, such that you have little space left for packing.

Static apnea is a term for holding your breath while relaxed. For static apnea drills better suited to kayaking, practice breath holding using orca breathing. Blow out and gasp in, doing a quick orca breath, and hold for 5 seconds. Repeat this orca breath and 5-second hold five times. Hyperventilation should not be a problem because you're holding your breath for several seconds and not taking more than one deep breath at a time, but stop if you get dizzy. Try a series of five 10-second holds. Most people can do this fairly comfortably with only a little practice.

Pyramid practice increases the length of breath holds to a peak, then reversing back down. Using one orca breath between each breath hold, hold for 5 seconds after the first breath, 10 seconds after the next breath, 15 seconds the next, then back down to 10 seconds, then 5, and stop. When this becomes easy, try double pyramids—hold twice at 5 seconds, twice at 10, twice at 15, etc.—and even triple pyramids. You'll build confidence by training to reach a peak well beyond the time you need for a roll. Then, as you descend back into the 5- or 10-second breath-hold range, still well within the time limit for a typical roll, it'll seem easy.

Don't bother trying to master triple pyramids. Start easy and build up to whatever level presents a comfortable challenge: If you attempt a double pyramid and can't hold your breath twice at 15 seconds, just do one. Building past the 20-second range goes well beyond the times required for rolling and wet exits.

While the short breath-holdings here should be fairly safe, realize that serious free divers who routinely practice holding their breath for several minutes at a time occasionally develop a heart arrhythmia. As with any new exercise program, check with your physician first. And if you are serious about learning how to hold your breath for minutes at a time, take a course taught by free-diving professionals.

Dynamic Apnea Drills

Dynamic apnea, holding your breath while exercising, is much more relevant to kayakers. Walking pyramids is a dry-land drill that is particularly effective. Walk at an easy pace, take an orca breath, and hold your breath for five steps. Take another orca breath and hold for ten steps, breathe, hold for fifteen steps, and so on. Practice single, double, and triple pyramid drills.

If you start feeling dizzy, stop—don't fall and hurt yourself. Until you're familiar with how your body responds, practice on a lawn or other soft surface. While it isn't that common to get dizzy and fall, it is a possibility. Once you are comfortable with the walking drills, it's time to take to the water.

Practice paddling pyramids in shallow water with a partner standing at your side. While the likelihood of your passing out while practicing is slim, if you do manage to hyperventilate and pass out upside down, you'll want someone there who can quickly right you. Paddling pyramids are performed using the same progression as walking pyramids, only you count strokes instead of steps. Those with solid rolling skills can take an orca breath, paddle five strokes, roll; orca breathe, ten strokes, roll; orca breathe, etc. When you can do triple paddling pyramids to fifteen strokes with rolls in between, you are well on your way to becoming a master of breath control.

A challenging variation of most of these drills is the reverse breath hold, practicing the hold after the *out* breath, with your lungs empty. Take an orca breath in, blow it out, and do a roll or pyramid practice, either sitting, walking, or paddling. With a little practice, you'll be surprised at how long you can hold your breath even when you don't have any breath to hold.

My "evil rolling drills" are particularly challenging—more mentally than physically. If you are still learning to roll, you can practice them with a paddle float on the paddle to increase your breath-holding confidence without worrying about missing a roll.

A double roll is two rolls on the same *(continued next page)* breath hold. Work up to triple and quadruple rolls. Experienced roll-ers can do six rolls in 30 seconds on a single breath.

Doing reverse breath holds for double or triple rolls is particu-larly evil but teaches you to remain calm and perform even if you can't get a good breath before going over.

The roll-and-hold drill is a rolling pyramid. Capsize, count to five, roll up, orca breathe, capsize, and count to 10 (yes, that's right, while upside down underwater). This can be extremely chal-lenging in cold water: An ice-cream headache may get to you. In a swimming pool or warm water, however, this drill can really help teach you to relax and take as much time as you need to set up and execute a nice, clean, unhurried roll. By learning to relax while missing your roll several times in succession—and training yourself to grab a quick orca breath between each attempt—you can dra-matically increase your ability to remain calm under pressure. Train yourself to get used to missing a half dozen or more rolls. Practice this with a buddy nearby. Next time you go over in the real world, you won't be so worried about running out of breath after only one or two attempts.

A friend of mine invented arithmetic rolls: He would capsize with a dive mask and solve a simple math problem on a dive slate before rolling back up. Holding your breath calmly underwater is as much a mind game as it is a physical skill. By practicing these drills, you'll gain mental confidence as well as the muscle memory that lets your body take over and tell your mind to "Chill out, we've got plenty of oxygen in here."

With daily practice of the dry-land drills, you should quickly see big improvements in your ability to hold your breath comfortably. Even drills two or three times a week should give noticeable results in a week or so. I often hold my breath while walking down the street, standing in line at the grocery store, working at the computer, or even sitting at stoplights. These drills have added confidence to my already-bombproof rolling skills. They've even breathed new life into my rolling practice!

the students should be given kayaks with medium to large cockpits that will assure an effortless exit in the event of a capsize. The students should not be given spray skirts. The BCU recommends that introduc-tory classes be held on calm waters where spray skirts aren't really necessary. If an instructor thinks that spray skirts must be used, they should be of a type that will come off easily if a capsized student sim-ply pushes out of the cockpit. Many of the plastic boats on the market work well for beginning paddlers because their coamings do not grip spray skirts as tightly as do those of composite kayaks.

It is not possible to predict whether a student will panic on a first wet-exit attempt. Some may panic even if they're prepared for the capsize, are wearing nose clips, and have practiced getting in and out of the boat under the water. Even in instructor-supervised situations where the student has reviewed exactly what to do after capsizing, has taken a full breath, and capsized when ready with no paddle in hand, some students still require immediate assistance by the instructor. Instructors must accept that any student might become confused, disoriented, or panicked on their first try at the capsize drill. The instructor must be prepared to act immediately to get that student upright or out of the boat.

Afterword

Robert Beauvais is survived by his wife and two teenage daughters. His house in Mattapoisett, Massachusetts, opened onto a saltwater cove and marsh. He had thought that paddling a double kayak with his wife, Diane, through the marshes, coves, and bays bordering Buzzards Bay would be a great way to get some exercise and enjoy the marine environment available from his backyard. I greatly appreciate the interest of Mrs. Beauvais in putting this unfortunate incident into the public record.

Editor's Note

Following this incident, a case was filed against the kayaking school and eventually settled out of court. The author of this article was retained by the prosecution as an expert on sea kayaking. His initial draft of this report was provided to the attorney for the defense, and the attorney's comments and those provided by the instructor were considered and, where appropriate, incorporated in the account and analysis of this incident. The original publication of this article in Sea Kayaker *magazine was postponed while the case was pending.*

12

One Paddler's Achilles

Doug Alderson

On a calm summer afternoon, Patrick Simard set out to paddle alone near his home in Victoria, Canada. Patrick was a skilled kayaker who liked to paddle for fitness. He had a good roll and had experience paddling and rolling a kayak in surf. He had taken a number of courses and clinics to keep abreast of effective paddling techniques and maintain good judgment for sea kayak touring, and over the previous year he'd concentrated on developing his offside roll.

His plan was to launch from Cattle Point and cross Baynes Channel to paddle out to Strongtide and Chatham Islands. The air temperature was about 70°F, but the water was in the mid-fifties, so under his PFD and spray skirt he wore a 3-mm wetsuit. The arms of the suit chafed a little, but Patrick put up with it knowing that the sleeves of his suit would keep him warmer in the cold British Columbia water than a sleeveless Farmer John suit.

The wind was calm, and the sea was smooth. Visibility was more than a mile through light overcast. The marine forecast was for continued calm weather throughout the day. The flood tide, pushing eastward from the Pacific Ocean and through the Strait of Juan de Fuca at a speed of 2 knots, accelerated as it curled around the southern tip of Vancouver Island. The tidal stream through Baynes Channel, well known for its strong currents, would be running at about 4 knots at its peak.

Patrick launched from Cattle Point at 2:30 and headed along the Vancouver Island shore, then across Baynes Channel to Strongtide and Chatham Islands. The crossing was uneventful, and Patrick had only to make a small ferry angle to compensate for the current. After a short time exploring the shores of the islands, Patrick headed back across Baynes Channel. The tide was now flooding near its predicted maximum of 4 knots, and Patrick had adjusted his course to the west to make a good ferry angle that would set him on a course back toward Cattle Point.

A seagoing tug crossed Patrick's path, and he set up to surf its wake. The waves were only 2 feet high and didn't provide much of a ride. Patrick was relaxed and unconcerned about the tug's wake. After it passed, he noticed a larger wake closing in on him from a different direction. Three feet high with a breaking crest, this wake promised a better ride. The tidal current probably contributed to the wave's steep slope and slightly breaking crest. The source of the wake was a mystery, possibly a large freighter out in the shipping lane.

Before Patrick had time to set up for surfing, the wake hit him broadside on his right. Patrick let the crest pass beneath the kayak, but the back side of the wave was surprisingly steep. He began to capsize down into the trough and prepared to high-brace into the trough as the kayak slid down the back of the wave. He had to reach well down with his paddle to reach the water. He capsized only far enough to dip his shoulder in the water; his brace kept him at the surface but didn't right the kayak.

After a quick sculling stroke to hold him at the surface, Patrick put additional effort into a second attempt to high-brace, but he lost his grip on the paddle with his right hand and capsized fully. Something had happened to his right arm. He released the spray skirt and exited his kayak. He emerged and held onto his kayak with his left hand. His paddle was floating nearby, and as he reached for it, he realized that his right shoulder was dislocated.

While in the water, he assessed his situation. He could see the tug that had made the smaller wake heading away. A sailboat, the only other vessel in the area, was also heading away from him. Although his right shoulder was badly injured, it wasn't very painful for the first few minutes; however, with the joint between his upper arm and shoulder now distorted, his arm and hand were weak and unresponsive.

He tried to keep his injured limb very still; he held onto the boat with his left hand and held the paddle with his weakened right hand. The flooding tide was pushing Patrick out of Baynes Channel into the open waters of Haro Strait. He drifted in the current for about 15 minutes before he saw a sailboat under power approaching him from the northwest. With only one good arm, it was very difficult to hold onto the kayak and raise his paddle above the surface to signal for help, but fortunately the sailboat responded to his signal and altered course toward him. By the time the sailboat reached him, Patrick had drifted a mile or more from where he had capsized and was approaching the much-less-traveled waters bordering Haro Strait.

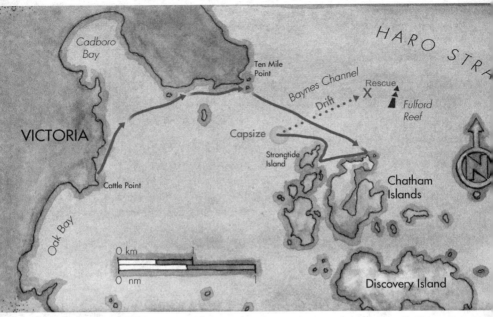

Christopher Hoyt

The skipper of the sailboat put a boarding ladder over the side, and Patrick passed over his kayak's bow line and began the difficult task of getting up on the first step of the ladder. He had been in the water for 30 minutes but was still comfortably warm, and although he was seriously disabled, he was not in excessive pain. With Patrick and his kayak aboard, the sailboat skipper headed to shore for the emergency medical treatment that Patrick needed.

Patrick felt cold and began to shake. The pain of the dislocation increased rapidly, and his hand had grown numb. The sailboat's small motor struggled to make progress against the current. It took another half hour before they made it to a marina in Oak Bay. At the dock, Patrick's kayak was locked up securely before his rescuer drove him to a nearby hospital.

LESSONS LEARNED

When we are close to home and out for an afternoon of paddling, the familiar surroundings tend to lower our perception of risk, especially if we know that emergency rescue services are readily available. Patrick had often paddled to the Chatham Islands, and for him there was nothing unusual about paddling alone across that busy channel in a current running up to 4 knots. This section of the Victoria shoreline is a popular area for experienced local paddlers to practice their skills, and many make the crossing of the channel to Discovery Island. While many consider the area a local playground, it has also been the scene of a number of kayaking accidents.

Afterwards, Patrick felt that he had been lulled into a false sense of security by the familiar and seemingly benign circumstances and had not been sufficiently alert at the time the breaking wave arrived. He recalled feeling very relaxed at the time he capsized and believed that his nonchalant response to the approach of the wake had resulted in a poorly executed high brace and the subsequent disabling injury to his shoulder, the Achilles' heel of any kayaker.

To his credit, he had reduced the risk of cold-water immersion by wearing a wetsuit. He had also taken several kayaking courses and had practiced his skills to the point of feeling prepared to perform a self-rescue if it became necessary. His training contributed to his ability to remain calm throughout his capsize and wet exit, but he was unprepared for the injury to his arm and the obstacle it created in getting back aboard his kayak.

Many of us train and practice to be stronger, more skillful kayakers but fail to consider the possibility that we may be incapacitated to some degree by injury, illness, or exhaustion. We regularly make a risk assessment before we depart the beach based on weather reports and tide tables, the gear we have with us, and an assumption of continuing normal health and fitness. Chronic or traumatic injuries to a wrist, elbow, or shoulder are infrequent but common to sea kayaking. The possibility of injury should be taken into account in our training and in our assessment of risk.

Coping With Injury

It's common to practice bracing and rescue skills in rough sea conditions, but generally we don't practice techniques to perform self-rescues with a simulated injury or other impairment. The training regimens among Greenland kayakers, however, include a long tradition of preparing for the possibility of injury or entanglement while hunting. To recover from incidents similar to Patrick's, they developed rolls that kayakers could do with one arm. While the variety of Greenland rolls may not be possible to perform with contemporary kayaks and Euro paddles, practicing wet exits and reentries using just one arm could provide valuable insight into coping with an injury. It would be best to learn to deploy a paddle float or stirrup with one hand in a practice session rather than in a survival situation. It's also very important that paddlers have the mental preparation and decision-making capacity to make the most of these special techniques at the time they're needed.

Practicing Mental Preparedness

Capsizing into the trough of a steep wave is not uncommon. A sudden high brace into a deep trough can place a great deal of stress on the shoulders. After a failed brace or roll, the paddler's shoulders are again at risk, as a second attempt to high-brace is often aggressive and forceful and done from an awkward position. If you find yourself facing a situation that requires a difficult high brace, allowing yourself to capsize and roll back up can be a more controlled and safer response. Patrick later thought he could have avoided the injury by not struggling to high-brace. He felt certain that relaxing, allowing himself to capsize, and then rolling up would have been a simple, easy, successful alternative. Frequent practice of rolling and bracing in a wide variety of paddling conditions will help you stay relaxed and confident and better able to set up and execute a safe and controlled roll, with elbows low and close to the torso.

Physical skills are only useful when mental control is present. Practicing mental skills allows us to assess situations, choose plans of action, and implement our best bracing, rolling, wet exits, and reentries when we need them. Practice sessions that simulate injuries, distractions, changing circumstances, and limited performance times provide an excellent way to develop the mental agility necessary for effective rescues under difficult circumstances. Frequent practice will help us make assessments and decisions quickly even while under considerable stress.

Patrick had practiced wet exits and reentries but had not prepared himself to respond to an unexpected injury. After his capsize in Baynes Channel, he didn't think to use the pigtail towline he was wearing to secure himself to his kayak, leaving his uninjured arm free to raise the paddle or reach into the kayak for emergency equipment. Just as with physical skills we practice, the mental techniques we practice diligently will be the ones we have available at the time of unexpected circumstances.

It took three months of rest and rehabilitation before Patrick's shoulder was strong enough for him to paddle a sea kayak. He continued paddling but took his local waters more seriously and always carried flares and a marine VHF radio.

Shoulder Dislocations

The shoulder joint is formed by the junction of three bones: the collarbone (clavicle), the shoulder blade (scapula), and the upper arm bone (humerus). The rotator cuff is the name given to the group of muscles and tendons that hold the head of the humerus in the glenoid fossa, a shallow socket in the scapula.

The structure of the shoulder joint provides an extraordinary range of motion. The only contact between the bones of the shoulder and those of the torso of the skeleton is at the joint between the clavicle and the top of the sternum, so the integrity of the shoulder joint comes almost entirely from the muscles that surround it. Because it allows a wider range of motion than any other joint in the body, the shoulder is less stable than other joints, and two types of shoulder injuries are infrequent but well known among paddlers.

A shoulder dislocation refers to an injury to the joint between the humerus and scapula. A shoulder separation refers to an injury to the joint between the clavicle and the acromion, an extension of the scapula. When the shoulder is traumatically dislocated, the top of the humerus is usually displaced below and forward of its usual position in the glenoid fossa (anterior dislocation). In far fewer cases, and unlikely in paddling-related injuries, the top of the humerus is displaced to a position behind the shoulder blade (posterior dislocation).

Typically, the significant pain of a dislocation starts about 5 minutes after the incident. The pain starts as a dull throb and gets progressively worse. Soon after the trauma, the muscles become tight and hold the shoulder in its injured position. The muscles begin to spasm, and the victim cannot find any comfortable position for the arm. Without treatment, the pain can become overwhelming, leading to debilitating shock, if not unconsciousness.

Treating a Shoulder Dislocation

Occasionally an injury to the shoulder may only temporarily dislocate the humerus and allow it to return to its original position within the shoulder joint. In this case, a supportive sling can serve to minimize discomfort and prevent further injury until medical help is available. If the humerus remains out of position, however, potentially very serious complications are present when treating the injury. The pain and the damage will grow progressively worse, and emergency medical assistance should be obtained as quickly as possible.

A hospital or appropriate clinic will choose the best of several procedures to relocate the humerus into its shoulder socket. As with setting a broken bone, the patient will be well medicated to relieve pain and relax the tense and spasmed muscles. Advanced wilderness first-aid courses may cover field treatment of a dislocated shoulder, but believe me, I have witnessed four anterior shoulder dislocations, and all of the victims were in severe pain. Any field treatment would have been excruciating and overwhelming for everyone involved. Typically, victims cradle their injured arm and aren't inclined to let any nonmedical person move it. Some padding and a sling to support the arm in its displaced position are likely the safest—and maybe the only—option available prior to transporting the injured paddler to a medical facility.

A long process of healing and rehabilitation begins after the dislocation is treated. The patient might be paddling again in 3 months, but it may take up to a full year to regain normal strength and a full range of movement. The shoulder may never be quite the same again. Patients who have sustained a shoulder dislocation can develop chronic instability and often suffer recurring dislocations. Surgery may be necessary to tighten up and/or repair torn ligaments.

Preventing Shoulder Dislocation

The shoulder is most stable when the elbows are positioned well below the shoulder and well bent. The shoulder is unstable and prone to traumatic injury when the elbows are near or above the level of the shoulder. The shoulder is most vulnerable to dislocation when the elbow is at or above shoulder level with the elbow behind the shoulder and the arm externally rotated (palm rolled to face upward). The leverage on the arm and the possibility of dislocation are further increased when the arm is extended with a straight elbow.

Imagine driving your car with your left hand on the steering wheel and your left elbow by your side. Your right arm is extended and your right hand is hooked over the top of the passenger seat; your left shoulder is in a safe position, but your right shoulder is not.

In a high brace, the wrists are above the elbows. Contrary to what the phrase "high brace" suggests, the working paddle blade should remain as low as possible, and the hands shouldn't be much above the shoulders. The forearm closest to the working blade should remain near 90 degrees to the paddle shaft, and the elbows should be well bent and near the torso. In a low brace, the same rules for the arms and elbows apply, but the wrists are below the elbows. The very common tendency in both braces is to extend the arm closest to the working blade, but that only reduces grip strength and places the shoulder in an unstable and weakened position.

The remarkable range of motion in a shoulder provides us with the ability to manipulate a paddle to control a sea kayak. Deprived of that joint's supple strength, our independent progress comes to a stop. We should all pay heed to our shoulders and routinely practice the best exercise and paddling techniques to keep our shoulders safe and strong.

13

The Loss of a Son
An Accident on Lake Superior

Grant Herman and Gail Green

When a fellow kayaker dies in your home territory, it generates an amazing number of emotional, personal, and professional responses. Many of us in the Midwestern United States consider Lake Superior and the Apostle Islands National Lakeshore to be jewels of the sea kayaking world. After an accident that occurred in our region last year, we've been engaged in a collective soul-searching and analysis of the facts surrounding the death of a young man. (Names in this chapter have been changed out of respect for the family.)

At about 10:15 in the morning of August 19, 2004, Peter and his son Michael, a tall, slender, athletic 23-year-old, launched from a frequently used put-in, known locally as Meyers Beach, on Mawikwe Bay in southwest Lake Superior. They were intermediate kayakers and had paddled the area's sea caves before. They'd also recently been swimming in the area; Peter is a dedicated swimmer and often swims long distances in cold water. Both paddlers were in rotomolded 17-foot sea kayaks with foam bulkheads and rubber hatch covers.

The air temperature was in the low sixties, and a small craft advisory was in effect. It was windy that morning, increasing in strength throughout the day. At the Devil's Island Buoy, about 26 miles from the put-in, the west winds were blowing steadily at 25 knots with gusts clocked at more than 40 knots. Bark Point, a significant peninsula that juts out from Lake Superior's south shore about 6 miles southwest of their launch site, masked the effect of the westerly wind and sea at the put-in site. Peter later reported that waves at the put-in were 2 to 3 feet high, and both paddlers had some trouble launching their kayaks, but otherwise the conditions evident in the area seemed within their abilities.

Once underway, they had a good time playing in the waves as they gradually made their way east-northeast along the coast. Peter had originally thought they might cross to one of the islands farther

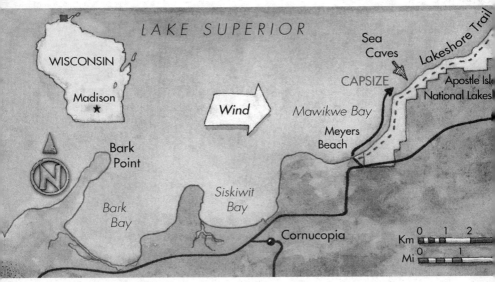

Christopher Hoyt

up the coast, but in light of the conditions they opted to stay closer to the mainland shore. The two headed toward some cliffs and sea caves that form a headland of eroded sandstone stretching the better part of 3 miles with only marginal opportunities for landings.

On this day, the west winds wrapping around Bark Point were creating waves running 4 to 6 feet. Where they were rebounding from the cliffs and caves, they created clapotis: irregular, exploding waves. Independent observers estimated that the waves later that day were 6 to 8 feet high outside the caves, and in the caves themselves were topping out as high as 12 feet.

Beyond the point where the sandstone cliffs emerge from the beach, there is no reasonable escape route from the water. Farther downwind, a steep, rocky headland juts out into the lake. The cliffs there took the full brunt of that day's strong west winds.

The caves in the cliffs mark where the wind protection of Bark Point ends. The full force of the wind combined with unforgiving, formidable shoreline features suddenly and dramatically changed the sea conditions for the paddlers and created what became the pivotal moment of the incident. As they paddled past this point of no return, their margin for error rapidly diminished.

The father and son made it only 50 yards or so before Michael went over. He was wearing shorts, a T-shirt, and a PFD. (Peter later noted that they'd worn Lycra wetsuits on a previous trip to the area.) The water temperature was 55°F.

Despite the extremely rough seas, Michael was able to get on top of his overturned kayak, but Peter was not outfitted with a towline, so he was unable to tow his son away from the cliffs and caves. Eventually, they decided to abandon that boat, and Michael got up on the back deck of his father's boat. The exact position he took on the aft deck as Peter attempted to paddle him out of the cave area is uncertain, but an accepted method for this kind of rescue is to have the swimmer "cowboy up" from the stern end of the kayak or side-mount directly behind the cockpit while the paddler sculls for support. The swimmer then stays low on the deck, face down, holding onto the waist of the paddler's PFD or the cockpit coaming. The swimmer's feet are held slightly out to each side to add stability to the kayak.

In the course of trying to paddle around the corner to relative safety, Peter also went over and bailed out. The waves pushed both men into one of the caves. They lost contact with their remaining kayak. (Both boats were found the next day a mile and a half from the cave, intact but badly beaten up.)

His strength drained by chaotic waves and cold water, Michael slipped into hypothermia. Three times over the next hour or so (the time estimates provided by Peter to the park ranger on the beach as they awaited the rescue boat are fuzzy), the two were separated in the daunting conditions in the cave. Finally, Peter could no longer get a response from his son and realized he could not swim out of the cave with him in tow. He also realized that he himself would not last long if he continued to stay in the cave. He made what must have been an agonizing decision to leave the cave and swim for help.

Peter was able to swim around the corner to the northeastern end of the beach where hikers walking a trail above the beach saw him struggling in the water and called 911 on their cell phone. The call was immediately forwarded to the Bayfield County Sheriff's office. Peter, unaware of this phone call, swam to shore and ran down the beach to the put-in (about a mile) where he made contact with another passerby, who made a second call to 911. Immediately after notification from 911 and the Bayfield County Sheriff's dispatch, the Coast Guard contacted the Apostle Islands National Lakeshore (APIS).

At that time, the main Coast Guard crew was assisting a sailboat struggling in the high winds to get into harbor on the south end of Madeline Island, 25 miles away. Since the sailboat's situation was not considered a life-threatening emergency, the Coast Guard boat immediately abandoned that task and headed for the sea caves, arriving there 47 minutes later. This was a Herculean effort considering the distance and the headwind of 25-plus knots.

While the EMS and U.S. Coast Guard systems were ramping up for the rescue attempt, APIS personnel rushed to Meyers Road to coordinate the rescue. They had the radio capacity to deal with the four different frequencies utilized among the various agencies. While the National Park can assist in basic rescues within the park, its crews are not specifically trained for and do not have the rescue craft to handle sea conditions of this sort. Meanwhile, on the off chance that it might be quicker to approach the sea caves from the west, the Coast Guard headquarters in Bayfield sent a second, smaller Avon craft by road to the launching ramp at Cornucopia, a town 3 miles southwest of Meyers Beach.

As it turned out, the larger Coast Guard boat traveling by water got there first. To pinpoint Michael's exact location, the crew needed to talk to Peter. An APIS ranger at the put-in got Peter on the radio to guide the Coast Guard to the exact location of his son. After a short search, the Coast Guard boat spotted Michael, still in the cave. They launched a rescue swimmer dressed in a survival suit and high-flotation PFD, connected to a 100-foot tether. He swam into the maelstrom and retrieved Michael. The crew hauled them both back on board about 2 P.M. CPR was initiated immediately, and Michael was stabilized for the bumpy 14-minute boat ride to Cornucopia.

In the meantime, APIS personnel had arranged for a Life Flight helicopter from St. Luke's hospital in Duluth, Minnesota, to meet the Coast Guard boat in Cornucopia. The Coast Guard officer who had been performing CPR during the boat rescue stayed with Michael during transport. APIS personnel transported Peter by car (about an hour and a half drive) to the hospital. The hospital staff took over administering CPR when Michael arrived at the Duluth hospital around 3 P.M. Emergency room doctors and nurses hooked him up to a heart-lung machine and worked on saving him until he was pronounced dead at 10 that night.

LESSONS LEARNED

Following this incident, Peter told APIS personnel about the sea conditions he and his son had encountered and about their attempts to get out of the situation into which they had paddled. He further offered some background that influenced his judgment that day. He had paddled at the sea caves the year before with friends in what he also rated as "wavy" conditions. In that earlier excursion, he and his companions wore wetsuits, and the conditions had remained much more benign. He had also called both the Coast Guard and Park Service for weather reports before launching.

Peter said that when he went paddling outside his normal paddling locations (north-central Wisconsin inland lakes), he typically listened to the marine shore forecast and gathered information and recommendations from park headquarters and local outfitters. He hadn't called from home for a report this time, however. Cell phone coverage at the launch area was unreliable, so he hadn't been able to call for a forecast from there.

Peter reported that on a previous occasion he had seen two kayak outfitters go out with what he believed were novice paddlers in conditions he thought similar to those on the day of the accident, so he thought it would be OK for him to go when the wind and waves were somewhat greater than he had previously paddled in. While the conditions that he and Michael launched in were *(continued page 132)*

CROSSING THE LINE

Christopher Cunningham

When I was a senior in college in Maine, my classmate Eben occasionally let me use his VW Bug to drive to Massachusetts to visit my sweetheart. I once made the drive on a cold winter evening. The Maine Turnpike was clear, as it was always well plowed of snow and sanded when temperatures dropped below freezing, and there were few other cars on the road. I drove at the speed limit, if only because Eben's Bug wouldn't go any faster without a good tailwind. I was driving in the right-hand lane as I approached a turnpike overpass that curved to the right. I had just started the turn and had the steering wheel cranked slightly clockwise, but when I hit the deck of the overpass, the Bug didn't follow the road. Sliding over black ice, it took a tangential trajectory toward the other side of the road. I eased off the gas as I crossed all four lanes, and I reached the far side of the overpass just as I slid onto the left shoulder. Then the tires gripped the bare pavement, and the cocked front wheels pulled me back into the turn before I skidded off the road. Another 20 feet of overpass, and Eben wouldn't have gotten his car back in one piece.

While sliding across the overpass I had a sensation of weightlessness at the moment I was released from the lateral pressure of the turn, and then I was gripped not by fear but by disbelief. Of course I knew about ice on overpasses, but none of those I'd already driven over that evening had been glazed with ice. There were no reflections on the road's surface that would indicate the presence of ice, no ruts on the median from *(continued next page)* cars that might have skated off the road before me. Once I lost traction, only the car's momentum would determine my fate, and there was nothing I could do but watch and wait.

In retrospect I can think back to a point about 100 yards before the overpass, an unremarkable spot on the pavement—but the point at which I could have started braking in order to stop before I got to the ice. Because I was not expecting the bridge ahead to be glazed with ice, I missed the opportunity to slow down. The father and son in this chapter might have passed a similarly unnoticed place on the water where there were only more waves like those they had already paddled—but a place from which they would slip into the influence of the geography on either side of them.

Most of the time, we can see trouble looming ahead and avoid it. Sometimes we can stop right at its threshold without crossing over into it. But at other times we may recognize we are in trouble only when we are irretrievably in the midst of it; we've crossed an invisible line beyond which the forces already in motion have gained a momentum that exceeds our ability to change the course of events.

Kayaking safely requires looking ahead in both time and space. We're looking for dangers that might lie ahead but, more importantly, also for the points at which we still have an opportunity to avoid them.

not too bad, in his estimation, those they faced later in the day were significantly more challenging for their skills and equipment.

Local kayak outfitters frequently use Meyers Beach for their outings when conditions are fair. Aware of the forecast for worsening weather on that day, they had cancelled or redirected their day trips to more protected inland locations. Paddlers familiar with the local kayaking community might have noted the absence of outfitters or any other paddlers evident at the put-in on the day of the accident.

The waves in the vicinity of Meyers Beach were manageable, even fun, for Peter and Michael. When they reached the cliffs, however, the reflected waves created clapotis, or what Peter described as "washtub waves," which neither of them were familiar with. Waves of this sort, also called egg-carton waves, are completely unpredictable in both their direction and size. They require exceptional flexibility and lightning-quick bracing.

As most paddlers' skills and knowledge increase, they typically attempt a corresponding increase in the difficulty of terrain and sea conditions. With this progression comes a need and even a responsibility to continue to educate themselves with more in-depth aspects of safety issues. This includes knowing how sea conditions are affected by elements that aren't evident in the immediate vicinity.

It's also important to know how landforms affect conditions for paddlers. Coming out of a lee (an area protected from the wind) can be marked by dramatic increases in wind velocity and wave height. Wind coming around the end of a lee can be intensified. Steep cliff walls reflect waves rather than dissipate them as a sloping beach would. Waves that are manageable coming only from one direction can be threatening when reflected. Crossing wave patterns created by reflected waves can nearly double the height of waves. Peaks can get so steep, even to the point of breaking, that kayaks are easily capsized. Being able to predict how landforms will affect waves and wind by looking at a chart is an important skill.

Paddlers should read environmental signs and changes at all times and continually reassess their plans accordingly. Even for experienced sea kayakers, nothing is ever static with paddling. The same place and apparent conditions can become a whole different story with a slight change in wind direction or the addition of leftover swells from a previous unknown storm.

Your assessment of conditions needs to have some safety buffer. Set out in conditions below your experience threshold so you can accommodate unexpected worsening conditions. It's not just wind that occasionally gets paddlers into trouble while paddling along the sea caves of Lake Superior; wakes coming across the lake from unseen ships miles away can suddenly and drastically change conditions near the rocks. It's important to be alert regardless of the conditions and to have plans for making a quick retreat.

After the accident, personnel from the rescue agencies involved—Coast Guard, EMS, and APIS—met to discuss their respective roles and deal with the issues that surround a rescue with a fatality. The incident was especially poignant for some Coast Guard members who were contemporaries of the son. Cooperative protocols among the agencies were streamlined, all elements of the incident were documented, and reports were filed. The response by agency personnel was systematic and thorough.

Since the incident, Peter worked with park rangers in the hopes of erecting a sign to warn kayakers who embark on paddling trips to the sea caves of the potential danger. He also urged the rangers to install a phone near the put-in so paddlers can call for weather reports and marine advisories.

While these agencies deal effectively with the aftermath of an accident, our local paddling community works to prevent such tragedies by providing opportunities for those interested in sea kayaking to get off to a good start. The local Inland Sea Society hosts an annual sea kayak symposium in June that introduces novices to the sport and teaches how to have fun paddling on Lake Superior in a safe and responsible manner. An excellent source for instruction is the American Canoe Association, which offers a wide range of courses in many areas throughout the country (www.americancanoe.org). Retail outfitters are an additional source for information and referrals for instruction, guided trips, and sea kayak rentals.

This was the first death related to sea kayaking in the Apostle Islands National Lakeshore. The islands have claimed many mariners over time and will no doubt take more in the future. Over the last 10 years, sea kayaking has become more popular with the general public, and many people are buying kayaks and learning skills that are appropriate for small inland lakes. It's exciting for them to visit Lake Superior, as hundreds do each season, but the Apostle Islands paddling community hopes that through this tragic incident will come an increased awareness of the need for higher skill levels, better equipment, and good judgment when paddling this inland sea. Informed paddlers enjoy a depth of experience that can be on one side of a very thin line between what happened in this tragedy and what makes rougher conditions a dance on the waves.

14

Three Rescues

Rob Casey

On a cold and very windy December day in 2004, my friend Dave and I launched our kayaks from Golden Gardens Park in Seattle and headed toward Meadow Point, on the north side of the park. The air temperature was in the low forties, but we were dressed for winter paddling with gloves, several layers of synthetic garments under our dry suits, and two skullcaps each. The waves were 3 to 4 feet high, and the northeasterly winds were blowing about 15 to 20 knots, creating a tide rip off the point. Perfect conditions for surfing wind waves in our kayaks.

KITE OVERBOARD

The conditions were also perfect for kiteboarding, and there were half a dozen kiteboarders off the point. After about 30 minutes of surfing, we noticed a red and white kite down in the water about a hundred yards farther out from us. The kite's inflatable spars kept it afloat and arched up above the water, making it highly visible. Spars also keep a kite from collapsing so that it can, in theory, be relaunched from the water.

We watched the kiter for a bit, but there was no indication that he was having any luck getting the kite airborne again. We decided to go over to check on him. He had lost his board, leaving him with only his wetsuit and inflated kite for buoyancy, and he had no PFD. His kite lines were crossed, and the increasing wind made it very difficult for him to perform a self-rescue, a technique with which a kiteboarder can get his kite airborne again and use it to drag himself through the water to the beach without a board. When we got close enough, he explained his situation to us, and we all agreed to tow him back to shore.

We asked the kiter to grab onto Dave's stern while I secured a line to Dave's boat so I could assist him with the tow. Within a few minutes, both kayaks, including my rudder, got tangled up in the kite lines trailing in the water. The web of lines created confusion and a bit of panic among us, as we feared that if we capsized, we would have a serious problem.

After several frustrating minutes spent freeing ourselves and releasing my towline, we chose to approach the kiter again from upwind, on the side opposite the kite and its lines. Around the time of our second effort, a sailboat passing by under power approached and the people on board asked if they could help. We said that we

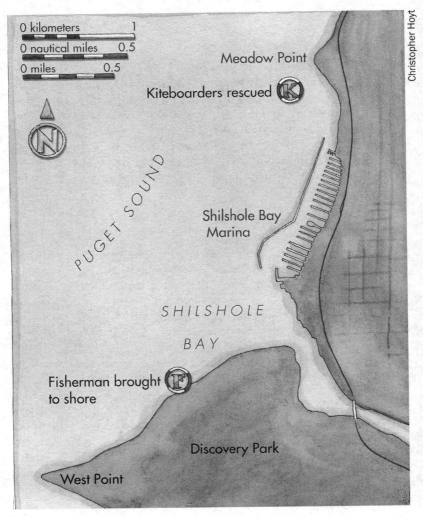

Christopher Hoyt

0 kilometers 1
0 nautical miles 0.5
0 miles 0.5

Meadow Point

Kiteboarders rescued Ⓚ

PUGET SOUND

Shilshole Bay Marina

SHILSHOLE

BAY

Fisherman brought Ⓕ to shore

Discovery Park

West Point

did need assistance, but there must have been some misunderstanding because they continued on and left us.

I asked the kiter to hold onto my stern as I towed him back to shore. After about 10 minutes of very hard paddling downwind toward shore in choppy seas, I realized I wasn't making any progress. The wind was blowing us south, away from the beach and toward the rocky breakwater of the marina south of Meadow Point.

We asked the kiter to separate himself from the kite so we could get him back to shore more quickly, but he didn't want to lose the costly gear or let go of the flotation it gave him. We told him that Vessel Assist could be contacted to retrieve his kite later and that by holding onto our boats he would be safe. Once he released the kite, I started back to shore. This made paddling a bit faster this time, but it was still slow going dragging him through the water.

I had training for paddling with a swimmer on the aft deck, but the waves were so large now that I was concerned that I might capsize. I thought of calling the Coast Guard on my VHF, but in the rough seas, I felt uncomfortable letting go of my paddle to grab the VHF out of my PFD to make a call. I didn't want to take the risk of becoming a swimmer myself. We were so close to shore that paddling the kiter to land seemed to be the best course of action.

As we neared shore, I could hear fire trucks and an ambulance coming into the park, and I saw a small crowd of people lining the shore. Someone on shore must have called 911.

After another 10 minutes of difficult paddling in large waves, we finally arrived at the boat launch just inside the marina where the fire trucks and ambulance were waiting for us. A medic evaluated the kiter's condition and soon after released him without treatment. The kiter was OK, thanks to his 5 mm wetsuit.

DÉJÀ VU

About a month later, at the same location and in similar conditions, I went to surf wind waves with another friend, Jory. As we carried our kayaks to the water, a woman ran to us from a group of people lining the shore and frantically pointed to a kiteboarder who had been down and in the water for some time. She asked us if we could go out and check on him. I asked the woman to call 911, and Jory and I paddled out.

Once we arrived at the kite, we spoke to the kiter. He had lost his board and his lines were crossed so he couldn't right the kite again. This kiter was wearing a PFD and a helmet. We asked if he wanted a tow back to shore, and he said yes. I told him I had recently rescued another kiter and had some experience with *(continued page 140)*

PIW

Christopher Cunningham

One warm evening in June, my kids and I packed up a picnic dinner and headed for the beach. Lots of other folks had the same idea. The parking lots serving the beach were full, and there were hundreds of people on the shore. Sailboats tacked only a few dozen yards offshore, and board sailors zipped back and forth across the wind. Kiteboarders skimmed across the water, towed by their massive crescent-shaped kites.

After eating, the kids and I walked to the water's edge to throw rocks. While skipping stones, I noticed one of the kiteboarders about 150 yards out struggling with his kite. It had come down and was floating on the water. The inflatable spars that give the kite its shape were folded, creating an angular shape like the Rock of Gibraltar. I watched to see what the boarder would do. I'd heard that the kites could be launched from the water, but I'd never seen one down before and was curious to see how it would get airborne again. The sun was low in the sky behind the kiteboarder so it was hard to see anything more than the dark spot of his head above the surface of the water.

Kiteboarders usually wear wetsuits, so I figured he had some time to get his kite set up and get underway again. Five minutes passed and the sail was still in the same position. Two powerboats raced out from the marina and passed between the boarder and the beach. Ten minutes passed. A dozen sailboats passed by him on their way back to the marina. While the boarder himself was not very visible, his sail stood a good 6 feet or more above the surface of the water. Ten more minutes passed. I saw a group of three kayakers on a course that would take them close to the downed kite. The lead paddler appeared to be wearing a T-shirt and had no PFD. As he drew even with the kite, he veered over to it, and his two partners followed.

I thought the kayakers might be able to help get the kite airborne again, but I was concerned that the kite might take off suddenly, catch one of the kayakers in its shrouds, and capsize him. Eventually, the kite began to shrink. It looked as though the kiteboarder had given up on relaunching it and was trying to fold it up so he could ride back in with the kayakers.

After the kite disappeared, I saw the boarder's head come up on the aft deck of the kayak. The paddler in the T-shirt turned toward shore, apparently to tow the boarder back to the beach. To my surprise, the two other paddlers resumed their original course and left the first kayaker to make the tow on his own.

I couldn't believe what I was seeing. I looked up and down the beach. There were dozens of people around me. Surely many of them had seen the kite down, but no one was paying any attention. There were other kiteboarders in the water and on the beach, but none of them seemed to notice, either.

Nearly half an hour had passed since I first spotted the downed kite. As the sun closed in on the horizon, the kayaker was making little or no progress toward the beach. It would start getting dark in a little more than 30 minutes.

I scanned the beach to see if anyone had a pair of binoculars I could use. If the kayaker wasn't wearing a PFD, as I suspected, I felt sure that he would not be experienced enough to make a quick recovery in the event of a capsize. Certainly the two other paddlers who had left the rescue had no idea how difficult it could be to paddle with a swimmer on board. I watched as the kayaker's stroke slowed down and the kiteboarder slid back into the water but remained by the kayak.

Even if he were wearing a wetsuit, he must have been getting cold. The water couldn't have been more than 50°F, and the beach was still a long way off.

I walked over to a couple sitting on a beach blanket and asked to borrow their cell phone to call the Coast Guard. A committee boat for the sailboat race was anchored about 200 yards from the beach, and there was a chance they had a radio and were monitoring Channel 16. I hoped the Coast Guard could broadcast a call to get the committee boat to rescue the boarder.

While I was making the call, an outboard skiff came speeding toward the marina on a course headed right for the swimmer. I was relieved to see it slow down. The kiteboarder, after spending more than half an hour in the water, was taken aboard.

I walked down the beach to intercept the skiff as it came ashore. The boarder climbed over the side with the huge bundle of wet fabric. No wonder the kayaker had given up: With that much weight and drag, he didn't have a chance of making any progress.

A woman I took to be the kiteboarder's wife took him by the arm. His face was drawn with exhaustion and ashy with cold; he seemed dazed. "It looked like you had quite a struggle out there," I said. He told me his kite had come down and flipped and he had no way of turning it back over. I asked him about the kayaker. He didn't remember much about him. "I had my head pressed on the deck," he said.

My kids and I walked back to the car. I *(continued next page)* kept looking out to see the kayakers. The three were back together, small silhouettes in the streak of fading sunlight that stretched across Puget Sound.

It was hard to shake the image of that downed kiteboarder surrounded by dozens of boats and within sight of hundreds of beachgoers, his own wife, perhaps, among them, and no one was reacting to the situation. The three kayakers, to their credit, came to check it out, but only one attempted a rescue. The other two, I'm sorry to say, left and never looked back.

I've always thought of boaters as a special community: a group of individuals who for the most part have good sea sense and an awareness of other vessels nearby. I grew up with the assumption that all boaters keep their heads on a swivel, taking inventory of everything on the water and in the sky. That perspective no longer seems to be shared by many boaters. They may have the same tunnel vision they use when they drive their cars.

The failure of so many boaters to observe and interpret the kiteboarder's situation was disturbing. While we may all be out on a beautiful day having fun, it is still possible for someone to be in serious trouble and in need of help.

As boaters, we take care of each other no matter what vessel we are aboard because it's the right thing to do. Kayakers might be among the smallest and slowest vessels on the water, but we have eyes and ears and a responsibility to come to the aid of anyone on the water who appears to need assistance.

this situation and asked that he drop the kite. He said that he didn't want to lose his kite. After we let him know that Vessel Assist could help retrieve his kite, he released it.

A sailboat under power heading to the nearby marina passed within shouting distance. I asked Jory to go over and ask if they could pull the kiter out of the water. He spoke to them, but strangely, the sailboat circled us but never came nearer. We wondered if they were afraid of catching the kiter's lines in their propeller. I shouted again for assistance as they continued to circle us several times, saying nothing. Frustrated by the boaters' unwillingness to help, we decided to continue our rescue without them.

Rather than try to tow him as I had towed the other kiter in the previous rescue, I instructed this kiter to climb on the aft deck. I had him wait for a cresting wave and then pull himself up on my stern deck just as the wave pushed him toward me.

As we neared the beach, I heard fire trucks coming toward the park. Once we arrived at the park's boat ramp, a paramedic came down and checked the kiter's condition. Jory and I then paddled our kayaks back out in search of waves to surf.

A LEAKY BOATER

A few months after rescuing the two kiters, I was out paddling with my friend Todd about a mile south of Meadow Point heading toward West Point. We came across a PFD floating in the water, and then some floating debris. On shore, a group of four joggers and a fly-fisherman were trying to get our attention and were pointing to a guy hanging onto a canoe paddle with a line attached to an overturned boat. He had capsized while trying to urinate over the side (a very common cause of boaters falling overboard) and had been in the water for 30 minutes. He'd had a PFD in the boat but hadn't been wearing it. He was trying to swim his boat back to shore, which we later found out was anchored to the bottom by a 12-pound lead ball and 55 feet of downrigger line.

We offered our help and asked him to climb on my aft deck so I could take him ashore. He was too exhausted to do so and instead held onto the stern as I paddled him to shore, just 50 feet away. We dressed him in the dry clothes, rain shell, and emergency plastic blanket that I keep in my boat. His condition appeared to be dire: He was exhausted and incoherent and could barely speak. He definitely needed medical attention, and we were at a semiwilderness park beach nearly a mile from regularly traveled roads.

I thought the circumstances warranted making a VHF call, even though regulations prohibit use of a marine VHF while ashore, so I broadcast a Mayday. I had neglected to check that my radio was set to Channel 16, the hailing and distress frequency, however, and my call went out on 14, the Coast Guard's vessel traffic frequency. Radio reception was pretty scratchy, and the Coast Guard asked me to repeat myself a few times.

After about 15 minutes we heard sirens and saw a police boat coming from the marina a half mile to the north. I shot a flare to draw them to our location. The police boat landed on shore, and at that same moment paramedics, who had come to the park by ambulance, emerged from the woods on foot. A couple of minutes later, two television news helicopters were hovering overhead. The paramedics took over, dressed the boater in more warm clothing, wrapped him in blankets, and walked with him on the trail back to the ambulance.

Todd paddled out to the capsized boat and flipped it right side up. He cut the downrigger line, and the police took the boat in tow. It was getting dark, so we headed back to our put-in, surfing on the wake of the police boat.

LESSONS LEARNED

As kayakers, we may often find ourselves paddling in the midst of boats, kiteboards, canoes, and other watercraft on very busy waterways. We must be aware of our surroundings and not assume other people out on the water share that awareness. Many recreational boaters who go out on the water go to relax and "zone out." Others don't have or use proper safety gear. Although we may be in the smallest boats on the water, we can often be the most helpful.

As you learn in first-aid classes, you must assess a situation before approaching someone in need of help. It's important that you don't wind up in trouble and then require assistance yourself. While rescuing the first kiter, we didn't take into consideration the possibility of getting tangled up with the kite lines. We were fortunate that we didn't capsize after both our boats got caught up in the lines. From our experience with the first rescue, we made the decision to approach the second kiter from the upwind side to avoid entanglement with his kite lines.

It's to be expected that someone in the water will want to avoid abandoning expensive equipment. Both kiters had to be convinced that their kites had to be left behind. The boater could have swum the short distance to shore, reducing his time in the water, if he hadn't tried in vain to tow his anchored boat.

Persisting at a task that is obviously failing is cited in some studies as a symptom of hypothermia. If someone seems hypothermic or you're in considerably difficult seas, focus on saving the person, not the gear. If the kiters had been better dressed for being in the water, as I was in my dry suit and insulating layers, or if weather conditions had been more favorable, I might have asked either kiter to deflate his kite, roll up the lines, and put the assembly on my stern deck, then climb on deck on top of the kite for the paddle to shore.

When chatting with members of the kiteboarding community after the second kite rescue, we found that the kites, in addition to being expensive, are the only flotation device many kiters have. Many kiters don't wear PFDs. Kiters also rely on their kites to be a highly visible marker if they need rescue.

As for which type of rescue technique worked best, the stern-deck rescue is certainly the most efficient way to paddle a person in the water to safety. If the person keeps his weight low and his legs angled out to the side, there is little loss of stability. Once on deck, the person conserves energy by being out of the water, and this also allows better boat speed by reducing drag.

The presence of many other boats on the water may suggest a margin of safety, but unfortunately, you can't always depend on other boaters to be aware of and react appropriately to mishaps on the water. Our experience shows that the sight of a kite in the water doesn't always prompt other boaters to offer assistance. Even in heavily used waterways, you can't count on a quick rescue.

Staying safe and being able to effect a rescue both require being alert to our surroundings, having and wearing the proper gear, and practicing rescue training regularly. By being prepared to take care of ourselves, we can be ready to help others.

15

Duck Island Rescue

*Leif Erickson, David Workman,
and George Gronseth*

STARTING OUT

Leif speaking

On August 20, 2005, I set off with two other experienced kayakers, Morris Buckner and David Workman, on a kayaking trip to Main Duck Island, located near the eastern end of Lake Ontario, where we planned to camp overnight and return the next day.

My interest in the 10-mile crossing to Main Duck Island started several years ago. I was a member of the Cataraqui Canoe Club of Kingston, Ontario, and had met two kayakers who had made a successful crossing and were enthusiastic about the seclusion and scenery the island had to offer.

Most of my kayaking experience has been touring on the St. Lawrence River, a waterway that's more sheltered than Lake Ontario. Ontario is the smallest of the Great Lakes, but with an area of over 7,000 square miles, it can develop ocean-caliber waves.

On August 20, it was warm and overcast; the water temperature was 73°F, which was unusually warm for this area, so we didn't feel it necessary to wear wetsuits or paddling jackets. We checked the marine forecast before leaving. The weather was to be perfect. Nothing in the conditions forecast gave us any second thoughts about the crossing. We had standard kayaking equipment, including deck compasses, GPS, spare paddles, paddle floats, bilge pumps, throw ropes, flares, and a cell phone.

We launched before 9 A.M. from Prince Edward Point near the eastern extremity on Prince Edward County and headed east between Timber and False Duck islands. Lake Ontario was calm, but the waves picked up after we passed between the islands and got out of the shelter of the headland. Ahead, we would pass north of three shoals and cross a shipping channel.

We were traveling east on a heading to go to the north of Main Duck Island. As the southwest wind increased, the waves were building up from the west end of Lake Ontario and were coming up behind us at an angle from the southwest.

I was hanging back to keep an eye on the others. With the wind hitting me on the stern quarter, I had to work to keep my kayak, a Nordkapp HM, from broaching.

The waves were about 3 feet high as we traveled across, and in the area of the shoals they grew two to three times higher and became much steeper. I wished I had worn my paddling jacket.

I checked my watch. It was almost 11:30. We were on track for getting to the island in time for lunch if we could just manage the short distance that remained.

I looked up and saw that Morris had capsized. Dave had heard Morris's whistle blasts and had turned around. I had a difficult time seeing Morris in the water, but I continued paddling until Dave and I were both beside Morris and his kayak. I estimated the waves to be at least 6 feet high with larger ones breaking before they washed over us. It made it difficult trying to get Morris back into his kayak.

While I was hanging onto his cockpit and our paddles, my kayak was lifted almost on top of his and was being tipped onto its side. Morris, a large man, was having trouble getting onto the back deck of his kayak, and I was having trouble keeping his boat steady.

We were in conditions well beyond our ability to perform an assisted rescue. A nearby Kingston weather site recorded the winds at that time as 17 mph. I estimated that the waves peaked at about 10 feet. We decided that I would try to tow Morris's kayak. Morris hooked his throw rope between the kayaks from my stern loop to the bow toggle on his kayak, and I tried to tow his Current Designs Solstice kayak with him hanging onto it. We were a mile or so from the island, and I hoped to paddle us into its lee where we'd have a better chance of getting Morris aboard.

The drag of Morris in the water stopped me dead in my tracks. When the next set of large waves hit me, I broached but performed a low brace and recovered. Another big set hit me, and the drag on the towrope caused my kayak to capsize. I bailed out, and with Morris holding my kayak, I reentered by climbing from the downwind side over the cockpit and onto the back deck. I dropped my legs in and turned around to face the bow. After I fastened my skirt, I started to clear the cockpit with the pump mounted on the aft deck, but it was very awkward for me to use. I switched to a hand pump, and as I used it, water poured in where I had pulled the spray skirt back slightly for the pump.

I resumed towing Morris, and again a large wave broached my kayak. The towline prevented me from side-surfing, and with the push of the waves I capsized again. Conditions had deteriorated, and we weren't going to be able to get ourselves out of trouble. Morris tried to use his cell phone to call 911, but there was no signal. Another set of large waves broke over him, and the cell phone, no longer protected inside the dry bag, was now waterlogged and out of commission.

We decided that Dave should paddle his plastic River Runner R5 (13 feet by 24 inches, with a fixed add-on skeg) to Main Duck for help if any boats were docked there. His kayak didn't have bulkheads or flotation and could sink if capsized. A giant wave washed over Morris and me, and I came up for air only to be hit in the head by my kayak. Dave took off for the island. Morris grabbed the bows of our kayaks and I grabbed the sterns, and we tried to swim them toward shore. We both realized it was futile, but it gave us something to focus on, and we didn't think it would be too long until help would arrive.

After about an hour, Morris became seasick. Although the water was 73°F, we were being slammed by waves and had to hold our breath when they went over us. Our arms were getting bruised, and I had to try to keep away from the rudder on Morris's kayak. When I saw a sailboat in the shipping channel about half a mile away, I pulled a flare from my PFD pocket and fired it. The sailboat passed by. An hour or two later, a ship passed about a quarter of a mile away, and even though it was close enough, it didn't see me waving my yellow-bladed paddle. My other flares weren't readily available, as I had inadvertently placed them inside a hatch in my hurry to get underway.

DASH TO THE ISLAND

Dave speaking

My muscles were tensed to the max. I knew that if I made a wrong move, I'd capsize and all three of us would perish. Fifteen minutes into my paddle, I heard a huge roaring behind me and was thrust surfing at full speed on a rogue wave. I tried my best to keep my kayak going straight but began to broach. I teetered from side to side as I went over the crest.

I decided to aim for the closest shore rather than the harbor. There was a house at the nearest point of land, and I hoped that someone would be there. The shoreline features slowly seemed to be getting bigger, and I tried to judge how far a swim it would be if I went over. I knew the rule about staying with your boat, but if I went over, I was planning to ditch my kayak if I could not reenter. My white kayak would be nearly impossible to spot in the whitecaps.

I had severe doubts whether I was going to make it. Waves were breaking over me. My skirt had a poor fit, and I was taking on water. I knew if I went over, the skirt would pop off and the kayak would fill with water instantly.

My upper body was cramping from the strain of hard paddling. The waves pounded me into an area that was all rocky ledges, and I came close to capsizing several more times. About 45 minutes after leaving Leif and Morris, I beached the kayak and ran to the house.

I discovered that it was abandoned and in complete disrepair. There was a trail next to it that I felt confident led to the docks I'd seen on the chart. I remember telling myself, "Go slow, pace yourself." I began walking. That didn't feel right with my friends in peril, so I started to jog. I have bad knees that eventually lock up if I run.

If I found someone docked at the far side of the island, I could have them put out a distress call if they had a radio. If no one was there, I planned to set a fire in hopes of attracting someone's attention.

I reached the dock in about 25 minutes. No one was there. I walked to an abandoned cottage on the point of land near the dock. All the windows were smashed out, and the door was missing. I had matches but hadn't packed a striker for them. Fortunately, I found a book of matches on a shelf.

My four attempts to start a fire with sticks were unsuccessful. I tried several times to ignite a mattress I found in the house, but the wind blowing through was too strong.

Frustrated, I went out on the porch and found one of the floorboards missing with some dried grass underneath. I took some of the mattress stuffing and shoved it under the floorboards and lit it. As before, it went up instantly but then went out. This time, however, I saw a small coal, so I blew on it until it began to smoke. I had some good coals going, but I had inhaled the smoke and started to cough heavily. Finally I got a small flame and soon had a fire going nicely.

I looked to see if there were any boats near the island. When the whole cabin was in flames, I stood on the point hoping someone would come along. There was no one to be seen or activity of any kind on the water. All I could do was wait. I knew I had to stay right where I was. If any help was coming, this was the place where it would arrive.

After about an hour, the flames started to peter out. Nearby within an old foundation I found a pile of about 30 car tires, which I knew would provide plumes of black smoke. I climbed into the foundation and lifted the first tire. It had a wasp nest inside. The wasps swarmed around me, but I was not stung. I tossed a few more tires out, then ran toward the cabin with the first tire. The heat was so intense from the fire's coals that I could only get within 50 feet of it.

I could almost feel the skin cracking on my forehead. I gave the tire a kick to roll it into the fire. I did this continually until there were no more tires to burn.

I then found four tire inner tubes. The first one I tossed toward the fire was wrapped around a large snake that went flying along with the tube. I threw all four inner tubes into the flames. By now I had a good pyre of black smoke. I hoped someone might spot it. I was also hoping that Leif and Morris would see it and have hope that I'd made it to shore and was trying to get help.

It was now about 3 P.M. I didn't want to leave the signal fire, but I couldn't stand around doing nothing, so I decided to head back to my kayak to go out searching for Leif and Morris if conditions permitted. I walked along the shoreline in case I could spot my friends trying to come in. There was no trail along the shore, so I made my way through waist-high grass. The area was teeming with short, thick snakes.

I spotted a sailboat coming from the north, and I began waving my arms and blowing sets of three short blasts on my whistle. I was sure that they had seen me, so I walked back to the bay waving my arms all the way. The boat dropped anchor in the bay and lowered a rowboat. I waded out in the water as the rowboat drew near. I explained my predicament to the rower, Captain Bruce Brown. He quickly told me to hop aboard.

Back on his boat, *Atreides,* he tried unsuccessfully to reach the Coast Guard or any other emergency vessel. His crew—daughter Charli and her friends Cynthia and Greg—raised the anchor, and we headed out of the bay. It was now 3:30, and Leif and Morris had been drifting for 4 hours at a speed I guessed to be about 1 to 2 miles an hour. They could have drifted as far as 8 miles from where I'd left them. We left the shelter of the bay and headed out into the wind.

Captain Brown started a search pattern to the east of where I'd left Morris and Leif, all the while calling Pan-Pan on his VHF radio. Greg offered me some water, my first drink since the capsize, and Cynthia gave me a pair of binoculars. I headed to the bow and scanned ahead. The 40-foot sailboat was taking a beating in the waves, and water was cascading right over me. I could hear pots and pans crashing about belowdecks. About an hour later, Captain Brown raised the U.S. Coast Guard, but the connection was weak. They thought we were reporting two missing kayaks, not two missing kayakers. They said they would put out a notice to have ships keep a lookout for two kayaks. Then radio contact failed, and we were unable to contact them again to explain the severity of the situation.

At the 8-mile limit of our search area, we turned to the north for a quarter mile, then headed back on a parallel course. Shortly afterward, we made clear contact with the U.S. Coast Guard. They contacted the Canadian Coast Guard, who initiated a search-and-rescue operation. It was 3:45 P.M.

WAITING FOR RESCUE
Leif speaking

We saw smoke on Main Duck Island and knew that Dave had made it ashore. We also knew that his signal fire meant there wasn't anyone there. Later, a sailboat passed within a quarter mile of us—which we later learned was the *Atreides* skippered by Bruce Brown coming from the north toward Main Duck Island—but they didn't hear Morris's whistle or see me waving my paddle.

We were drifting east along the north shore of the island but weren't making much progress toward it in the approximately 4 hours we tried to swim the kayaks to shore. I was really feeling the effects of hypothermia. I had stopped shivering and had muscle cramps. I was starting to fear for our lives. If we missed the island, we would continue on toward Wolfe Island about 12.5 miles away, crossing the shipping channel sometime in the night.

We'd had nothing to eat since an early breakfast and nothing to drink after 10 or 11 in the morning. My spare water bottles were lost when I capsized, and the bite valve came off my hydration backpack and let it empty when I wet-exited.

When the waves died down to about 3 feet, Morris suggested that I reenter his kayak, the more stable of the two, and try to tow him to shore with it. It took a couple of tries, as I was getting weaker, but with Morris holding the kayak I was able to get aboard.

Maybe Morris felt too weak to attempt to get on top of the kayaks. I didn't think I had the strength to pull him out of the water without his help. I checked the front hatch of my kayak for the rest of my flares but discovered they weren't there. That meant they were in the rear compartment. Strapped over the aft hatch cover were my tent, sleeping pad, and spare paddle. I decided to leave the flares there and start paddling. I considered abandoning my kayak, but its yellow and red deck would give us more visibility than Morris's dark green kayak. I also didn't want my kayak drifting away and diverting any rescuers away from their search for us. Morris attached a line to keep it in tow.

I paddled for over 2 hours and made some progress toward Main Duck Island. I was feeling warmer after I got out of the water, but I was very tired, hungry, and thirsty. Morris was in the water the whole time hanging onto the stern and was in worse condition with more severe hypothermia and seasickness. He was getting lower in the water, and my concern for him was increasing.

Sometime around 5 P.M., I noticed a ship to the northeast and a Canadian Coast Guard boat and a sailboat coming from the north. They were a long way off but heading in our direction. After a while, I could hear the sound of an aircraft and soon saw a search-and-rescue C-130 Hercules aircraft doing a search pattern from Main Duck Island north to the shipping channel.

The Hercules then seemed to circle above us, its landing lights flashing. After a while, a Cormorant search-and-rescue helicopter circled over us. They dropped a strobe and a flare, then came closer. Spray driven by the rotor wash pelted us as two rescue swimmers jumped into the water and swam over to us. The one on my side said he was surprised to see that I had gotten back aboard the kayak and he was happy to find us alive. I told the swimmers Morris had been in the water for about 6 hours and was seasick.

Both aircraft were from Canadian Forces Base in Trenton, Ontario, about 50 miles away. Subsequent reports said that the Joint Rescue Coordination Centre got the emergency call at 3:45 P.M. and we were found at 5:42. We spent over 4 hours in the water before the Coast Guard was notified of our situation, and a total of more than 6 hours passed before our rescue, which would have been too late if the water temperatures had been colder as they are most summers.

The search-and-rescue vessel *Cape Hearne* from Kingston came close to us and pulled Morris aboard. I was reluctant to abandon the kayaks, but the rescue swimmer told me not to worry about them. I was pulled aboard. We were taken inside the vessel where it was warm. One of the rescuers told me that Dave was on the sailboat I'd seen and had initiated the rescue effort. Morris and I were walked to the foredeck to be hoisted up to the helicopter and taken to Kingston General Hospital. I started shivering again, and the rescue swimmers were pleased to see this indication that I was warming up.

THE RESCUE

Dave speaking

Looking over the bow of the *Atreides,* I saw a bright light fall from the helicopter. We were still quite a distance from the action, so couldn't see what was happening. We continued our course and came directly to both kayaks, which were tethered together, drifting downwind from the location of the helicopter. Had the Coast Guard not found Leif and Morris, it seemed evident that Captain Brown would have.

We tried to tow the kayaks, but Leif's was nearly full of water and the extra weight broke the tether. I suggested trying again, knowing that Leif would be very angry with me if I left his boat. Captain Brown decided it was unsalvageable, and we let it go adrift. We managed to keep Morris's boat and picked up a paddle and a pump that were floating nearby. We motored to the sheltered bay at Main Duck Island.

At 5:43 P.M., the Coast Guard vessel *Cape Hearne* pulled up alongside us and to my relief informed us that both kayakers had been airlifted to Kingston General Hospital. They told us that one person, they couldn't say which, was nearly unconscious and would not have lasted much longer. Captain Brown said that I would be welcome to stay aboard the *Atreides,* but the Coast Guard officer vetoed that, saying, "No, he's coming with us. We came out to rescue three people, and three people are going back." We loaded Morris's kayak onto the *Cape Hearne.* They had picked Leif's kayak up after we set it adrift from the *Atreides* and all the floating gear they could find. Later Leif, Morris, and I took inventory, and the only thing missing was one of Leif's sandals.

RECOVERY
Leif speaking
At the hospital, Morris and I were put into beds with covers that circulated warm air around our bodies. Our vital signs were monitored, chest x-rays taken, and blood tests performed. My temperature climbed up to 96°F. We were given some dry clothing to wear, and after we had some soup and sandwiches, we were released.

LESSONS LEARNED
George Gronseth
It's easy to identify the mistakes made in this situation that could have been avoided and problems that could have been dealt with in better ways. But before going into what went wrong, we need to ask ourselves, if we were at the put-in with this group of three, would we have joined this trip?

River Kayaks and Open Water
Would you have gone if one of your friends planned to use a river kayak? River kayaks and recreational kayaks are generally slower than sea kayaks, but I've been on several sea kayak trips with clubs where someone showed up with an old 11- to 13-foot river kayak. In all but one case, the paddler in the river kayak either outpaced the

group or had no trouble keeping up, much to the surprise of those in 16- to 18-foot touring kayaks.

The Duck Island incident, ironically, doesn't illustrate the risks of making an open-water crossing in a river kayak. Dave, who was in a river kayak, was the only member of the group who made it to the destination without capsizing, but that had more to do with his skill than the seaworthiness of his boat. His use of a river kayak would have left his friends with fewer options and put them at greater risk if things started going wrong for him.

Most river kayaks and recreational kayaks lack sufficient buoyancy to do deepwater reentry rescues. Dave recognized the trouble he'd have if too much water leaked through his poorly fitting spray skirt or if he capsized and had to wet-exit. River kayaks have no bulkheads, so they have to be equipped with float bags for buoyancy.

To be truly safe, kayaks used for cruising should have backup flotation—bulkheads plus float bags, for example—and there's often no way to give river kayaks backup buoyancy. They generally lack deck rigging needed for a spare paddle, paddle tether, pump, self-rescue device, chart, compass, etc. Whitewater paddlers are never far from shore, so many items considered basic for sea kayak safety are unnecessary for running rivers.

Exposure During Crossings

If your open-water kayaking experience was limited, would you go on a trip with a 10-mile crossing? I'll bet most sea kayakers with 20-plus years of experience like these guys had would go, especially if the weather forecast was benign. When there's no wind, no current, and no surf, the main challenges of a long crossing are stamina and bladder control. If the weather forecast calls for more wind than the group can handle, then it's an obvious no-go.

But there's more to making a safe crossing than simply choosing to cross only when the weather forecast is favorable. There's never a guarantee that the weather will stay calm, not even when the forecast is benign. At least twice in my 25 years of sea kayaking, I've been caught in gale-force winds that had not been predicted in the marine weather forecast. Some squalls caused by weather cells can be too localized to be predicted by the weather service.

The essence of evaluating the risk of making a crossing is to consider the worst-case scenario. To do this, you need to understand a bit of oceanography and marine weather. The trip here is a simple example. On Lake Ontario, there's no tidal current, and if winds had been light for a couple days prior to the trip, then there wouldn't have been any swells. Without swells, there would have been no surf un-

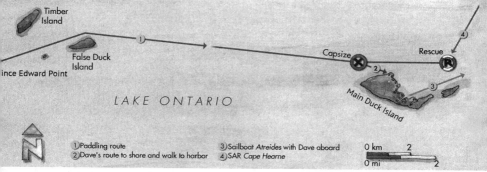

Timber Island
False Duck Island
ince Edward Point
LAKE ONTARIO
Capsize
Rescue
Main Duck Island

1) Paddling route
2) Dave's route to shore and walk to harbor
3) Sailboat *Atreides* with Dave aboard
4) SAR *Cape Hearne*

0 km   2
0 mi   2

Christopher Hoyt

less the weather had changed for the worse, and even then, the wind would have had to blow for a while before the waves got big enough to be of much concern for experienced paddlers.

When the seas (wind waves) are somewhere between 1 and 2 feet, most sea kayakers will start using their paddles to brace. Seas bigger than about 2 feet can require significant bracing skill, and seas of 3 feet or more may require expert-level skill to handle safely.

Waves and Fetch

In deep water with no current, three factors determine the size of the seas: wind speed, how long the wind has been blowing (duration), and how far the wind has blown unobstructed over the water (fetch).

In ponds and small lakes, the fetch is short. Waves can't grow very big on a small lake regardless of the wind speed and duration. Kayakers in coastal and inland waters often take advantage of the limits on water conditions imposed by a short fetch.

Lake Ontario is not a small body of water, however. For the crossing in this story, a wind from the southwest would have a fetch of 75 nautical miles, enough distance for a 20-knot wind of sufficient duration (10 hours, according to *Waves and Beaches*, by Willard Bascom) to produce "fully developed seas" of about 8 feet, the same size of waves that a similar wind would create on open ocean.

In this story, the wind had already been blowing for an undetermined length of time before they started the open crossing. The 8-foot wave height predicted for a 20-knot wind is an average height, not the biggest possible wave for those conditions. Ten percent of waves will be 1.3 times higher, or 10.4 feet, and one percent of the waves will be 1.7 times higher, or about 13.6 feet. Although very unlikely, it is statistically possible for a single wave to be 2.5 times higher: 20 feet.

If conditions were calm when you started and the forecast benign, and you agreed to head for shore if and when any wind came up, then the worst case would be if the wind came up when you were in the middle of the crossing. Under ideal conditions, an experienced group of paddlers might expect this 10-mile crossing to take about 3 hours. So if the wind came up when you were halfway across, it would take about 1.5 hours to get to shore. With 20-knot winds blowing for 1.5 hours, the wave height would then be about 2.2 feet, which is getting into advanced skill-level conditions. Shorter crossings would shorten the time on the water and the time the wind had to develop waves.

For crossings longer than 3 to 4 nautical miles, even under ideal starting conditions, you need either a high level of rough-water paddling and self-rescue skill or a lot of confidence in the weather forecast. If the wind is blowing 15 knots or more before you start a crossing, it's going to be rough out there.

The Devil in the Details

Let's see what we can learn from some of the specific details in this story.

I was surprised that on two of the three occasions these kayakers used whistles, they were heard. Perhaps the signal worked because Dave and later the sailboat were downwind of the whistle. I've tested a variety of whistles, and none have been impressive in winds above 20 knots. When signaling to someone upwind, the whistle's range may be only 20 to 40 feet. Air horns are significantly louder but less reliable. The best ones I tried lasted only about a year in a saltwater environment, others only a few weeks or months. So I gave up on air horns and went back to just carrying a whistle, mainly because it meets the legal requirement to carry a sound signaling device.

When paddling near shore within your swimming distance on a small lake or other sheltered water, you might get away with a leaking spray skirt and a kayak without sufficient flotation. For long crossings, the need for a seaworthy boat is a given. Kayaks should have backup buoyancy in both ends: bulkheads plus gear in dry bags, gear in dry bags plus a sea sock, etc. Safety gear—flares, VHF radio, etc.—needs to be in good working order and carried where you have access to it without having to open the compartments that provide buoyancy.

Protect your flares from moisture by storing them in a fully waterproof bag. Because of the short time that they're visible, flares won't always bring results, but as a matter of policy I would have fired a flare at the point when Leif realized they "were in conditions well beyond our ability to perform an assisted rescue." Don't wait until you see a boat to fire at least one flare. Because of the curvature of the earth, there could be a boat beyond your line of sight but still in a position to see your aerial flare. If everyone in Leif's group had carried a pack of three flares in their kayaks, or better yet, tucked in their PFDs, a lot of flares would still have been available if they'd seen a boat.

Cell phones need to be in fully waterproof bags (not ordinary ziplocks) designed to allow use while sealed. A submersible VHF radio is a more reliable means of calling for help because it broadcasts a signal to any other VHF within range.

Water at 73°F is somewhat forgiving but still cold enough to cause hypothermia even just with exposure to splash and spray. So on a long crossing keep some extra clothes and a dry top or paddling jacket accessible.

Leif's failed attempt to get Morris back in his kayak may have gone better if Leif had rafted up on the downwind side of Morris's boat. With the swimmer on the upwind side of the rafted kayaks, there would be less banging of boats, and the swimmer could use the wave action to assist him in getting up onto his kayak instead of the waves pushing his kayak over him, forcing his legs to drift beneath it.

Leif used Morris's throw rope for towing, but sea kayakers need to carry a tow system. It should attach near the center of the rescuer's kayak, either to a strong cleat just aft of the cockpit or to a quick-release belt around the kayaker's waist. If the towrope is attached to the stern of the kayak, the drag of the kayak in tow can stop the rescuer from turning or holding the chosen course.

With a little practice and a properly designed towing system, towing a kayak isn't very difficult. But towing a swimmer is slow, hard work no matter how you go about it. It's better to tow someone in or on a kayak than to tow a swimmer. Even if this group couldn't get Morris back into his cockpit, perhaps they could have had him lie sideways across two kayaks and towed this raft with the third kayak.

The most effective way to use a handheld bilge pump in rough seas is to lift the bottom of your PFD up and shove the pump down between the spray skirt and your belly. This way is slow and awkward, but you can pump with the spray skirt completely sealed. Practice it.

Ongoing Practice

Sea kayakers need to practice their reentry rescues at least once a year. Rescues may seem simple, but without practice, you may miss important details. Try rescue techniques you haven't done before. It's good to know a variety of rescue techniques because no single method works in every situation.

For most two-person assisted-reentry rescues, it's best to have the swimmer reach over the rescuer's kayak as the swimmer climbs up onto his or her own kayak. This makes both the swimmer and the rescuer more stable. The rougher the conditions, the more critical this is.

As your experience grows, you may become more comfortable paddling in rougher conditions and taking on longer crossings. As you take on higher levels of risk, you need to find controlled situations to test and practice your rescues in the conditions you're likely to find yourself in.

16

A Sudden Storm
A Texas Squall Brings Two Kayakers Their 15 Minutes of Fame on the Evening News

Ken Johnson and Tim Hamilton

STARTING OUT
Ken speaking

Tim Hamilton and I kayak 8 to 12 miles at least twice a week in Corpus Christi, Texas, pretty much year-round. Tim is 40, a fitness trainer in very good physical condition, and a skilled kayaker who has paddled for two and a half years. I am 74 and retired 15 years ago to kayak fulltime. Tim and I are both strong paddlers with above-average speed and endurance. Both of us are somewhat impulsive and confident, and we've never spent much time packing safety gear into our kayaks.

We paddle Performa fiberglass kayaks manufactured by Mayan Seas of Mexico (a company for whom I am the Texas distributor). They are 16.2 feet long with a 23.5-inch beam, weighing about 55 pounds each. There is no rudder or skeg; they're designed to handle in a very wind-neutral manner, with slight leecocking (tendency to turn away from the wind) in heavier winds that is normally easy to compensate for with standard edging and slight turn strokes. Both kayaks have paddle leashes, full deck lines and bungees, forward and rear hatches, a day hatch, and a compass.

On the morning of November 30, 2006, I had packed my gear inside the cockpit. I had a paddle float and sponge on either side of the seat, water bottle and towrope under my legs, and my life jacket and

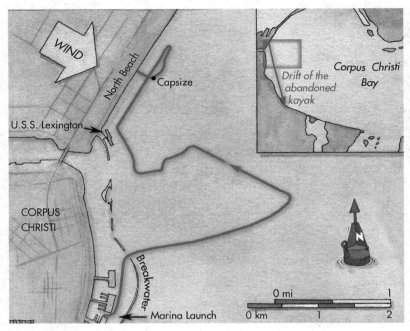

Christopher Hoyt

pump secured on deck under the rear bungee. I carried my dry top on my lap, ready to put it on if I needed it. Tim had a sponge and a shirt inside the cockpit, and on deck he carried his three water bottles under the front bungee and his PFD under the rear bungee.

Our story, which begins with Tim's account, started out as a typical outing for us but ended up being anything but typical as we and our concepts of safe paddling were literally blown away in just 5 minutes. All wind speeds and temperatures described here were verified with local weather reports, and the timing was verified by time markings on photographs taken and in the police logs.

Tim's Perspective

That morning in Corpus Christi began much like every other day over the previous several weeks. It was unseasonably warm and humid, with light to moderate south-southeast breezes off the Gulf of Mexico. Ken and I were well aware that a pretty serious cold front was on its way, yet we were rarely deterred from our usual Thursday morning paddle on Corpus Christi Bay.

We had both looked at the weather reports several times prior to leaving, having heard that high winds would accompany the front's arrival. Looking carefully at the NOAA forecast, I saw that gusts as high as 50 mph were expected around noon. If you have ever experienced the arrival of a Texas northerly, you know that they can sweep in powerfully, with temperatures plummeting and howling winds gusting and switching directions abruptly.

I calculated that we could get our customary 2-hour paddle done in just enough time to be off the water before the really big winds hit. The plan was to launch from the Corpus Christi marina, head north across the bay, and if we were lucky, enjoy a tailwind both ways.

Ken and I launched at 8:15 a.m., with an air temperature of 75°F and a 10- to 12-knot wind out of the south. I opted to paddle without a shirt or a dry top, as I was confident we'd be out of the water before the front's arrival at around noon. I tucked my PFD under the rear bungee, snapped the spray skirt on the cockpit, and dipped the paddle in the water.

We headed outside the breakwater and decided to head northeast toward the shipping channel. The sun was rising, and the morning was gorgeous. I worked my muscles up to good warmth as we cruised at our usual 4.5 to 5 mph. I saw a tanker approaching well off on the eastern horizon and thought maybe we'd head toward it, turn around there, and perhaps surf its wake back. I had done this once before and enjoyed a long exhilarating ride across the bay.

Less than an hour after we launched, the sky began to cloud over and the wind and waves began to change direction, shifting to be more from the southwest than the south. At the time, there was no real change in wind speed or wave height, and perhaps that lulled both of us into a false sense of security. We did decide to abandon our course to the tanker and instead began to surf the wind-generated waves across the shipping channel to the west.

Waves were maybe 2 to 2.5 feet high at that point, and we caught a few as we headed downwind. I decided to do my usual practice rolls and executed several of them, rolling over to both sides and once or twice with the paddle out of position. A glance at my watch showed it was 9:07 a.m.

Ever the slave to ritual, and not wanting to cut our trip short, I suggested to Ken that we paddle northeast along North Beach for perhaps another 30 minutes or so. "I'll follow you," Ken replied, as usual. At that point we both noticed the sky swiftly darkening to a deep shade of black off to our left rear quarter to the west-northwest. At 9:27 Ken snapped a photo, and we both quickly agreed to turn around and hustle back to the marina.

The front had arrived two and a half hours ahead of what we had expected. We paddled southwest, parallel to the beach, which was about a half mile away on our right. At 9:29 Ken took one last picture of the storm clouds. Off in the distance, a flock of birds, stark white against the black sky, flew up and scattered like debris in the wind. At this point, we had felt no change in temperature or wind. Seconds later, I felt an icy wind hit my right shoulder and wrap around my bare torso. Instantly the wind whipped up to a ferocious level, throwing spray and threatening to rip the paddle out of my hands.

It was difficult to stay upright. Within moments, I knew I had to turn to my right and head directly into the northwest wind (as indicated on the map) blasting straight off the beach. I was about a quarter mile from the beach at that point, and its lee would provide the closest refuge. If I couldn't make it to the beach, I would be swept out into the open bay and across the shipping channel. If the waves harassing me now weren't trouble enough, those farther out would be monsters by comparison.

Try as I might, however, I could not turn the kayak into the wind. I stroked as hard as I could on my left, edging the boat as much as I dared, as my anxiety level rose. The blasts of wind against my right side repeatedly forced me to brace hard on my left. The wind shrieked around us. White spray and foam streaked across the water as waves hammered the boat relentlessly. Fear set in with the growing realization that I couldn't turn into the wind and would not likely be able to make it to the beach. I could just see myself being swept out into the middle of the bay. Although we frequently kayaked in rough conditions and enjoyed paddling in winds of 20 to 30 mph and surfing waves up to 4 feet or so, I had never experienced wind this powerful.

At 9:35, I chanced a look around to see how Ken was faring. Just then, a strong gust of wind hit me and I capsized. Because of my state of panic, I utterly failed to even consider rolling. I let go of my paddle and ejected from the kayak immediately. Fortunately, the water temperature was still in the 60s. I instinctively grabbed onto the kayak and ripped my PFD from under the bungee. It was awkward putting on the PFD in the rough water, and before I could fasten it, the kayak was whisked away from me by wind and waves. I swam toward it, away from the beach, as hard as I could, but I couldn't get any closer. I buckled down and swam as fast as my heart would allow, and somehow I grabbed a deck line.

I was torn between staying with the boat, which was rapidly being swept out into the open water of the bay, or swimming for the beach. I let go of the kayak, thinking to swim to shore, but clutched impulsively at my paddle as it floated past, still attached to the deck by its leash. As soon as my fingers tightened on it, the cord snapped with a hiss and a recoil. The final decision to abandon my kayak had been made for me. I tossed the paddle aside and began swimming for shore.

All the while, I hadn't been able to catch sight of Ken. In the back of my mind I assumed he too was being swept helplessly downwind, also unable to turn into the wind. I tried repeatedly to zip up my life vest, but it was next to impossible with the beating I was taking. It felt like someone was hurling buckets of water directly into my face, the waves coming so fast one after another. Only with great determination and focus did I finally zip it up while treading water in a half-vertical and half-laidback position.

Then I focused on swimming. I kept looking at the buildings on shore, but they were not getting any larger. I swam hard but kept swallowing seawater every time I raised my head to breathe. I tried the backstroke, which kept the water out of my face, but I was pushed farther away from shore. I kept alternating between the two, and then I heard Ken yelling at me. Incredibly, he had managed to stay upright, turn into the wind, and reach me. He was yelling at me to grab his stern.

He made several passes, but the wind blew him sideways and away from me several times before we could connect. He was able to avoid getting spun completely broadside to the wind again, and at one point I actually helped steer him back into the wind by pushing his bow. At last, with great relief, I grabbed his stern, then stroked with my free hand and kicked. We got absolutely nowhere. Ken is a big man and a seasoned, strong paddler, but the winds were blowing 50 mph and gusting higher, and he was attempting to tow a 185-pound man.

Finally, I told Ken just to paddle in and I would swim. I let go of the kayak and just swam. Ken did not paddle on but stayed beside me as I swam in. Eventually, after what seemed like 30 minutes (but was actually 15), I felt the sandbar under my feet. I was more exhausted than cold as I got out of the water at 9:50 A.M. I was stung by sand blasting from the beach. I staggered under the force of the wind as sand scoured every exposed bit of my skin.

The air temperature had plummeted, and with the wind chill it felt like it was in the thirties. I was greeted by police, EMTs, and several news crews. Nearby in Corpus Christi Bay, someone visiting the aircraft carrier USS *Lexington* had seen us from the flight deck and called for emergency help at 9:40. The police and marina patrol arrived at North Beach at 9:46. By 10 A.M. we had dragged Ken's kayak safely up on the beach and were in the backseat of a police car driving over the Harbor Bridge back to the marina to pick up Ken's car and trailer to collect his kayak.

Meanwhile, my kayak was taking a journey of its own across Corpus Christi Bay. It traveled 5 miles in about 3 hours and landed in a residential area near a public park. A passerby spotted it coming ashore and waded in to fish it out before it reached the shoreline. I was extremely grateful that it had been spared getting bashed on the rocks. When I retrieved it, I was quite amazed to find it undamaged. There wasn't even any water in the hatches. Aside from a few surface scratches, there was no damage.

Ken and I ended up on the 5, 6, and 10 o'clock news.

TIM'S LESSONS LEARNED

There are certainly some lessons I learned from this experience. Not allowing for a margin of error with the forecast can be deadly. Weather conditions can change very quickly. I failed to show proper respect for Mother Nature, and that cost me. I'm willing to accept a certain amount of risk, and I enjoy the challenge of big waves and rough conditions—it's exhilarating. But to go several miles out, without proper clothing, not wearing a PFD, and allowing for no margin of error in the forecast was foolish.

Another important lesson for me was a new perspective on how much practice is required to make bracing, turning, and rolling reliable skills. In spite of my confidence with rolling, my technique was still not reflexive. It's one thing to roll in relatively calm conditions when I'm intending to capsize and roll. Practice in controlled conditions has no resemblance to a roll in "combat" conditions. I needed more work in rough-water rolling. That skill may have made it easier for me to remain calm and to roll on the day of the storm. If I'd been able to recover quickly from the capsize, I think I would have had a fair chance of simply paddling ashore.

Remaining calm in an emergency is essential. Panic leads to disaster. Had I remained calm and executed a stronger, more purposeful turn stroke, I might not have capsized. Panic shortens your movements and freezes you up, and you become rigid and paralyzed. None of that helps you deal with your situation. I'm fortunate that this story had a good outcome and that all I lost was my carbon-fiber paddle. That can be replaced. This experience was humbling and instilled in me a greater respect for Mother Nature and an understanding of how quickly things can turn ugly. I will be back out in the bay, but as a much more cautious kayaker.

KEN'S PERSPECTIVE

It's funny how last-minute changes in your routine can have a profound effect on your paddle. When Tim emailed me about paddling Thursday morning and mentioned 10- to 20-mph winds, I knew he wanted to surf the waves those winds would produce. So I teased that he had omitted the part in the weather report that mentioned gusts to 50 mph. He replied, "Details, details," and I anticipated another exciting surfing day like many we had enjoyed before.

I arrived at the launch site early and was suited up with a poly shirt and dry top, wearing my PFD, which was rare for me. On the Texas coast the weather is usually warm, if not hot, and the water temperature in the bay is pleasant for swimming nine months out of the year, rarely dropping below 60°F in the winter. But for this outing, I wanted to try out my new waterproof camera, and I could use my PFD's pocket to keep the camera available for quick shots.

By the time Tim arrived, I was sweating and feeling overdressed, and he looked quite comfortable in just his bathing suit, so I changed into my bathing suit and stuffed my dry top in the cockpit in case we ran into cold rain. My PFD went under the rear bungees as usual because I don't like it chafing on my bare skin. I hung the waterproof camera around my neck and stuffed it inside my spray skirt.

It was a beautiful sunny day with a nice warm temperature, and although we did see the skies darken up and a fast-moving shower pass over us, the sun soon came out again, the wind abated, and we decided to extend our paddle for another half hour along North Beach, the northern shore of Corpus Christi Bay. At that point I thought about heading back early to be sure we'd beat the storm, but I didn't want to be the one to quit if Tim still wanted to paddle.

I soon noticed a very black sky moving in behind us and yelled to Tim, "Here it comes again!" thinking it was another band in advance of the front. But as Tim and I watched it darken, we decided it was serious and turned around to paddle the 3 miles back to the marina to try to get off the water ahead of the storm. At 9:30 A.M. we turned around to head for home, paddling parallel to the beach on our right. Within 5 minutes, the temperature dropped from 75° to 50°F and the wind jumped from 14 mph to a steady 42 mph with gusts to 54 mph (wind speeds as reported on an hourly NOAA weather report).

When the wind hit, I knew Tim and I were in trouble. I had suggested we head toward the bow of the *Lexington*, a little more downwind, to get us in the harbor entrance to paddle back to the marina. He was aiming a little more upwind to the right, trying to edge a little closer to the beach. Both of us were only able to paddle parallel to the beach with the wind on our right beam. There was still no panic at this point, although I decided we'd be better off trying to paddle upwind half a mile to reach the beach rather than paddle downwind 3 miles back to the launch point at the marina.

I saw Tim capsize at 9:35, a little forward and upwind of me, closer to the beach. I was unable to turn my kayak fully into the wind and waves to come to his aid. It took me what seemed like 15 minutes (it was actually 5) paddling as hard as I could to finally turn into the wind to reach him, and by that time he had already lost his kayak and paddle and was trying to swim against the wind and waves to reach the beach.

He was able to hang onto the stern of my kayak and get some rest, but because we couldn't make any headway into the beach that way, we decided that we would try to reach the beach with him swimming and me paddling alongside so he could grab my kayak if he needed a rest. This was paddling at a slower pace for me to avoid getting ahead of Tim.

The closer we got to the beach, the more protection we felt in the lee, although I still had to be careful not to let the kayak broach and be carried away from Tim as he swam. We reached the beach at 9:50. Tim had been swimming 15 minutes for all he was worth but was still able to walk up on the beach and help me carry my kayak inland where it could be tied to some trees so it would not blow away.

When I got out of my kayak at the beach, I put on the dry top that I'd stowed in the cockpit. I hadn't missed the dry top while I was paddling and had actually felt warmer paddling in the kayak than I did on the beach after I'd put on my dry top. I also had heavy fleece pants and jacket in my car.

The wind and sand blasted us, and it was difficult to walk against the wind. I was really relieved and too happy at being ashore to think about being cold or tired. After stowing my gear and answering questions from the reporters, we were lucky to get a ride in the police car back to the marina.

Tim and I were nearly blown away by the storm, but our assumptions about paddling safely were truly blown away. We were both amazed at the storm's speed and intensity. It arrived two and a half hours early, with sudden winds that increased nearly fourfold in velocity and a temperature drop of 25 degrees. There was no gradual buildup to this front. In just 1 to 2 minutes we went from enjoying a comfortable paddle to fighting for our lives.

When paddling I wear a cowboy hat for shade with a string tie under my chin, and I was surprised when the wind hit and it blew off my head. It was swinging wildly from side to side on my back with the chin cord around my neck beginning to choke me. It was very disconcerting, but I had no time to fix that. I had to keep both hands on the paddle and paddle for all I was worth.

I am a powerful paddler and have always felt in control of my kayak. This was the first time I was ever on the verge of being out of control and unable to turn sharply into the wind. During the broadside gusts it was all I could do to paddle parallel to the beach and keep from being blown downwind. Only when there were some very brief breaks between gusts was I able to get my bow pointed directly into the wind. I didn't have much leeway in trying to point the bow even slightly. A few degrees off the wind and I'd start to broach. Both Tim and I love the neutral way the Performa handles, not requiring a skeg or rudder. In previous heavy winds and waves we had experienced times when we'd have to edge and do a strong turn stroke to counter a moderate leecocking, but we'd never had to fight to get the bow into the wind.

Tim has a reliable and technically beautiful roll, and he practices it faithfully. He is also very nimble with other self-rescue techniques and does his reentry faster than anyone else I've paddled with. I was shocked to see him bail out of his kayak after he'd capsized. I was also shocked to discover that it was impossible for me to control my kayak well enough to reach him promptly and help him do an assisted reentry.

When I finally reached Tim and had him hanging onto the stern of my kayak, I was stunned at how futile my paddling was. I took long, powerful strokes into the wind, but it felt like the kayak was locked in cement. I could hold my own and not drift back, but I couldn't advance toward the beach against the wind. I was amazed that I couldn't tow Tim to shore with my kayak even with his swimming assistance. Swimming along seemed the only option for getting to the

Ken Johnson

nearby beach. The only other option for us was to have Tim continue to hang onto my kayak while it drifted away from shore into the open bay. There I would surely have had trouble remaining upright. As it was, even a few hundred yards from shore, every wave was breaking with foam.

I was also surprised to be in conditions where it was impossible for me to retrieve Tim's kayak and paddle, knowing how much he loved both. I would have jeopardized my own safety if I'd tried to chase down his gear.

KEN'S LESSONS LEARNED

We'd been lulled by year-round warm weather into thinking we could leave our PFDs on deck. In an emergency, you need it on you. Your paddle leash needs to be very strong; if it's all that connects you to your kayak, it has to hold in extreme conditions. Practice your braces, rolls, and reentries in really rough water where you'll blow ashore if anything goes wrong. This will also give you practice for remaining calm in really hectic conditions.

Give yourself a wide margin of safety when anticipating approaching storms, and don't hesitate to be the first to suggest a rapid return to shore. When in doubt, stay close to shore, especially with an offshore wind or chance of one. Stay close to your partner when you paddle together. Have a bombproof paddle-float outrigger procedure as a backup in case you get swept out in really rough water. Dress for the water and the worst anticipated weather, or at least have the clothing you need readily accessible so you can put it on well before the dire weather hits. Turn and head for the nearest shelter at the first sign of oncoming bad weather. Focus on remaining upright and not capsizing.

17

Crossing Lake Michigan

Paul McMullen
and Brian Day

THE COURSE OF EVENTS
Paul McMullen

My goal was to cross Lake Michigan unassisted in an 18-foot kayak. I would leave from Grand Haven, Michigan, and paddle west for Milwaukee, Wisconsin, a distance of 82.6 miles across an unpredictable and dangerous body of water. I estimated it would take me 16 hours and I'd spend most of that time paddling at night.

I wrote up a float plan indicating my departure time, estimated speed, navigation route, description of my vessel, and estimated time of arrival at my destination. I carried with me a cell phone, a waterproof GPS device, extra batteries, flares, and a strobe light. I also had an emergency position-indicating radio beacon (EPIRB) that would alert rescuers, if needed, and pinpoint my location within 100 meters.

I rented a kayak for the crossing, one that was longer and faster than the kayak I owned. On board I carried a hand pump, an extra paddle, and a paddle float, and I wore a wetsuit and a life vest. I packed food and water for five days, pain reliever, and sunscreen. I trained for six weeks for the trip including a 70-mile, 13-hour trip down the Muskegon River from Big Rapids to Lake Michigan just two weeks before. At the age of 34 and in excellent physical shape after a career as a track and field athlete, I felt I was well prepared for the challenge.

I packed up the kayak I'd rented for the crossing and faxed my float plan to Coast Guard Station Grand Haven and Coast Guard Sector Milwaukee. I didn't ask the Coast Guard's permission, but notifying them of my attempt would give the resources responsible a targeted search area if needed. Sending float plans directly to the Coast Guard is not standard procedure, but I'd been on active duty with the U.S. Coast Guard from 2003 to 2005, trained as a surface swimmer.

The on-duty officer at the Grand Haven station knew me and deemed it appropriate to take my float plan.

On September 7, 2006, I pushed off at 5:00 P.M., telling my very worried wife I would come back no matter what. The weather was beautiful with an air temperature around 68°F and a water temperature of 70°F. The sun was setting right on the bearing I needed to follow to Wisconsin, and the full moon would be rising as the daylight faded.

I felt quite comfortable in my kayak while I was underway. Only when I stopped to eat and to call my wife did I feel unstable in the waves. I expected my cell phone to work across the relatively flat expanse of the lake, but the waves made the signal inconsistent. At 25 miles offshore, there was no signal at all. While I was trying to make one last call to my wife, the three ziplock bags in which I stowed the phone blew away. I stowed the phone in another ziplock that held several dose-size packets of Tylenol. Once I realized the limits of the cell phone coverage, I decided I would have to paddle hard to get within range of the cell coverage in Wisconsin where I could call again and reassure her that all was well.

After the sun set, the light from the moon rising behind me made it possible to see the white crests of breaking waves. I used the stars to help me maintain my course, and every 30 minutes or so I would take a new bearing with my GPS and steer for a new star. I saw only one other vessel through the night, a sailboat out in the middle of the lake heading due north. I didn't signal my presence to them, as it was midnight and it looked like the autopilot was engaged and the crew sleeping.

Everything was going well, but the waves continued to build in the early morning hours and the wind began to howl out of the southwest. This was the weather I had anticipated, but thought I would be within sight of Wisconsin by the time the wind picked up. Occasionally a wave would break over the bow and splash me in the chest. I could feel water sloshing around my legs. The spray skirt kept most of the water from breaking waves out of the cockpit, but it leaked a little. To get the water out, I had to open the spray skirt and use the hand pump while watching out for larger waves that could fill the cockpit I was trying to empty.

For 2 hours in 3- to 5-foot waves, I paddled hard toward the setting moon with a furious intensity to get close enough to Wisconsin for cell coverage. When the sun came up shortly after 6:00 A.M., I watched the speed on my GPS and noticed that I was not going as fast as I needed to. I would miss my original estimated time of arrival by hours. Around 8:00 I pulled out my cell phone to call my wife. The phone was swimming in a water-filled ziplock bag. The foil corners

EPIRB AND PLB RECOMMENDATIONS

Brian Day

Because of the problems associated with early emergency position-indicating radio beacons (EPIRBs) operating on 121.5 MHz, the Coast Guard now requires the use of 406 MHz beacons. These EPIRBs use 406 MHz (a restricted emergency frequency) to contact satellites in Earth's orbit and use 121.5 MHz as a secondary homing signal for rescuers to follow. New 406 MHz personal locator beacons (PLBs) are generally smaller than EPIRBs and thus better suited for kayakers, and offer the best odds of rescue, particularly if equipped with a GPS transmitter.

The satellites involved in processing the 406 MHz emergency signal can calculate your position, but not as quickly nor as accurately as they can relay the position information that is coded into a GPS-equipped unit's 406 MHz signal. Equip yourself with an EPIRB or PLB that is equipped with GPS and your location, accurate to within 100 meters—and the information you provide when you register your 406 MHz device—will go almost immediately to the U.S. Mission Control Center (MCC), which contacts the appropriate regional Rescue Coordination Center (RCC) to initiate a search.

The unique identification number of the PLB or EPIRB allows the MCC to retrieve the beacon's registration form. The registration form includes the name, address, and phone numbers of the user and the phone numbers of two emergency contacts. Users can access their information online and update it as required, even on a daily basis. Registration of 406 MHz PLBs and EPIRBs is required by law. The units may be registered at no cost with NOAA at www.beaconregistration.noaa.gov. More information on PLBs, EPIRBs, and their associated satellite systems can be found on the U.S. Coast Guard Navigation Center website at http://www.sarsat.noaa.gov/emerbcns.html.

of the Tylenol packaging had punctured holes in the bag, and my cell phone was dead. I screamed out loud and began to calculate a new ETA. With the wind working against me I was making just 2 mph, so the 30 miles I had ahead of me would take another 15 hours.

The wave action was getting to my stomach. I was regularly burping up chunks of dried apricots and energy bars with a tinge of lemon-lime Gatorade. It quickly became apparent that it was time to make some important assessments. The first was to recognize that I was in distress. I instantly felt a sense of guilt that I was going to worry my loved ones and a sense of disappointment that I wasn't going to complete the crossing. It was, however, a relief to make the decision to call for help. I'd been paddling without my life jacket to avoid chafing my arms. I pulled it out from under the bungees on my forward deck, put it on, and activated the EPIRB secured to it.

After having paddled 52 miles from Michigan, I was 30 miles from Wisconsin. I started to calculate the response time and figured I would see a Coast Guard helicopter dispatched from Air Station Waukegan, Illinois, in about 30 minutes. I checked the EPIRB: The antenna was up, the red light was flashing, and it was beeping. I scanned the horizon for any boats or aircraft, but I saw nothing but blue waves and sky. Forty-five minutes went by, and the Coast Guard helicopter should have been drawing near. The horizon was empty, and I began to think of plan B—to paddle my way out. I had a decision to make: Do I go toward Milwaukee for 30 miles at 2 mph or do I retrace the 52 miles to Michigan with the wind at my back?

I decided to wait a couple more minutes to collect my thoughts. To the south, I spotted a vessel with a red hull and a white superstructure and a plume of smoke trailing. At first I thought it was the Coast Guard's 41-foot motor lifeboat, but I couldn't figure out why it was coming from the south. It was probably 10 miles away, and it kept coming right for me as if it knew where I was. When it got within approximately 5 miles of me, I could see that it was a Great Lakes freighter. I was so focused on trying to get into position so that the ship's crew would see me that I completely forgot about the flares that were stowed in my cockpit.

I paddled to position myself so the ship would pass to the east of me and its crew wouldn't be looking into the sun to spot me. I stopped 75 yards to the ship's port side to avoid its formidable wake. I could read the name on the side, *Joseph L. Block*. It was an iron-ore freighter over 700 feet long, obviously empty, riding high in the water and steaming north at about 14 knots. As it approached, I could see a man's silhouette on the deck, so I filled my lungs with air and whistled as my dad taught me as a kid. The first shrill sound must have caught the crewman's attention, and the second and third whistles got him to lock his vision on me. I began to wave my arms in the international signal for distress, as I had been taught in the Coast Guard. I watched the guy run back to the bridge to notify the captain about seeing me.

I was so excited to have been seen that I experienced something the Coast Guard calls "a loss of situational awareness." I was so focused on watching the guy run the several hundred feet from the bow to the bridge of the ship at the stern that I didn't notice the approach of the freighter's wake. Running counter to the wind waves, the wake created a sudden steep, towering wave crest that caused me to capsize. The next thing I knew, I was underwater. I quickly told myself, "Relax and live." I started to pull the spray skirt off but realized my legs were very stiff from not moving from a sitting position for 16 hours. I was running out of the quick breath of air I gasped before I went over, and I was pinned to the aft deck of the kayak because of the buoyancy of my PFD. Finally, I was able to pry my legs out of the cockpit and get to the surface to inhale a breath of fresh air.

It took about a half a mile and 30 minutes for the *Joseph L. Block* to make the turn and return to me. Meanwhile, I was attempting to reenter the now-swamped kayak. I inflated my paddle float, crawled belly down on the aft deck, and got my feet in the cockpit. When I tried to twist around to get into the sitting position, I capsized again. I tried unsuccessfully two more times to get back aboard before I abandoned my effort and waited for the *Block* to return. They found me swimming in the water next to my swamped kayak, waving my paddle over my head. The *Block* was about 100 yards away from me, and I knew the captain wouldn't be able to maneuver much closer. I had to abandon my kayak and gear and swim to the ship. While I was swimming, the $3,000 cost of the rented kayak came to mind. I had already put down a $1,500 deposit on the kayak as a condition for using it for the crossing.

The ship lowered a metal basket from a loading crane. I climbed in, and the crew cranked me up the side of the ship. I watched the kayak float away and said, "Man, is my wife going to be mad now."

Once on board, I quickly identified myself to the crew and said, "Please call my wife and let her know I'm OK, but don't tell her I lost the kayak." It was 9:30 A.M., just when I said I would call to let her know I was OK. Moments after I gave my name, age, and phone number, I started to vomit uncontrollably. A 728-foot freighter doesn't move as much as an 18-foot kayak in 3- to 5-foot waves, but I was hit with a bad case of motion sickness as soon as I got on board. The crew quickly attended to me. They literally took the clothes off their backs to warm me, then wrapped me in blankets.

I repeatedly thanked Lloyd Suzewski, the crewman who spotted me, for saving my life. I sensed a certain excitement in the crew in that they'd had the opportunity to execute a real rescue after enduring countless practice drills. Each crewmember who came up to me asked what I was thinking to try crossing the lake. Then they'd ask next, "Are you gonna do it again?" They all reiterated how lucky I was that they had come across me. I said over and over again how grateful I was and told the captain I was sorry for inconveniencing him. He said, "Don't worry about it, Paul. I'm just glad you're OK."

I asked the captain if he'd picked up the signal from my EPIRB. It had seemed to me that he steamed directly to my location as if he knew I was there. He said, "We heard nothing on our radio. In fact, the guys took the EPIRB off your life jacket, and even though the red light was flashing and the beeper was beeping, it wasn't transmitting." This EPIRB was supposed to signal satellites to transmit a frequency that special receivers picked up in a 1,000-mile radius. The frequency received would make an annoying fire-alarm sound over the ship's radio, but mine, purchased just days before the trip, appeared not to produce such a signal. [These devices no longer function in this way; see later discussion and the sidebar about EPIRBs.]

The captain of the *Block* contacted the Milwaukee Coast Guard

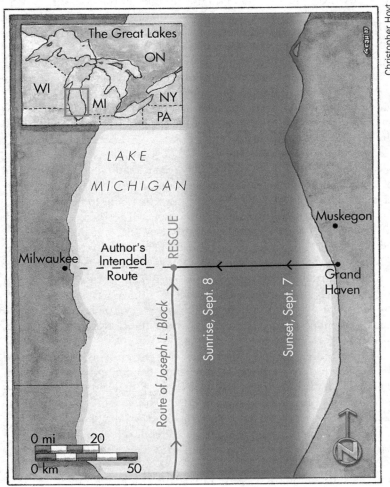

Christopher Hoyt

by radio. They dispatched a 41-foot motor lifeboat to transport me to shore and arranged to have an ambulance waiting to get me to the hospital to check me over. The well-trained crew from Station Milwaukee transferred me off the freighter flawlessly. The ride into Milwaukee took 2 hours. The skies were sunny, but the lake was still rough. I had no problem with the pounding of the boat going over waves, but when the boat slowed for a routine engine check, I began vomiting all over myself and passed out. When I came to, I saw that I had made a big mess not only all over myself but also all over the boat. I couldn't figure out what had happened. Apparently the bucket I'd used to collect the contents of my stomach had fallen to the floor, spilled, and rolled all over the inside of the boat in the rocking waves. At that point, I got a little more worried about my condition and asked the crew to keep a closer eye on me. I apologized for the smelly mess I caused. "Don't worry about it," they said. "Work has been slow lately, and it gives the younger guys something to clean up other than toilets."

We got into Milwaukee, and with two guys on each arm, I slowly made my way to the ambulance where I was quickly transported to the hospital emergency room. The triage nurses looked me over and started an IV, saying I was very dehydrated. Blood tests indicated I had paddled so hard that there were by-products of muscle breakdown in my blood. This condition has a long name I can't remember, but apparently it can become fatal due to the stress placed on the kidneys to filter out the high protein concentration. The ER doc wanted to admit me for overnight observation, but I was eager to return to my wife, so I begged him to reconsider. He consulted with a kidney specialist and agreed to release me because of my age and fitness level.

I got to a phone and called my wife. The number of swear words she used gradually diminished during the course of our conversation, but the word "stupid" persisted. I caught a cab to the Lake Express Ferry dock for the 7:00 P.M. ferry back home. The Coast Guard Station was close by, so I dropped in to say thanks.

I slowly limped into the station. My right heel was numb from reduced blood flow for several hours, and my left hamstring was cramping. The officer of the day greeted me and said, "I have good news. You're one lucky guy. The captain of the *Joseph L. Block* put out a call on the radio for any vessels in the area to assist. The fishing vessel *Joslyn* showed up after you got on board. They searched the area and located your kayak. It's sitting undamaged on the dock over at the ferry terminal and ready to be loaded." I shook his hand happily but winced when he gripped my palm, which was covered with blood blisters.

I limped around the terminal in mismatched sweats carrying all of my soaked clothes in plastic grocery bags. When it came time to board the ferry, I had plenty of help carrying the kayak aboard.

I hobbled into the ferry lounge looking terrible and feeling worse. I found a comfortable seat for the two-and-a-half-hour journey back across the lake to Muskegon. I hadn't slept in 36 hours and quickly fell fast asleep. I was awakened by a crewmember when we docked.

My wife was understandably still mad, but her face wore a "glad to see you again, you stupid idiot" smirk. The ordeal had left me peculiarly unaffected by the emotional storm of worry and anger I had caused at home. I focused only on getting to bed and sleeping off my haze of exhaustion. The next day, I tried to explain myself and to acknowledge the distress I had caused.

But the question of why I had attempted it continued to surface in my thoughts and conversations about the crossing. Reinhold Messner, arguably the world's greatest mountain climber, describes in one of his many books finding moments of complete self-sufficiency when climbing. For me, crossing Lake Michigan was never about the accomplishment but about creating a moment of self-sufficiency in the midst of challenging a formidable obstacle. It was about learning something about the human spirit and answering questions that I have about myself: How will I respond to fear and pain? Will I be able to make the decisions I need to make to survive? What are my limits?

On the lake, I found myself in a state of absolute concentration. I saw everything as logical. There was no danger. I felt truly alive; that has always been my reward for taking on risk. This time, though, I found my limit and slipped beyond self-sufficiency.

LESSONS LEARNED

Brian Day

Sea kayaking offers many opportunities for personal challenge and discovery. The commitment of a long crossing of open water, whether it's done to reach some far-off island or to push personal limits, is among the most challenging experiences a kayaker can have. Long crossings always come with a degree of exposure to hazards. While these hazards can be mitigated with proper planning and fitness, they cannot be completely eliminated. Small errors in planning, problems with equipment, and bad weather can easily compound into an emergency situation. For the solo paddler, the challenges and the stakes are even higher and the resources for dealing with emergencies more limited.

Weather and Planning Conspire

At first glance, the greatest obstacle to success in Paul's crossing was the weather. Headwinds slowed his progress significantly and led to his decision to abandon the attempt and use his EPIRB to signal the Coast Guard for assistance. It is important, however, to examine the choices that Paul made both during the planning process and once he was on the water that contributed to his failure to complete the crossing.

Research into prevailing wind conditions and adjusting his plan as needed could have minimized the chance that Paul would encounter a headwind on his attempt. The prevailing winds on Lake Michigan are from the west. Had Paul chosen to begin his crossing in Wisconsin rather than Michigan, he would have increased the likelihood that any wind that materialized would have pushed him along toward success rather than slow his progress.

Paul chose to paddle in September for the higher water temperatures, but regional wind speeds are higher then than they are in the summer months. To do the crossing from east to west despite the prevailing winds, Paul could have scheduled his attempt from June through August, when average wind speeds across the lakes are less than 5 knots. This would have minimized the chances for a headwind impacting his speed across the water but would have exposed him to colder water temperatures in the event of a swim.

Having seen the weather forecast, Paul knew that headwinds would materialize at some point during his paddle. He believed that he would be within sight of his destination by the time the wind picked up, but the weather turned sooner than expected. By choosing to launch rather than delay and wait for a more favorable weather window, he took a calculated risk. Unfortunately, he overestimated his paddling speed in calm conditions, and underestimated the effect that the wind would have on his progress.

Planning and Pace

Paul had predicted that he would be able to paddle at over 5 mph for the duration of the crossing, expecting to complete 82 statute miles of paddling in 16 hours. This estimate was based in part on his 70-mile training paddle on the Muskegon River two weeks before his attempt. It's likely that Paul overestimated his pace by failing to correctly deduct the speed of the river's current from his overall speed. Paul did his training run in 13 hours, for an average of almost 5.4 mph over the course of 70 miles—very fast. On that river run his GPS registered a speed of 6.5 mph while he was paddling, and Paul believed his estimated 5 mph average for the crossing was safe. Unfortunately, without knowing the exact speed of the river current, Paul had had to guess at his training pace. Had the river been moving at 2 to 2.5 mph, his actual speed would have been much lower than predicted. This turned out to be the case.

Small changes in speed over the water can result in large increases in the time that a passage requires. If Paul had maintained 4.5 mph and had paddled continuously with no rest, he would have needed slightly more than 18 hours to complete the crossing. If his pace had been closer to 4 mph, he would have taken 20 hours. However, it is difficult to paddle continuously over such a long distance. Breaks to eat, drink, and relieve your bladder all add time to a long crossing. Over the course of 20 hours, just 5 minutes spent each hour resting will result in an additional 1.5 hours on the water.

Speed on the water and duration of passage are important factors in how hard you choose to push yourself physically. Paddling for 16 hours is very different from 22. If Paul had expected his crossing to take closer to 22 hours at his maximum pace, he might have lowered his estimated speed to account for fatigue. He might also have chosen to paddle more slowly and take scheduled breaks to maintain his energy reserves, even though this would have increased the time required to complete the crossing. Finally, if he had used a more accurate estimate of his pace, Paul might have chosen to cancel his attempt rather than try to race the weather that he knew was on the way.

Paddling at Night and Alone

Night crossings involve special hazards, among which are seasickness and disorientation. On a crossing of this length, it is impossible to avoid night paddling, and paddling alone at night brings its own set of problems. The standard rule of thumb for sea kayaking is "No fewer than three on the sea." A strong group has more options for self-rescue, and more heads to evaluate hazards. Without another paddler to raft up with during breaks, a solo kayaker must expend energy just to maintain his or her balance. This can make rest stops anything but restful. A kayak bouncing up and down constantly challenges the paddler's sense of balance, and stopping to pull snacks out of the cockpit or consult a GPS unit can become a trial.

Even when night visibility is good, it is easier to succumb to motion sickness at night than it is during the day because the visual horizon is not as distinct. For most of the night Paul was able to maintain his balance, even while pumping out and eating, but by morning he was suffering from nausea and dehydration. It's likely that darkness contributed to his nausea, and the fact that he was alone made it impossible for him to raft up with another kayaker to get any truly recuperative breaks.

Equipment Problems

Paul encountered several problems on his attempt due to his use of unfamiliar equipment. He had rented a Necky Arluk III for the crossing because he wanted a kayak that would be faster than the Wilderness Systems Cape Horn 15 he had been training in. The Arluk was faster, but the increased speed came at the expense of stability. The rented boat turned out to be less stable than he was accustomed to, and the twitchiness of the hull was a challenge when he stopped for breaks. The Arluk also had less foot room. Paul had previously paddled in running shoes, but the smaller hull of the rented kayak made his shoes a snug fit. As a result, Paul was in considerable pain for much of the trip. His large shoes made it impossible to shift positions in the kayak to improve his comfort and blood flow, and the instability of the boat made it risky for him to try to remove the shoes. A final equipment problem was a leaky spray skirt that allowed water from breaking waves to enter the cockpit of the kayak. Paul found it necessary to stop from time to time to pump out his boat using a hand pump. He didn't have a sea anchor, so while he was pumping, the headwinds were pushing him backward toward his starting point. The distance he lost during these breaks had to be paddled twice.

Call for Help

By morning, the combination of headwind, dehydration, nausea, and fatigue from his intense exertion to get back into an area of cell phone coverage had taken its toll. Thirty miles off the Wisconsin shoreline, Paul's GPS showed a net speed of 2 mph. From that point, at that speed it would take him another 15 hours of continuous paddling to reach his destination. Paul realized that in his condition he would be unable to complete the crossing, and the time had come to call for help. His cell phone had been disabled by water damage. More effective waterproofing for the cell phone could have prevented this damage, but Paul might still have been out of range to use the phone to call for help.

Cell phones are designed to work within a network of land towers, and tower-to-tower connectivity is what gives cell phones their worldwide range. The effective range between a cell phone and the nearest tower varies from model to model but often does not extend beyond 25 miles even over flat terrain or water. Paul had checked the range of his cell phone in an informal way before using it on the trip. Walking across the top of a 200-foot-tall sand dune in Michigan, he had watched his phone switch from Eastern (Michigan) time to Central (Wisconsin) time. He assumed that the cell phone was connecting to a tower in Wisconsin, over 50 miles away across Lake Michigan. On the crossing, he discovered that the effective range of his phone was much shorter than he had expected. A second test after his crossing attempt confirmed that the cell phone's range was not adequate. Using his new phone on a recent cross-lake ferry ride, Paul was unable to get a signal beyond 21 miles from shore.

Considering their limited range and vulnerability to water damage, cell phones clearly are not an adequate means of summoning help when far from shore. That's especially true for kayakers, who are low in the water and usually have wet hands. A handheld submersible VHF radio would have been a more effective means of communication, particularly for contacting the Coast Guard and any other vessels in the area. Waterproof VHF radios are affordable and readily available. Both the Coast Guard and commercial vessels monitor VHF Channel 16, which is used for hailing and emergencies. As a Coast Guardsman, Paul was experienced in the use of VHF radios and in their protocol but chose not to carry one because he had been confident that his cell phone would be effective.

EPIRBs

Paul carried an EPIRB as his final resort for contacting help. He used an ACR Mini-B 300 ILS Personal EPIRB. ACR sold the Mini-B as part of an integrated person-overboard system for use by larger surface vessels. The transmitter's small size and affordable price made it attractive to kayakers at the time, but it was a poor choice when it came to bringing help in a hurry.

The Mini-B beacon was an older Class B device that transmitted only on 121.5 MHz, not a newer, more effective 406 MHz model. The signal from a Class B EPIRB could be picked up only by specially equipped surface vessels and some satellites, but there was so much interference and congestion on the channel that false alerts accounted for 99.8 percent of the signals received. It could take several satellite passes before an actual emergency was confirmed and a response mounted. The Coast Guard reported the average detection time for a Class B EPIRB at 4 to 6 hours, with times of up to 12 hours possible. The device had to be activated for this whole time period to give the best chance of detection. Because the system was unreliable, NOAA then planned to phase out satellite monitoring and use of Class B EPIRBs by February of 2009. After that time, satellites would receive signals only from 406 MHz beacons. [In 2013, NOAA's website states: "All Class A, B, and S EPIRBs operate on 121.5 or 243.0 MHz and have been phased out."]

When Paul was rescued, the captain of the *Joseph L. Block* told him that the *Block*'s radio was not receiving any signal from the beacon. The Coast Guard rescue boat crew activated and tested the device a second time. They confirmed that Paul's EPIRB was not transmitting. The EPIRB itself appeared to be operating correctly, showing a positive indicator light and emitting an audio tone. Paul returned the EPIRB for a refund shortly after he arrived back in Michigan. He did not contact the manufacturer to have the device tested.

Did Paul's EPIRB fail to transmit? Without a test by the manufacturer, it is difficult to know for certain. A representative of ACR indicated that no 121.5 MHz beacons had been activated in the Great Lakes region on the date of the incident. Does this mean that the beacon failed? Not necessarily. One of the reasons that Class B EPIRBs were phased out is that it took so long for their signal to be effectively picked up by satellites. It's possible that the device was not activated long enough for a satellite to move into position to receive its signal. If the *Joseph L. Block* had not crossed Paul's path, a satellite might have eventually received the signal from his beacon, but help would not have come for many hours.

Although the *Block*'s captain told Paul that his beacon wasn't working, it may be that the *Block* wasn't listening for the beacon's signal on the correct frequency. A Class B beacon like the one Paul carried could not be heard on a standard VHF radio. A specialized radio direction finder (RDF) was required to detect and home in on its signal. The *Block* wasn't equipped with this RDF equipment, so the captain of the vessel would have been unable to check to see if Paul's beacon was transmitting. Mariners on the Great Lakes had historically used a different kind of locator beacon, a Class C. The Class C beacon (phased out by February of 1999) transmitted on VHF Channels 15 and 16 with an audible tone. These beacons were then used extensively on the Great Lakes, and it is possible that the crew of the *Block* assumed that Paul's beacon was one of this type.

The Coast Guard incident report also indicates that the EPIRB failed to work. Paul had filed a float plan with the Coast Guard in Grand Haven and Milwaukee, and that float plan included the type of beacon that he was carrying. The 41-foot utility boat that Station Milwaukee dispatched to the *Block* was equipped with RDF equipment that could pick up a 121.5 MHz beacon, and crewmembers would have known which frequency to use if they'd had a copy of the float plan. The report does not offer any specific information about how the beacon was tested, so it's unclear whether the crew used the RDF equipment to check the device. Once they had Paul on board, their priority was not to check his beacon, of course, but rather to transport him to medical care.

Regardless of whether Paul's EPIRB was transmitting or not, the fact remains that he would have been much better served by a different beacon. Class B beacons were being phased out because they were ineffective. Paul was fortunate to have the *Block* pass by close enough for a crewmember to see him. If this hadn't happened, he might have had to wait for hours before any search efforts were initiated. In contrast, a newer, GPS-equipped 406 MHz personal locator beacon (PLB) would have pinpointed his location and conveyed his distress signal in minutes and could have brought help within an hour of being activated.

Skill Level and Fitness

Paul trained extensively for his crossing, and as a former world-class athlete he was in above-average physical condition. He had paddled in rough water and surf on Lake Michigan and was confident in his ability to stay upright in challenging conditions. However, his experience in closed-cockpit kayaks was limited. Most of his surf paddling was done in a sit-on-top kayak, and he estimated that he had only 40 hours of paddling experience in a decked boat. Paul had practiced wet exits and paddle-float self-rescues but had never needed to reenter his boat after an unintentional capsize. When he attempted to reenter his kayak in rough water in his exhausted condition, he was unable to do so.

With Paul's training on the Great Lakes as a cutter surface swimmer with the Coast Guard, he was familiar with conditions on Lake Michigan but had limited experience with long-distance kayak journeys. The seamanship skills he developed during his three years of service didn't automatically translate into solid sea kayaking tools.

Final Analysis

Paul's experience offers many lessons to paddlers who are considering a long crossing. Proper planning is critical to safety and success. You must know your personal limits and your average pace in a variety of conditions. You need to be familiar with your gear. It's safer to paddle in a strong group rather than to venture out alone. It's important to have plans in place to deal with emergencies, and backup plans if necessary. Don't rely on a single piece of equipment for navigation or to call or signal for help in an emergency.

Paul was fit, had experience on the water, and had professional emergency training, but it was a stroke of good luck that led to his timely rescue. His lack of kayak touring experience caused him to overestimate his pace, launch under questionable circumstances, and push himself to exhaustion—all mistakes that might have been avoided if he'd had more experience in the cockpit. There's no way to eliminate all risk on a long crossing. Indeed, the elements of risk and challenge might motivate a kayaker to paddle open water in the first place. But risk can be managed and minimized. More time and experience paddling long distances in a sea kayak could have increased Paul's chances of success by helping him to eliminate the risks that he didn't need to take.

18

The Cape of Storms
Solo Kayaker Lost While Rounding Brooks Peninsula

Doug Lloyd

Brooks Peninsula, the dominant promontory along Vancouver Island's rugged west coast, 10 miles long by 6 miles wide, protrudes farther into the open Pacific than any other westerly Canadian headland. It divides the region's paddling opportunities into the distinctly exposed weather of Brooks Bay to the north and the more paddler-friendly waters of Checleset Bay to the south and east. With unique, weather-intensifying topography, its steeply peaked, reef-fringed profile is constantly harassed by wind, weather, and tide. Mariners consider Brooks a formidable navigational hazard. Cape Cook, Brooks Peninsula's blunt outermost corner, was called the Cape of Storms by Captain James Cook, and sees only a small number of paddlers pass by each year. Most kayakers who round Brooks do so anxiously.

On July 13, 2006, at the peak of the prime paddling season, 60-year-old Brian David Grant left his home in Victoria, British Columbia, and drove to Gold River, the terminus of Highway 28. There, he loaded his kayak, a faded red-over-white Current Designs Pisces, along with his gear and provisions aboard the paddler-friendly MV *Uchuck III*, which steamed away at 7 A.M. on the 10-hour scheduled run to the small coastal village of Kyuquot, a word meaning "Land of Many Winds."

Kim Letson, a retired military logistician, kayaker, and co-owner of a guide service operating in the Kyuquot Sound basin at that time, met the athletic, tanned solo paddler aboard the *Uchuck III* during the coastal freighter's run.

Kim recalls the conversation Brian had with her and some of the other twenty passengers. Brian, like the other paddlers, was very down to earth; there was nothing bombastic or foolhardy about him as he related stories of his earlier paddling pursuits. His approach to kayaking was notably "low-tech," as she put it, but he was a "real kayaker" according to Kim, who had seen a lot of paddlers arrive in Kyuquot Sound with an abundance of up-to-date gear yet little experience. His demeanor was completely sensible. He was water wise and competent, with every indication of a quiet confidence and knowledgeable assurance about his paddling. Kim added that Brian exuded a youthfulness that belied his 60 years of age.

The *Uchuck III* was running late that day; seas were rough for most of the passage to Kyuquot. Brian had time to show Kim his charts and share some of his paddling plans. Kim pointed out some of the special places along the route to Jackobson Point, his primary goal as far as she could tell.

When the passengers of the *Uchuck III* disembarked at Kyuquot, Kim remembers Brian on the dock, surrounded by piles of dry bags. He was packing his kayak in preparation for his first night out in the Mission Group islands, possibly to the back of Spring Island. Kim offered to host Brian at her facility, but Brian said he preferred to be alone. She assumed he would have had enough experience and knowledge to be aware of the potential dangers the waters south of Brooks Peninsula could pose to small craft. Kim attempted to caution him about the exposed 8-mile crossing from the Mission Group to the Bunsby Islands. Brian told her he'd kayaked in the area before.

Kim doesn't recall Brian mentioning planning to paddle around to the north side of Brooks. The last she saw of him was the next day as he set out northwest across the still morning water for the Bunsby Islands.

Little else is known about Brian; later on, his partner shied away from the media (and chose not to be interviewed for this article). Poppy Hallam, a media contact for the Port Alice Royal Canadian Mounted Police (RCMP), said that Brian's family had described him as a very safety-conscious individual. Those in the paddling community in Victoria who knew of Brian were not well acquainted with him. He was said to be friendly but usually sought solitude rather than companionship. He kept his kayaking simple and relied on good judgment and common sense in lieu of high-tech electronics and all the latest gear.

The RCMP reported that Brian kept daily journal entries during his paddling trip, but his journal wasn't made available for this article. It isn't known if Brian was disciplined in logging weather and sea state to better predict local weather patterns during his two trips to Brooks Peninsula.

Much of Checleset Bay on the southeast side of Brooks Peninsula offers sheltered exploring if directly in the lee of Brooks or among the major island groups where little precautionary planning is needed. Many experienced paddlers returning to the area prefer, as Brian did, to head to the more secluded and sheltered beaches near Jackobson Point. From there, the experienced paddler can explore nearby caves, inlets, and lagoons, then take a side trip to the outer coast of Brooks or to Solander Island when conditions permit.

As a solo paddler, Brian had the freedom to kayak when and where he wished, but he had only himself to oversee the important logistics inherent in route setting, contingency planning, and keeping a good margin for error. Thorough planning is especially important for kayakers making forays involving open water, offshore islands, and inlets subject to tide and wind influence. Paddlers with base camps in this area typically keep a keen weather eye and note local changes in the weather to augment information gleaned from weather radio broadcasts. Kayakers familiar with paddling the west coast of Brooks Peninsula typically know and understand the signs of these changing weather patterns and their effects on local paddling conditions.

LAST CONTACT

On July 15th, Roy Massena of Spokane, Washington, and fellow paddlers, Scott and Andrew, crossed paths with Brian near the Acous Peninsula, 5 miles or so west of Big Bunsby Island, while he headed toward Jackobson Point on Brooks Peninsula. The trio of experienced paddlers was three weeks into a thirty-four-day circumnavigation of Vancouver Island and had rounded Brooks the previous day. The time and place of the chance meeting suggests that Brian spent July 14 in the vicinity of the Bunsby Islands. The weather had cleared after a light rain in the morning, promising a beautiful day. Brian told the three paddlers traveling south that he was headed out toward Brooks Peninsula and would be eventually returning south again to catch the *Uchuck III*.

Roy said he and his paddling partners had the impression that Brian was somewhat unprepared for the exposed paddling he was setting out to do, though it isn't clear if he announced his full intentions regarding rounding Brooks Peninsula to the north. Brian did not appear to the men to have any real immersion protection. A picture taken of Brian during the encounter shows a rigid North Water foam paddle float under the rear bungees of the Pisces. The three men wondered if Brian would be able to perform a successful self-rescue with the loosely secured float in a really cold, rough-water emergency.

Brian was wearing a yellow, lightweight anorak with wrist seals, a blue PFD, a brimmed white cotton hat, and sunglasses. He had a chart in a deck case, a deck-mounted compass, and paddling gloves on deck. He was using an ergonomic, lightweight carbon-fiber Werner paddle with small- to medium-size blades. His spray skirt appeared to be sound and secure. Brian finally left the three men astern and headed toward Jackobson Point.

On July 16, two paddlers from Calgary, Alberta, rounded Brooks Peninsula and landed at the end of the beach opposite from Brian's camp near Jackobson Point. Peter Rowland and his wife, Susan Adamson, had left Port Hardy on the northeast coast of Vancouver Island on July 2 for the village of Zeballos, another 60 miles of paddling southeast along the coast. Peter and Susan visited with Brian for the next two days. They were impressed with his attitude and level of experience, though they noted his lack of immersion apparel. During those two days, Peter formed the impression that Brian was a conservative paddler who would not put himself in a high-risk situation, at least no more than paddling solo on Vancouver Island's rugged west coast already suggested. They discussed both the unique aspects and perils of paddling alone.

During their initial exchange on the afternoon of the 16th, Brian wanted to know if the couple had a marine weather forecast for the next few days. Brian had a VHF radio, but the charge of its one rechargeable lithium battery was too low for routine regular use. Peter recollected that Brian had no way to recharge the battery and did not carry a backup radio or backup alkaline batteries and the adapter required to use them in the radio. This necessitated Brian saving battery power for the end of his trip in case he needed to contact the *Uchuck III*.

Peter and Susan each carried a radio and offered to lend one to Brian for the two days they were camped nearby so he could check his own marine forecast information. While Brian declined the offer, over the course of those two days he nevertheless continued to ask a number of times for daily Environment Canada marine weather forecast information.

On the evening of July 16, Peter and Susan used their charts to show Brian some of the technical issues and hazards important to note when rounding Brooks, including their impression of wind, wave, and swell considerations. Peter indicated on the chart some of the landing spots and emergency refuges he knew of.

Brian said he wanted to paddle from his current camp, round Cape Cook, and back as a day trip. While Peter and Susan didn't directly try to discourage the plan, they reminded Brian he needed a perfect weather forecast because he would be doubling his expo-

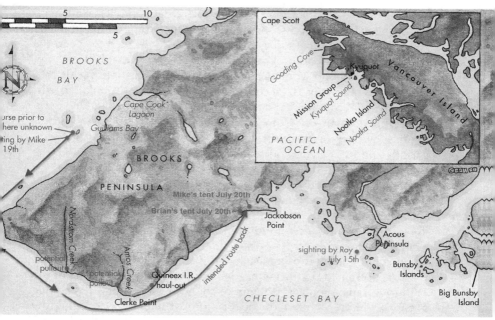

Christopher Hoyt

sure by going twice past Clerke Point and its reef, twice along the completely exposed shoreline of Brooks, and twice through the reefs between Solander Island and Cape Cook.

Peter recalls querying Brian about those proposed distances— a 26-mile round-trip to Cape Cook—because he first assumed Brian was hoping to only go as far as Cape Cook to take a look at Solander or perhaps poke his nose around Cape Cook for a few minutes. At the point where Brian started talking about paddling beyond Cook into Brooks Bay, Peter asked him why he didn't plan to carry his camping gear to avoid being forced to return back on the same day. Brian replied he was accustomed to paddling long days and preferred not to have to haul all his gear along.

The following morning Peter and Susan saw Brian returning from an early morning attempt around the peninsula. A brisk breeze and choppy seas off Clerke Point, it turned out, had sent him scurrying back to camp. Conditions that morning were similar to, if not better than, what the couple had experienced during their rounding of Brooks the previous day, confirming their impression that Brian was a conservative paddler who avoided questionable conditions. Peter said that Brian carried a robust, wood-laminate spare paddle but doesn't think it was on the aft deck of his kayak the day Brian made this first attempt.

The couple spent another evening with Brian, and he asked again about the weather forecast. Brian spoke of his disappointment in not getting to Cape Cook and beyond and said he'd decided to spend the 18th exploring Jackobson Point, an area just to the east of his camp, and in all likelihood would leave the next day for his return south.

On Tuesday, July 18, according to Environment Canada records, the 4 A.M. forecast for Vancouver Island North was changing again with winds northwest 15 to 20 knots easing to 10 to 15 that afternoon, then backing to southerly at 15 knots overnight, with cloudy periods and fog patches. Seas were forecast at near 1 meter with the outlook for moderate to strong southeast winds.

The 18th turned out sunny and calm. Peter and Susan packed up and headed out around noon to continue their trip, waving, and shouting good-bye to Brian as they passed near him while he was paddling back to camp after a morning excursion in the immediate area. They were not able to give Brian the revised forecast information, and it is not known if Brian listened to the forecast on his own radio.

It is presumed that Brian headed out early on the morning of the 19th for an unannounced attempt to round Brooks Peninsula. Setting out in his lightly loaded kayak, Brian most likely was running the outside of Brooks with a following breeze. He would have made good time without having to paddle against the more typical northwest headwind. The 4 A.M. weather forecast for the 19th was: "Winds light rising to southeast 15 to 20 knots this morning and to 25 to 30 knots in the north this evening. Cloudy. Chance of showers. Fog patches. Seas less than one meter building to 1 to 2 meters this evening. Outlook: Moderate southerlies becoming moderate northwest."

With the exception of fog, these would seem to be passable conditions for a push north. However, Environment Canada's *Marine Weather Hazards Manual*, second edition, details localized effects on weather created by the peninsula. Weather approaching from the southeast deflects around the peninsula, creating a band of intensified wind along the outer coast from Clerke Point to Cape Cook. Because of the shape of the outer coast of the peninsula, the effect created by a southeasterly is far worse than that created by a strong northwesterly. While the southeasterly winds may have offered some advantage when Brian set out that morning from the south side of the Brooks Peninsula, the forecast was unacceptably poor for his return to camp. As well, a strong southeast wind will flow over the top of Brooks and curl into a vertical eddy on the north side of the peninsula, often with enough force to create a strong onshore wind along Brooks Bay. The eddy can generate choppy seas and surf where you would expect to find a calm in the lee. It's never safe to assume easy landings on the peninsula.

The automated weather station on Solander Island 1.4 miles southwest of Cape Cook recorded a southeast wind rising steady to 15 knots at 6 A.M., then to 25 knots just after noon.

Mike Jackson of Victoria, British Columbia, and his companions, Pete and George, were camping at Cape Cook Lagoon. They were on the second day of a trip from Gooding Cove to Cougar Creek in Nootka Sound. On the 19th they had intended to take a run out to Cape Cook, but upon hearing the forecast for the strengthening southeasterly they decided to sleep in. There was a southerly wind spilling into Brooks Bay, with cool, gray, drizzly conditions casting a pall over the area. After a leisurely breakfast, the three experienced paddlers paddled farther along the peninsula to check out the route to Cape Cook. The wind continued growing stronger and, while settled on the beach at Guilliams Bay midafternoon, they saw a solo kayaker a half mile away in a red and white kayak heading south toward Cape Cook. Mike believes the kayaker they saw at about 3 P.M. was Brian Grant.

If it was Brian, he had about 31 miles to go to get back to his camp. He had already paddled at least that far—it's not known how far he paddled before turning around—suggesting he had made a predawn departure. In his lightly loaded boat, he would have been capable of covering a lot of territory relatively quickly.

Mike knew the kayaker was going to be faced with a stiff southeast gale, but he was too far away to hail the kayaker. Mike commented that he was standing on the beach in his dry suit shivering in the cooling air. Had Mike known the kayaker was heading to a camp on the south side of Brooks, he said he would have advised the kayaker about the forecast and gladly offered him food and shelter for a forced layover. Mike assumed the kayaker was paddling on a day trip to the cape from North Brooks, not from South Brooks, and would turn back upon encountering poor paddling conditions. As far as anyone knows, Mike and his companions were the last people to see Brian alive.

Meanwhile Peter and Susan, as well as some friends they had met up with, were holed up on South Brooks. Peter recalls strong winds building all day and having to rerig tarps that were flapping loose during the frequent rain squalls. He noted it was a particularly bad day for anyone to be on the water.

There are small, boulder-strewn pocket beaches just around the cape from the north, but most paddlers find landings in them an unacceptable risk in surf. Solander Island Station was reporting wind from the east-southeast at close to 30 knots at 6 P.M. At that time, Brian was probably very near Cape Cook and would need at least an hour and a half to get to Clerke Point. He would have been struggling in a stiff headwind and boisterous seas. The light rain had turned to showers. A small flood tide, made much stronger by current induced by the strong southeasterly wind, may still have been running against Brian's direction of travel. Waves would have been steepening over the reefs along shore.

The wind would have been pushing Brian not only backward but also offshore. The more intense conditions typically found around a major headland would have made Brian's passage truly difficult. By 8 P.M. the wind had increased to over 30 knots with gusts at 40 knots.

Mike and his fellow paddlers had listened to the evening forecast on the 19th and knew the winds were not expected to ease until midday on July 20, so they decided to sleep in. The 4 A.M. forecast for the 20th (had they listened to it) would have confirmed their decision to stay ashore: The gale warning continued, with winds southeast 20 to 30 knots and southeast gales 35 to 45 knots near the headlands. Winds were forecast to ease to southerly 15 to 25 knots that morning and then to light wind later in the afternoon. Winds would turn northwest at 15 to 20 knots by the evening. Fog patches were expected to dissipate in the morning, then redevelop overnight with an outlook of moderately increasing strong northwesterlies.

When Mike, Pete, and George got up, they broke camp and paddled to the staging beach they had scouted the day before. The 10:30 A.M. forecast confirmed the lighter winds they were looking for. They continued on for Cape Cook. At the cape, the winds became light just as predicted. Fog rolled in and dogged them until they were off Amos Creek. They gave the reef off Clerke Point a wide berth and soon had both capes behind them. With relief they paddled along the south shoreline of Brooks Peninsula to their next campsite.

At the end of the day they had covered nearly 21 miles. Mike later commented that the calm conditions they had patiently waited for had paid off.

Mike, Pete, and George set up their tents near Jackobson Point at the eastern end of a wide sandy beach. They saw a tent on the western end of the beach and noticed it appeared to be unoccupied. They guessed a local outfitter had set up the tent to reserve a prime spot on the beach. The following day they paddled to Spring Island and there asked outfitter Mike Simpson about the tent. Simpson indicated the tent wasn't one of his. Mike and his companions thought nothing more of the matter and continued their journey south. Brian's tent sat abandoned.

MISSED RENDEZVOUS

As a matter of routine, all kayakers traveling aboard the *Uchuck III* are asked to record in the reservation book their rough planned itinerary, with their names and the number in their party. If paddlers making arrangements for later pickup miss their rendezvous with the *Uchuck III*, the captain calls in a missing person report to the Canadian Coast Guard. Paddlers who have not scheduled a return trip are asked for a float plan with their destination end point and finish time and asked whether they left a float plan with a reliable person. If the boat's crew were contacted by police or search and rescue at a later date, this information would help narrow the search area. Paddlers who appear ill prepared may be denied passage aboard the *Uchuck III*.

On July 24, the *Uchuck III* arrived at the rendezvous point, the northernmost tip of Nootka Island, to pick up Brian. Brian wasn't there, so Captain Fred Mather called the Coast Guard. A missing kayaker notice was issued over the marine radio weather broadcast, naming the paddler. The following morning, the Regional Operations Centre in Victoria initiated a joint Canadian Coast Guard and Canadian Armed Forces search-and-rescue operation. The two closest available vessels began looking for Brian. A Cormorant helicopter and Buffalo aircraft from the 442 Squadron at Canadian Forces Base Comox assisted in the search effort.

Mike Jackson heard the missing kayaker alert on the weather radio. He, Pete, and George were at the time gale-bound on a small islet in the Nuchatlitz, north of Nootka Island. Hearing the alert at around 10 P.M. on the 24th, the three men connected their sighting of the solo kayaker and the unoccupied tent. Mike called on Channel 16 on his 5-watt handheld VHF. Radio repeater stations carried his transmission to the Tofino Coast Guard Station. He got an almost instant reply. Mike provided the Coast Guard with the location of the tent and the coordinates of the location where they had seen the kayaker they thought was Brian.

On the 25th, authorities inspected Brian's tent. All his camping gear remained there, including his sleeping gear. In Brian's journal, found there, the last entry, according to Poppy Hallam, was dated July 18th. There was no entry for the 19th to suggest Brian had managed to return to his campsite after rounding Brooks. The search for Brian continued until Friday, July 28, 2006. On July 31 the *Victoria Times Colonist* released Brian's name to the public along with details of the search. No sign of Brian or his kayaking gear reported thereafter, so his disappearance remained an open file with the RCMP.

LESSONS LEARNED

Many consider a reliable, waterproof, handheld VHF radio to be an absolute necessity on the remote, rugged shores of Vancouver Island's west coast. Not only can a VHF radio provide up-to-date weather forecasts and sea-state information, but it is also an invaluable tool for summoning help and reporting important marine activity. VHF is the standard means for calling other boaters. A VHF radio with a rechargeable battery can be easily charged with available solar rechargers. Backup battery trays using AA batteries are an option with most VHFs. A small weather radio also can be used for routine forecast information, extending the battery life of the VHF.

New devices are now available for summoning help, including GPS-equipped tracking devices like the SPOT Satellite Personal Tracker unit and small, reliable personal locator beacons (PLBs). (See the sidebar in Chapter 17.) Response times can vary once authorities are alerted of an emergency. The Canadian Coast Guard will summon any vessel in the area to assist. Around the end of each May through Labor Day weekend, a fast-response rigid inflatable boat (RIB) is stationed at Nootka Island. In addition, the 442nd Squadron of the Canadian Air Force provides search-and-rescue services for the British Columbia coast and strives for a 30-minute response time weekdays and a maximum 2-hour response time weeknights and weekends. Flying time to the scene from the air base in Comox, on the east coast of Vancouver Island, 130 miles southeast of the Brooks Peninsula, can add to the time between a distress call and rescue. Even with good communication equipment, paddlers must be prepared to wait a considerable length of time for help to arrive. Self-sufficiency is essential for paddlers visiting Brooks.

Brian was not wearing the kind of immersion apparel prudent for paddling in an area where water temperature is about 48°F. Along an exposed coastline that is subject to quickly changing weather and sea states, dressing for the water temperature is doubly important. A solo paddler lacks the relative safety provided by group travel and in rough water can face difficult and time-consuming reentries.

If Brian was able to clear Cape Cook, he may have tried to land along Brooks Peninsula's blunt nose either at Nordstrom Creek (a dubious option when the swell is from the southeast) or Amos Creek just before Clerke Point. Neither is an easy landing, and boulders and reef-fringed shoreline make navigation tricky in rough water and decreasing visibility.

If Brian had managed to reach Clerke Point, his options for rounding the point would not have been good. Swinging wide around the Clerke reef would have exposed him to the building gale and taken him into an area where boomers break heavily and unexpectedly. Alternatively, on a course closer to the point, Brian would have been in the midst of some extremely difficult paddling in smaller but constant breakers near shore. In either case, wind, waves, and reduced visibility would have turned Clerke Point into a vast minefield of boomers that would be difficult to distinguish from whitecaps.

With few exceptions, surf landings along the southeast side of Brooks Peninsula would have been difficult in a southeasterly gale. It is doubtful Brian made it that far. If he had, it is likely debris or some remains of his boat would have washed ashore. Bill Crawford and Rick Thomson of the Institute of Ocean Sciences in Sidney, British Columbia, indicated the strong northwesterly flow created by the storm off the blunt end of Brooks would normally wash flotsam out into deep ocean water. As this is where Brian likely came to grief, it is unlikely that any trace of him will ever be found.

While Brian had told Kim and Peter that he had paddled the Brooks region before, his boat-handling skills are unknown. Paddlers attempting the outer shores of Brooks Peninsula must have (and typically do have) a reliable roll and strong bracing capacity. They must be able to make significant headway into strong winds in the range of 20 knots for 2 hours or more. Just as importantly, their solo recovery skills must typically include a strong, device-free reentry and roll or cowboy rescue, along with some way of hands-free bailing. Cockpit fit and boat control are priorities. Deck gear must be well secured, normally kept to a minimum. A paddle tether and even a personal tether (a kayaker-to-kayak tether used only outside the surf zone) might be considered. Skill with surf and dumping breakers is a prerequisite for paddling the north and west coasts of Brooks. It isn't known if Brian left his spare paddle back at shore for his second attempt, as he did with his first, or if this was a factor in his demise.

Sound judgment and seamanship skills are especially important on the exposed coast of northern Vancouver Island. Waiting for a break in the weather is only prudent at all major headlands, especially those hazardous sections on the Brooks Peninsula. Having plenty of time built into the schedule to allow for changing conditions and waiting out storms improves the odds and helps kayakers avoid accidents.

In addition to the risks Brian took by paddling alone and without immersion wear, he set himself up for failure by deciding to make North Brooks a day trip. By leaving his camping gear behind, he presumed he'd be able to make a round-trip. In an area where changes in the weather can be sudden and can dramatically change the paddling conditions, paddlers need to be able to take the earliest opportunity to go ashore and to wait out foul weather. When under stress, as Brian must have been when conditions soured, perseveration—clinging to a task or goal that no longer makes good sense—can cloud decision making. Every mile that Brian put between himself and camp was a mile he may have felt driven to paddle back, even though his nearest refuge may have been farther away from camp. If he had been traveling with all of his camping gear, it's not likely he would have felt compelled to struggle into the brunt of the storm.

It is unknown if Brian had an up-to-date weather forecast the morning of the 19th. Peter did not recall specifically discussing weather patterns with Brian but felt that even without the forecast, a paddler of Brian's experience should have known the signs of poor weather approaching, including shifting winds rising to the southeast, rain, and building seas. Peter was even more puzzled that Brian held back on the 17th, and then again on the 18th, a nearly perfect day, but then headed out on a day when the weather was obviously taking a turn for the worse. With the pressure to be back at Nootka by the 24th, Peter wonders if Brian's ambition may have trumped common sense.

Brian may have thought the southeast wind would not build as severely as it did, or perhaps he thought it would moderate during the afternoon enough to get back around, underestimating his travel time. Either way, his planning appears to have been based upon a best-case scenario. The adage "Hope for the best, prepare for the worst" should have been heeded. Captain Fred Mather indicated it was his understanding this was Brian's third attempt to make it around to Brooks Bay from South Brooks. Having made good progress outbound from his camp, Brian may not have realized how careless he was becoming as he paddled north.

Most kayakers paddle around the Brooks Peninsula as a one-way trip. Paddlers planning a two-way trip should treat each passage as a separate trip, provisioning themselves for the possibility of having to wait out poor weather hampering a return trip. Idyllic conditions are rare here. Paddlers have reported conditions changing from pleasant to barely manageable within 30 minutes along the exposed portion of Brooks.

The *Pacific Coast Sailing Directions* from Fisheries and Oceans Canada calls the waters off Brooks the most dangerous on the British Columbia coast. Cape Cook can be a very rough place to be at the wrong time. Mike Jackson and his partners Pete and George had been exhausted by their 18-mile run around the capes in good weather. They could not imagine how Brian could have been successful returning to his camp with his progress thwarted by the adverse conditions he was heading into when they last saw him. Mike believes Brian would have made little progress from Cape Cook to Clerke Point and most likely capsized and perished not long after rounding Cape Cook.

By all accounts, Brian was an intelligent man, an experienced kayaker, and a strong paddler in excellent health. He was familiar with the general area. We may never know the exact circumstances of Brian's disappearance off Brooks Peninsula. It seems obvious, though, that his judgment was flawed this time out and that the consequences of his decision to paddle around the peninsula were fatal.

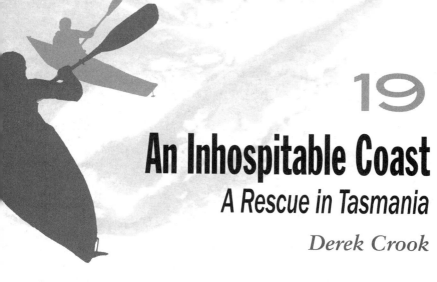

19

An Inhospitable Coast
A Rescue in Tasmania

Derek Crook

We all know the saying, "Haste makes waste." While on a recent solo kayak expedition around Tasmania, I found out the exact meaning of those three words the hard way.

While paddling around the eastern and northern coasts, I met many fishermen who had fished the west coast of Tasmania. They all had a story to tell about someone whose boat had gone down while fishing along that coast. They explained how the ocean swells travel from as far away as Africa before crashing on that coast, and there aren't very many places where you can hide from the sudden storms that plague the area. As one fisherman put it, "It's downright inhospitable."

On January 27 of 2008 I arrived at Conical Rocks on the west coast of Tasmania at noon. This was my third day paddling on the west coast, and I had experienced high winds in the early afternoon on each of those days, but this time was different. There were telltale clouds warning of an approaching storm.

As I pulled up to shore I was greeted by a man named Heath. He and his family and friends were spending the Australia Day weekend at some beachside cabins. Heath invited me to stay in one of the cabins and wait for better weather. The storm quickly brought heavy rainfall and high winds. After I was settled in, I was invited for a dinner of fresh-caught crayfish and abalone. Heath expressed his concern for my safety while paddling the southwest coast and gave me lots of advice on the weather patterns. In particular, he said to be wary of southwest winds that combined with the southwest swell and caused the waves to double or triple in size. He had seen waves cresting over the largest rocks on the reef nearby. That would put them at well over 50 feet high.

The next leg of my journey consisted of 35 miles of paddling to

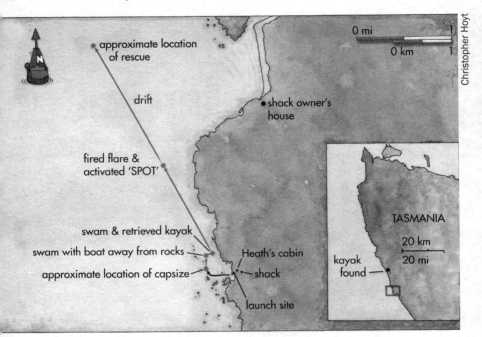

Christopher Hoyt

approximate location
of rescue

0 mi 1

0 km 1

drift

shack owner's
house

fired flare &
activated 'SPOT'

TASMANIA

20 km

20 mi

swam & retrieved kayak

swam with boat away from rocks

approximate location of capsize

Heath's cabin

shack

launch site

kayak
found

reach Macquarie Harbor from Conical Rocks, and there weren't any places in between where I could land safely in the event of a storm.

Before leaving the cabins for home, Heath gave me a weather update. It sounded like the conditions were going to be ideal: light southerly winds with a 1-meter swell. "It doesn't get much better than that in these waters," Heath said. He said that I could stay in the cabin as long as I liked. I just had to shut off the water and lock the place up before I left.

After spending two nights there waiting out the storm I was feeling well rested. At 6:30 A.M. on January 29th I stood beside my kayak and studied the weather and water conditions. I wanted to be sure the weather forecast was correct before setting out on what was going to be the most dangerous leg of my journey so far. The sky was gray and the wind was blowing southerly at about 10 knots. That was consistent with the forecast, but as I watched the waves crash on the rocks in the distance I had my doubts about launching. I was thinking about waiting another day and was about to start unpacking when I decided to paddle out to the reef to check out the conditions there.

The reef consists of large, tightly spaced rocks near the shore; one sticks up out of the water at least 50 feet. A quarter mile or so north and farther away from the shore, the rocks were smaller and farther apart. Some lay below the surface.

The water was flat and calm inside the reef near shore, but as I paddled north the water erupted into confused seas caused by reflecting waves from the rocky shoreline colliding with the incoming swell. It looked like a bit more of a challenge getting out through that than I liked, and I was having second thoughts about proceeding at that point. Once I was away from the end of the reef, I was free of the reflecting waves and things got a little smoother, as I anticipated they would. I gave the end of the reef a wide berth. I had a healthy respect for rogue waves and would always paddle the extra distance to be on the safe side.

When I turned around and started paddling south, I felt the full intensity of the wind and waves against me. It felt good to be finally on the water again, and after two days of rest I felt like I was ready to take on the challenge in spite of the headwinds. But I paddled for only about 15 minutes and quickly realized I was making little progress. I'd made that mistake in the past of pushing on against strong headwinds only to gain a mile or two in an hour. With a 35-mile paddle south to Macquarie Harbor, continuing on was totally out of the question.

I turned my kayak away from the reef to face the swell head-on before making the turn downwind. The waves seemed to be building by the minute, and I had to be very careful not to capsize while executing the turn. At this point I was becoming a little apprehensive about the sudden weather changes that can occur there. Paddling downwind was effortless compared to paddling upwind, and it took a fraction of the time to make it back to the end of the reef. I took up a position just beyond the end of the reef and with some difficulty turned the boat into the wind and waves. I paddled east toward a cliff, using it as a reference point, as I knew how close I had to come to it in order to make my way through the narrow opening between the reef and the shore. The waves were rolling under me at a fast clip, and it was difficult to focus on any one particular spot for very long. I began paddling south in the direction of the area that I had come out of, and then I came to a sudden stop when I saw a wave curling and crashing less than 100 feet in front of me. I sat there with a frozen stare waiting to see if that was just a rogue wave or not. It didn't take very long before another wave came crashing down in front of me. I thought for a moment that I was in the wrong place, so I checked my location again only to confirm that I was in the right place. I realized that the wave heights were substantially higher than when I launched, and now the waves were sweeping right over the rocks that comprised the reef and breaking in the center of the area out of which I had paddled. I wasn't going to be able to make it back along the same route. I felt a great sense of urgency, as the nearest safe take-out was Sandy Cape, almost

20 miles north. I quickly decided to paddle south along the outside of the breaking waves in search of a way back to the beach from which I had launched. I advanced slowly among the rocks while keeping an eye out for any that might be just below the surface, until I found myself positioned between a very large rock on my right and some smaller rocks on my left. The waves were now passing through this area and building rapidly in height and speed before breaking, and I realized I was putting myself at risk of being slammed onto a submerged rock if I advanced any farther.

I held my position and looked for some way out of this situation. The reef's distance from shore narrowed as I paddled south, and the rocks that comprised it were much larger and more tightly spaced. I began to formulate a plan that I thought was my only chance to make it in off the water, but I wasn't in the best position to attempt it yet. My plan was to advance along the reef as far as I could and find a place where I could escape through the rocks and into the lee of the reef. As I advanced, I realized that there was no turning back as the waves and rocks didn't afford the area I needed to complete a turn in the opposite direction. Rocks that were normally submerged suddenly appeared in front of me as the troughs passed over them. I'd never been in a situation as bad as this before, but I held my composure. Waves were rushing toward me at an unrelenting pace, and there was no use trying to find a pattern in them. I relied on my intuition and prayer. I advanced ever so slowly, constantly keeping an eye on the waves building to my right in case I had to make a mad dash and head right into them to avoid a wave breaking onto me. I couldn't paddle back or bail out now, and I was thinking that I had made a huge mistake in getting in too close. If a larger-than-normal wave came, I would be thrown onto the rocks. A few smaller waves passed under me, and that allowed me some time to focus on a possible escape route. I saw an opening between two rocks with room to pass through, and it was just a matter of outsprinting the oncoming waves to get to the shelter of the reef. A wave could break onto me at any time, so I glanced quickly over my shoulder and then at the place I had to be to be out of danger. I dug my paddle in and pulled with every ounce of my strength. I began to make some forward progress, but it wasn't anywhere near what I thought it should be, and as I looked back I saw a huge wave building. The water was receding faster than I could paddle forward against it, and I knew that the wave was going to overtake me. I lined myself up so that the bow pointed in line with the direction of the wave. The wave struck and I was soon standing almost vertically on it. My bow started to dig in as I slid down the face. I was in danger of pitchpoling onto my face, so I leaned all the way back, just enough to get the bow to rise slightly. I began to accelerate and for a split second I felt I was going to shoot out and outrun the break, but suddenly I was upside down and underwater while the boat was sucked away from me and my paddle was ripped from my grip. I was held under by a large mass of foam and water, and I tumbled underwater for quite some time. I surfaced unexpectedly and felt a huge sense of relief that I was still in one piece.

I looked around, saw my yellow dry bag a few yards away, and swam for it. In it were items that I could use to survive if I made it to shore, and it also offered flotation and a means to protect myself if I was tossed onto the rocks. While paddling toward it, I felt fortunate to find my paddle also. After I secured these items, I looked around and spotted my kayak upside down about 100 feet away and drifting toward the rocky shore where the waves would pound it to small pieces in no time. Swimming against the wind and current in the direction of the beach I had launched from would be impossible, so my best chance for survival was to recover my kayak. I swam as hard as I could to make it to the boat before it was swept onto the rocks. In what seemed like less than a minute I looked up and saw that I had closed the distance on the boat, which hadn't moved very far toward the rocks. The waves reflecting from the shore must have been holding it off the rocks. My optimism peaked as I gained distance rapidly. I swam holding onto my paddle in my right hand and

The bow of the author's broken kayak was found by campers on a beach over eight miles north of where he'd capsized. Derek Crook

with my dry bag tucked under my right arm. A few yards from the kayak, I swam into my video camera. I looped a finger around a strap on the housing. With all the gear I was hanging onto I could grab the kayak only with my left arm around the bow, which was nearest as it pointed away from the shore. I believed I could do a self-rescue, but my feelings of success ended quickly when I realized that only 50 feet separated me from the rocks.

When I reached the kayak, I had let go of my gear to free my hands to right it. I thought it would just take a few seconds to lift and rotate the bow, but both my attempts—the second using all my strength—failed. I had to lunge over the middle of the kayak, grab the cockpit coaming, and use my weight to roll it over. This worked on my first attempt. I saw that the rear hatch cover and neoprene inner cover were gone and my gear was floating out as the stern compartment filled with water. My paddle was drifting away, so I swam after it and grabbed it, my dry bag, and camera, and then swam quickly back to the kayak. I tossed the gear into the cockpit, and while holding onto my paddle I swam to the bow and grabbed the bow toggle and tried to tow the kayak away from the rocks. At first the kayak didn't move at all. I began taking long hard kicks, and after several steady pulls the boat started to move.

I soon had the boat positioned far enough away from the rocks that I could attempt a reentry. The stern of the kayak was half full of water, which caused the kayak to list, and with the bow sticking up out of the water, it was very unstable. I decided the best and quickest way to rescue myself was to lie on it as on a surfboard and paddle with my arms. After attempting this for a while and not making any forward progress, I tried using my paddle. That didn't work, so I tried sitting up and straddling the boat with my legs. The wind and current were against me, and I was slowly losing ground and being swept farther north and away from the only place I could land safely. I decided to toss the dry bag and try to sit in the cockpit and paddle, but I was only able to make a few strokes before I capsized. I tried several more times to sit in my kayak and paddle, but I couldn't stay upright for any more than a few strokes.

The kayak's stern eventually filled completely with water, and the bow pointed upright at a 45-degree angle. It was impossible to sit in the cockpit. I didn't know how long I'd been in the water since the first capsize, and it wasn't until I started feeling the effects of the cold water that I checked my watch. To my surprise it was 10 A.M., meaning that I had been in the water for about 3 hours. I felt a sense of hopelessness because I had exhausted myself attempting every possible self-rescue that I could think of, and now I faced the grim reality that I wasn't going to make it without assistance.

I knew that there were a few people living in some cabins along the coast near the Pieman River and thought I would fire a flare and see if I could get someone's attention. I had a pen flare ready in my lifejacket, and it was quick and easy to fire it off. I watched it soar straight up and was really impressed by it, so for some reason I decided to fire another one. While attempting to screw the second flare onto the firing pen, I dropped the flare into the water and lost it immediately. I knew I had a small bagful, but they were all missing, so I tossed the firing device into the water. I opened the day hatch and pulled out the SPOT messenger device I'd stored there. I quickly turned it on and watched the green light blink, indicating that the unit was powered on. Then I pressed the 911 button to signal for a rescue.

There was nothing else I could do but try and stay with the boat and hope rescue was on its way. The waves were getting larger, and I was feeling the effects of hypothermia. Hanging on was no easy task as waves rolled me off the kayak several times. My strength was diminishing quickly, and I had inhaled and swallowed a lot of seawater, which seemed to weaken me more. I didn't know how long I could survive before blacking out, and I knew I didn't have enough strength left to climb back onto the boat if I rolled off many more times. Fortunately, I found that if I lay over the cockpit with my arms stretched out in front of me and my legs spread outward in the water, I could balance myself and stay on the boat without using too much energy.

I felt a sensation of warmth come over me; a drowsy feeling tempted me to close my eyes and fall asleep. I'd had a previous experience with hypothermia and was aware of the symptoms. I knew that as the blood circulation to my brain diminished, I'd feel myself drifting into a deep sleep.

At some point in time I remember thinking that I wasn't going to make it, and saw myself as being "one with the seabed" as opposed to being "one with the boat." This image sparked an intense will to survive, and along with that I remembered a promise that I had made to my daughter, Natalia, a student in the Royal Winnipeg Ballet. I'd told her I would see her perform in Winnipeg when I got home from the trip. I repeated to myself, "I'm going to be there to see her," as I fought off the drowsiness.

Every now and then I glanced up into the sky to see if there was anything there, but looking up detracted from the concentration I needed to stay upright, and with my limited muscle control I needed to stay focused to keep myself on top of the boat.

Suddenly I heard the sound of a motor, and when I looked to my right I saw an aluminum boat with two people in it speeding toward me. At this point I had been hanging onto my half-sunk kayak for about an hour and a half from the time I pressed the 911 button on my SPOT messenger. I had so little strength and mobility left that it was all I could do to stay on the kayak. I don't remember how I was pulled aboard the skiff. Paul Lees, the driver of the boat, later told me he called out for me to get in the water and swim away from the kayak. Apparently I was reluctant to let it go. They had to come alongside the kayak, a tricky maneuver that put them at even more risk.

When they finally had me in the boat I said, "Thank you." Paul said, "Don't thank me yet, we have to make it back first!" I felt helpless lying on the cold bottom of the aluminum boat as we made our way back. The skiff slammed head-on into the oncoming waves. I prayed we wouldn't capsize, as I knew that I wouldn't be able to help myself if we did.

We made it back to shore, and I was transported by a vehicle a few miles to a cabin. (I have no memory of the ride.) Wrapped in warm clothing and lying by a fire, I started to warm up.

Sometime shortly after arriving at the cabin, the search-and-rescue (SAR) helicopter arrived, and the paramedics aboard attended to me. I was transported by the SAR helicopter to a hospital in Burnie, a small town on the northern coast. I was treated for hypothermia and saltwater inhalation and kept overnight for observation. I was really surprised when I looked up from my hospital bed and saw Heath and his daughter Carmen standing next to me. He had heard on the radio that I had been rescued and came to the hospital as soon as he could. He offered me some clothing and a place to stay and said he would be back to pick me up the next morning. He handed me his cell phone so I could call my wife, Shirley, and let her know that I was alive.

It was 11:30 P.M. in British Columbia when I called Shirley, and when she heard the phone ring, she told me later, she started shaking. Before the trip I had told her that I was so confident of my abilities to self-rescue that I would press the 911 button only if I had no hope at all for surviving on my own. She had seen the 911 message in the email notification from SPOT and feared the worst. When she picked up the phone and heard my voice, she cried and told me she thought I hadn't survived.

The local news media wanted to interview me for a story about the rescue. During the interview the reporter asked me what had given me the determination to survive. I told her about the promise I had made to my daughter.

Later that evening I was introduced to Dean Wotherspoon, who was in charge of SAR in the Tasmanian Police Department. I recited a list of the safety gear that I'd had with me. Although I'd lost almost everything, he took my word for it that I'd had all the required safety equipment.

Heath arrived with some much-needed clothing. I was soon at Heath's home. I called Shirley, and we made plans for her to wire some money to me. I called the airlines and changed my flight to the following week. I wanted to shake hands with and thank the guys who saved me, so I asked my friend Heath for a big favor. It's not an easy drive back to the "shack," as he calls it, but Heath didn't hesitate to arrange to take me back to Conical Rocks to help me search for my gear.

Conical Rocks was a 4-hour drive from Burnie. When we pulled up to the shack where Paul lived, he was clearing some land by the edge of the water. It was there that he first saw me with his binoculars as I drifted out beyond the breaking waves, heading northward. There was no hint of recognition of me in his eyes when we drove up, but when we were just meters away he did a double take. He later said that he never expected to see me again.

I learned a lot about Paul Lees, the man who saved my life. I wasn't surprised to learn that he had rescued two other people over the years. I decided to take it upon myself to see that he was officially recognized for his unselfish acts of heroism. Jade Shadbold, the other man in the skiff, wasn't around for me to thank.

Later on, during my conversation with Paul, the subject of my age came up, and I remarked that I was going to be 52 in April. Paul looked at me with a sideways glance and asked me, "What day in April?" I said, "April 17th." Paul replied, "That's my birthday too!"

Peter Wells, a camper whom I'd met while kayaking down the west coast found my digital camera, intact, on a beach eight and a half miles north of where I'd been rescued. When he looked at the pictures he knew it was mine as some of the images were of him and his family at the dinner he'd invited me to share. A little farther down the beach, at the mouth of the Interview River, Peter found the broken-off bow of my kayak (see photo earlier in this chapter) along with a few other pieces of my equipment. The Tasmanian police came along soon after that and he handed everything he'd found to them. The officers let Peter know that I was okay. While I was back at Conical Rocks I walked the shoreline hoping I might recover some of my gear. I found the dry bag with my wallet and identification documents. The police later met me there and returned both my camera and the kayak's broken bow.

LESSONS LEARNED

Although the SPOT device hadn't been directly responsible for my rescue, I'm sure it would have been, had I not been pulled from the sea first by Paul. In addition to that, if we had capsized in the aluminum boat, there would have been three people needing rescue, and help was on the way. I won't paddle without it because I know first-hand how conditions can change so rapidly, and one day your luck may run out. If you are planning a trip in a dangerous place, it is an affordable and accurate device for pinpointing your location. (See also the sidebar on PLBs in Chapter 17.)

If you're about to paddle waters that you are not familiar with, you need to find out what you're up against. There is no substitute for local knowledge from the people who live in the area you'll be paddling. During a trip, fishermen you may encounter can provide you with valuable firsthand information that you will never find while researching an area on the Internet or in books.

Kayaking is a sport in which survival equipment and skills are a must. Whether you're going on a leisurely paddle along the shore or planning a longer trip, you need to have your safety gear with you. But more importantly, you need to have it accessible and ready for use. As you become more confident in handling your boat, you will likely venture farther and seek challenges that will test your skills. Sea conditions can change rapidly, and you may suddenly find yourself in a situation as I did, where you are no match for the wind and waves. If you end up in the water, you have to be able to perform a wide variety of self-rescue techniques in adverse conditions. You also have to be able to call and signal for assistance.

In hindsight, my accident could have been prevented, and I know how. When I was standing on shore uncertain about the weather conditions, I should have stayed ashore and waited for the weather to improve. I had suspected that there was a chance that conditions weren't good, and as a solo paddler I should have erred on the side of safety and stayed ashore. When I realized I couldn't make it back to the launch site and there was nowhere else to land, I shouldn't have risked racing through waves toward shore. Going through the zone where the waves were breaking posed a high risk of capsize and poor chances for getting safely ashore. I should have either waited the storm out or signaled for help. It is easy to delay calling for help until the situation gets desperate. Taking stock of the situation early and calling for help before embarking on a risky course of action can be the best option.

After the capsize, when the hatch cover had come off and the stern was full of water, it was a mistake for me to make repeated efforts at self-rescue. If I had activated my SPOT device upon realizing my kayak was swamped and unseaworthy, I wouldn't have spent nearly as much time in the water exposed to the elements. While I survived several hours in the water, the cold severely depleted my energy and my ability to help myself. Being dressed for immersion would have extended the time that I had before hypothermia set in.

In addition, my safety gear should have been attached to me. If I hadn't reached my kayak before it landed on the rocks, I wouldn't have been able to activate the SPOT device and signal for search and rescue.

I had two flares in my PFD, but the rest were in my kayak and ultimately were lost. My first flare fired easily but it was very challenging to reload the pen while swimming in rough water. Signaling devices need to be easy to use while in the water bobbing around, hanging onto the boat and gear.

I should also have spent more time testing my kayak and preparing it for a capsize in breaking waves. The hatch lid and neoprene cover should have been secure enough to stay in place when the wave that capsized me broke over the deck.

Believing that rescue was on its way made it possible for me to fight the drowsiness and resignation brought on by hypothermia. I was determined not to succumb to the cold. What I learned most was never to give up hope.

Johnstone Strait Rescue
Rescuing a Stranger

Paul Thomas

I n September 2007, my wife, Cindy, and I, along with our friend,
Conrad, embarked on a weeklong kayaking trip along the northern
shore of Vancouver Island. We planned to explore Johnstone Strait
and the cluster of islands at its western end. We had been in the area
before and looked forward to another trip to what we think is one of
the most scenic kayaking areas in North America.

The three of us all had sea kayaking experience and varying degrees of training. Conrad, the most experienced, had been paddling
sea kayaks for over 40 years and had taken many wilderness kayaking trips of up to a month's duration. His rescue training included one
formal kayak rescue course, significant informal training, and regular
practice on the water. I had been paddling sea kayaks for 12 years and
had considerable experience with multiday trips. My formal training
included a couple of two-day sea kayaking courses that both featured
self-rescue and assisted-rescue training in the pool. I had also read
anything I could get my hands on related to kayak safety, including *Sea Kayaker* magazine articles and a variety of books. I'd found
Sea Kayaker's book of safety stories, *Deep Trouble*, to be especially
educational. Cindy had had comprehensive whitewater canoeing and
whitewater kayaking training and had taken a number of day trips
in sea kayaks.

At Johnstone Strait we were dressed for immersion because the
water temperature in the region was approximately 48°F. Each of us
wore polypropylene long underwear, a wetsuit, a fleece jacket, a rain
shell, and a PFD.

Our trip began at Telegraph Cove, a small Vancouver Island community at the western entrance to Johnstone Strait. The marine forecast was for southeast winds to build throughout the day, possibly to
gale force, but the calm water in the lee of Vancouver Island made the
paddling near the shore easy, so we headed east hugging the coast.

Cindy and I were paddling our Northwest Kayaks Seascape 2 double, and Conrad was in his Seda Viking single.

After a couple of hours of leisurely paddling, we stopped for lunch on the beach at Kaikash Creek, 6 miles from Telegraph Cove. As Cindy and I began to unpack our lunch, Conrad spotted what looked like a capsized kayak out in the channel, perhaps three quarters of a mile from shore. The upturned kayak was clearly visible through binoculars, but it was a miracle that Conrad had seen it without them. At first we wondered if someone was practicing self-rescues, but it didn't seem likely that a paddler would have chosen to do so in a busy shipping channel. The area is used by cruise ships, tugs, and a wide range of other commercial and recreational marine traffic.

The kayak remained capsized, so we scrambled back into our still fully loaded boats and sprinted toward the capsized kayak. As we neared it, we found a kayaker, Don, in the water, holding onto the stern of a kayak paddled by Curt. Don's kayak had drifted away and was being pursued by a third paddler, Dan, who was now well out of shouting distance.

We later learned from Don and Dan that the trio was on a multi-day trip from Telegraph Cove. They had set out in rented kayaks the day before and had camped on shore overnight. The next morning, they embarked on a day trip with empty boats. They did not have a VHF or weather radio and were unaware of the day's marine forecast. Don, an experienced canoeist but novice kayaker, had capsized in the choppy water beyond the island's lee. Waves were approximately 2 feet with winds of 15 to 20 mph. Don was unfamiliar with a wet exit and had been unable to release his spray skirt despite several attempts. He later recalled being underwater for "a long time." Eventually, Curt had somehow managed to help Don do a wet exit and make it to the surface before he ran out of air. (Tragically, Curt was later killed in a motorcycle accident, so his account of events is unknown.) Since none of the three paddlers had rescue training, Curt may have reached down in the water to pull Don to the surface between the two kayaks, then helped him free his spray skirt and exit the kayak. Alternatively, Curt might have managed to remove Don's skirt underwater.

Once he was on the surface, Don had "no idea" how to reenter his swamped kayak, so he held onto the stern of Curt's kayak and let his own boat slip away. Curt began to tow Don toward shore, and Dan paddled after the swamped and drifting kayak.

By the time we arrived, Don had been in the water for at least 15 minutes (the time between Conrad's sighting and our arrival on the scene). To our dismay, he was not wearing a wetsuit or a dry suit. (We couldn't see what he was wearing while he was in the water, but it turned out that he was clothed in shorts, a *(continued page 207)*

WHAT IF?

Christopher Cunningham

When we practice sea kayaking skills, our focus is usually on our paddling partners. It's natural to prepare for taking care of our own. Playing the "What if?" game is a popular way of preparing for the unexpected. What if you capsize and dislocate your shoulder trying to roll? What if someone in your group capsizes and doesn't roll up or wet-exit? As you and your partners become more proficient and knowledgeable as kayakers, you'll acquire a set of skills that will help you cope with almost every situation you're likely to encounter—at least when it comes to helping each other. If you spend enough time on the water, however, you may find someone else who needs help. That can open up an entirely different set of what-ifs.

In this chapter Paul Thomas recounts his experience of coming to the aid of a stranger. In Paul's practice of assisted rescues he'd never asked himself or been asked by his instructor: What if the person in the water weighs well over 250 pounds, has lost his kayak, and is weak due to cold? While the swimmer in this case had wet-exited his kayak, the prospect of rescuing him presented challenges that Paul and his group had never considered. While their training didn't provide them with specific tools and techniques for getting a big guy out of the water, the radio call they made to bring larger boats to the scene quite likely saved his life.

Rob Casey, a friend of mine, paddles a lot in the waters of Puget Sound near the *Sea Kayaker* office. There's a lot of boat traffic in the area. A ship canal here connects Seattle's extensive inland waters with the sound. The entrance to a 1,400-slip marina lies a few dozen yards to the north. At the far end of the marina is a busy launching ramp and, beyond that, one of Seattle's most popular beaches. Rob likes to surf the wakes of the ships that travel up and down the middle of the sound, and I see him out there at all hours of the day. He usually paddles solo, so he doesn't have paddling partners to take care of, but he's had no shortage of boaters to assist. In recent years he has rescued six or seven people, among them a fisherman who had capsized his outboard skiff and a shorts-and-T-shirt novice kayaker who had capsized in cold water in the midst of heavy powerboat traffic. Rob has also rescued two kiteboarders with their kites in the water (see Chapter 14). Kiteboarders are reluctant to abandon their expensive kites, and the tangle of kite lines is a rescuer's nightmare.

In this same area I've hauled a couple of capsized sailors out of the drink, towed a disabled powerboat, and escorted a cabin cruiser through the fog to the marina. A few miles to the north I watched a 50-foot commercial fishing boat run aground at full speed. Its prop was still turning hard when I beached my kayak nearby, climbed aboard, and found the crew of three in the wheelhouse all fast asleep. No lives hung in the balance, but I kept them from burning up their engine.

When you throw other boaters into the picture, the what-if game becomes infinitely more complex. Obviously you can't foresee every eventuality, but you can prepare and equip yourself, at least, to do something. As Paul Thomas discovered, making a VHF radio call to bring other boats to the scene can make a lifesaving difference.

Practicing what-if scenarios will make you more familiar with the possibilities and the limitations of your gear and skill. The practice also fosters the mental agility that is an essential part of any rescue. When someone is in distress you often have a sense of urgency, but that shouldn't put acting ahead of thinking. Assessing the situation is an essential first step. Make sure that it is safe to approach, and then decide what needs to be done. When one of your kayaking partners bails out, you may be able to respond quickly with a drill that you've practiced, but in situations where you encounter a what-if scenario, the first challenge is a mental one: thinking through the problem to an effective solution. That too gets better with practice.

T-shirt, and a hooded sweatshirt.) Don was coherent, was not shivering, and was able to clearly answer my questions: "Are you wearing a wetsuit or dry suit?" and "What is your name?" Curt was attempting to tow Don to shore, but Curt was visibly shaken and exhausted by his earlier efforts at freeing Don from his overturned kayak, so the two of them were making scant progress.

Realizing the gravity of the situation, I used my VHF handheld radio to try to call a commercial fishing boat about a mile east, heading away from us. Unfortunately, the boat was not monitoring Channel 16, the emergency frequency, even though monitoring Channel 16 is required of all commercial vessels. (I later learned from a tugboat captain that failing to monitor the emergency channel is a common occurrence.) I fired a flare with my Olin 12-gauge flare gun, but they did not see it, perhaps because it was behind them.

As there were no boats in sight and we didn't know when or even if help would arrive, I concluded that our best course of action would be to continue towing Don to shore, which seemed well within reach, and then warm him in a sleeping bag that we had aboard.

Before resuming the towing of Don toward shore, I sent out a Mayday call. It was picked up by the Coast Guard in Comox, 120 miles away, via their extensive antenna network. I gave a verbal description of our position and described the situation. The Coast Guard then broadcast an urgent request for assistance to all boats in the area, letting them know where we were and that we would be heading toward shore towing a paddler (Curt) and a person in the water (Don).

Conrad departed to help Dan get Don's capsized kayak to shore. This seemed completely logical at the time, and I don't think we even discussed it.

I connected my towrope to Curt's kayak, then Cindy and I began to paddle our double as hard as we could toward shore, as did Curt with what little energy he had left. It's an understatement to say that paddling a loaded double while towing another kayak that in turn is towing a swimmer is incredibly difficult and very slow; it felt as though we were tied to a tree. Periodically I yelled back to make sure Don was still coherent and holding onto Curt's boat. Each time he answered that he was still OK. My greatest fear was that he would let go because of exhaustion and hypothermia. If that happened, I had no idea what we would do next.

Meanwhile, Conrad and Dan caught Don's swamped, drifting kayak. Conrad pulled the bow onto his deck in order to dump the water, but the waves were so large that he feared capsizing and abandoned that effort. He connected his towrope to the capsized kayak and started for shore, although the opposing tide and the difficulty of towing a swamped boat made his progress extremely slow. Dan did not have a towline nor any experience with rescues, so he could not contribute to the effort.

After Cindy and I had been paddling for perhaps 15 minutes and were within a few hundred yards of the shore, a call came over the VHF from a park warden. She was on her way to the scene but could not see us in the moderate chop. I answered that I would fire a flare in 10 seconds, did so, then got back on the radio. I repeated the sequence a second time, and the warden then came straight to us in a 20-foot Zodiac. She assessed the situation and asked that we hold onto her boat while she tried to get Don out of the water. Don was quite heavy, and the cold water had rendered him completely inert, so the warden had a great deal of difficulty getting him over the transom of her boat. The large tubes of the Zodiac made it impossible for either Cindy or me to get out of our double and into the Zodiac to help. Don's helplessness was not surprising, since he had been in the water without thermal protection for at least 30 to 45 minutes. If not for his extra body fat, he would have been in very grave danger. (The warden later told us that earlier that summer, a kayaker without thermal protection drowned in the same area after being in the water for approximately 45 minutes.)

A large commercial whale-watch boat also appeared, seemingly out of nowhere. The crew had heard the Coast Guard announcement, headed for the area, and then spotted the flares I fired for the warden. As soon as the warden had Don in her Zodiac and wrapped in a blanket, she rushed off to the whale-watch boat, now only 50 yards away, and Don was hoisted aboard. The crew took him to the warm galley as another large Zodiac arrived with a Coast Guard medic crew. The medics stripped off Don's clothes, "all of them," he later recalled sheepishly, and worked at rewarming Don for about half an hour. Once they judged Don stable enough to transport, they took him back to Telegraph Cove, where he was transferred to a waiting ambulance and taken to a regional hospital about 10 miles distant for further warming and monitoring.

Don was released from the hospital late in the day, but he had no idea where he was, had no wallet or money (both were in his tent at the campsite), and did not know how to rejoin his friends. Eventually he managed to call his daughter, who faxed credit card information to a nearby hotel. Don spent the night there, then came back to Telegraph Cove by taxi the next morning and met his enormously relieved friends later that day.

LESSONS LEARNED

Being involved in a life-or-death incident made me take a close look at my actions, gear, and training. In hindsight I realized that while I did several things right, there are also several things that I should have done differently.

I made a grave mistake by continuing Curt's efforts to tow Don to shore. While the relatively short distance to shore provided an illusion of safety, moving him through the cold water only hastened his heat loss. We should have rafted two kayaks and attempted to pull Don out of the water and across the rafted boats, then towed the combination to shore or waited for help. Don's weight and our lack of practice rescuing swimmers may well have prevented such a rescue, but it certainly should have been our first line of defense. *(See Editor's note 1.)*

Though I had felt confident that my previous training made rescuing another kayaker well within my capabilities, I was not prepared to rescue a swimmer not in our group. My future training and practice will not just focus on self-rescue and helping other paddlers reenter their boats but will also include rescuing swimmers. Had the shore not been within reach or skilled medical personnel close by, failing to get Don out of the water promptly would probably have cost him his life.

Splitting up our group to save Don's swamped kayak was also an error. While abandoning a kayak may be a difficult choice to make, the first priority is to attend to the person in the water. Kayaks are replaceable, and in many cases lost kayaks are later recovered. Had Conrad remained on the scene with Don, we would have had three kayaks to work with. Again, we should have rafted up and done whatever we could to get Don out of the water and onto the decks of two rafted kayaks. The third kayak, most likely the double, could have towed the raft. If we had failed to get Don on deck, we could have at least partially supported him between two kayaks, reducing exposure and drag. While there were two of us in the double, a double isn't as versatile in rescues as two single kayaks. Our double may be quite stable, but two kayaks side by side would make a better base for rescues, and the two paddlers would be well positioned to work together. In a double, only one of the two paddlers could assist a swimmer.

In the future I'll also carry more flares. I had only three cartridges for my flare gun, and I used those quickly. Had we been on the water longer or more difficult to find, such as in fog, three flares could easily have gone unnoticed. I now think nine flares should be a minimum. I prefer the gun variety over the pencil-type aerial flares because the gun can be fired with one hand. Handheld flares with a long burn time would also have been helpful when the warden was approaching and called to ask us to help her locate us. They might also have attracted the attention of other boats that may have been in the area but not visible to us.

I should have attached my towrope to a deck cleat or around my cockpit coaming, rather than using the integral waist belt for towing. My back took the force of two paddlers working at maximum effort and could easily have been injured if the tow had been prolonged. To be sure, a tandem pulling a kayak and a swimmer is a worst-case scenario for a waist-mounted towing system, and the option to switch to a deck-mounted towing point would have been very useful.

Though I always carry a sleeping bag, even on day trips, it can only be effectively put to use ashore and can safely treat only mild cases of hypothermia *(see Editor's note 2)*. In the future I'll also carry a space blanket or survival bag that can be deployed and put to use

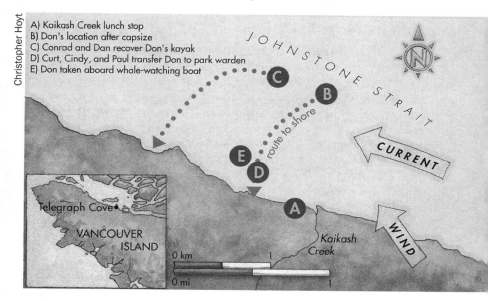

Christopher Hoyt

A) Kaikash Creek lunch stop
B) Don's location after capsize
C) Conrad and Dan recover Don's kayak
D) Curt, Cindy, and Paul transfer Don to park warden
E) Don taken aboard whale-watching boat

JOHNSTONE STRAIT

CURRENT

WIND

route to shore

Telegraph Cove

VANCOUVER ISLAND

Kaikash Creek

0 km   1
0 mi   1

while afloat. A survival bag or blanket in our readily accessible emergency equipment would have reduced Don's heat loss if we'd pulled him out of the water.

I feel that making the VHF Mayday call at the outset was the right thing to do. Even if we had been able to get Don ashore, the treatment we could have provided would not have been a good substitute for professional medical attention. In Don's case minutes mattered, and we were very fortunate to have prompt assistance from a team of trained medics.

It is worth noting that the outfitter who rented kayaks to Don, Curt, and Dan made what appear to be a number of errors in judgment. First, the outfitter allowed the three paddlers to venture out in notoriously cold waters wearing only street clothes. Second, according to Don, the outfitter provided no rescue or reentry training whatsoever, either by video or by live demonstration; nor were they informed about what sort of safety gear their rented boats contained, where it was, or how to use it. Third, the outfitter did not alert them to the weather forecast or the effect of local winds and currents *(see Editor's note 3)*.

Outfitters have a responsibility for contributing to the safety of those renting boats. Had Don, Dan, and Curt been better informed, they might not have been so cavalier about paddling across Johnstone Strait and might have avoided putting Don's life in jeopardy. I'm glad that Cindy, Conrad, and I were able to come to his assistance.

Sea Kayaker's *More Deep Trouble*

Editor's Notes

1. In stressful situations, perseveration—the tendency to continue with a counterproductive or ineffective course of action—is common. In this case, two efforts, towing Don and recovering his kayak, were already in progress. While both could be reasonable in other circumstances (most notably in warmer water), in this case they were not. The quickest thing to do is to join in an ongoing effort, but the most effective thing to do is to assess the situation and change the course of action, if necessary, to remedy the most critical concerns.

2. Having someone get into a sleeping bag with a hypothermic victim has long been regarded a field treatment for hypothermia. In mild cases it can be helpful, but in more severe cases, warming the skin, particularly of the limbs, can pose a risk to the heart. Hypothermia victims should also be treated very gently and, if at all posible, kept horizontal.

3. Paddling in a lee is dangerous for the uninitiated. The calm water alongshore lures paddlers to venture away from the land, but as they leave the protection of the lee, the force of the wind and the size of the waves can increase quickly and dramatically, making a retreat to safety difficult if not impossible.

21

A Rocky Rescue
A Deceptively Gentle Swell Puts a Bay Area Kayaker in a Tight Spot

Gregg Berman and Ciaran Eustace

Gregg speaking

I enjoy kayaking among the rocks outside San Francisco's Golden Gate, so I was happy to see a post from Bill Vonnegut about paddling north from Rodeo Beach. When I heard there might be a lot of paddlers from our club, Bay Area Sea Kayakers (BASK), for this outing, I was delighted at the chance to kayak with some folks I might not have seen in a while. I even thought the large group might afford the opportunity for a little rescue practice. Ultimately there were about twenty-two people on this trip. Another smaller contingent of four to six BASK kayakers started shortly after our group.

We paddled off the beach into 3- to 4-foot waves. Most of the waves we encountered after leaving the shore were much smaller. On this relatively benign day we headed north up the coast, much closer to the rocks than is typically possible for the area. With this sort of club trip it is not likely, nor necessarily even desirable, for everyone to stay in one large pod, so it wasn't long before we were in groups of about four to six people.

We stopped to play in the passages into caves and through arches, and we rode waves through slots between rocks or over them. Groups split apart, swapped members, and merged into new groups. That there was not a single paddler that day who lacked the skills or experience for these conditions made this an easy affair. There were capsizes with and without wet exits, as well as a few simple rescues throughout the day, but we were all having a great time.

Ciaran speaking

It was a nice day with very little wind and maybe 2-foot swells. Usually they're bigger than this. Shortly into the paddle, Tony Johnson and I negotiated a small pour-over (place where the water flows over a rock) at the same time. I tried to make a hard left turn to avoid Tony. I went over and rolled back up again. No big deal. I hit the pour-over a few more times, and I have to say, I was having fun. Then I got hung up on a rock and went over again. With my bow stuck on a rock, I blew my first two roll attempts. As I was setting up for a bombproof roll, I saw someone's bow next to my boat, so I did a bow rescue instead. Conditions seemed very calm, and my guard was probably down a bit. I paddled back outside and someone asked, "How many times have you been over already?" I answered, "Two," then thought to myself that this was going to be a long day—possibly a 14-mile paddle—and I should probably dial it down a bit.

Gregg speaking

Because of my penchant for play and exploring, I usually find myself taking up the rear in the group on any rock-garden trip. As I rounded one bend, a large arch came into view. A large group of people were floating a bit outside the arch. It seemed as if they were just casually chatting, but then I heard someone say something about someone getting flushed from "there." I didn't know where "there" was, but then I saw Ciaran abruptly appear, flushed from a cleft in the rock. He was out of his boat and hanging onto a toggle. Just as suddenly as he appeared, Ciaran and his boat were sucked back into the crevice. Several of us started shouting at Ciaran to just let go of his boat and swim out, but I couldn't tell whether he could hear anyone.

Ciaran speaking

To the right of a big arch that some kayakers were playing in was a small slot. I had been observing the slot for a short time when I saw someone do a little pour-over inside the slot and come out at the front of the arch. I watched a little longer and decided I was going to go for it. So much for my decision to dial it down.

I went into the slot on the next surge but wasn't fast enough and landed on top of the pour-over. No big deal, I figured; I would just wait for the next wave to carry me through to the front of the arch. The next wave came in, but instead of washing me through to the front of the arch it sucked me back into the rear of the slot. I had completely failed to anticipate this. I went into combat mode. There was a lot of whitewater around me as I went over. I rolled back up, tried to paddle forward in the slot, but it was only 3 to 4 feet wide.

The next surge came in and pushed me back even farther and rolled me upside down again. I thought bailing out was not an option and would make things very difficult. It was too narrow to roll, but I managed to push off the bottom to right myself. I headed for the exit only to be hit again by the incoming surge and sent back again to the rear of the slot. I think I went over again and managed to right myself by climbing up the side wall. There was no room to roll. At that point I was feeling this was becoming a bad situation and attempted to rush for the exit again. The next surge sent me flying backward again. My boat got stuck sideways between the two walls, and I was sucked out of the cockpit. I hadn't been unintentionally out of my boat in about 3 years and thought, "This isn't going to be good." The water pulled me down and beneath what seemed to be an underwater ledge. I was held there for what felt like a long time. When the surge subsided, I made for the exit again, grabbing my boat along the way and trying to swim with it and the paddle. I guess this was instinct: "Never lose your boat or your paddle."

After the surge came in and out a couple more times, I could no longer hold onto my boat, so I let it go. The boat was pushed back and forth, crashing into me a bunch of times, so I held onto it again. I even thought, "If I hold onto the boat, I might get washed out to the exit with it." At one point I tried to climb on top of the boat, but that didn't help any. I was held under the ledge for about 20 seconds at a time and was drinking a lot of water.

Gregg speaking

Though the outside swell didn't rise above 3 to 4 feet, its effect was amplified in the tight confines of the slot, causing the water to slosh in all directions at once, creating standing waves in a clapotis effect. Given the way the water was sucking in and out of there, creating lots of strong currents and whirls and alternately exposing the mussel-encrusted rocks and pounding them with whitewater, it seemed debatable as to whether another boat in there would make the situation better or worse.

Jeff, a Class V whitewater boater, paddled his whitewater boat into the melee and attempted to rescue Ciaran. He left me with the bag end of his towrope, but I very quickly had to let go because it was not long enough and my holding onto it prevented Jeff from paddling in. Even with a slack rescue line, Jeff went in. By this time Ciaran, despite wearing his PFD, was repeatedly disappearing beneath the waves. He would be gone only for a few seconds, but those seconds seemed to stretch out when he did not immediately pop to the surface.

Ciaran speaking

After about 10 minutes in the slot I was feeling fatigued. Jeff Hastings came in with his small blue riverboat and tried to extract me. We both got bashed around back and forth in the surge. Jeff rolled at least once, but no matter what I did, I couldn't seem to hold onto his boat. Jeff is a very strong kayaker, and at first I really thought he was going to drag me out of there. He also inspired me to keep fighting. He told me to let my boat go, which I think I did, but I was concerned about it hitting me again. I felt like a pin in a bowling alley.

Someone threw in a throw rope. I grabbed it and started to take up the slack. After I pulled in about 50 feet, I realized there was no tension on the other end, so I let it go. The next surge wrapped the rope around my body and legs, which I managed to brush off. I ended up in the back of the slot again, under the ledge.

Gregg speaking

Jeff reached underwater a few times to pull Ciaran to the surface. Unfortunately, Jeff was getting banged around pretty hard as well and went over a few times, but he always managed to roll up. Once when the area was sucked partially dry by the incoming swell, I saw Jeff's boat wedged upside down between two rocks inside the crevice. It's a testament to his skill that he didn't end up out of his boat himself. Still, despite all Jeff's efforts, Ciaran didn't have the strength to hold on when Jeff attempted to extricate him. And the longer Jeff's boat was being tossed around in there, the greater the chances of injury to Ciaran and the chances of Jeff becoming a victim himself. Ultimately, Jeff was forced to abandon his efforts in the slot.

At some point during all of this, Ciaran's boat finally washed out, and Bill and others grabbed it and took it out of the way. I could see Ciaran's expression clearly during one of the times he came to the surface. The look on his face was grim at best.

Ciaran speaking

Jeff, my boat, and the rope were gone. I felt myself being sucked under the rock and let go a bunch of times. I certainly got my money's worth out of my helmet. It was a pity it did not cover all of me. I felt like I was in a giant toilet lined with rocks being flushed every 10 to 15 seconds. I had no energy left and could not fight anymore. I felt I had done fifteen rounds with Mike Tyson and was set up for another fifteen. I realize now that after all that struggling, I was not getting close to the exit at all. First I was angry, and then I was accepting of my fate. I was quite sure I would die. I told myself that my wife and kids would be OK and tried to picture them. It came to a point that I thought I could go under the rock only one, maybe two, more times and that would be it. I had swallowed a lot of water but still had not inhaled any. For a fleeting moment, I considered inhaling water to bring the inevitable end on more quickly. Then I pushed this idea out of my mind. I only hoped it wouldn't take too long and not hurt too much.

Gregg speaking

I was desperate to try another tactic and thought about climbing onto the rock outcropping close to the arch. I paddled to the side of the arch, figuring the currents would be easier to deal with there, and scouted the options. I hadn't yet committed to that decision, however, and went back to check on Ciaran's progress. Tony, a very experienced sea kayaker, had the same idea about climbing onto the rock, but he had committed to a course of action. He told me he was going to jump out of his boat and clamber onto the rock and asked if I would take care of his kayak. I agreed and suggested we do it on the arch side of the rock I had just scouted. Full of adrenaline, Tony was already heading in that direction. He and I paddled to the north side of the rock outcropping. Once there, Tony quickly exited his boat and swam to the rock. I held his boat and tossed him my rescue belt. By this time Jeff had arrived near us, probably also thinking of jumping on the rock. As I was already exiting my boat, Jeff instead helped organize folks to take care of the kayaks after I'd released them to swim to the rock.

When I arrived at the rock, I set my paddle as high up on the rock as I could without it being in the way of the precarious available footing. At some point, I have no clue when, my paddle was washed away by the waves repeatedly washing over the rock. By this point, Tony had thrown a line into the slot. Fortunately it landed right over Ciaran's shoulder. He was now wedged toward the back of the crevice, and while still splashed by the waves, he was no longer in the water and being battered about.

Ciaran speaking

After about 20 minutes, I heard Tony's voice and then saw him standing on a rock above and to the left of me, about 20 feet away. I was in a daze at this point. My arms and legs no longer worked. To be honest, I found him a little annoying. I figured these were my last moments, and I wanted to be in peace. He was disrupting this. Tony is a great friend and kayaker and consistently manages to inspire me; he seems always to say the right thing at the right time. I remember him saying, "Be strong, Ciaran." It is something he says a lot. He kept saying, "Grab the rope, grab the rope." I made one last attempt, figuring he was not going to go away, so I may as well make an effort.

Gregg speaking

At this point Ciaran had been in the water probably about 15 minutes. He was hypothermic and physically exhausted from his struggles, had swallowed lots of water, had been beaten by the rocks and his own boat, and was now suffering a post-adrenaline-rush crash. There was no way for him to climb out from his perch, and neither was jumping back into the water an option.

Tony had to very forcefully yell at him to "Stay strong!" while giving him directions for what to do with the rope. Despite the wave noise, Tony heard the click of the carabiner around the rope; he gave the word and Ciaran jumped back into the water. During brief moments the surge pulled him toward us, allowing us to reel in the rope. But it seemed most of the time we were tugging for all we were worth to keep him from being pulled back into the crevice. The opposing forces of the fast-moving water rushing like a river in the crevice, and Tony and I struggling against it, caused Ciaran to slide just beneath the surface as the water rushed over him. Seeing that made us more determined to hold on, and we eventually worked him alongside the rock we stood on.

Ciaran speaking

It took everything I had to wrap the rope around myself and click the carabiner onto it. The rope tightened around me as Tony pulled me out toward the exit. He tried to pull me up. Then I noticed Gregg Berman standing behind him, also holding the rope. I saw the next surge coming down and tried to hold onto the rocks. I don't know if I was any help. We all nearly ended up in the slot. They pulled me farther and farther toward the exit and then up onto the rocks. Gregg reached out and said, "Take my hand," which I did. At this point I actually thought for the first time that I might make it. I was completely exhausted.

Gregg speaking

We were at least 10 feet above Ciaran, and the rock was too steep to even consider attempting to haul him up its face. From my position I was able to back up to a lower but more wave-washed portion of the rock while maintaining my hold on the rope. Once I was set, we timed it and Tony let go of the rope and I pulled Ciaran, now in a much weaker part of the current, the last few feet to the rock. As he got there, I yelled for him to take my hand and initially got no response despite the fact he was looking right at me. I yelled again, and he slowly reached out his hand. It was a struggle for Tony and me to haul him onto the rock. Initially he just lay there facedown trying to recover. I was now more afraid that he was going to be washed off the rock, and no matter which direction the water might take him, it would not have been good. I barked like a drill sergeant that no matter how tired he was, he had to move his butt higher up the rock. While Ciaran attempted to crawl, we hauled him higher onto the rock just before the surge washed over the spot where he had just been lying.

Ciaran speaking

Tony and Gregg held on to me, asked me questions, and tried to get some life back into me. I told Tony, "I have to rest. I can't move anything." I had never felt so helpless. I guessed this was what being paralyzed feels like. At least once a wave almost washed us off the rock, so we moved up higher.

Gregg speaking

As we turned Ciaran over, I noticed how dark purple his face had become. He was conscious and talking, even if totally spent. I quickly checked him over, and he eventually was able to sit up. Ciaran had fought beyond what we might typically be capable of and was completely exhausted. I wanted to get some calories in him before he crashed further. I always keep a few strips of fruit leather or energy bars in my PFD. Initially Ciaran could not eat, though he ultimately managed to slowly get some of the food down his gullet.

Gregg and Tony get Ciaran clear of the slot. Bill Vonnegut

Other members of our group were rafting kayaks so Ciaran could be hauled away from the rocks to a landing site. Ciaran was lucid and had some energy coming back, so he, Tony, and I decided that if we could get his boat on the rocks and get him in it, that would be the best solution. His boat was brought to us, and Tony and I held it in place while Ciaran climbed in and took up his spare paddle. When the swell rose again and the group in the water was ready, we pushed and Ciaran easily slid down the steep rock to the kayakers waiting below to catch him.

Ciaran speaking

Tony and Gregg pulled the boat up onto the rocks, and I managed to climb back in. They snapped on my spray skirt, assembled my spare paddle, and launched me down the rocks into the water. I managed a little brace and stayed upright. It took all I had to stay upright.

Gregg speaking

Tony and I then moved to the farthest seaward portion of the rock to prepare to reenter our boats. It wasn't until someone offered me my paddle that I even realized it had been gone. I jumped in the water and paddle-swam to my boat, and Tony swam to his. At this point Elizabeth and a few others were rafted up with Ciaran and supporting him. We all agreed to do a rafted tow, with another paddler holding on to Ciaran to support him while we headed back to Rodeo Beach. I clipped on and started a tow. Anders quickly offered to help with an in-line tow and attached to my bow. Tony clipped to Ciaran's boat as well, so now we had both an in-line and a husky tow on the same boat.

After we'd covered about half the distance back to Rodeo Beach, Ciaran regained enough strength to balance himself without being rafted with a supporting paddler. With just a single boat in tow, the work was much easier. He still had a kayaker paddling on either side of him, though, just in case. By this point he was much more communicative and doing much better. We all even joked about the new cliff feature we would name in his honor: "Ciaran's Crack." We decided to paddle to the southern part of the beach. It was farther from our cars but had much smaller surf. As we neared the beach, Bill paddled in first to assist with the landing. Before crossing the surf zone, we disengaged our tows for the paddle in. Ciaran said that he had lost his contact lenses and could barely see. I jokingly promised him I'd go back and look for them. We didn't want to risk any more calamity with a collision in the surf, so with Bill on the beach to catch Ciaran, I escorted him the last couple hundred feet through the surf zone. We timed it well and had an uneventful landing.

We all headed up to the cars, and as we were getting Ciaran changed into dry clothes, Lynnette, Tony's wife, appeared. She had been hiking on the bluffs overlooking the coast. When she saw the contingent with Tony's boat moving "too slowly" back to the beach only a short while after launching, she knew something was amiss and came to meet us. There had been talk of getting Ciaran to a hospital. Jeff had been worried about the risk of secondary drowning, a condition in which your lungs fill with your own body fluids up to 72 hours after a near drowning as they try to clear themselves of any contaminants. There had also been talk of someone driving him home. At this point, however, his breathing was doing great. Despite the large amounts of water he surely swallowed, it seemed little had entered his lungs, as not once did I notice him cough from the time we pulled him onto the rocks till we got him safely back to the put-in.

With his strength returning, warm clothes, plenty of food, a public place with lots of resources, and Lyn and Anders to stay with him, we decided to just let him rest and recover before determining whether he was safe to return home on his own. The rest of us headed back to the water to reconvene with the rest of the group. Anders stayed there quite a while, and Lynnette talked with Ciaran for at least 3 hours in the parking lot to help him sort out his experience.

GREGG'S LESSONS LEARNED

I had heard of BASK long before and joined shortly before moving to California. BASK provides ample opportunity for a whole host of training sessions, most of which are free or only of minimal cost to members and are run by other members. The club also promotes classes conducted by professional instructors. Each summer we select about a dozen lucky participants to take part in our annual month-long skills clinic. You would be hard pressed to find a more thorough mental and physical course on paddling. On this particular outing, being in a club like BASK gave the group an advantage. Most of the participants were either graduates or instructors of the BASK skills clinic. Most had organized or participated in club skills and rescue practice sessions. And we all had the benefit of the online forum on a wide range of topics, with lots of lively discussion on all aspects of paddling.

Ciaran commented that he had already had a few problems that day and should have dialed things down a bit. That's a judgment call only he could have made.

The people on the water I respect the most, regardless of skill level, are not those who blindly rush into everything they see or try to impress or keep up with or be cajoled by their friends. The people who most impress me are the ones who have the personal strength to say, "You know, I think I'm going to pass on that," or "I'm just not feeling it today." That is not to say you shouldn't push yourself or be complacent, but rather you should push yourself only when you feel it appropriate. On some days it may be appropriate and on others not. I look for that attitude in those I paddle with and try to cultivate that sensitivity in myself.

Tony, Bill, and I had no indication that something was amiss when we approached the scene where Ciaran was in trouble. Perhaps everyone was just too involved in what was going on and didn't expect the situation to continue as long as it did. It should be common practice to blow a whistle, raise a paddle, or in some way alert others to an emergency situation. If things are resolved for the best, then great, no harm done, but if they are not, then more resources become available when more folks are aware of something going on.

After we delivered Ciaran to the beach, most of us resumed paddling. Later in the day I helped rescue someone else I saw come out of a boat. Calling it a rescue seems ridiculous compared to the earlier events, and I did not blow a whistle before going in. I should have, however, in case it turned out to be more involved. At another time near the end of the day, I also capsized in the rocks, and while I rolled up and got out fairly quickly, would it have been prudent for those who witnessed it to alert others until I was not only upright but free of the rocks? A simple whistle blow to alert others just to be on the lookout would likely never hurt. And if an incident continues, being more vehement in your signaling to actually draw others near then becomes imperative.

Some of the group members later asked me about the decision to call or not call the Coast Guard. Anders had wondered whether he should push the alert on his satellite messenger. Deciding when to use distress signals is a worthwhile debate. This situation had continued to drag on in a manner that nobody expected, but then, the worst is never expected. When should a call be made, and how do you decide? Should it have been done in this case?

When I spoke with the Coast Guard following the rescue of Ciaran, they said to call any time you suspect trouble. They recommended calling early. They further stated that calling on VHF Channel 16, instead of by cell phone, had the advantage of reaching not only the Coast Guard but also other boat traffic in the area. A commercial or recreational vessel nearby could potentially respond even before the Coast Guard arrived on scene. In our situation, a fishing boat had been within close sight. They might have been able to get Ciaran to safety without our having to put him back in a kayak to leave the area. Instead, they remained unaware of our plight.

I always carry food in my PFD in case of hypothermia, fatigue, or even just getting cranky from lack of food. For Ciaran I wished I'd had something other than a very chewy fruit leather. In a truly weakened state such as Ciaran's, or for a diabetic reaction, it simply takes too much energy to chew and swallow that food. In the future I will carry a tube of glucose paste or cake frosting in a PFD pocket. These tubes are small, and the paste need not be swallowed (though it can be) because it is absorbed through oral membranes. Thus it is less likely to induce vomiting, is more quickly absorbed into the bloodstream, and is a readily available source of energy.

A warm beverage is great and can be helpful psychologically as well as physically. Be careful, however; if it is too hot, dilute it with a cooler liquid to avoid the risk of burning the recipient.

I was happy to have my paddle for the swim to and from the rock. I often practice swimming with a paddle just for fun. It comes in handy when wearing full kayak gear, and for short distances it dramatically improves your swimming speed and power when done right.

Although the rescue knife I carry on my PFD is used mostly for spreading peanut butter or cutting foam for outfitting, it's great to have when it's really needed. If something had gone wrong while pulling Ciaran in, for example, it would have been invaluable. I keep it on my left shoulder for easy grabbing with my right hand. I have used it many times to cut sea birds free from fishing line. A knife that won't be corroded by saltwater is best for the marine environment.

It is important to be aware of the possibility of secondary drowning. If someone gets too much water in the lungs, the lungs may fill with fluid from within the body later, requiring medical treatment even if the person seems to be fine. This is true in both salt and fresh water. Of course, the importance of being certified in first aid or wilderness first aid along with CPR can't be overstated. While Ciaran managed to avoid inhaling any water, at least two of us in the group knew to look for signs of secondary drowning before we determined he was safe to go home.

Regardless of how long you've been paddling or what your skill level is, taking advantage of additional training is always worthwhile. After more than 17 years of paddling and teaching, I know that the more experience I get, the more I realize I have to learn. Every change in your gear or routine merits more practice. Something as simple as a new whistle on your PFD can throw a whole new wrinkle in your T-rescue if it gets caught on your deck lines as you try to climb out of the water.

You never know what an emergency will require of you. Anything you can add to your bag of tricks to help you assess situations and solutions just might make a very big difference. Practice every-thing and practice often. Tony and I have both paddled extensively and participated in numerous training sessions, including practicing self-rescues and swimming to and from rocks with a boat in tow. Jeff's attempts to perform a rescue by kayak, while valiant, did not work. Had Tony and I remained in our boats, there would have been little else we could have done for Ciaran. I believe it was our training that prompted both of us to come to the conclusions we did, inde-pendently, and made it possible for us to swim to the rocks to gain a position where we could help with Ciaran's rescue. Tony's decision to dump his boat and climb on the rock may have saved Ciaran's life.

CIARAN'S LESSONS LEARNED

Three weeks after the accident, I went paddling again for the first time. We did the same trip and made it all the way to Stinson Beach this time. The waves were much bigger than last time, and we all stayed outside for the most part. The slot beside the arch looked a lot different.

I have been paddling for about five years now and consider my-self a reasonably good kayaker. It still bothers me that I did not see the danger in that slot. It did not look like a big deal at the time—nothing I hadn't done before. I hope I recognize a situation like this in the future. I can't say for sure that I will, however, and this does bother me. But I don't want to start second-guessing everything I do. I hope I will get my "mojo" back soon. I love kayaking and want to keep going out for as long as I can still get my dry top on by myself.

I truly believe that if Tony had not dumped his boat and climbed up on the rocks, I wouldn't be here now. And I don't think I would have responded to anyone else's voice when I believed I was in my last moments.

I can't thank everyone enough who helped in my rescue. Because Tony, Gregg, and Jeff took action, my 11-year-old daughter and my 8-year-old son don't have to say, "Yeah, we miss our dad. He died in a kayak accident."

Acknowledgments

Thanks to Tony Johnson, Jeff Hastings, and Elizabeth Rowell for helping piece together the events. After this incident, Glenn Nunez set up a rescue practice and Q & A session with the local Coast Guard station. Finally, thanks to all of the Bay Area Sea Kayakers for pro-viding critical training, support, and feedback when events like this happen.

22

Rescue in Alaska
A Rising Wind Overpowers
Two Visiting Kayakers

Gadi Goldfarb

THE DECISION TO GO

I had been thinking about paddling in Alaska for a long time. Many kayakers I know have paddled there, most of them in organized groups, and almost all of them in Prince William Sound. My friend and fellow kayaker, Albert, instantly accepted the idea of paddling in Alaska but proposed a different Alaskan destination, the Kenai Fjords.

We both were committed kayakers. I'd been kayaking for six years year-round, along the Mediterranean coasts of Tel Aviv and Herzlia. I had made a few kayak trips in Greece, visited Wales during summer and winter for the intense BCU Five Star training, and joined the three-man Ireland expedition, paddling 400 miles clockwise from Dublin to Galway. I felt quite comfortable in tidal races and in surf zone and have a good roll.

Albert had been paddling for four years. He had never taken serious advanced kayak training; he could roll but his roll was weak. He had done a couple of kayak trips in Greece and paddled for two weeks in Alaska with a strong group, both in Prince William Sound and in the open sea.

Our plan was to explore the Kenai Fjords launching in Seward, rounding the Kenai Peninsula and taking out after roughly 300 miles at Homer.

FIRST EIGHT DAYS

On the bus from Anchorage to Seward, our driver updated us on the weather situation: "We've had a very dry summer this year [2009],

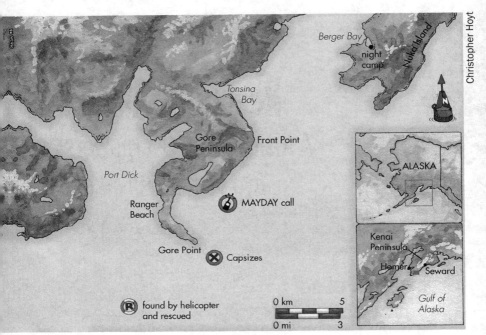

very unusual, but now, at last, we're getting the first real rain." We could see the dark clouds from the bus window. At Seward it was already raining heavily, and we were informed that the wind outside Resurrection Bay was southeast at 45 knots. Alan, the local kayaker who helped us with the kayaks, commented on that: "You wouldn't believe what beautiful weather we've had all this summer, but we always knew that when the storm would come, it would come big." We decided that even in this weather we could start our trip if we kept to the sheltered water inside the fjords and bays. We left on the next day, planning to stay in Resurrection Bay until the conditions improved.

We were paddling rented NDK Explorers, the same model that both of us own and paddle at home. Both of us carried NOAA nautical charts of the area on our kayak decks. We each had a compass mounted on the foredeck. Albert carried a simple waterproof Magellan GPS in his day hatch. He carried a backup Garmin GPS packed below deck. I had an ICOM waterproof marine radio, kept in a waterproof bag that was attached to my deck. I also had a McMurdo PLB (personal locator beacon) with GPS in a pocket on the back of my PFD. In a dry bag deep in my day hatch, I had two aerial flash rockets.

While on the water we both wore dry suits with one layer of fleece and a hat. Each of us used a paddle leash and had a spare paddle on deck.

The constant rain stayed with us for the next eight days, usually accompanied by wind and fog. We continued our trip, cautiously passing from one fjord to another, always having escape plans ready and often using them. On one occasion we had high and rising choppy seas and strong wind just before the narrow McArthur passage, but we found shelter safely in Chance Cove, which was one of a few escape places that we prepared for that day. On another occasion we were surprised by the enormous strength of the tidal race at the entrance of the Northwestern Fjord; it was clearly impassable, so we camped on the western side of the upper Harris Bay. It was the only place that day without big surf and suitable for landing. We didn't have a day without a new challenge.

By July 29 we had covered 155 nautical miles and more than half of the distance to Homer. On that day we camped at Berger Bay on Nuka Island. It was a beautiful gravel beach with a place for the tent and a natural place for our kitchen. We had a fresh salmon that I caught, and it was our first camp almost without rain. What else does a kayaker need?

THE PLAN FOR THE DAY

We knew that Gore Point is often a difficult place. It has high cliffs, unpredictable currents, and rocks all around. But Gore Point was not our main concern. We worried more about the day following our rounding of the point. On that day we would have to leave very early to catch the flood. It was the only way to continue west from Gore Peninsula and cover the long distance to reach the first landing spot. To set ourselves up properly for the following day, our objective was to pass Gore Point as quickly as possible and camp at the first place that presented itself. We knew of one potential campsite, Ranger Beach, located on the west side of the base of the Gore Peninsula. It is a sandy beach, and the landing should not be a problem with the usual southwest winds. Ranger Beach was located 15 miles from our camping site on Nuka Island. At that point in the trip we were in good shape and could easily paddle at 4 knots, so we figured the entire way with the favorable wind and current would take less than 5 hours. That was the good news. The bad news was that the last 11 miles, everything south of Tonsina Bay, offered absolutely no place to land. It is all high cliffs, and we knew very well from the previous days that even in a moderate swell we would do well to stay at least a mile away from land. We hardly had any rain that evening, and our weather forecast, for a change, was not bad. The last forecast that we got by satellite phone text message from our weather support man in Israel was for wind ESE at Beaufort Force 3 to 5, with waves at

1 to 2 meters coming from the south-southwest. The VHF reception was very bad at our campsite, but what we were able to make out seemed to be a forecast that was no different from our satellite phone forecast. Before we retreated to our tent that night, we watched the northern lights on the horizon. We felt encouraged by our prospects for the following day.

THE GORE POINT DAY

We left our camp on Nuka Island at 1 P.M. The sea was very quiet, and there was almost no wind. It was foggy but not too bad; visibility was about 2 miles. We decided to paddle in the same manner as we had on the previous days, keeping within sight of land. It made navigation easy, and we could quickly determine our location based on the shoreline shape and the mountain relief. We headed west and then southwest toward Tonsina Bay. Very soon after we left, we started to feel some wind, north-northeast at Force 3 to 4. This direction was unusual and not as forecast. The wind was, however, ideal for us, and I had nothing to complain about having it help push us along. In about an hour we saw Tonsina Bay on our right side. Our speed was very good, the weather was great, and we continued south to Front Point.

On our way to Front Point the wind changed to northeast but still was at Beaufort Force 4. There were only occasional whitecaps. The only thing that worried us was that the fog was becoming worse. We could still see the land from about 1 mile away, but it was behind a barely transparent screen of fog. We worried that our view of the land might disappear within minutes. But the sea conditions were not bad at all at Front Point, and we continued to Gore Bight.

The 3 miles from Front Point to Gore Bight took about an hour, and within that span of time everything changed. The wind grew stronger with frightening persistence. In an hour the wind had changed from a friendly Force 4 to a challenging Force 7. The direction of the wind changed as well from northeast to east.

At 3:30 P.M. we were two miles northeast of Gore Point in a rapidly strengthening wind and in waves reaching 8 feet and coming from all directions. We still could see some shape of the land to the north, but the fog obscured any hint of Gore Peninsula. (The log kept by the captain aboard the nearby fishing vessel *Vigilant* noted: "15:30 . . . Gore Point, Winds 45 miles per hour, Seas 10 Feet.")

I had to brace constantly just to stay upright. Albert was much less experienced in a sea like this, and I knew his situation had to be much worse. We were pushed by the wind toward the most intimidating place on the whole Kenai Peninsula. The locals considered it the best location to find interesting debris that has been driven ashore by wind and waves.

It was absolutely clear to me that we were in serious trouble. I called out to Albert, "I think we should call for help." He quickly agreed.

We brought our kayaks alongside one another. Albert held my cockpit with both hands while I took the VHF radio from my deck and attached it by the wrist strap to the clips in my PFD's right pocket. Then I switched the VHF on, set it to Channel 16, and pressed the transmit button.

"Mayday, Mayday, Mayday. We are two kayakers two miles northeast of Gore Point. We are still in the kayaks but cannot paddle and we are drifting in the strong wind."

I had very little hope that anyone would receive our message because we hadn't seen any other boats since we left Aialik Bay five days earlier. We hadn't seen anyone on shore either. To my surprise, the call was answered. The blowing wind and the fact that English is not one of my native languages didn't help. I could understand only part of what came across the radio. I heard: "This is . . . Star . . . specify your position." I didn't know who had responded to my call. I replied "Please wait."

In the strong wind and high waves Albert and I concentrated on keeping the kayaks rafted together. I put the VHF into my pocket, then held Albert's cockpit while he retrieved the GPS from his day hatch. We couldn't make any mistakes now. He switched the GPS on and held my cockpit as the coordinates appeared on the GPS screen. I took the VHF out and relayed our coordinates using numbers as well as the words "degrees, minutes, seconds, north, west." (It was explained to me later that I should have used only digits, since everything else only made the reception more difficult.) The VHF came back: ". . . sending the boat . . . will come in one hour and fifteen minutes. It is a big black boat; you will see it." I was not so sure that we would see it in the fog. The hour we would have to wait seemed like a very long time—too long a time.

I looked at Albert and said, "Let's activate the PLB."

Albert took the PLB out of the pocket on the back of my PFD, and opened the safety. "The lights are on," he said.

We were so focused on operating our electronics that we didn't look around even though we knew we were drifting. Suddenly Albert glanced up and said, "Gadi, look!"

I looked and saw the landscape looming over the fog. The land wasn't the coast we'd been seeing to the north. It was to the west. It was the Gore Peninsula. We were drifting very fast in a very bad direction. There was very little chance we would survive being washed ashore on the peninsula. The only solution was to paddle away very fast. We needed to move about a mile south to avoid getting washed ashore.

I called on the VHF: "This is the two kayaks; we will try to paddle south and get around Gore Point."

We started to paddle again, bearing east-southeast to make sure our real progress was to the south. Our effort was mostly against the wind now, and it helped our stability to have the waves coming over the bow. But the farther south we moved, the worse the sea conditions became. It wasn't surprising. The sea around the end of a headland is always the worst.

It was hard to say how much time passed, but at some point we had the Gore Peninsula behind us. Now, without the danger of being thrown on the rocks, we could try to get to the peninsula's west side where we would probably be protected from the strong wind and waves. We continued to paddle west, but the sea was the worst we had met that day. The 11-foot waves coming from the south-southeast were constantly breaking in the strong east wind. One cresting wave hit me from the left and turned me over. The water wasn't as cold as I expected. I noticed it wasn't as salty to my tongue as the Mediterranean and felt like I was turned over in a river. My roll is quite reliable, but when I was nearly upright, another blow turned me over once again. I made a much more aggressive attempt and came up expressing my feelings in my native Russian language. I realized that if the waves could capsize me, they could do the same to Albert, and he probably wouldn't be able to recover by rolling. Albert was on my left, and I reduced the distance between us to about 30 feet. A few minutes later a wave crashed violently on both of us. I did a high brace and survived.

Then I looked to my left after the wave passed and saw the white bottom of Albert's kayak. Albert had bailed out and was holding onto a deck line. The strong wind made it difficult to maneuver alongside him, but I eventually reached his kayak. I didn't dare try to empty the kayak, so I just made the rescue and got Albert back into a cockpit full of water. We had a hand pump on my deck, and I hoped we could use it to empty his cockpit. We rafted up and started to pump. We had only partial success. We got some water out, but the process was very slow, and we had to protect the cockpit from the waves.

I asked Albert if he thought we should try to paddle toward land. He said that he preferred to stay rafted together and wait for rescue. That was quite understandable. The water remaining in his cockpit made his kayak less stable. The wave that had capsized Albert had washed away his hat and glasses, despite the fact that both had been tethered. Albert's glasses are a very strong *(continued page 235)*

U.S. COAST GUARD REPORT

U.S. Coast Guard Petty Officer 1st Class Sara Francis

A jagged, rocky coastline stretched out under gray skies and seas. The wind howled at more than 25 mph, hurling rain against the exposed faces of the two figures being tossed about. Not another soul in sight for miles as the figures looked south toward their destination, Homer, about 100 miles away.

Gadi Goldfarb and Albert Kachesky had traveled about 100 miles in the eight days they been paddling. Caught in a storm, tired, alone, beset by 20-foot swells, they made a call for help. The distress call was heard by the crew of the fishing vessel Inlet Sunrise and relayed to the Coast Guard Command Center in Anchorage.

The flight crew wriggled into two layers of long underwear, dry suits, and life vests. Helmets in hand, they headed for their helicopter aircraft. About 30 minutes after the call came in, the blades were turning and the rescue crew was en route.

While the aircraft was in flight, the crews of the fishing vessels *Vigilant* and *Northern Mariner* passed to (continued next page)

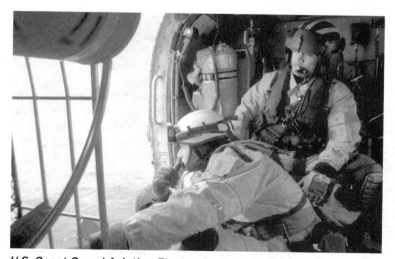

U.S. Coast Guard Aviation Electronics Technician 2nd Class Tito Sabangan (right) and Aviation Survival Technician 1st Class Chuck Ferrante (left), crewmen aboard an MH-60 Jayhawk helicopter from Air Station Kodiak, scan the Gulf of Alaska for two kayakers in distress. U.S. Coast Guard photos/Petty Officer 1st Class Sara Francis

Search and Rescue controllers at Sector Anchorage that they were within about a mile of the kayakers' relayed position and would assist. The Inlet Sunrise continued to help with communications but was engaged in fishing and couldn't break away.

With rescuers on three platforms closing in, Kachesky and Goldfarb huddled together in their kayaks. They activated their 406 emergency position-indicating radio beacon (EPIRB) to help rescuers locate them. The location of a transmitting 406 beacon can be determined within approximately 3 miles by the first satellite pass and to within 1 mile after three satellite passes. The 406 EPIRB uses the Cospas-Sarsat system of polar orbiting satellites with worldwide coverage. About a half hour elapses between satellite passes. The EPIRB/PLB the men were using was not GPS enabled, so location coordinates were not transmitted. Instead, the helicopter crew vectored in on their exact position using the VHF radio signals.

As the helicopter drew closer, its crew began to hear the kayaker's transmissions over the radio. The rescue swimmer, Aviation Survival Technician 1st Class Charles Ferrante, had just transferred from Air Station Cape Cod, Massachusetts. This was his second duty day, and he'd been in Kodiak only for three weeks. Ferrante was on the radio working with Kachesky and Goldfarb to try to establish their location.

"They had an ICOM handheld radio, which is how the pilots located them," said Ferrante. "It basically saved them since we could not DF [direction find] on their 406 EPIRB, which seemed a little dated, but the radio is the same radio we use as helicopter rescue swimmers."

Avionics Electrical Technician 2nd Class Tito Sabangan, the flight mechanic in the third year of his tour in Kodiak, scanned the horizon for a flash of color that might be the two men. The helicopter arrived in the area at 4:18 p.m., about a half hour after departing Kodiak.

The crew tried to use the radio signal to search for the men. "Sir, please give me a long count, 10 . . . 9 . . . 8 . . ." said Ferrante. Goldfarb responded. He repeated the count several more times.

"Locating the kayakers was a bit of a challenge due to the low visibility, the search pattern's close proximity to land (which made maneuvering a little restrictive), a lot of radio traffic from the good Samaritans [the fishing vessels Vigilant and Northern Mariner], and a language barrier with the kayakers that made communications hard," said Sabangan.

The rescue crew used Goldfarb's VHF radio transmissions to vector in on the kayakers. After a half hour on scene, a red and yellow dot—the two rafted kayakers—came into view. The crew of the fishing vessel *Vigilant* arrived right on their heels.

Ferrante donned his fins, hood, and snorkel and prepared to drop into the water. The helicopter came into a low hover about 40 feet above the water, several hundred yards from the kayakers. It was necessary to drop the swimmer at a distance to prevent upending the kayaks with the 120- to 140-mph rotor wash from the helicopter. As a swell passed under the door, Ferrante pushed himself out of the helicopter for a 20-foot free fall into the frigid ocean. After a quick thumbs-up to Sabangan, Ferrante began his swim over 20-foot swells toward the kayaks.

"They're OK," radioed Ferrante when he reached the kayakers. "Tired, cold, mildly hypothermic, but OK."

Ferrante offered the kayakers a choice: They could be hoisted by the helicopter or they could go aboard the Vigilant. In the end they chose the *Vigilant* because they could take their kayaks. Over the next 30 minutes Ferrante swam the kayaks alongside the Vigilant and assisted each man out of his kayak and onto the fishing vessel.

According to Ferrante, the sea state made getting the men out of the kayaks a bit of a task. It caused the fishing vessel to pitch and yaw.

"During the first attempt to get near the fishing vessel, the vessel almost ran us over with the starboard quarter," said Ferrante. "Later I found out this was due to the captain of the fishing vessel leaving the pilothouse to help his only deckhand. Once he left the pilothouse, the vessel went broadside into the seas and the back of it came right at us."

Ferrante was forced to push off the fishing vessel and swim the two kayakers away to safety.

"It was difficult to communicate with the deckhand due to the wind and seas," said Ferrante. "I had the deckhand throw a life ring to us. He was dead-on with his throw."

Ferrante dragged the men out of the kayaks and, one by one, put them into the life ring. Then the deckhand pulled them to the vessel and Ferrante pushed them up on deck.

"I would have to say that I believe putting them on the fishing vessel was harder than if we had hoisted them to the helicopter," said Ferrante "The pilot and I discussed this prior and during the evolution. After three attempts I decided I would give it one more try. I knew we could have hoisted them to the helicopter safely, but they would have had to leave their kayaks behind and there was a good chance the men would have ended up in Kodiak with us. If I could safely get them on the vessel that was *(continued next page)* heading to Homer, I would. In addition to safety being the number one priority, I thought of what I would want the rescuers to do if I were in their shoes."

With the men on board, all that remained were their kayaks. One by one they were hefted onto the deck of the *Vigilant*.

"This was not an easy task, but I timed the seas and leaned on one end of the kayak to get the other side up for the deckhand to grab," said Ferrante. "We then had to flip it to get all the water out, I kicked hard and as long as I could to get the kayaks up on board."

Top: Aviation Survival Technician 1st Class Chuck Ferrante holds onto a life ring and two kayaks as crewmen from the fishing vessel Vigilant *tow him toward the vessel to take the weathered kayakers aboard. Above: Aviation Survival Technician 1st Class Chuck Ferrante swims to the kayaks.* U.S. Coast Guard photos/Petty Officer 1st Class Sara Francis

In the helicopter Sabangan and the pilots maintained their hover, watching and waiting. By 6:00 p.m. all was well. The two very cold, very tired, and slightly nauseated men were safely aboard the fishing vessel headed to overnight in Port Dick with plans to transit to Homer the following day. Sabangan leaned out of the aircraft door and sent down the hook. Ferrante clipped in on the other end and was hoisted back aboard. With all parties safe and accounted for the helicopter crew headed back to Kodiak, arriving at 7:05 p.m.

"Despite all the challenges of this case, the H-60 helicopter once again proved that it is a very suitable search-and-rescue platform," said Sabangan. Kachesky and Goldfarb were well prepared: They had all the gear they needed, wore dry suits, and took multiple means of communication. That's what led to their successful rescue. Wearing gear to stay alive and being heard made all the difference. Having a radio and a properly registered PLB saved their lives in a beautiful but unforgiving environment.

prescription, and he had never even tried to paddle without them. I looked around and couldn't see any hint of land; the fog was obviously stronger than before, and we were also drifting out farther. I looked at the GPS, which was now dead, just a black screen. I agreed that the best thing right now was to keep our raft upright and to wait for rescue.

As we were moving away from Gore Point, the wind remained strong but the seas became more regular. The waves were still big, but now they came from only one direction. A strong rain had started, making the visibility even worse.

We couldn't put our paddles at 90 degrees to the kayaks. The wind was shaking our raft structure and threatened to take our paddles away. So we had no other choice but to put the paddles under the deck lines. They were not as vulnerable to the wind there, but they were not in the best start position for us if we failed to keep the kayaks rafted and needed the paddles to roll. We had to pay attention to every wave. It was all about having the kayaks at the right angle to meet the wave. All the waves came from Albert's side. My left hand was on Albert's kayak and on each wave I pushed the far side of his kayak down in a kind of low brace edging without a paddle that gave us some control of our stability. While we were rafted up, we maintained contact with the ship over the VHF.

"This is two kayaks; we are drifting in strong wind."

Ship: "Do you see any land around?"

"Negative, we are in fog; we don't see any land."

I later learned that the captain of the ship was not confident that we had actually succeeded in getting beyond Gore Point and was searching for us in the worst place, on the east side of the point. This is why he asked the question about land more than once.

"We activated our PLB. Do you have our position?"

No answer. Sometime after, the ship responded, "We turned on our searchlights. Do you see us?"

"Negative, we see nothing. We activated our PLB; do you have our position?"

Ship: "Do you have any flares?"

Deep inside my day hatch I had a dry bag that had come with the kayaks. I knew that we had flares in there, but I didn't think it was worth the risk for one of us to let go of the deck to open the day compartment and grope for the flares. Even if we had been able to find the flares, I didn't believe that they would be able to see them when we hadn't been able to see their searchlights.

I replied on the VHF, "Negative, we don't have flares. We activated our PLB; do you have our position?"

The ship continued searching quite a long time, but they couldn't find us. Then we got a new message. "A helicopter is coming for you. It will direct us."

After some time we heard a transmission from the rescue helicopter. It was hard for me to understand every word: ". . . radio . . . count . . . ten . . ."

What I got was enough. "One, two, three, four, five, six, seven, eight, nine, ten. Should I do it again?"

Rescue helicopter: ". . . count . . ."

"Should I count again?"

Rescue helicopter: "Yes, please count."

"One, two, three, four, five, six, seven, eight, nine, ten. Should I do it again?"

Rescue helicopter: "Yes."

This back and forth continued for some time. It was explained to me later that I had been asked to count repeatedly to provide a continuous radio transmission so they could find our direction.

Rescue helicopter: "Great! The signal is stronger now!"

In a minute we saw a big red helicopter coming out of the fog just above us. It was a moment I will never forget.

"We are in good condition," I said on the VHF. "We can wait for the ship."

A few minutes later the helicopter dispatched a rescue swimmer.

He approached us with a huge smile on his face. "Hi! I'm Chuck." It seemed he would jump on our kayaks and shake our hands. "How are you?"

"Albert lost his hat and glasses but we are well."

"What are you doing here?"

"We are paddling nine days from Seward to Homer. The weather changed suddenly."

"Where you from?"

"We are from Israel."

"Israel? Really?! You are quite far away!"

In a few minutes we spotted the *Vigilant* with all its searchlights on. It was bouncing up and down on the waves, and our first attempt to reach the ship with the kayaks didn't go well. But Chuck was very cool and very efficient. We were told to leave the kayaks and climb up using the ship's tethered life ring. The ship's crew pulled us aboard. Chuck held onto our kayaks and helped the *Vigilant* crew haul our boats aboard. In short time we were safely aboard with all of our gear.

It was 6:00 P.M. Two and a half hours had passed from the moment we had transmitted our first Mayday.

The fishing boat *Vigilant*, a 58-foot fish tender, was handled by captain Dennis Magnuson and the deckhand Quinn Tavfer. We couldn't imagine a better welcome than what we got on the *Vigilant*. Fortunately for us, the *Vigilant* had been nearby in Port Dick Bay collecting salmon from three smaller fishing vessels. We stayed aboard the ship for two days, and when it was full of salmon and ready to head home, we were dropped off at Homer.

LESSONS LEARNED

Be Alert

We had allowed ourselves to be distracted from our safety procedures. Our routine was to get a weather forecast via the satellite phone text message and listen to the weather radio twice a day to get the regular updates at 4 A.M. and 4 P.M. Even though we didn't have reception for the weather radio at our campsite, we still could have paddled out from shore and probably had reception out on the water. With the good weather around us, the forecast for fair weather we had gotten a day before and the general feeling that conditions would likely improve after the eight days of rain we'd been through had blunted our senses, and we didn't maintain a necessary level of alertness. The radio forecast had drastically changed that day. If we had received it, we would have heard the gale warning. We did ultimately receive an SMS message announcing the change in the weather forecast, but it was received by our satellite phone, when we were already on the fishing boat, after a delay of more than 12 hours.

Be Well Equipped

Both the PLB and waterproof VHF radio were necessary. If we had had only the PLB and not the VHF, we would have had no knowledge about a rescue being launched until it got to us. At least 2 hours could have passed while we waited and wondered, and that would have been highly unpleasant.

According to the Coast Guard, the location of a transmitting 406 PLB beacon like the one we had can be determined within approximately 3 miles in the first satellite pass, and to within 1 mile with three satellite passes. In our situation of very poor visibility along with our fast drifting in the wind, it would have been very difficult not only for ships but also for the Coast Guard helicopter to find us without the radio signal.

The fact that our VHF radio call was heard by the fishermen was just good luck. The annual salmon season in Port Dick Bay lasts only twenty days a year. Without large vessels around, our PLB would have been the only means to call for help.

We had flares, but they were stowed deep in the day hatch. In the fog they might not have done much good, but as a rule, safety flares should be kept handy and ready for use.

Match Your Trip to Your Abilities

Albert is a good kayaker, strong both physically and mentally. However, I knew that he didn't have much experience in rough seas and that he didn't have a combat roll. As compensation for that, we had allowed extra days in our itinerary and had decided not to paddle if we were not sure of the conditions. As it turned out, we had bad weather for all nine days and still paddled.

You cannot make any assumptions about the conditions you will be in at sea. Even if you listen to the weather radio five times a day, sometimes the forecast still will be terribly wrong. You should be prepared for the worst. For our trip, the solid Five Star training would have been essential for *both* of us.

23

El Viento Norte
A One-day Scouting Trip Becomes a Battle of Survival for Experienced Guides off Costa Rica's Nicoya Peninsula

Christian Gaggia

In the fall of 2002 I was asked to join a small group of experienced guides finding routes and campsites for a new branch of a sea kayak outfit on Costa Rica's Nicoya Peninsula. It was a paddler's dream, being paid to paddle bath-warm waters along wild, undisturbed shores. Compared to the cold water we were used to, the warm seas and light breezes of the tropics seemed like child's play.

Three of us would guide fulltime, and several more partners would help out around the base and fill in on trips when necessary. Most were either guides or had a good deal of on-water experience.

In late November we arrived at our base, the fishing village of Pochote, about 3 miles to the northeast of the town of Tambor in Bahia Ballena (Whale Bay). Bahia Ballena is situated on the southeast tip of the Nicoya Peninsula, where the Pacific meets the Gulf of Nicoya. Surrounded by tall, jungle-covered hills, the bay is usually protected from inclement weather and ocean swells. Outside the bay, however, the gulf is generally subject to the conditions of the ocean, along with weather that occasionally comes from the mountains to the north. This coastline is quite rugged and undeveloped, with cliffs plunging into the sea and isolated rocky beaches. Farther into the gulf, the beaches are sandier and more accessible and allow for easier landings.

The plan was to spend a few months familiarizing ourselves with the area and scouting for potential campsites. Literature on the area

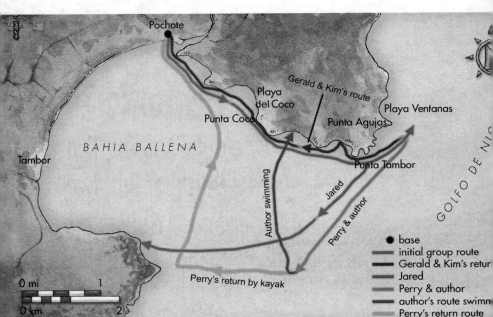

Christopher Hoyt

was scant, and current atlases and marine weather reports were nearly nonexistent, so we relied on personal experience and conversations with the locals. The fishermen seemed to gauge the weather by sticking a wet finger in the air. Weather radios, charts, and tide tables were a foreign concept, and their knowledge of the weather and conditions was based entirely on personal knowledge.

We had several VHF marine radios, but there were no weather channels or coast guard stations within range. Some information could be gleaned from the NOAA website, but Internet access was a 45-minute drive away and not a feasible option every time we wanted to go on the water. The waters of the Gulf of Nicoya were new to all of us, but given our collective experience, we felt confident that we would be able to understand this new area quickly. The gentle breezes and warm ocean temperatures lent a sense of ease to the place, and the fear I had of the cold waters of the Pacific Northwest seemed to melt away.

On the afternoon of January 20, about a month and a half into our tenure in Costa Rica, we set out to do some more exploration and to build some small tables at the primitive campsites that we shared with the local fishermen. We strapped a few bundles of rough-cut teak onto the backs of the tandem kayaks and set out from Pochote along the northern side of the bay en route to Playa Ventanas (Windows

Beach), about an hour and half southeast around a large point, Punta Tambor.

There were five of us: Kim and Gerald in one expedition-size tandem; Perry, our supervisor, and I in another; and my friend Jared in an expedition single. The four of us in the tandems were fulltime guides and had a wealth of on-water experience. Jared was the least experienced but had been on a number of kayak trips with me back home and had gotten some time on the water in Costa Rica.

Our tandems were sluggish, older expedition boats with front, rear, and center compartments with leaky bulkheads. The bulkheads in Jared's kayak were in better condition, and his hatches were sealed drum-tight.

We were lightly equipped. It was to be another short paddle, just some quick work, lunch, and home again. We had paddled this route repeatedly, and it was an easy, routine voyage. We carried one VHF for the group behind a seat in our boat. We all had bilge pumps and paddle floats and wore PFDs, with our spray skirts on us but not attached to the coamings, because when they were in place the sun turned the cockpits into ovens. If conditions dictated, we could always pull them on. We almost always paddled shirtless, carrying a shirt in the boat in case the sun got too intense. When it got too hot we could pull up on a beach and swim, even though that was scarcely refreshing. The water was warm, but at least it washed the sweat off.

This was a far cry from paddling our native waters. All the usual precautions and gear we took there stayed on the shelf here: float plans, air horns, compasses, flare guns, the ten essentials, and even the VHF sometimes. Our preparation for kayaking was all but absent; you dragged your boat across the sand. You could jump in the boat in the morning, have a quick paddle, and be home for lunch. Our friends at the base knew we were going out, but it was such a routine endeavor that it was hardly discussed. We were just going around the corner, so sharing a plan and rescue arrangements with them would have seemed odd. This was a daily venture.

We had been on the water nearly every day for 50 days and had become quite familiar and comfortable with the sea and weather conditions. The mornings were always calm and quiet, and then around 2 P.M., a brisk breeze would blow up off the Pacific until the sun went down around 6 P.M., after which it would be calm again. The breeze was generally a 10- to 15-knot southerly, sometimes a bit harder but never howling. Once in a while, when a good swell was coming in from the Pacific and a hearty breeze was blowing onshore, conditions would get a bit rough, but it was never more than a bit of a challenge and some fun. This day the sky was clear and there was a breeze rustling the trees, and there was nothing unusual. We paddled close to the coastline in a tight group with Gerald and Kim leading. Perry and I were close behind, and Jared was to our left. We cruised along the northeastern coastline of Bahia Ballena at a brisk clip toward where the bay meets the Pacific and the Gulf of Nicoya.

Near Punta Coco the intensity of the wind increased slightly. The water far out in the gulf appeared to be getting choppy, but where we were it was still relatively calm. Gerald and Kim forged ahead as we stayed back with Jared, who was paddling a bit slower. Near Punta Tambor, the far tip of the large arm we were following, the wind was more intense, and out on the gulf I could see whitecaps in the channel. We were now out of the protection of the bay and exposed to the Pacific swell coming in from the south. I mentioned to Perry that things looked a little nasty, but we both kind of shrugged it off and decided it would be best to catch up to Gerald and Kim. They had no radio, so we couldn't call them with our VHF. We hollered to Jared that we would have to push to catch up and get onto a beach as soon as possible. As we came up on Punta Tambor, the wind grew stronger. Paddling was a struggle, and we communicated with Jared in shouts and hand gestures. Gerald and Kim were barely visible ahead. We had moved off the sheer rocky coastline as it was littered with large, sharp rocks. A part of me wanted to turn around, but we needed to catch Gerald and Kim; besides, we weren't all that far from Playa Ventanas.

We rounded the point about 150 feet from shore. Jared was pushing hard, and we were doing the same. The wind out of the northeast was exceptionally strong and continuing to build. We were paddling almost directly into it. The sea was a mess. The swells coming in from the Pacific from the south were slamming head-on into the wind and creating giant walls of water. Swells were rising and dumping every which way. Jared was visibly disturbed. He mouthed something at me over the wind and made a circular gesture with his finger. He spun his boat around, and I yelled at him that we should stick together, but the wind drowned out my voice. He was soon out of sight.

Perry and I pushed on as hard as we could. We could barely hear each other, but I managed to catch the sound of an expletive from behind me. Perry had spotted Gerald and Kim's kayak swamped in the churning water with them clinging to it. They were about 30 yards in front of us, and about 100 yards off of Punta Agujas. I guessed that they had attempted to turn northwest to make the approach to Playa Ventanas and had been hit broadside by the swells.

A monstrous break had set up off of Punta Agujas, making it impossible to access Playa Ventanas by kayak. We were in way over our heads now, in the worst conditions I had ever encountered in a small craft.

We approached Gerald and Kim with our bow directly in the wind, riding up and down on the swells, and assessed what to do. Their cockpits were filled with water and their deck was awash. Large swells were dumping on them as they clung to their boat. Gerald was rapidly pumping water out of his cockpit, but it was refilling as fast as he could empty it. We had performed rescues, both practice and real, and they always went relatively easily and smoothly in calmer water. This was a different story. The swells lifted the kayaks up and down like battering rams, and we did not come anywhere close to them for fear that our boat would come down on their heads. Except for heading straight into the wind, our boat was nearly unmanageable. We cautiously attempted rescues several times, but the risk was far too great that someone would sustain a serious injury. All the techniques that make sense in books and work well in practice situations were useless to us now. A tow was out of the question because of the sheer weight of the water-filled boat. They waved us off.

After a bunch of hollering, it was decided that Perry and I should head home to get help. We trusted Gerald and Kim to their own safety. We didn't want to end up in the water ourselves or injure someone while making dangerous attempts at rescues. It went against our better judgment to leave them, but we felt like our hands were tied. Jared, the least experienced, was out alone and must have been in need of help too, and we were doing nothing but creating a safety hazard.

Perry and I turned around without capsizing. With the wind now at our backs and pushing us due southwest, we paddled as hard as we could, perpendicular to the giant dumping swells underneath us. We surfed wave after wave to escape from the mess at Punta Agujas. We both knew we needed to turn northwest to get back to Bahia Ballena and into more protected waters, but we had strayed quite a ways from the coastline in our effort to get away from Punta Agujas. To get where we wanted to be would now require paddling for a mile parallel to the large, breaking wind waves. We feared we would be rolled as soon as we made the turn, so we continued southwest, waiting for a moment when the time seemed right to turn.

Waves were breaking underneath and around us. The wind showed no sign of letting up, and we were too far from land. After some deliberation, we decided that we would have to turn back toward the bay and hope for the best.

We turned parallel with the waves and leaned into the oncoming crests. Within seconds a giant wave broke over our boat, ripping off my loosely attached spray skirt and flooding the cockpit. Moments later, a second wave pounded the boat and rolled us over. We both recovered our paddles, but we were floating in a yard sale of seat cushions, sandals, safety gear, and wood. The boat had righted itself, and Perry quickly crawled in the rear while I tried to steady it from the opposite side. I grabbed one of the pumps that was still strapped to the boat and hooked my elbows over Perry's cockpit coaming and began pumping like a machine, while Perry kept the boat upright and into the wind. At this point I felt that all my training and practice had gone out the window and I was just trying to survive.

We were hit by another large dumping wave, powerful enough to break my tenuous hold on the kayak and spin the boat broadside out of my reach. I lunged for it, but with its broad side to the wind it spun around and moved away quickly. Panicking, I yelled as loud as I could, but I only caught glimpses of Perry. Within 30 seconds I couldn't see him anymore.

There were still remnants of kayak gear floating nearby in the water, including one of the teak planks. I seized it for extra flotation. I floated for a second, resting, dumbfounded, and almost in shock. I was alone in the Pacific Ocean, but I felt almost calm. The past several hours had been so fraught with adrenaline and exertion that to float there was almost otherworldly.

Then I snapped to and assessed my situation. It was hard to estimate how far offshore I was, but the sheer cliffs we had been near just a while ago were way farther away than I had ever seen them from a kayak. I guessed I was several miles south-southwest of Punta Tambor. I had no choice but to begin swimming. I held the teak plank under my left arm and stroked with my right and kicked. I focused on the land and stroked, my mind almost empty.

I was so full of adrenaline still that if I was feeling any fatigue, I wasn't registering it. I had a single focus, and strangely I did not feel fearful or have any thoughts of anything but what my body was doing. There were no worries of sharks or anything of the sort. It was just "Go!"

After what seemed like at least an hour and a half, the sun was getting lower, but the land seemed no closer than when I had begun swimming. A wave of panic rose in me as I wondered if I was fighting a current as well as the wind and whether I would reach shore before exhaustion set in. I had a moment of clarity and thought, "You can live or die." I remember seeing in my mind a line between the two and thinking, "Live!" I began my sidestroke again at a furious pace.

I swam like an automaton for what felt like hours, with only slight pauses. I was afraid to stop for too long, fearing I would realize how tired I was and not be able to continue. Gradually the shore got closer. Although in my first hour and a half of swimming I felt that I had gone nowhere, now I was finally moving.

The daylight faded rapidly. The wind had calmed slightly, but the water was still full of sloppy swells. I was extremely fatigued, running only on willpower and adrenaline. The coast grew larger in the darkness, and I used every last bit of strength I had to bring myself to it.

The waves were still banging up against the shore, and there was no beach in sight. I realized that if I didn't get out of the water soon I would be completely exhausted. The area was littered with rocks, and I crawled onto one of the larger ones with my last ounce of strength. I was still about 40 feet from shore. I let go of the piece of teak, and at that moment I realized how exhausted I was. It was around 7 P.M. and almost dark. I had been in the water since about 2:30. I'd had nothing to eat or drink since before the weather had turned foul, as my food had been in a small dry bag in my cockpit. I'd been in the hot sun all day. I was completely drained.

I wasn't sure exactly where I was, but I knew I had come ashore between Playa Ventanas and Playa del Coco, not far from Punta Coco. I remembered that there was a rocky beach about a half mile around the point toward Pochote, and I briefly considered getting back in the water and attempting to swim around the point, but I was in no shape to do such a thing.

Hours passed. I watched a lightning storm over the glow of the capital city of San José, but the sky stayed clear over the gulf. The wind still blew, but without its earlier ferocity, and the only lights in the area other than the stars were lights passing back and forth across the gulf several miles from where I sat.

I realized that the lights were the Costa Rican Coast Guard, combing the water for my body. It was humiliating. Then a worse thought crept over me. "What if they are looking for the bodies of my friends?" A sense of panic enveloped me. The lights eventually disappeared.

I spent the night on that rock in a sort of half-conscious upright doze, awakened every few minutes by a swell spraying me with water. I was beginning to feel slightly chilled from being wet for so long, even though the night temperature was in the high seventies. The night passed slowly. I anxiously awaited the first light so I could get off the rock and back to Pochote. I wanted to see what had happened to the others and to let whoever was still at the base know I was OK. Waves pounded the rock all night. When the first shards of light broke, I prepared to make my exit.

Shore was a series of large, jagged rock faces plunging into the sea. If I could make my way to the riprap at the base of the rocks, I could then climb up one of them to a ledge that ran along the tops of the rocks. From there I could find my way home.

I was worried that if I didn't time my swim to shore right, I would be hammered up against the rocks by the swell. I surveyed the water for an appropriate time to jump in, and then made the plunge. I swam a few of the swells toward shore, and after the last one passed and crashed against the rocks I made a mad charge to climb up on the riprap and get a hold on the rock face before the next one broke. I was acutely aware of my exhausted state as I began climbing the jagged rock face. About 12 feet up I had a gripping fear that I might fall, break my legs, and then be pounded by the incoming surf. I calmed myself and continued slowly up to the ledge.

From there, after a long bout of scrambling, bushwhacking, and swimming across a mangrove swamp, I was back at the shores of Pochote.

About 5 hours after I had left the rock, I staggered onto the beach in front of our house and was met with the calls of the local kids. One grabbed me by the hand and hustled me up to our yard, where there seemed to be a countless number of people. Everybody took notice of my arrival all at once and let out a collective gasp. I was told the whole crew had made it back intact. We were all speechless and expressed our thankfulness for being back together through hugs, tears, and laughter.

Perry had lost sight of me within seconds of us becoming separated. He was in a frenzy to locate me but was helpless in the water-laden boat. He continued to surf with an open front cockpit in the breaking seas. He navigated across the mouth of the bay and paddled back into Pochote into the oncoming wind waves that had filled the bay. He was first to arrive in the late afternoon, and when he realized no one else had returned, he rapidly began searching for a local fisherman with a motorized panga to take him out to search for us. A friend of ours, Camareno, had a boat but said that the conditions were too rough to go out in and they would have to wait. They then called the Coast Guard. Search and Rescue would be dispatched from Puntarenas, roughly 23 miles across the gulf on the mainland. It would be several hours before they could arrive.

Gerald and Kim had managed to reenter their swamped boat, keep it upright, and slog along the coast toward Pochote. They found a rocky cove just big enough to get the boat out of the water so they could empty it. They waited for the wind to die down, and just before sunset they made the push back to Pochote. On their way into the bay, they spotted Perry and Camareno in the panga coming around one of the bay's small headlands. Gerald and Kim had figured they were the only lost sheep and were excited to see Perry, but when they saw the grim look on his face, they understood things were far worse than they had thought. They continued straight on into Pochote. After several minutes outside the bay in the panga, Camareno decided the conditions were too rough to continue searching in the oncoming darkness. They headed back in. All they could do was wait.

Jared had capsized shortly after his departure from us. He was thrown from the boat but was able to get ahold of it. He repeatedly attempted to reenter and pump but was continually rolled by the heavy seas. He was unskilled in the use of the paddle float and other self-rescues; he attempted to enter by crawling up on the deck, only to be dumped off again. This cycle went on for a while, until he was too fatigued to continue. He grabbed the boat and held on for dear life. He kicked and stroked in an attempt to drive into the bay. Eventually, just after dark, he emerged from the water just to the south of the village of Tambor. He had been in the water for close to 6 hours. He knocked on the door of the house of a local fisherman, who immediately recognized him as one of the missing kayakers—the story had spread quickly—and arranged a taxi for him back to Pochote. Reunited with Gerald, Kim, and Perry, the four of them could only wait to see if I turned up. They spent a tense night next to the phone waiting for word from the Guarda Costa. In the morning I arrived.

The days following the incident were spent doing interviews with the Costa Rican news. It was embarrassing. The coverage was sensational, inaccurate, and just plain fabricated. It was reported that Jared and I were international students and had gone on a kayak trip to the nearby Islas Tortugas and had jumped out of our boat in fear of the weather. A local fisherman claimed he had heard that an upturned kayak was found and went searching for the lost foreigners. He said he found us all, plucked us from the water, and gave us a stern lecture about the dangers of the sea and *El Viento Norte*. He was proclaimed a hero.

El Viento Norte, the North Wind, was what had turned our day into a nightmare. Apparently it is an annual weather event that takes place sometime around the middle of January and lasts for several weeks. The wind builds up in the north and makes its way down the Nicoya and out to the Pacific, wreaking havoc. It was well known by all of the locals and fishermen that you don't venture out if there is any sign of wind during this period. All the locals seemed perplexed we hadn't known about *El Viento Norte*. Somehow this fact had passed us by in all our conversations with them. Weeks afterward, I was talking with a hotel owner who was also somewhat of a mariner. He had read of the incident in the papers and told me that the wind had blown over 60 knots that day.

We never heard anything more from the Guarda Costa, and I felt a bit ashamed that they had gone out looking for us, but I was thankful they had been there if we needed their help.

LESSONS LEARNED

This event was a huge wake-up call for me and changed my attitude about the outdoors entirely. The biggest lesson was not to become too comfortable in my abilities or too complacent about my environment. I had been kayaking almost every day since the previous April. I had spent many springs and summers guiding on a daily basis. I had worked on fishing boats and sailboats and had grown up on the shores of a moderately protected body of water that was cold year-round. I felt at home in boats and around the water. I figured if I had handled myself this long with no incident in much more extreme environments, Costa Rica would be a breeze.

The warm water and predictable weather made me feel like nothing could possibly go wrong. The respect and healthy fear I had for the sea near home faded because that cold, biting water was absent. "The water is warm; what's the worst that can happen?" I grew lazy in my judgment and concern for safety. Paddling in this friendly, laid-back environment made me forget about the real dangers of the ocean and the weather that comes with it. Safety and equipment measures that I would have taken back home without a second thought became distant memories. It was so easy to forget about safety equipment when I could just drag my boat from the yard to the beach in two minutes and be floating along in gentle swells without a life jacket or spray skirt, poke up the coast, jump out, and have a swim. I have always had a lot of respect for the forces of nature, but overconfident and nonchalant this time, I headed out underequipped into conditions that should have warned me to turn around.

There were things we should have done differently. We felt complacent and ignored an important part of safe paddling—planning—which led us to become spread out and out of communication. If we had stayed in a group, we could have collectively made the decision to turn around before the weather grew worse. If we'd each had a VHF radio on our PFD, we would have been able to call our front kayak and have them turn around. Later, when things got bad, we could have radioed the Coast Guard, but the one radio we had was untethered and ended up at the bottom of the Pacific.

The swamped double kayaks presented a level of difficulty that we were unaccustomed to. We had practiced many single and double rescues, but only in relatively calm conditions where the boats took on little water and the rescues were performed without incident. In dumping seas the boats nearly filled to capacity, making them unman-ageable and incredibly heavy. In the rough water the weight of these water-laden boats created a serious danger for anyone trying to get close. Towing the swamped kayak would have been an impossibility. We had always used double kayaks on our guided trips because we felt the stability was important for inexperienced paddlers, and there-fore safer. But my experience this day made me question their man-ageability in these situations. I'm not sure what would have happened in cold water. I felt that I was a practiced rescuer, but this experience humbled me and made me rethink my training and my ability to react in a serious situation.

The effort we spent pumping was in vain and, looking back, was perhaps a reflex response because we felt there was no other course of action. Much of this wasted energy could have been saved. An elec-tric pump or a foot pump could have helped ease the situation, as it would have allowed for us to be in our boats with our skirts over the cockpits and our hands on our paddles to attempt to control the boat. Boats with lower-volume cockpits and well-sealed bulkheads would also have made this situation more manageable.

Jared, even though he'd had some time on the water, was the least experienced of all of us and shouldn't have been in the single. He was unpracticed in self-rescues and boat handling in rough water. He didn't have a roll. As it turned out, he was familiar with the concept of the paddle float but had never used one, and he didn't even attempt using it in his capsize. I feel personally responsible for his lack of safety training. We had been on a number of day trips, but safety had just been a discussion, not something we'd practiced. To his credit, he was a good athlete and was strong enough to swim his kayak ashore, but strength alone does not always save one's life, certainly not in colder water.

Without a PFD I surely would have drowned. I am sure the same holds true for Jared. I was extremely exhausted, and I needed every bit of help I could get to make it in the churning sea. Wearing the PFD allowed me to float when I needed to rest. If I had needed to tread water, I would have quickly been overcome with exhaustion.

Our VHFs didn't pick up any signals in the area, so radio contact was a moot point. We usually brought them but were never able to use them except boat to boat, which had never been necessary. If we had brought more than one this day and had them properly acces-sible, we would have been able to radio each other and potentially our own base, if someone had been monitoring a VHF there. We did not have a flare gun with us on this particular trip, as we had become lazy about bringing it. Flares are less useful in remote areas; if we had fired one at the first sign of trouble, it's quite unlikely that there would have been anyone in the area to see it. But flares would have played an important role once the Coast Guard was on the water.

When exploring the developing world, one needs to take into account that the safety measures we count on back home just aren't the same. We have an extremely tight safety net in place in North America consisting of well-trained rescuers with advanced technology. Places like Costa Rica do not possess the same wealth and technological equipment. The infrastructure is not as developed, and the equipment isn't as modern. To assume you will be rescued is foolish. It must be assumed that you are on your own. This fact makes our nonchalance all the more unjustified.

If I'd had an EPIRB or PLB with me, it would have provided my location, via satellite, to the Search and Rescue Satellite Aided Tracking (SARSAT) Mission Control Center in the United States and then to Costa Rican authorities. It is a testament to Costa Rica's organization that upon receiving a call they were able to deploy as quickly as they did to search for us.

We had done our research to the best of our ability. There was little written nautical information about the area, and our conversations with the locals seemed to turn up little we needed to be wary of. Our own experience indicated that the weather was predictable and generally friendly. I believe not knowing about things like *El Viento Norte* are part of the danger of exploring a foreign area. You might miss something that may be common local knowledge.

Any person who has ever been in a crisis situation knows that making decisions isn't always simple. I would have liked to have performed a rescue of Gerald and Kim instead of leaving them floating, and I would have liked to have not gotten so far offshore with Perry, but it was just the way that it happened. Sometimes these situations take on a life of their own, and the equipment that is supposed to save you, and all of the things you are trained to do, just don't work. It just becomes a scramble to survive.

The best advice I can offer is this: As a paddler it isn't worth taking these risks. Don't become too comfortable, and don't take anything for granted. You can still be relaxed and confident, but don't become complacent. Develop a good skill set and always carry the proper equipment, but don't let them replace a healthy respect for, and might I say fear of, the sea. It is a fickle place, and a little fear could save your life.

Editor's Note

Names have been changed at the request of those involved.

24

Cold and Alone on an Icy River

Randy Morgart

On Friday, February 19, 2010, the weather was better than it had been in some time, with temperatures in the upper thirties and overcast. I couldn't make a Saturday trip with friends, and I was in the mood to paddle solo.

My plan was to launch into the Mississippi River from the gravel ramp at the Foley, Missouri, access, 3.5 miles above the Winfield Lock and Dam and paddle upstream in the calm, slow-moving water sheltered from the main channel by a string of islands. On my return I could easily pop out into the main channel and return downstream to my car. I realized the risks of paddling alone. Even my wife, who rarely paddles, had heard enough discussions that she voiced some concern about my decision to paddle solo in the Mississippi River. The Foley access is one of the closest to my home, and I paddle there frequently either solo or with the St. Louis Canoe and Kayak Club. It had been a long time since I unintentionally flipped a sea kayak, and far longer since I had to wet-exit, so I felt quite secure paddling in a familiar setting on calm water.

Getting my QCC 700 kayak ready to go, I stowed my spare paddle, a two-piece Euro blade, on the front deck. I'd paddle with my mainstay Greenland paddle. My paddle float and pump were already in the aft compartment, often stowed there during transport, and I decided to leave them there. I felt they wouldn't be needed for a flat-water paddle, although they were still available. I knew there was phone service in the area, so my cell phone joined my wallet and car keys in the dry bag along with the basic gear I always carry. In the back hatch with that dry bag were some snacks and a sports drink in case I chose to land along the way. Over my insulating poly base layer I wore splashproof nylon pants, a fleece pullover, and rubber-soled booties with waterproof socks. A breathable rain jacket, knit

Randy Morgart

watch cap, and waterproof neoprene gloves completed my gear. I had a hydration pack and new camera secured to the PFD I was wearing.

At the river's edge there was an apron of ice about 3 feet wide and not quite a quarter inch thick. I used a fallen tree branch to clear a path through it. Launching into the slough and paddling near the shore brought me in sight of a few bald eagles, several pelicans, and other waterfowl, most just out of camera range. The large flights of waterfowl passing high overhead were a sign that spring was on the way.

Widely scattered rafts of ice were drifting in the gentle current; I took several photos of one and even tried setting my camera on the ice for a self-portrait but was unable to get far enough away for a decent picture. Once I heard a loud ripping sound and turned to see the gentle current shred the quarter-inch ice over a log snagged on the river bottom. A few times I heard a loud metallic racket in the distance. Not being able to determine the source of the sound, I assumed it was coming from the lock and dam downstream.

After an hour of zigzagging up the slough taking pictures, I reached the head of Jim Crow Island. I heard more metallic clanging, first upstream, then across the main channel. It finally dawned on me that the noise was caused by rafts of ice striking the marker buoys in the navigation channel. Thinking this would make an interesting video, I headed out to the middle of the river to the nearest buoy.

While there were more and larger rafts of ice moving down the main channel, it was still no problem crossing between them. It was amazing to see how the quarter-inch-thick sheets of ice moving a few miles an hour could knock the several-hundred-pound buoys about so violently. I took a video of the buoy as I drifted downstream with the ice.

I had to pick a route through the ice floes as I headed back. While there was a clear path down the left side of the river, from this distance I wasn't able to see an easy way to cross the channel to get back to the landing. An hourglass-shaped sheet of ice beside me left only about 30 feet of ice blocking an easy crossing. I decided to become an icebreaker, something I've done several times before although usually in a plastic kayak rather than in my Kevlar boat.

Ice breaking in a kayak is fun, but you don't move very fast. You chop the paddle down to punch a hole in the ice, then use that as an anchor point to slide ahead until the boat's weight breaks the ice beneath it. With only 6 to 8 feet of ice left between me and open water, I brought my paddle down to make one last anchor point, but instead of punching a hole in the ice, the blade hit and skidded across it. I was suddenly upside down. I made two unsuccessful attempts to roll up, and while both attempts got my head above water, neither was good enough for me to stay upright. I'd never had a problem with the gasp reflex underwater, but I was definitely gasping when I surfaced.

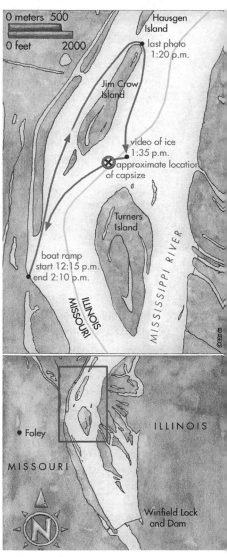

I bailed out and came up on the left side of the boat. My first thought was: "You have minutes to do something." I could feel the icy water on my legs. I had chosen not to wear a wetsuit, assuming I wouldn't need one for a flatwater paddle. Previously our club's coldest day out paddling had been 9°F, and I had worn a dry suit that day, but the suit had worn out since then and I hadn't replaced it. Unfortunately, on this day, the coldest I had paddled solo, I was in trouble wearing only a poly base layer and a fleece pullover under nylon pants and a waterproof jacket. Only my neoprene gloves worked well in the water. My cap had fallen off in the water and I threw it into the cockpit, but I didn't notice the cold on my head.

I turned the boat upright and popped the cover off the back hatch. It

Christopher Hoyt

was a simple matter to grab the paddle float. I had it mostly inflated before I thought to put it on the paddle. During my paddle-float rescue, I put my foot on the paddle to climb in and the boat leaned over, taking water into the cockpit and open back hatch. I knew this wasn't working but didn't immediately grasp why. Thinking it was better to call for help too soon rather than too late, I opened my dry bag and found my cell phone. I was afraid I would drop it into the water so I held it over the open hatch. That made it hard to see the keys to dial 911. The call to 911 failed twice; then I noticed there wasn't any signal strength showing on the screen. This seemed odd, since I'd heard my phone signaling an incoming message shortly after launching and I'd made calls from the shore on other days.

I thought that if I could swim the boat through the remaining ice, the current would carry me toward the car while I worked on a self-rescue. It soon became evident I could not swim through quarter-inch ice as fast as I needed to. The thought crossed my mind that maybe I should tie myself to the boat to make it easier to find my body, but I wasn't willing to give up yet.

It then dawned on me that I had not finished inflating my paddle float. That explained the failure of my first self-rescue attempt. I blew more air into the float and tried again. I was able to get myself belly-down on top of the boat and took a moment to slide the paddle under the bungee more securely. As I started to rotate my body upright, a wrong shift of my weight dumped me back into the water on the other side of the boat, away from the outrigger. This was probably the low point for me. Fortunately, the partly flooded boat did not flip and dump all my gear into the water. I once again repeated my mantra for the day—"you have only minutes"—and kept moving. Pulling my marine radio from the deck bag, I struggled to control my gasping, then made a Mayday call twice and listened for a reply. Silence. I changed the power from 1 to 5 watts and tried the Mayday call again. Still no reply. That's when it really sank in that I was on my own.

Moving the paddle float to the right side, I saw my pump in the hatch and put it in the cockpit. Then, gingerly climbing onto the flooded boat, I was able to get completely out of the water. I took a minute to rest. The rest of the paddle-float rescue went just as it's supposed to with one hitch: As I sat up in the cockpit, I realized I was on top of my pump. If I'd had feeling in my lower extremities I'm sure it would have been uncomfortable.

A couple attempts to reach the pump convinced me the flooded boat was too unstable to risk pulling the pump out. It was under my right hip on the seat, and the float was now on that side. I'm not sure of my thought processes at the time, but I didn't feel I could get it out without shifting my weight to the left and capsizing again to that side.

I knew I couldn't survive going in the water again. Deciding not to remove the paddle float, I very gingerly retrieved my spare paddle. The 3 inches of water in the cockpit didn't help with the cold I felt or my stability. Working through the remaining ice was uneventful, however, and soon I was in open water.

Paddling back was a slow, methodical process. I remember trying to reach the pump once or twice and was stopped by the boat's lack of stability. I remembered a chemical hot pack in my jacket pocket. I felt around but it was under my PFD and I wasn't willing to tempt fate by trying to get it out. I did take a moment to drink from my hydration pack. I hadn't realized till then how thirsty I had become.

It was still about a half mile to the car, and for the last several minutes I had noticed my vision getting dark *(continued page 256)*

DESCENT INTO COLD

Christopher Cunningham

A few years ago, my friend Tim and I were trying out some new gear and doing some reentry drills. Tim, wearing his paddling wetsuit, had been in the water off and on for about 20 to 30 minutes. By the time we headed for shore, he was feeling cold but not uncomfortably so. We loaded the kayaks on Tim's van and headed for my house. Tim's not a bad driver, but in less than a mile he breezed through two four-way stops. The cold water, apparently, had left its mark.

Many articles about hypothermia include graphs depicting survival time in cold water, but it's more important to think about where hypothermia begins than where it ends. "Survival" times, after all, are well beyond the time we are able to help ourselves.

Neither of my own experiences with hypothermia was brought on by immersion. The symptoms were the same as in the water—they're just slower to unfold. My first experience happened in Boston on Christmas Eve in 1975. I had spent the day traipsing around town and in the evening went to wait for my girlfriend to get off work. I hadn't bothered to eat lunch or dinner, and my feet were soaked from walking through the snow and slush on the sidewalks. I was cold and tired, and while I waited for Jay, I sat on a dry patch of sidewalk and leaned against a brick wall. I felt the wall pulling the heat from my back, and the numbness in my feet and hands crept inward. I knew I should stand up to conserve my heat, but I was too tired to care. When Jay appeared, I got up and we started walking to the subway station. Warm air was coming up the stairway, but when I was halfway down the stairs, the cold that had *(continued next page)* enveloped my limbs reached my stomach. My legs buckled and my abdomen seized up, and I doubled over. Then I started to sob. Not out of pain or fear—it seemed for no reason at all. I warmed up on the train, and when I got home, I sucked down some honey straight from the bottle and wrapped myself around a radiator for half an hour.

The second time, I was rowing down the Mississippi River. It was late December. I had promised to meet someone at a landing downstream from Nashville. It was dark when I arrived at the landing. There was no one there, and I couldn't find a break in the stone revetments where I could come ashore. I continued downriver looking for a place to land. Spray from the bow of my boat splattered on my back and glazed my jacket with ice. After an hour or more, I found a small patch of sand and grass. My arms and legs had that same numb feeling I'd experienced in Boston, but this time I was acutely aware of the state I was in and fully focused on the tasks I had ahead of me. I got the tent set up, but by the time I had enough twigs gathered to start a fire, the cold had hit my core. I was grunting like a weight lifter as I fumbled with my stiffened hands to light a match. I warmed my hands around the fire, and when they could function again, I got my stove going and boiled water for a hot drink.

Cold, whether it gets to you gradually while you're paddling or wraps around you quickly when you're in the water, has significant effects even in the early stages of hypothermia. It can cloud your judgment. It's better not to think of hypothermia in terms of how long you can survive. The real question is how long you have before you make your first bad decision and how long you have before you're unable to help yourself.

around the edges and a roaring in my ears that almost covered the usual river noises. I don't really remember shivering much during the paddle. Pulling into shallow water and attempting to dismount resulted in landing on my butt in 6 inches of water. My next attempt got me on my feet, and I dragged the boat ashore. I immediately went to the car and got it started.

Before long I had wet gear spread out all over the landing. My PFD and wet clothes were scattered on the ground, the roof racks, and roof of the car. I changed into dry clothes but I didn't remove my soaking briefs. I don't know why, but that certainly caused me to take longer warming up.

Back in the car, I got a couple drinks of Gatorade, but I was soon shivering violently. I found a chemical hot pack and stuck it to my shirt near my armpit. Weighing my options, I knew I couldn't load my boat, but I wasn't willing to leave it unattended.

With my cell phone now working, although slightly damp, I called my friend Mark. He lived nearby and we often shared rides to and from trips. As soon as I spoke, Mark asked what was wrong with me. Hearing I'd taken a swim and needed help loading my boat was all it took to get him on the way.

A few minutes later a car with two men and a pickup with another guy pulled up. Seeing the debris field between the car and the water and taking one look at me, the pickup driver came over and asked if I needed help. They all offered to load my boat, so with minimal instruction and even less real help from me they pumped it out, put it on the roof rack, tied it down, and helped me pick up the scattered gear. I was still shivering violently, so the pickup driver urged me to get back in the car, saying he'd stay till Mark got there. Most people on the river are decent, hardworking souls. These guys were some of the best.

Within a few minutes Mark arrived, and the pickup driver left before I could properly thank him. Looking over the situation, Mark took my Gatorade and began heating it on an alcohol stove he'd brought with him. I have to say hot grape Gatorade tastes terrible, but it felt really good!

Sitting in my car, Mark gave me another hot pack and found that I had turned the car's blower on high but hadn't turned the heat up. He dialed it up and that helped warm me, but not nearly as much as the warm drink. Fortunately, Mark had put it in a spillproof cup or I would have worn it. He still had to do a lot of coaching to get me to drink. I tended to just hold the warm cup, pant, and shiver unless told to do otherwise.

The warm drink worked its magic quickly. Even though Mark had offered to follow me home and help unload, by the time we

Randy Morgart

reached the highway I told him I could make it on my own and we parted ways. I had nagging thoughts that someone may have heard my Mayday call and started an unnecessary search, so I phoned the lock and dam to make sure someone knew what happened. The lady who answered the phone told me they only monitor Channel 12 for lock operations and do not monitor Coast Guard Channel 16. No search had been initiated.

When I got home, I put together a timeline from time stamps on the camera and cell phone. The 911 calls hadn't been completed, so they didn't register in the phone log.

About 12:15	Launch
12:21	First photo
1:20	Last photo at the head of Jim Crow Island
1:35	Video of buoy
2:21	Called Mark
3:40	Called lock and dam

Time was a very relative thing that day, but I estimated I spent about 10 minutes in water that was thirty-something degrees. Assuming I dumped about 10 minutes after taking the video and called Mark about 10 minutes after landing, that left 16 minutes for my paddle from near the head of Turners Island to the ramp just over a half mile away.

LESSONS LEARNED

I had filed a float plan. My wife knew where I was going and when I planned to be back. However, given the limited survival time in cold water, a float plan may only indicated where to look for my body. The single best thing that I did was never give up. Every time one attempt failed, I moved to the next. While I was making calls for help, I was thinking of what to try next. I knew that even if my call for help reached someone, I had to get back aboard my kayak. Staying in the water till help arrived would have been fatal. Paddling upstream first is always a good idea. Whether you're tired, hurt, or just late, it's always best to have the easy downstream or downwind leg at the end of the day.

What I did wrong: Not listening to my wife. Even if things go well, that's always a bad idea. Going solo is not necessarily wrong, but when you do, it influences every decision you make from then on. Going into the navigation channel was probably OK, but my decision to cross the channel between ice floes was questionable. Deciding to break through the ice was definitely a bad choice. Getting among ice floes at any time can be dangerous. If the ice had jammed up on an island or sandbar, the current would have crushed the floes together. Being caught in its midst would be dangerous for a person in a boat and almost certainly fatal for a swimmer.

Not dressing for immersion in 30°F water was a critical mistake. I didn't own a dry suit then, but even my wetsuit would have kept me much warmer. Proper cold-water immersion wear would have kept me better composed, making fewer mistakes and achieving self-rescue more quickly. I wear a wetsuit when paddling whitewater where the odds are good I will roll and probably swim, and the protection it offers makes a big difference.

Several weeks after the incident, a friend pointed out a sale on semi-dry suits. My wife insisted I get one, so I did. I wasn't going to repeat the mistake of not listening to her.

Doing a radio check before launching would have told me no one in the area was monitoring Channel 16. The lock tenders monitor Channels 12 or 14, and while they have no capacity for rescues, they could have called 911 for me.

I hadn't been practicing rolling last summer as much as usual. In the ice I think I rushed and overpowered the Greenland paddle. The paddle works best for me with a very slow sweep and more of a gentle knee lift than a hip snap. I feel my roll is less reliable with a Euro paddle, but with it I complete half of my rolls in cold whitewater. All of my failed rolls have been in shallow whitewater where I'm bouncing off rocks and can't seem to get set up properly. In the past I have sometimes dealt with an unsuccessful roll by switching to a sculling roll, which may have worked in the ice had I thought to try it.

I demonstrate paddle-float rescues at our club's safety clinics, but because it's a technique I feel confident with, I don't regularly practice it. More practice may have helped it work the first time. Leaving the paddle float and pump where they were stored in the back hatch was another critical mistake. Had I placed the pump and float in their normal position on the back deck, when my first reentry attempt failed, the kayak's buoyancy would not have been compromised by water getting into the open rear compartment. Had the pump been secured in its place, it would have been available to clear the cockpit after my successful reentry. Without the pump under me I would have had my weight lower in the boat and therefore would have been more stable. Getting the water out of the kayak would also have restored its stability.

I survived the day more intact than I had any right to expect. I had two palm-size bruises on my right thigh, perhaps from sliding out of the thigh brace during my wet exit, and right calf, probably from the coaming. I also had some numbness of the skin in my midsection. My doctor said it was inflammation of the nerves. It's almost totally gone now and improving. He also said my darkening vision was possibly low blood pressure brought on by shock or hypothermia. He explained that initially during submersion, all the blood vessels constrict, forcing blood into your core. As hypothermia gets worse, you lose the ability to constrict the vessels and they relax, dropping your blood pressure—the same effect as shock. The doctor thought that dropping blood pressure would also have caused the roaring in my ears.

I think about that day a lot, and it will definitely influence my decisions about future trips. Two days after the swim, my wife and I went to see the movie *The Wolfman*. One of the characters is in an 1880s mental institution, and as part of his "therapy" he's strapped to a chair and lowered into a tank of ice water. That was hard to watch and caused me to tense up so much that my wife asked if I was OK.

Time can take on new meaning as quickly as a kayak can flip. Resting on a warm beach, we can while away a few minutes with barely a thought. Submerged in icy water, gasping repeatedly as your body reacts to its warmth streaming away in the current, every thought races past and you try to grasp their importance and cling onto the thoughts that will help you. Our comprehension of the water can change just as quickly as we make the transition from kayaker to swimmer. Sure, it's just a flatwater paddle—so what if it's colder than last time I was here? It's easy to dismiss such concerns because we have no intention of swimming. But we can't control the water, and that's part of what draws us to it. When we make that sudden transition from kayaker to swimmer, the outcome hinges on choices we've already made, maybe days before, when we were on land, warm and dry. Good decisions should come and go instinctively. But you will ponder a poor decision for the rest of your life, be that decades or minutes.

EPILOGUE

Since this article was first published in *Sea Kayaker* magazine, I've felt I did not emphasize enough that the biggest mistake made that day was becoming too casual about a trip that I had taken many times before. Since then, the saying that "it's just a flatwater paddle" has become a cautionary statement repeated by our club members when someone considers taking a too casual approach to safety on the water. They say familiarity breeds contempt. While I never feel contempt for the rivers I paddle, the complacency that I let familiarity breed that day was nearly my undoing.

Randy's video, "Ice on the Mississippi River," showing the river ice colliding with the buoy, can be viewed at www.seakayakermag.com/ Resources/links.htm.

25

Michipicoten Island
Atypical August Winds Turn an Annual Summer Outing into a Struggle to Survive

Robert F. Beltran and Roger Schumann

ROBERT'S STORY

I had been fascinated by Michipicoten Island ever since I became aware of it 43 years ago. This heavily forested island located in the northeastern part of Lake Superior is uninhabited by humans, seldom visited, and awash with wildlife, sandy beaches, rocky coastlines, and jagged cliffs. My partner, Judy, and I took a kayaking trip to Lake Superior every year. We usually went late in the summer to enjoy the cooler weather and fewer mosquitoes, but our 2010 trip began near the very end of August. We planned to visit Michipicoten Island and begin our trip from Michipicoten First Nation land near Wawa, Ontario. The island itself is 15 miles long and 10 miles across. We'd cross to the island about 35 wilderness miles from the put-in.

I had been kayaking the Pukaskwa region of the Canadian north shore of Superior most summers for 24 years. I'd made the full 110-mile trip from Hattie Cove to Michipicoten Harbour twice. Judy and I had made the nearly 10-mile crossing from Northern Ontario's remote Pukaskwa region to Michipicoten Island for the first time the previous year. Despite my long-standing interest in the island, until our 2009 trip, time limitations, weather, and caution regarding the unpredictable nature of Lake Superior had kept me from making the crossing.

The paddle out to the island had been a joy in fine weather, and the return crossing had been even nicer; we'd only wished time had

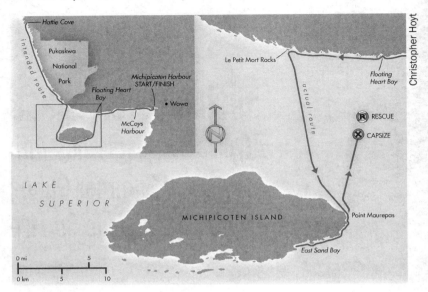

not constrained our explorations of the island. We had promised ourselves we would return.

Judy and I felt prepared for the 2010 trip. We were using a
21.5-foot Current Designs Libra XL, a tandem sea kayak I'd had for
15 years. It had a great deal of cargo space and considerable seaworthiness. We'd added two deck mounts for sails that we would
use if the winds were favorable. We dressed for immersion with
2-mm shorty wetsuits that protected the body parts most vulnerable
to heat loss: the body core, armpits, and groin. Over the wetsuits
we wore long-sleeve paddling jackets. We also wore neoprene socks
and neoprene sleeves on our forearms. I had deliberately chosen the
shorty-style suits after hearing a Coast Guard medical doctor report
on his studies of body-core heat loss in cold water. The study found
that shorty wetsuits protected the shoulders and armpits better than
Farmer John wetsuits. With neoprene on our lower arms and from
our calves down, only our heads, elbows, knees, and parts of our
hands were exposed.

Our plan was to paddle from the put-in at Michipicoten Harbour
to Floating Heart Bay, make the crossing to the island, and explore its
perimeter and larger streams. We would then cross back to the mainland, go 40 miles north to Hattie Cove, and paddle back to our starting point. If we had more bad weather days, we expected we would at
least make it to Hattie Cove and shuttle overland back to our vehicle.

The previous year I'd felt vulnerable near the middle of this passage, so I purchased and registered an ACR personal locator beacon

(PLB) as a precaution. When activated, it sends a distress signal and location coordinates (via satellite and a Rescue Coordination Center) to the appropriate search-and-rescue team. (See the "EPIRB and PLB Recommendations" sidebar in Chapter 17.) It was our security blanket not just for paddling but also for mishaps that might occur on land while far from a road, a telephone, and maybe even another human being. At 63 years old, and with Judy not much younger, I felt the PLB was a prudent addition to our safety gear. The model we chose also allowed us to send daily "OK messages" and our location coordinates to our loved ones.

We filed our float plans using ACR's web-based trip registration service. If we activated the PLB, the U.S. and Canadian coast guards and ACR would have key information available, including our intended route, the type, size, and color of the kayak, and the colors of our paddling jackets. They would be able to keep our contacts apprised of our status until the rescue was complete. I would keep the PLB tethered to my person so I could activate it even if I were separated from the kayak.

Our trip in 2010 was colder, windier, and wetter than any prior year. The first two days were quite warm, and the winds were moderate, but after the first stopover at McCoy's Harbour, we spent three to five nights at almost every campsite awaiting a break in the weather. Lake Superior can be formidable, and most days we were confronted with 20- to 30-mph winds.

After spending three nights at Floating Heart Bay (the closest approach to Michipicoten Island), we were presented with strong northwest winds and predictions for more of the same, so we decided to put off the crossing and instead proceeded westward, hugging the north shore for protection from the wind. The coastline here roughly parallels that of the island for the next 15 miles. We could cross from another point if the opportunity arose or continue to our turn-around point at Hattie Cove and catch the island on the return leg.

Our strategy worked fairly well until we got to Le Petit Mort Rocks in the afternoon. Here, the shoreline begins to arc gently northward to the west of Floating Heart Bay, and once beyond Le Petit Mort Rocks, the shoreline was no longer providing us adequate shelter from the northwest wind. After about an hour of being pummeled by wind and mounting seas, we decided to turn around and overnight in a cove above a small beach behind the "little death" rocks.

Contrary to the earlier weather reports, the next day was fair and mild, with a light north wind. The latest weather reports indicated the northerly would last no more than a few hours, then change to a west wind. We saw this as our opportunity to cross, and we did, using our sails to speed our trip. Fortunately, the fair weather window remained open long enough for us to make it to the island's East End Lighthouse at Point Maurepas—but no longer. The wind shifted just before we arrived, and then the wind and waves rose suddenly right after we landed.

Once we were on the island, the unfavorable weather pattern returned. We spent two nights at the lighthouse, then another mild day paddling around to East Sand Bay, a deep, southeast-facing scoop out of the island's southern shore. The fifth day opened with a gale from the southeast—a howling, sandstorm wind, alternating with cold, driven rain. Weather radio indicated conditions were more benign everywhere else. The gale lasted a full 24 hours, and then the wind turned to the west, and for the next two days we watched leaping waves march past the bay.

Judy and I reviewed our situation and our calendar. We were not making the progress we intended. Approaching the equinox, daylight was diminished by several minutes each day, and the air temperature, already below normal, was following suit. Nights were sometimes at or below freezing, and days were now typically around 50°F. We decided to head back to the mainland.

The next day, winds were fairly stiff, but from the west. By hugging the south shore as it arced northeastward, we felt conditions would be favorable for our return to the East End Lighthouse. The wind rose and shifted to the east that evening, and we spent the next day listening to the waves pound the rocks, periodically checking the kayak to make sure the waves weren't reaching high enough to grab it from the boulder ridge where we had secured it.

The next morning, we admired a spectacular sunrise but decided to ignore the old mariner's saying, "Red sky in morning. . . ." The winds were gentle and from the southeast, and the weather report was for the wind to change to the southwest and increase to around 20 miles per hour in the midafternoon. We thought we could be across by then, and if we weren't, we would be close to land and able to make safe harbor before the sea rose too high. We also took comfort from the fact that, in a worst-case scenario, we did have the personal locator beacon. So we packed up and shoved off. We decided to strike out to the northwest, with the wind directly at our backs, headed for Le Petit Mort, the same bay where we had departed from the mainland.

Within a half hour of our departure, the gentle southeast breeze became a brisk southeast wind. Apparently the sequence of events was not to be a wind shift followed by a rise in wind speed. The wind speed was rising first. By then, however, the prospect of fighting the wind to get back to the island was daunting, and we figured that the southeasterly would help us get to the mainland before it changed direction.

Our reluctance to reverse course and return to the island was part of our undoing. Yes, it would have been very difficult to fight the wind and waves if we had turned around, but plowing into the waves, able to see the oncoming peaks, anticipate their effects, and compensate accordingly would have afforded us much more directional stability. A heavy following sea knocks the stern to the side, and since the top of a wave is flowing forward, the boat must be moving even faster than the water in the crest in order for the rudder to function. I became fatigued by constantly correcting for direction and compensating, after the fact, for wave impacts.

As we got farther from the island, occasional waves crossed from the southwest, even though the wind had not yet shifted. These were a nuisance, as they crossed the southeasterly waves at roughly a 60-degree angle, and where they met, the combined crests peaked while the troughs deepened. I expected we'd experience crossing waves for a short period of time after a wind shift, but the wind was still from the southeast. As we would learn later, this herringbone pattern of waves, well known by experienced mariners and called the Witch's Grin, is caused by a 90-degree shift in wind direction and was accentuated by the waves from the south wrapping around the island and intersecting.

Then the wind changed—2 to 3 hours before we expected it to—and grew stronger. Building southwesterly waves intersected the well-established southeasterly waves. We decided to change course to avoid being broadsided by the growing southwesterly waves and started steering a little east of due north, aiming for Floating Heart Bay. Judy and I struggled to keep moving forward, but we were getting knocked side to side. Where the two wave patterns converged, waves would occasionally toss a column of water into the air that appeared fully double the other wave heights.

Slowly, the mainland appeared closer and the island behind us more distant. We took some comfort when the GPS told us we were at least halfway. The wind was stronger than anticipated, and by now the waves seemed over 6 feet in height and the peaks higher yet. (We later learned the waves were up to 10 feet high.) The shore disappeared from view about half the time.

I felt the stern swing violently to the left as we listed to the right. Almost at the same time, a large wave crest from the right washed over my shoulders, burying the aft half of the boat while the forward half seemed to pitch upward as it was thrown to the right. I felt the kayak roll into the curl of the wave and I knew there was no coming back. I shouted in outrage at the elements even as my mouth filled with water. And then I was upside down.

OK, we've all been taught that all you have to do is roll back up. Try that in a fully loaded tandem in heavy seas—especially when you've never done it very well in practice in a single. Nonetheless, I tried. The kayak barely rotated. I evacuated the cockpit and bobbed to the surface.

Judy was already out and hanging on. She asked if I was OK. I sputtered affirmatively and asked her the same. I didn't notice the water temperature. With our two-piece shorty wetsuits, long water socks, paddling jackets, and water shoes, we weren't completely exposed, but I knew we couldn't afford to stay in the water for long. We both had our paddles, which were attached by paddle leashes to our paddling jackets. We also were both wearing backpacks carrying hydration packs. These provided some insulation as well as flotation.

I decided the first order of business was to attempt a self-rescue, so together we righted the kayak. I dispensed with the paddle-float approach and had Judy hold one side of the kayak while I pulled myself up from the opposite side onto the rear deck. The kayak promptly tipped over again. The second attempt worked better, and I reentered the cockpit. The waves within the cockpit surged back and forth, causing an eerie water-clap sound like you'd hear at the back of a sea cave. I contemplated whether I should empty the cockpit with the bilge pump or have Judy get in first. A crashing wave suggested I'd never get the spray skirt on, much less be able to empty the cockpit in these seas. Then another wave sent me over, throwing me a good 6 feet from the boat.

My paddle was between my legs and one leg was wrapped in the leash. I had to get untangled before I could swim back to the kayak. By the time I had myself straightened out, the boat was 20 feet away. I was upwind of the kayak, and the wind was blowing it farther from me. Judy was holding on to the lee side of the kayak, watching the bilge pump float away. For the first time ever, I had failed to secure the bilge pump tether to the kayak. Had Judy pursued it as it floated away, we both could have been separated from the kayak. Waves were breaking over my head, and I swallowed some water.

We didn't have a throw rope. I had always thought of it as something to assist another boat, and we always went alone. If Judy could have tossed one to me, letting it trail upwind of the drifting kayak, I could have reached it and pulled myself to the boat. We later learned that 15-meter throw lines are required boating equipment in Canada. I tried to swim to the boat, but my tethered paddle was like a sea anchor. I reorganized myself and used the paddle to swim, albeit clumsily. I slowly approached the kayak, then put on a burst of speed to catch up. I gained on it somewhat more quickly but soon ran out of steam. I had to catch my breath, but the crashing waves kept that from happening. By the time I recovered, the boat was 30 feet away. I tried again and again, without success. Judy watched me with a look of desperation.

At this point it was clear to me we were not going to self-rescue. I wasn't even sure I was ever going to catch up with the boat. I fumbled and found the rip cord on the belt pack for my inflatable life vest. It promptly inflated but was so rigid that it was difficult to pull over my head.

It was clear we were going to need help if we were to survive. I opened the pocket on my spray skirt and pulled out the PLB. I hated having to do this. I'd never before gotten myself into a situation I couldn't get myself out of. But I had no other choice. I unwrapped the antenna and uncovered the red emergency button. I pushed it, held it 2 seconds. Had I held it 2 seconds? Was my sense of time even close to accurate? The PLB's display showed that it was sending coordinates, and its strobe began flashing. It would do this, presumably, for 48 hours. I knew we wouldn't last 48 hours in Lake Superior, so either that would be long enough to summon assistance or it was a moot issue. I tucked it into my PFD where it was generally above the water and its GPS was well exposed. It was still tethered to my spray skirt so I wouldn't lose it.

By now the kayak was a good 75 or more feet away from me. Judy appeared not to have inflated her vest yet. I began to paddle-swim toward her, but that was awkward. I had never practiced swimming with my PFD inflated. I swallowed more water as waves crashed over me. I tried different approaches, once even holding the paddle aloft like a sail, hoping the wind might move me toward her and the boat. It seemed they were receding ever farther, disappearing except when they bobbed up on top of a wave. Once I saw Judy had righted the boat, but then it was over again. Once more it was up, and she was in it. "Good girl!" I spluttered aloud, but then it was over again. Why didn't she inflate her life vest? Finally, I could see the vest inflated, but not on her. She appeared to have her arm looped through it.

I was starting to feel the cold. I didn't know how long it had been. I looked at the distant shore and thought, "Is this how it ends? If help doesn't arrive, this will be how it ends." I looked for the kayak. I wasn't even sure where to look anymore. I began to despair. I flashed on a scene from the film *The Perfect Storm*, where the last surviving crewman from the submerged fishing boat bobs to the surface in his PFD and the camera pulls away, revealing the vastness of the sea—and how hopelessly lost he is in it. I chastened myself for being such a media creature that I would even think of such a thing in this situation.

Then I saw Judy and the kayak, so far away, Judy with that desperate, searching expression on her face, looking for me. I had been swimming in the wrong direction. Then I thought, "No, it will not end this way!" I resolved to make it to her side. The only way I could possibly catch her would be to paddle-swim as efficiently as possible, at a rate I could sustain for a long time. If I could travel just a bit faster than the kayak was drifting, I could catch it—if I could keep it up long enough. I didn't know how long it would take for rescue or if rescue was in fact on its way. If rescuers found me by homing in on the PLB and strobe, I needed to stay close to Judy so she'd be found quickly. So I swam using the paddle. It was hard to estimate how long. Paddle, breathe. Paddle, breathe. Ignore the breakers. Swallow water. Breathe, paddle. It occurred to me that at least I wouldn't get dehydrated.

I was closer. I could see Judy and the kayak more frequently. This was heartening. It seemed Judy was turning the kayak into the wind. "Good girl!" I thought again. "That will reduce the windage and help me catch up!" But then it was parallel to the waves again. At one point it appeared I was almost even with *(continued page 270)*

RISK HOMEOSTASIS

Christopher Cunningham

In 2004, the Recreational Boating Product Assurance Division of the United States Coast Guard released a report titled "The Efficacy of Sponsons on Canoes and Kayaks." The review of sponsons (a type of flotation device) was, as the report put it, "part of an effort to identify worthwhile strategies and equipment to increase boating safety."

The most interesting part of the report was its presentation of risk homeostasis theory: "The theory states that when a person engages in any activity, they are constantly maintaining the risk level they are comfortable with, regardless of safety precautions." So, if paddlers add sponsons to their boats to increase their safety, the theory suggests they are likely to take on riskier activities. In balance, the level of risk hasn't been decreased but remains the same. This theory has most often been used to explain the unintended adverse effects of safety devices: an increase in fatalities associated with mandatory use of seat belts, an increase in accidents among taxicabs equipped with ABS brakes, and a higher incidence of poisonings after the FDA required childproof lids on medications. The devices all performed as they were expected to, but in response to the presence of the devices, people changed their behavior and became less cautious.

In this chapter Robert Beltran speculated that having a PLB influenced his decision to launch for a long exposed crossing. A

PLB is an invaluable tool for initiating a rescue. Its signal is picked up by satellite and instantly conveys your position coordinates to search-and-rescue teams. That may be reassuring, but it's a bit of an abstraction. As Robert and Judy now know, the blinking light on a PLB may be an effective call for help, but they still had to go through hell and survive long enough to be rescued.

So we often have to learn things the hard way. Anyone who has taken a spill on a bicycle discovers you can be badly hurt even if you're wearing a helmet. Anyone who has a child soon finds out that you can childproof a house but you still can't turn your back on a toddler. No device is as good as having the knowledge, experience, and judgment that will keep you from having an accident in the first place.

Problems arise when the perceived level of risk is lower than the actual risk. The law in many states requires cars to stop for pedestrians at crosswalks, for example. Drivers rarely do, however, so while a crosswalk may be perceived as a safe place to cross the street, it really isn't. Looking out for traffic is what provides the safety, whether you're using the crosswalk or jaywalking midblock. In the Coast Guard report, one source explained that "sponsons could even be dangerous because they create a false sense of security and may encourage paddlers to take risks they wouldn't take otherwise." The danger, of course, lies not with the sponsons but in the paddler's thinking.

The risk homeostasis theory is based on statistics, not a cause-and-effect relationship dictating that you'll necessarily be made less safe by the equipment you carry. The key element in safety is knowing how to keep yourself from getting into a situation that requires you to use your emergency equipment. We all take on risks every day. Those that we take while sea kayaking should fall well within our ability to make it back to shore in good shape before anyone thinks it necessary to go looking for us.

Sponsons, like PFDs, flares, VHF radios, and PLBs, won't make any of us safer paddlers. They can only mitigate the consequences of any trouble we might get into. The Coast Guard's report concluded that "sponsons may not be appropriate for every canoe and kayak activity, but there are applications that have proven beneficial to some users. As with other boating equipment, sponsons do not provide a single solution to all safety problems, and their use remains a personal decision by the boater." The same could be said about almost any piece of kayaking safety equipment. As another study on risk homeostasis concluded, "Indeed, safety is in people, or else it is nowhere."

it relative to the wind, but a hundred feet off to the side. I had to correct my course. As I drew nearer, I saw that the front hatch cover was missing. The bow was riding low in the water. Judy must have accidentally dislodged the latches while attempting to right the kayak or board it. The lower profile of the bow may have been what was allowing me to catch up. What I didn't know was that Judy was trying to scissor-stroke the kayak in my direction. Whatever was happening, I was finally getting closer. I was getting colder, and I was running out of energy. It must have been an hour by now that I had been chasing the kayak.

Just keep swimming. I had almost reached it before and had run out of steam. If that happened again, my energy was too depleted to make another attempt. I had to avoid the urge to put on a burst of speed. Just keep plugging. And I knew I must not grab for the kayak too soon; if I missed, or if it lurched out of reach, I'd lose momentum and then have to reorient the paddle. I waited until I was in contact with the kayak to reach for it.

I caught the rudder deployment lines with my fingers. Judy came around the bow to the upwind side and called back to ask if I was OK and if I had activated the PLB. I gasped yes to both, but I needed to rest. The waves were crashing over my head as the kayak and I bobbed up and down. I tried to use the kayak to elevate myself a bit in the water, my inflated life vest holding me somewhat away from the boat. I just hung there for a while, recovering. Once my breath and strength returned, I worked my way around to the downwind side of the kayak and Judy did the same at her end. I moved along that side to join Judy at the bow. I asked her about her PFD. "I can't get it over my head!" she replied. "I can't use both hands because I won't let go of the kayak!" We had never before inflated our PFDs, so we were inexperienced at actually getting them on, especially in a situation in the water when you don't want to release the boat.

I told her to hang on, and I pulled it over her head. It had not been easy to get my own PFD over my head, and it was harder still to do that for Judy.

"I'm going to try to reenter the boat again," I said. "Try to stabilize it from the upwind side—but don't let it get away from you!" I worked my way back to the rear cockpit while Judy went around the bow. After a couple of tries, I managed to get into the boat. It felt terribly unstable. Judy tried to get in, and we capsized. I reentered. We repeated the experience. The kayak just wasn't stable enough for her to get in too. We were less than fully practiced in self-rescue. Our practices had typically been in gentle, warm waters with low winds, using an empty kayak. Reentry of both kayakers in a flooded kayak with the stability of a half-soaked log was much more challenging.

In the process of entering and capsizing, my coiled paddle leash became tangled in the deck-mounted sail yoke. Judy too had her paddle leash wrapped on the sail yokes. We had kept the yokes mounted because of the inconvenience of stowing and retrieving them as needed. Our coiled paddle leashes compounded the problem in that they persistently fouled on everything they encountered. Judy was not able to release her paddle, but I got it loose for her by releasing the leash's Velcro fastening.

Judy gave up trying to get back into the boat and hooked her arm over the forward cockpit coaming and hung on. I tried to paddle, partly to maintain some stability, partly to generate some body heat, and partly to try, however incrementally, to move us toward the mainland shore still 4 to 5 miles to the north. Judy's drag on the port side of the boat kept turning us in that direction. Trying to overcome the drag using the rudder and paddling mostly on my left was only slightly effective. I know that at least once we turned in a complete circle. Eventually, I was paddling just to be doing something.

The chill was beginning to penetrate. We both had lost our hats. I could feel the heat leaving my body in the 25-knot wind. I was in the kayak, only half immersed, but Judy was still in the water. It had felt warmer in the water, but sensation can be deceptive. Survival was beginning to look less likely. I could keep believing we would survive as long as I was reasonably strong and our objective realistically attainable. But it had become apparent that even if we made shore on our own, we would be too hypothermic to survive. And at the rate we were chilling, we would never make shore. We had been heartened when I regained the kayak but dismayed by our inability to get us both into the boat without capsizing. Our inability to make progress toward shore was just as discouraging.

Our only hope was that the Coast Guard had received our PLB signal and were en route. We spoke of it circuitously. We told each other that we loved each other. Judy told me how she had feared she had lost me. I told her of the wrenching minutes when I couldn't see her or the boat. We kept hoping to see our rescuers and wondered how far they would have to travel. We didn't know how much time had passed, but it seemed like hours. I kept paddling. My arms hurt. My hands barely felt like a part of me, but they continued to follow my instructions and I held on to my paddle. The waves must have gotten more organized, with less of a southeasterly component, as I don't think I could have stayed upright if the herringbone peaks had been prominent.

I was weakening significantly and could feel the cold in my bones when I heard a deep drone. I saw a magnificent, huge, four-engine prop plane approaching us from the southeast, flying what seemed to be only a couple of hundred feet above the water. It was the Canadian Coast Guard search plane. We would later learn it had come all the way from Trenton, Ontario, some 90 miles east of Toronto. The C-130 aircraft was a beautiful sight as it flew directly over us. It seemed like forever before it turned and circled. It seemed to be flying a pattern and flew over us again only after completing it, then circled some more. We assumed it must be checking to be sure we weren't the only ones out here. But it also soon became apparent this aircraft was not going to rescue us. It was the search half of search and rescue, and the faster half at that. How far behind was the helicopter? We could only wait.

Time was elastic. The half hour it took for the U.S. Coast Guard helicopter to arrive seemed like well over an hour. It approached from the south, across Michipicoten Island, and pulled to a hover about 200 feet away. My arms were rubbery, barely able to brace the kayak against battering by the waves, and I hurt from chill and fatigue. My field of vision had closed down to a tunnel, and I didn't see the rescue swimmer leap from the helicopter. I looked over my right shoulder to see what looked like a finless dolphin slicing through the water at amazing speed toward us.

In a moment the rescue swimmer reached me and said, "We're going to get you both out of here. I'll take your wife first and come back for you." I would later learn his name was John. He then went to her, gave her a thumbs-up, and said, "You're going to be OK!" and told her the plan. He grabbed her by the loop on her backpack and towed her back toward the helicopter, placed her in the basket, and sent her skyward. When he came back for me, he said we had a nice kayak and nice equipment. I think I thanked him. At this point, I was only intermittently aware of things, as I was beginning to shut down, but when he said he was going to tip the kayak over so he could take me, I had enough presence of mind to reach behind my seat and grab the waterproof pouch tethered there. It contained a credit card and ID, some money, and most importantly, the car key. I wasn't capable of unclipping it, so as I fell out of the kayak, I just pulled until the cord snapped.

John told me to relax and let him do the work. He towed me through the water by my backpack strap at remarkable speed. The water felt so warm compared to the icy wind. He laid me on my back in the basket, which was submerged just below the waves, and told me to hold my glasses. As I rose through the air I turned my head to see our capsized kayak drifting slowly northward, presumably never to be seen again. I didn't care.

The prop wash from the chopper blades was intense and freezing. Whatever body heat I had left seemed to get sucked out of me on that ascent. I was helped out of the basket by one of the crew, positioned on the floor in the back, and given a blanket. Judy was sitting in the one spare seat in the rear. We both expressed our relief at being reunited and for our rescue. Then cramps set in my entire body, especially my neck. Mercifully, Judy didn't experience any cramping. A crewman put a radio-equipped helmet on me so the crew and I could hear each other. He pulled off our PFDs and our water socks, and said the heater in the cabin was cranked all the way up. It was stifling for them but good for us. John turned off my PLB and said he would love to learn the whole story.

When we arrived at the Wawa airport, the ambulance was waiting. We were each asked whether we could walk to the ambulance. For me, there was no way that was going to happen. Judy was able to walk the few steps to the ambulance.

We had spent over 3.5 hours fully or semi-immersed in the water. The Coast Guard reported the water temperature at 55°F. I was more hypothermic than Judy. The paramedics couldn't get a temperature reading on me using a forehead scanner. They immediately stripped the wetsuits and gear from us and wrapped us in warm blankets. Once we were in the emergency room at Lady Dunn Hospital, they were able to take ear-probe temperatures. Mine was 93°F, and Judy's was 95°. I was still cramping. They put us both under hot air blankets, and because my hypothermia was more severe, I was put into the trauma room and administered a warm IV, followed by warm liquids to drink. Judy recovered more quickly, and after 3 hours of treatment, we both enjoyed a hot shower. I learned later that it would have been dangerous, possibly fatal, to have taken a hot shower early on. Warming the skin too rapidly can cause a sudden rush of cold extremity blood to move into the body core, causing cardiac arrhythmia. We were given wonderful care, receiving the almost undivided attention of a physician and the ER staff for 4 hours.

After we had both recovered sufficiently, the hospital staff provided us with warm clothing and summoned a pair of community volunteers from the Wawa Area Victim Services program to return us to our vehicle, which we had parked not far from the hospital. One of the volunteers, hearing our story, told us we had been caught in the "Witch's Grin."

Five days later, we were contacted by Dave Wells, a kayak outfitter in Michipicoten Harbour near Wawa. We had provided him, the police, local fishermen, and anyone else we could think of with a list of the kayak's contents in case any of it were to show up. Dave told us that our kayak had washed ashore on a sand beach adjacent to his facility. It had drifted 35 miles to one of the few patches of sand in a coast that is nearly all rocks.

Dave and his staff had emptied the kayak of sand, brought it to their facility, emptied the hatches, and dried out the gear. The kayak was nearly undamaged. We lost my camera and some nonfloating items that had been stored in the cockpits, but recovered almost all the rest. Even my paddle was retrieved by local folks who turned things over to the police or Dave. Our GPS was found on the beach, still working.

After the accident I wondered if having the PLB had influenced our decision to proceed even when we had doubts about the crossing. I know it went through my mind that morning, weighing the factors, that if conditions turned really rotten and we got into trouble, we always had the PLB to fall back on. Would we have proceeded without it? I don't know the answer, but I know I will be wary of allowing it to influence me in the future. No doubt our family and friends will demand we carry one on future excursions (as if we weren't already convinced ourselves), and after this event, I expect they will be tracking our movements and status carefully.

Surviving a near-death situation can be a life-altering experience. In our case, it has served to cement the bonds between Judy and me. Seeing a loved one's life at genuine risk, especially knowing you may be responsible, can be more frightening than being at risk yourself. It reprioritizes your values in a hurry. Both of us are more aware of how precious we are to one another. The single strongest memory I have of that event is the image of Judy in the distance clinging to the kayak as waves intermittently heaved her into view, her face filled more with concern for me than with fear for herself.

We two aging, far less than optimally conditioned sea kayakers had capsized in Lake Superior under adverse weather conditions and weren't able to self-rescue, yet we survived thanks to a combination of technology and the extraordinary efforts of a team of people who have dedicated themselves to bailing the rest of us out of situations we should never have put ourselves into. Certainly, our experience underscores the importance of kayakers having a personal locator beacon for any but the most protected waters. Our only consolation in consideration of the public resources expended to save us is the hope that our case contributed positively to the justification for the U.S. and Canadian Coast Guard budgets. We cannot fully express our gratitude.

LESSONS LEARNED
Roger Schumann

When analyzing most kayak accidents, one rarely has to look very far beyond a few common basic safety measures to see what went awry. The majority of mishaps typically involve hypothermia plus one or more (too often all) of four basic errors. Paddlers who got in trouble were (1) not wearing PFDs, (2) not dressed for immersion, (3) paddling a kayak without adequate flotation, and/or (4) lacking adequate rescue training and practice for the type of trip attempted. There is often also a bad decision to launch, followed by one or more unexpected waves and/or gusts of wind and, voilà—deep trouble.

In this story bad things happened to paddlers who thought they were fairly well prepared. Both Robert and Judy wore PFDs as well as wetsuits, and they paddled a kayak that had demonstrated "considerable seaworthiness" to them for the past 15 years. They also had several years' experience in the area and carried a personal locator beacon "as a last resort" to get them out of just about any trouble they might get themselves into. In spite of their feeling well prepared for the trip, trouble did come, and it came in spades.

While stories of survival can be inspiring—Bob and Judy's determination after they found themselves in the water was no less than heroic—our goal is to avoid putting ourselves in circumstances where our survival is in jeopardy.

Back to Basics

Bob and Judy did wear PFDs, although the inflatable type they wore proved less than ideal when they ended up in the water. Although the PFDs ultimately did the job of keeping them afloat, despite the obvious operator error, standard PFDs that use foam for flotation would have caused them fewer problems, and the inherent insulating properties of foam would have kept them somewhat warmer. Bob and Judy hadn't practiced paddling, swimming, and doing rescues with their PFDs fully inflated. Bob told me that they just hadn't thought that practice was necessary. Making time to practice with the gear you will be using on a trip can help reveal any unexpected complications you might encounter.

While Bob and Judy had considered themselves dressed for immersion, they were not dressed for a capsize and wet exit in the middle of a 10-mile crossing in very rough conditions and in 55°F water.

Full wetsuits designed for paddling, or even dry suits and neoprene hoods, would have been better options. Had Bob and Judy both been warmer after Bob's long swim back to the kayak, they both might have been better prepared, not just physically but mentally as well, to explore and execute a wider range of reentry alternatives, such as deploying their paddle float (more on this later), that might have gotten them both out of the water and back aboard the kayak.

No immersion wear can assure survival in cold water forever, but what's more important than survival time is the added time immersion wear provides for clear thinking, adequate strength, and manual dexterity.

Most tandem kayaks are quite stable, especially when loaded with camping gear, but they can take on a lot of water after capsizing and lose much of their stability. With a hatch lost and the forward compartment flooded, Bob and Judy's tandem was made even less stable. Also, paddling a tandem kayak "solo," that is, without another kayak to help out and provide stability for reentries and pumping, definitely limited their rescue options. Other gear issues, such as getting tangled in paddle leashes and not having a throw line, compounded their problems. (Given their luck with the paddle leashes, however, I don't know if having another few dozen feet of throw line in the roiling water would have improved their situation much.)

The main lesson still left to learn before Judy and Bob attempt paddling solo in open water again—and the most important point, I believe, for readers to ponder—involves shifting our focus away from gear.

Focusing on things like tangled leashes and throw lines they wish they'd had and difficult PFDs is a bit off the mark—like "rearranging the deck chairs on the Titanic," as the saying goes. Certainly a throw rope could have saved Bob from the epic swim, but then what? And life jackets that didn't have to be awkwardly forced over their heads would have been much more helpful, for sure, yet still would have left them essentially in, or rather out of, the same boat: miles from shore without the skills to reenter their kayak, shivering and waiting for a helicopter ride to the hospital.

While the PLB certainly saved their lives, and their shorty wetsuits kept them alive long enough for the Coast Guard to save them, the fourth safety principle I listed above could have spared them the trauma and danger of requiring a rescue: Paddlers should have adequate self-rescue skills and practice for the trip planned.

Bob admits that they were "less than fully practiced in self-rescue." Bob had done some rescue training in calm conditions and had even managed to roll an empty single in practice. Judy's only background involved having taken a basic canoe course as a teen. They had not practiced at all together nor practiced rescues in a tandem or in a loaded kayak. Most importantly, they hadn't practiced in a loaded tandem together in conditions similar to those they could and did encounter on Lake Superior.

Bob mentions that his rescue "practices typically had taken place in gentle, warm waters and low winds using an empty kayak." Unfortunately, this is all too common an approach. While protected areas are a great place to begin your rescue training, allowing you a safe place to learn, it takes more than flatwater practice to develop the sort of self-sufficiency that might actually keep you from having to activate your PLB. Once you feel confident with your technique in calm water, a good next step is to move to a safe place to practice in more challenging conditions, such as off a wind-blown point where you're being blown back into a calmer area.

After that, the third step might be to head back to a calm area and practice in a loaded kayak, since it handles much differently from an empty one. While it might sound inconvenient to pack your kayak full of camping gear for a practice session, you can easily simulate a load by filling jugs of water held in place by float bags. You could also practice with an actual load of gear on the first day of a trip, in the shallows near shore as you're coming into camp. You don't even have to get your head wet; just jump out in waist-deep water and tip your boat over to see what it takes to get back in. Many paddlers I know resist this, because they say that they don't want to get wet and cold. But this would be a valuable reality check on whether their immersion gear is adequate for a capsize in actual conditions. If they aren't eager to get in the water to practice, it's a pretty good indication that they're not properly dressed. What you learn during an in-trip practice could provide you with invaluable information about how well you are equipped to carry out any crossing you may have planned for the days ahead. If Judy and Bob had done such a practice session before even considering their initial crossing to the island, they likely would have discovered the same weaknesses in their gear and skill in a much less dangerous venue. Knowing that the weather was worse than usual, they might then have reconsidered the crossing if they found any reason to be less assured about their current level of skill and the suitability of their gear.

The fourth step in preparation would be to practice in a loaded kayak out in rough conditions. Such a practice session would duplicate what Bob and Judy went through but without the dire consequences. Without a graduated series of practice sessions, the mid-crossing capsize they experienced was like learning to swim by jumping straight into the deep end of the pool.

By practicing before the cruise and the crossings, they would have discovered that their inflatable PFDs were difficult to deploy, and they could either have had a chance to figure out a technique for getting them over their heads more easily or else decided to switch them out for foam-type vests. They would also have learned that their shorty wetsuits were perhaps a bit skimpy for immersion in 55°F water and that they needed more thermal protection. And they might have prepared for the drill by making sure essential gear like the bilge pump was securely attached to the kayak.

They also would have discovered that the latches on their hatch covers were a problem. Fifteen years ago, when their double was made, the lever-and-slider systems for hatch cover straps were common and prone to release accidentally. Manufacturers have since addressed this problem in a number of ways—bending the end of the levers upward, putting jogs in the sides of the lever arms, or putting webbing with snaps on the slider—all to help prevent accidental tripping. Unfortunately, hundreds of the old closure type are still lurking on hatch covers, and they are susceptible to being tripped, especially in reentries when people are crawling over the decks. Regular practice would have revealed this problem and sent Judy and Bob to seek a solution. Ironically, as Bob pointed out, the flooded bow and the resulting change in the trim of the kayak may have been what made it possible for him to catch up with the kayak.

Bob's paddle leash was attached to his spray skirt, instead of his kayak, leading to his becoming tangled in it away from the kayak and precipitating his long swim. He and Judy found the coiled leashes they used were especially prone to tangles and snares. Practice would have exposed the possible problems with their paddle leashes and left them better able to weigh the pros (such as not losing your paddle) with the cons (entanglement issues) and to consider possible alternatives. (For more on the trade-offs and use of paddle leashes, see "Staying Connected: The case for paddle tethers," *SK*, Feb. 2000, available as a pdf file at www.seakayakermag.com under "Free Resources.")

Most of all, taking the time to practice gives paddlers a more realistic idea of their reentry skills, allowing them to make better informed route decisions. Crossings require a higher level of expertise in rescue skills and knowledge of alternatives. The greater the exposure, the higher the risk of bad conditions and greater need for practice in rough water.

My standard advice to students is not to paddle in waters that are rougher—or likely to get rougher—than they've practiced rescues in. To take this a step further, always add a set of conditions to your skills and equipment. Saying, "I've practiced paddle-float recoveries" won't help you make decisions as well as being able to say, "I've done solo reentries in 3-foot seas and 20-knot winds with a loaded kayak." Similarly, an assessment like "I'm dressed for immersion" is not as useful as "I can still function well in my immersion wear after 20 minutes in 50-degree water."

A rescue is something that happens to paddlers who don't yet have the skills to reenter their kayak after a capsize. Capsizing is in itself not the problem for kayakers. For those with a solid roll, it's just a momentary dunking. It is when paddlers end up in the water without the proper gear or regularly practiced skills to reenter the kayak that a capsize can become life threatening.

The major lesson to be learned from this incident is what can happen if you take a set of skills and equipment that may be adequate for touring in calm, warm water along a friendly shoreline, and then attempt to pull off a significant open-water crossing during a fluke of a weather window on a large body of cold water with a nasty reputation.

Exposure is a key consideration. It makes a big difference whether you are paddling 5 minutes or 5 miles from the nearest safe landing zone. On longer crossings, there is more time for conditions to change. Your decision to cross has to be based not on what conditions are like at the start but on what they could become before you make a safe landfall and how much strength you'd have left to deal with adversity, say several hours after leaving shore.

Bob and Judy's first crossing committed them to a second crossing, doubling their time of exposure. The brief weather window that allowed them to get to the island hadn't been forecast but was merely a break in a pattern of unfavorable conditions. They needed a second break in the weather to get back to the mainland. While I agree with their assessment that making the crossing back to the mainland was a poor decision, making the crossing out to the island in the first place set them up for trouble.

Once they ended up in the water, Bob mentions that he had a paddle float but decided not to use it for his reentry because Judy could stabilize the kayak for him while he got in. That strategy ended up being a good way for Bob to get himself out of the icy water, but while Judy provided the stability to allow Bob to get back in his cockpit, he was not able to brace well enough in the conditions for her to get back in without recapsizing them. Using a paddle float can provide much more stability than braces alone. Better yet, if both paddlers have paddle floats, especially ones that they've practiced with previously, they can provide enough stability on both sides of the kayak to help counteract the effects of confused sea conditions, such as those encountered by Bob and Judy.

Even with a pair of paddle floats deployed, there might not have been enough stability to remain upright in the teeth of the Witch's Grin, given some of the inherent issues with rescuing tandem kayaks. Although they are usually perceived as being a safer, more stable craft than single kayaks, after a capsize tandems pose several problems.

Their decks are generally higher and can make reentry more challenging than with single kayaks. The reentry sequence needs to be coordinated between the two paddlers. The large cockpits allow the entry of lots of water and for lots of sloshing (free surface effect) that creates instability. Bob was able to get back in the kayak for good once they drifted into the somewhat less confused seas beyond the Witch's Grin, and it is quite likely that paddle floats would have worked to get Judy aboard and kept the double upright, especially if the two had done a little rough-water practice beforehand.

While investing in a PLB is a good idea, investing in some rescue classes as well as some time practicing before heading out is an even better idea because the training can help you avoid the trauma of having to deploy a PLB. Expert guidance can be an invaluable source of advice and perspective, and nothing but actual practice—especially in at least some moderately rough seas—can reveal weaknesses in your gear or skills that might land you in trouble.

Practice your reentry skills regularly, at least every paddling season. Before every trip, ask yourself when was the last time you and your regular paddling partner practiced reentries. Did you practice together, in the same boats and conditions you are likely to capsize in? Reentry skills are perishable. When was the last time you checked the "expiration date" on yours?

26

The Right Place, The Right Time

Colin Mullen and Christopher Cunningham

COLIN'S STORY

Sea Kayaker magazine has a lot of stories about kayakers being rescued by other mariners: sometimes by the Coast Guard, sometimes by working seamen or pleasure boaters. Occasionally the tables are turned and kayakers come to the rescue. I had the opportunity to do just that this summer on Great Peconic Bay between the north and south forks of New York's Long Island.

On Monday, August 9, 2011, my girlfriend Dara Fee, her 17-year-old nephew Ryan, and I were enjoying a late afternoon outing on Great Peconic Bay. It was the first time Ryan had been kayaking. He was in Dara's P&H Delphin, Dara was in her Lincoln Canoe & Kayak Schoodic, and I was in my Tahe Marine Greenland T. We had paddled out of Red Creek Pond in Hampton Bays to Red Cedar Point and were on our way back. It was a short outing, less than 3 miles.

Dara and I were both American Canoe Association (ACA) Level 3 coastal kayakers. We were also ACA-certified trip leaders. I led numerous trips each year for North Atlantic Canoe and Kayak, a kayak club that both Dara and I belonged to. We were also members of Qajaq USA, a Greenland-style kayaking community in the United States. We had circumnavigated Manhattan Island and kayaked most bays on Long Island and Long Island Sound and had explored stretches of the Maine coast.

While paddling I always carried a VHF radio secured to my PFD. I always took visual and sound signaling devices, a paddle float, pump, first-aid kit, and a tow belt. Dara carried the same equipment.

We carried food and water appropriate for the length of the outing. If I was kayaking with Dara or other experienced kayakers, I usually stowed my tow belt along with my first-aid kit in my day hatch. I wore the tow belt on our August 9 outing because we were paddling with Ryan, a novice kayaker.

We were nearly halfway back to Red Pond when a white sailboat about 27 feet long passed in front of us about 35 yards ahead. There are a lot of boats sailing Great Peconic Bay, so this was not an uncommon occurrence, but this sailboat had a man being dragged through the water behind it at the end of a line. No one was visible aboard the boat, and only the jib was set. The boat was moving fast enough that the man in the water was apparently able only to hang on but not pull himself toward the boat. Dara and I, without speaking or even glancing at one another, started to paddle after the sailboat with Ryan following. After starting to pursue the sailboat, I hesitated, believing that I heard a faint yell of "Help" off to my left. I looked in that direction but I didn't see anyone in the water. I paddled after the sailboat again but couldn't shake a nagging feeling about the faint cry that I thought I'd heard. I once more turned my kayak to the left. It was clear that Dara would catch the sailboat, and I knew she could render whatever assistance was needed to the individual being dragged behind it.

Ryan was paddling after Dara, and I was confident that if Dara needed Ryan's assistance in helping with the sailboat, she would instruct him what to do. I'd watched Ryan paddling on our way to Red Cedar Point and was confident that he wouldn't capsize in the small 18-inch swells. Besides, Ryan was wearing a PFD, and even if he did capsize I knew he would follow the instructions that Dara had given

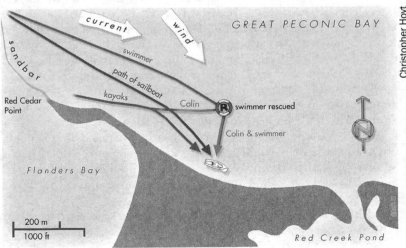

him before we set out: Hold onto the kayak to be more visible in the water, then wait for us to get him back into his kayak.

After paddling about 25 yards, doubt started to set in: Had I really heard a cry for help? Could that cry have come from the man being dragged behind the sailboat? Was I wasting time traveling in this direction when I should be trying to catch up to the sailboat? Just when I was about to change direction and continue chasing the sailboat and the man tethered to it, I saw a hand with outstretched fingers emerge from the water about 15 to 20 yards away.

Then, as if it had been a mirage, the hand was gone.

I glanced back over my shoulder and could see Dara now off in the distance rapidly gaining on the sailboat with Ryan not far behind her. I slowed down and continued paddling toward the spot where I had seen the specter of a hand emerge from the water. It didn't reappear. I continued to paddle but didn't see anyone in the water.

Then, directly in front of my bow, just below the water's surface inside a small swell, I was startled to notice a pair of eyes. The swell had brought the eyes almost up to my kayak's bow level just a few feet in front of me. The eyes seemed the size of golf balls. Emerging from the water once more was the hand, reaching for my bow. I applied some reverse strokes before the hand grasped my bow. I wanted to stop my kayak before the man did anything in panic that might capsize me. With just his fingertips gripping my bow, a head now emerged from the water along with the sound of a gasp for air. As I paddled backward I said, "Don't grab my boat—I'll tell you what to do!" I didn't want to risk capsizing if he tried to pull himself along my kayak's grab lines toward me. The man nodded, and I stopped back-paddling.

I instructed him to place his other hand on my bow and interlock his fingers. Once he had done this, I told him to let me know when he had caught his breath. When he once more nodded his head, I had him wrap his legs around the bow of my kayak and place his feet around the foredeck. The man seemed to be in his 50s, shirtless, tanned, barefoot, and heavyset but not overweight, with black hair and dark eyes. He appeared extremely calm while secured to my bow.

I hadn't done this swimmer rescue before with the Greenland T, but I had practiced the technique with my other kayaks. It is my preferred method for transporting a swimmer: I could see the individual on my bow and assess his or her condition as I paddled. I had no problem paddling distances with someone attached to my bow and didn't feel unstable. As it turned out, the Greenland T was very well suited for this rescue technique. Its long tapered bow allowed the swimmer to nestle right under the bow. He had no problem wrapping both his arms and legs around the kayak's narrow bow. With water temperature in the seventies this time of year, I didn't have to concern myself with the swimmer quickly becoming hypothermic. The Greenland T had very little freeboard, and if I had tried to carry him on the rear deck he would have submerged the kayak's stern and made it unstable. With him secured to the bow, I started to pursue the sailboat, which appeared to have come to a stop. My passenger, now that his life was no longer in jeopardy, regained his composure and was breathing normally. I had never been thanked so often and in such a short time span as when this man was clinging to my kayak's bow. He turned his concern to the sailboat, which was being carried by the wind toward a rocky shore.

It only took me a few minutes to paddle the approximately 100 yards to reach the sailboat. When I arrived, Dara was at its bow and the man who had been dragged by the sailboat now stood in waist-deep water, holding the line he'd been dragged by to keep the sailboat from running aground on the rocky north shore of Hampton Bays. The man on my bow, his shorts hanging around his knees, waded over to the sailboat and pulled an anchor out of the water and put it on deck. The anchor had been overboard and may have helped stop the boat as it drifted into the shallows near shore. There was no chain attached to the anchor, just a short line. The man I'd rescued climbed onto the sailboat's stern. With all modesty forgotten and no attempt to pull up his shorts, he started the small outboard engine.

Now with both men aboard, shorts up and engine running, they moved the sailboat away from shore while continuing to thank us. We didn't get their names or even take note of the name of the boat.

Dara and I, from the brief conversations we'd had with the sailors, put together the circumstances leading up to this incident. The two men had been sailing on Great Peconic Bay and decided to anchor near the exposed sandbar off Red Cedar Point. They dropped the anchor but left the small jib up. The anchor was tied to a short length of nylon rope. Without the weight of chain on the anchor rode, the anchor couldn't get a purchase on the sandy bottom. The line looked taut to them as if it were holding, but the boat was drifting slowly backward. The man I had rescued hadn't noticed the boat had moved and jumped off believing it was still in the shallows surrounding the sandbar. He found himself in water over his head. He was not wearing a PFD, and he couldn't swim. His companion, noticing the plight of his friend, secured a rope around his own waist and jumped into the water in an attempt to rescue him. The wind and current quickly separated the two. With just the jib set, the sailboat swung around on a downwind course and picked up speed. Soon it was moving fast enough that the man tethered to it could not pull himself along the rope to get back aboard. Within a few minutes the wind and current pushed the sailboat and the tethered sailor across our path.

I marveled at all the circumstances that fell into place to allow us to rescue these two men. Dara hadn't had her usual work assignment and had left work early; we'd picked that precise location and time to paddle; the direction of the wind and current had carried the men right across our path; I'd paid attention to the nagging feeling that I'd heard a weak cry for help; I'd looked in the right direction and noticed a hand emerging briefly from the water. We'd been very fortunate to be in a position to help the two sailors.

This was the second time I'd been able to help someone while I was out kayaking. Two years previously, two teenage boys had capsized a one-person, sit-on-top kayak in Noyak Bay, 12 miles to the northwest. I had gotten one of the boys back into the sit-on-top and towed the other back to shore with my kayak. I hadn't really thought much about that incident. I'd spent three years as a paratrooper with the 82nd Airborne in the 1970s and almost thirty years in law enforcement, so this hadn't been my first incident helping someone. I hadn't thought much of helping the boys out of a bind, but it was quite a different experience to see a man's hand reach out from beneath the waters of Great Peconic Bay.

LESSONS LEARNED
Christopher Cunningham

It's good to see that kayaks are not always on the receiving end of a rescue. There is a long-standing tradition of assisting mariners in distress: "Every master is bound, so far as he can do so without serious danger to his vessel and persons thereon, to render assistance to any person in danger of being lost at sea" (Article 10 of the International Convention on Salvage, 1989). There is also an obligation to keep watch while operating a vessel, not only to assure its safe navigation but also to respond to emergencies. The custom of assisting others is a central part of the maritime culture for one simple reason: On water we are out of our element, and without a sound vessel to carry us our survival time is limited. Kayaks may be small, but we are all mariners nonetheless. The diminutive size of our vessels may limit what we can do to assist others, but being alert to what goes on around us and prepared to take action can put us in a position to save lives.

The degree to which we prepare to go paddling usually increases the farther we are from home and the more isolated our destination. It makes good sense to be quite self-sufficient when help in an emergency would be, at best, hours in reaching us. But closer to home, while we may feel a greater margin of safety for ourselves, the likelihood of encountering other boaters in distress is much higher. Great Peconic Bay, where Colin, Dara, and Ryan crossed paths with the errant sailboat, is rimmed with piers and marinas. Just as most auto accidents occur within 25 miles of home, it's reasonable to expect that most boating accidents will happen in close proximity to the places boats are moored or launched.

The waters within view of the *Sea Kayaker* offices are a good example of an urban waterway. At the center of Shilshole Bay is a marina with 1,400 slips. To the south of the marina are a beach popular with stand-up paddlers and a canal leading to locks that lead to inland waters. About 65,000 boats pass through the locks each year. To the north of the marina are a four-lane launching ramp used by more than 10,000 boats per year and a popular beach frequented by kayakers and kiteboarders. The vast majority of boaters pass through these busy waters without incident, but a few get into trouble. I've pulled two capsized boaters out of the water while I was sailing and have towed a disabled fishing skiff behind my kayak.

We can't expect that other boaters will always respond to people in distress. A couple of years ago I was walking along the beach and saw a kiteboarder about 50 yards offshore. His kite had landed in the water and he appeared to have lost his board. He was struggling with a tangle of kite lines and it was clear he wasn't going to be able to get himself to shore. Even with a steady stream of power boats passing by him on their way in and out of the marina, no one stopped for him. (I tell the story of his eventual rescue in the "PIW" sidebar in Chapter 14.) Although this kiteboarder's sail in the water was an obvious sign of trouble, the signs are not always so easy to detect, like the faint cry that Colin thought he'd heard and could have passed without notice. For the two boaters that I'd pulled out of the water, there was literally nothing to see or hear. I had looked astern just to keep track of the other boats in my area. I'd been keeping a mental note of traffic nearby, so I recognized that one boat was missing. I turned around and headed to where I thought it had been and eventually caught sight of the low profile of an upturned hull.

Colin did well to pay attention to the sense he had heard something, especially when the sight of the sailboat dragging the sailor was so obvious and could have narrowed his focus. He could easily have missed the person in the water, a PIW in Coast Guard jargon.

A drowning person can be very easy to miss. We commonly associate drowning with crying out and thrashing in the water, a behavior referred to as aquatic distress. That can be true in some cases, but the signs of drowning are typically much more subtle. Mario Vittone and Francesco A. Pia, Ph.D., describe what they call the instinctive drowning response (IDR). In IDR, drowning people cannot speak or shout—their efforts are exclusively occupied with trying to breathe. Their mouths rise briefly above the water, then submerge again after a quick breath. They do not raise their arms or reach out or wave because they're pressing down in an effort to get their mouths above the water. They float vertically and don't kick to support themselves.

Colin approached the PIW with caution, knowing that a person in aquatic distress can be unpredictable and put a rescuer in danger. Emergencies necessarily create a sense of urgency, but it is important not to act too hastily. You can't be an effective rescuer if you make yourself part of the problem. Fortunately, Colin reached the swimmer in time and the swimmer had transitioned out of aquatic distress and could calmly grab his bow. As Colin discovered, people exhibiting the IDR typically relax when rescued.

The water wasn't dangerously cold, so hypothermia wasn't an immediate risk. Colin could afford to keep the swimmer in the water wrapped around his bow while he paddled toward shore and the sailboat. In cold water, a swimmer can be transported on deck to slow the onset of hypothermia. Our rescue practice is often directed at getting kayakers back in their kayaks, but to prepare for coming to the assistance of other boaters, practice should also include assisting a boatless PIW. If you are paddling with a group, a pair of kayaks can be rafted up to provide a stable platform to get a PIW on deck. Additional kayaks can tow the raft to safety. If your easily accessible emergency gear includes a space blanket, the PIW can be protected from the cold.

Colin had a VHF radio and could have summoned the assistance of a larger vessel if that had been required. In a life-threatening emergency, a Mayday call can bring other vessels in the area to assist while also enlisting the services of the Coast Guard. The Coast Guard can coordinate or assist in the rescue and prepare land-based emergency medical services to receive the rescued person. With submersible handheld VHF radios now available at under $100, there is little reason not to have one.

Most sea kayaker paddling is very much like the summer afternoon outing that Colin, Dara, and Ryan embarked upon. The benign conditions they paddled in were just the thing to bring other boaters out in numbers. Those times when we may feel least at risk may present us with situations where we can be of great service to others—perhaps even save a life—if we are well prepared and equipped.

27

In Awe, in Trouble
A Too-close Encounter with Gray Whales

Birgit Piskor, Perry Abedor, and James Michael Dorsey

MY STORY

Birgit Piskor

December 27, 2011, was just another day in paradise—or more specifically, another day at Los Cerritos, a relatively undeveloped stretch
of beach along the Pacific Coast of Southern Baja, about an hour's
drive up from Cabo San Lucas. That morning, Perry Abedor, a surfer
who lives on the property where I was staying, invited me out on his
tandem sea kayak to see if we could get some good sightings of the
gray whales that are so abundant this time of year. That sounded like
a fun, appropriately Baja-style adventure, so we gathered our gear
and headed down to the water.

It was a little tricky getting the double sit-on-top kayak through
the surf, but once we were past the waves the sea was relatively calm.
It wasn't long before we spotted whales blowing in the distance.
Excited, we paddled hard to see if we could intercept them. Sure
enough, there they were. We stayed a respectful distance away from
them and watched.

I had never been on the ocean in the presence of gray whales
before and had never seen the exquisite arching and slow languid
curve as their bodies reenter the sea, a curve that is endless and
achingly beautiful. We saw first one arching body, then another, and
then a third. It was grace beyond anything I had imagined, visceral
and deeply moving. Then as suddenly as they had appeared, they
were gone.

We had several more sightings that afternoon, each as exhilarating as the first, and for one glorious moment we were even able to keep pace off to the side of a small pod traveling south. By midafternoon we hadn't seen any whales in a while and contemplated heading home. We drifted quietly, breathing in the beauty of the open ocean, when we spotted two whales moving north. Perry tried to get their attention. He made a squeaky sound by rubbing his hand hard below the waterline against the plastic hull of our kayak. Whether that squeak meant anything to them or not, the whales seemed to have heard it because they turned and began swimming west. Here was our chance for one last encounter.

After several minutes of hard paddling to get closer to their new course, we stopped to wait. I said to Perry, "Wouldn't it be cool if the whales came up right beside us?" I recalled all of the photographs and films I'd seen of curious whales interacting with humans in small boats and allowing themselves to be touched. These peaceful encounters led me to believe that people can have a special, almost spiritual, relationship with these fellow mammals. What I mean to say is that I felt no fear, no fear at all for creatures that measure up to 45 feet and weigh over 35 tons.

Not 10 minutes later, a whale exploded out of the water a few feet behind and to the left of us. It was so sudden and so massive that I could not comprehend what was happening. Terrified and bewildered, I turned to grab the edges of the kayak to brace myself

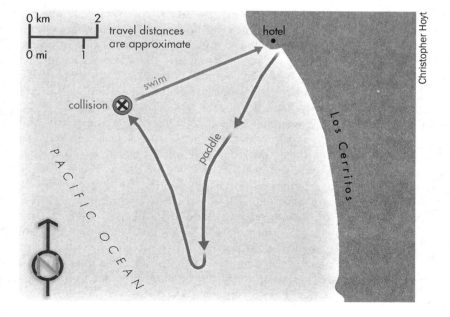

for the wave that would soon be upon us. In that moment, the second whale breached directly in front of me, rising and rising until all I could see was whale: no sky, no land, only whale. In that suspended moment, I knew I was dead. Yet there was no fear, no flashing of my life before me. I closed my eyes, bowed my head, and simply surrendered.

It turned out that Perry, sitting behind me, had kept his eyes open. He leaned way back and saw the whale twist and turn in the air and slam down directly on the kayak in the narrow space between us. I heard the mighty sound of the whale coming down, then felt a massive pressure as I was driven underwater. I opened my eyes, realized that I was still alive, and swam up through the swirling white water. When I surfaced, I saw that the kayak had buckled in the middle and was rapidly sinking. Perry was already up and uninjured, but I had sustained some injury that was causing pain in my right leg and lower back. By some miracle, neither of us was bleeding—these waters are thick with hammerhead and tiger sharks. The whales were gone, and Perry and I were easily 2 miles from shore.

Shock is a wonderful thing. It focuses the mind on the moment, on the task at hand, the actions that you must take to ensure your survival. I had no room for panic, no room for the horror of sharks and deadly jellyfish. Only one task existed, and that was to swim. To swim and make it to shore before the sun went down. After a quick hug in the water to celebrate that we were still alive, Perry and I began our swim.

I was thankful that I'd been a swimmer from way back and my work as a sculptor had kept my arms and upper body strong. I wasn't able to swim on my front due to my injury, but I was able to do the backstroke. It had always been a strong stroke for me. We swam and we swam until my hands went numb, but my arms kept moving. We were so far out that for the longest time it seemed like we weren't getting any closer to land. Fear began to seep in at the edges.

Eventually, it was clear that we were making headway and getting closer to land. While that was a massive relief, we had another challenge ahead of us; the current was pushing us northward, away from the long, sandy curve of Los Cerritos beach toward the rocky point that defines its northern end. The swell from the west had helped bring us in, but it had picked up and now huge waves smashed with killing force against those rocks. I had to place my trust in Perry's knowledge of these waters. We didn't alter our course until Perry told me to swim hard toward shore. I saw our goal was a single narrow strip of sand to the north of the point. This was our best chance to get safely ashore, for the rocky cliffs extended up the coast for quite a distance. Pain forgotten, I swam for my life. Perry was fantastic; staying just ahead of me, he shouted when to duck under the cresting waves and when to swim. Without him, I doubt I would have made it ashore alive. I reached the beach hypothermic, sobbing uncontrollably, and in shock. I was barely able to stand on my right leg, so Perry helped me up the beach, where we waited at the base of the cliff. People at the hotel atop the point had seen us, and help was on the way.

MY PERSPECTIVE
Perry Abedor

Birgit has given an accurate account, except I remember that both whales rose on the right side of the kayak. The first whale breached straight up, only 25 feet to the right of us. The nose of the whale reached 65 feet up while the tail was still in the water. It had to be 65 feet out of the water—these things were so giant. It was much larger than 50 feet, that's for sure.

It moved from west to east in a straight line and slammed into the surface of the ocean. It sent a 5-foot wave toward us. Birgit braced for the wave, then 10 feet away, when the second whale broke right through it, canceling it out. This second whale went straight up like the first. I watched it reach its apex, turn its pectoral fins, and come directly for our kayak. Had it continued in an easterly direction we wouldn't have been on a collision course, but it turned north. I watched the whale the whole time until it hit us. Its huge body extended most of its length to the north of us, but it was so close that the tail came right between Birgit and me. We were only about 5 feet from each other, with my legs extended between us. The force of the whale sent me 10 feet underwater, my whole body in pain. I don't know if the whale had hit me directly or if it was just the force slamming me down that caused so much pain. As I swam upward I felt all my limbs moving, so I knew everything was intact at that point. I clearly recall touching the whale for a split second as I reached the surface. It slithered right by my hand and I felt the slipperiness of his skin. I didn't

Perry stands with the bow of his kayak after it washed ashore three days following the incident.
Ron Adams

have my PFD on at the time, but I found it floating nearby and put it on. Birgit had been wearing hers.

I believe we were more than 2 miles out to sea, as Birgit estimated. I think it was 3 miles or more. The current was pulling us farther out to sea, and the more we swam, the more the current sucked us away from shore. I thought we were going to die out there. By the time we reached land, we had probably swum a total of 5 miles. I know this because I used to swim 4 to 5 miles in the ocean every day, and when we finally got back to shore I was totally spent. We made it to the beach about 45 minutes before the sun set.

Editor's Note

It can be difficult to estimate size and distance accurately, particularly when there is no frame of reference nearby. From the perspective of the kayak, the whale would have been seen in a foreshortened view and its length especially difficult to gauge, much as it is difficult to guess the height of a tall tree while standing next to its trunk. By the same token, judging a long distance to shore is difficult when you are sitting or floating close to the water's surface. An observer on shore who had been watching the kayakers when the whales breached—but who was unaware of the collision—put Perry and Brigit at "more than a mile from shore." Perry's and Birgit's estimates are presented here as they wrote them. Given the circumstances of the collision, any exaggeration is to be expected.

LESSONS LEARNED

James Michael Dorsey

Humans have shared the ocean with whales since long before recorded history, and there is evidence that kayaks can be traced back at least 6,000 years, so it is likely that paddlers and leviathans have had close encounters for at least that long. There is an account of a sperm whale that rammed the Nantucket whaling ship *Essex* on the morning of November 20, 1820. Many surviving crewmembers wrote accounts of it, and all agreed that after its companion had been harpooned, the whale attacked, ramming the ship repeatedly until it split its head open and died. Since then there has been only one recorded incident that I know of. In the mid-1960s in the Mexican lagoon and whale sanctuary where I have worked for 15 years, one of Jacques Cousteau's crews was in a Zodiac pursuing a gray whale; it breached underneath their boat and killed two crewmen. At that time, Cousteau was the only person actually investigating whale behavior. Little was known about whales, particularly where their comfort zone began or ended, so every one of Cousteau's encounters was an experiment. This one went badly. In 2010, there was a supposed attack by an orca against its trainer in a SeaWorld facility. My opinion is that confining an animal used to roaming hundreds of miles in a day inside a 40-foot tank is tantamount to locking a human in a closet, day in and day out, for several years; you can decide for yourself if this was an attack or the orca's inability to accept its environment any longer. (Orcas, by the way, are often categorized as dolphins, but the Cetacean Society International, the American Cetacean Society, and I consider orcas the largest of the toothed whales. Their behavior sets them apart from dolphins, placing them more toward the whale side.)

I consider both the *Essex* and the Cousteau events to be instances of instinctive self-defense rather than attacks. Both incidents happened long before the Marine Mammal Protection Act was enacted in the United States in 1972. While difficult to enforce, this law requires that mammals be given a 100-yard zone that is not to be encroached upon. It states that it is permissible to be closer if the mammal approaches, but unless a whale has shown itself previously, a kayaker might not be aware of its proximity. The Marine Mammal Protection Act applies in the United States, and Mexico and many other nations have similar laws protecting whales. (You can find links to summaries of many nations' laws at www.puertovallartawhalewatching.com/html/official_regulations.html.)

Gray whales are very much like humans. They breathe air, give live birth, nurse their young, and have hair and warm blood. In the womb, a gray whale has individual fingerlike digits that morph into a pectoral fin before birth, while a human fetus has finlike appendages that morph into fingers prior to birth. Only two living creatures have a soft spot on top of their heads at birth to allow for the growth of the brain: humans and whales.

Baby gray whales have almost no depth perception and are rambunctious and playful. In the spring 1984 Issue 1 of *Sea Kayaker* magazine are photos and an account of a gray whale calf capsizing a kayak in Magdalena Bay, Baja, Mexico. That incident can't be regarded as an attack. In their rush to investigate something new, young grays frequently ram into boats. I have seen this countless times in the sanctuary of San Ignacio, a gray whale nursery in Southern Baja, Mexico. During their first couple of years, baby grays are like human teenagers: curious, finding their way by experimentation, and often ignoring their mothers to make mischief. Occasionally juveniles have almost come out of the water right into my lap in their apparent eagerness to make contact. They do not know their own strength and have a compulsive curiosity. If something attracts their attention, they are drawn to it instantly without regard to consequences.

Birgit makes note of the fact that Perry made a squeaking sound by rubbing the hull of the kayak. This could certainly have attracted whales of any age. Recently a young gray breached next to a sailboat off the coast of California and landed on top of it. I have been told by many boaters that the creaking sounds of their rigging attracts whales. This may or may not be true, but it is certainly possible.

Unlike dolphins, orcas, and other toothed whales that navigate by echolocation, gray whales do not possess this ability and must rely on sound and eyesight to know what is around them. Grays do have some sensory receptors—dimples on their rostrum, or nose, with a single hair in each dimple—that pick up minute vibrations in the water and help them identify what is around them. In younger whales, this sensory ability is often not yet developed. Grays of all ages also frequently spy-hop, bringing their eyes out of the water to look around. Since their eyes face outward and down, they need to look above the water frequently to identify potential threats. Young whales do not always check their environs before surfacing. Think of a human teenager texting while driving or changing lanes without looking.

I have no doubt that these whales breached just as Birgit and Perry said they did, but I also believe they were most likely newborns or yearlings simply being reckless, as is their nature. The collision with Birgit and Perry's kayak was probably the result of a random breach, with no intent of harming the people or kayak. As far as I am concerned, it was simply an accident.

The size of the whales reported by Birgit and Perry was exaggerated, though understandably so. A length of 35 to 40 feet is average for a gray whale, and a large gray would weigh close to 40 tons. In two decades on the water among them, I have seen only two that approach a length of 45 feet. For a gray whale to have 65 feet of its body out of the water during a breach while its tail is still submerged would mean the whale had to be 70 to 75 feet long. There has never been documentation of a gray whale even close to 65 feet long.

The ocean is a vast place full of creatures of awesome size and power. When we paddle there, we are out of our element even under the best of conditions. We accept the risk that goes with entering the environment.

Most people—especially kayakers, who have the best opportunities to see marine life up close—are fascinated by whales, but we should never lose sight of the fact that they are wild animals, and it is best to avoid an area where whales are known to be. In this case Birgit and Perry knew there were whales in the vicinity and tried to watch them from a safe distance, but it seems they had no way to know that two grays would come so close until they breached.

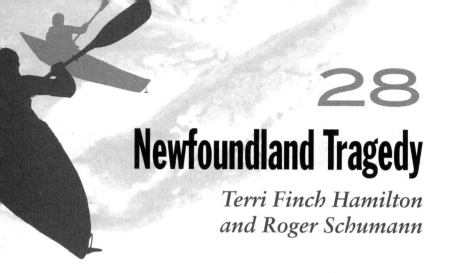

28

Newfoundland Tragedy

*Terri Finch Hamilton
and Roger Schumann*

WHAT HAPPENED
Terri Finch Hamilton

When Jim invited David, an engineer, to go kayaking to Michipicoten Island on Lake Superior, David was eager to go. He had canoed Isle Royale in Lake Superior, but this outing in 2009 would be his first big kayaking trip. They had a great time on the 11-day adventure, and at its conclusion Jim asked, "What should we do next year?" Jim wanted to go to Newfoundland. He had read an article in *Sea Kayaker* titled "Iceberg Alley, Newfoundland's Northeast Coast" (*SK*, June 2010) and was fascinated by tales of the Bay of Fundy. The bay has the largest tides on earth—a differential up to more than 40 feet—and Jim wanted to experience it. The plan was to do a three-week adventure in Newfoundland and Nova Scotia that included three kayaking trips of three to four days each.

Jim, a meticulous packer, paid special attention to his safety checklist: pump, bow line, paddle float, spare paddle, paddle leash, personal flotation device (PFD) with a whistle and compass attached, strobe light, first-aid kit, satellite emergency signal, GPS, local topographical map, and weather radio. "Making sure you have everything and knowing where you put it takes time," Jim said.

The friends drove to Nova Scotia and caught the ferry to Newfoundland. They arrived late Thursday night, June 23, 2010, at a Baie Verte campground on the northeast coast of Newfoundland. The mosquitoes were thick. David took a shower, but Jim went straight to bed. The weather radio said the next day would be clear and calm.

They woke up on Friday to a sunny morning and drove the 10 miles to Coachman's Cove. They started to pack their kayaks, a 2-hour task. Jim had a Perception Sea Lion (a 17-foot rotomolded touring kayak), and David would use Jim's Perception Scimitar (a 15-foot 6-inch rotomolded touring kayak).

The pair embarked under bright, clear, sunny skies, with just very gentle rolling waves and no wind. By lunchtime they were paddling along the open coast of the Atlantic. They followed the shore, taking in the seabirds, the green hills, and the rocky coast. They stopped to camp at Bishie Cove and found a green meadow near a waterfall where they could pitch their tents. The stream provided fresh water. They set up camp, relaxed, and made dinner. Jim was a bit of a camping gourmet, so he pooh-poohed dried, prepackaged foods in favor of fresh fish and steak. He toted a reflector oven for making pizza and brings arborio rice, dried mushrooms, and bouillon to make risotto. They built a campfire, chatted the evening away, and turned in.

Saturday morning was sunny and clear. Jim and David made breakfast and decided they enjoyed this campsite so much they would stay another night. They left their tents set up and headed out for a 1- to 2-hour paddle. They didn't load up all the gear but took just enough for lunch and safety. David wore a paddling jacket and paddling pants, both with splashproof but not watertight cuffs, and Jim wore a swimsuit and T-shirt. The air temperature was 75°F, and Jim knew that he'd be too warm in his paddling jacket and pants. Both men wore PFDs.

"We knew it was windy," Jim said later, "but the wind was coming off the shore. It was calm near shore, but the wind was churning up the water farther out."

The weather radio report said the day would be windy but clear.

"We knew that if we followed the shore, we would be protected from wind and waves. We would go paddling, have lunch, and come back. We'd stay where it wasn't dangerous. The danger was farther offshore, and we wouldn't go there."

They set out at about 11 A.M. After about 10 minutes of paddling, Jim turned around and paddled for 2 to 3 minutes back in the direction they'd come from as a test of the conditions.

"Conditions can affect you differently when you change directions. I did it to make sure we weren't being lulled into a situation where we couldn't get back to our campsite. I determined it was OK."

He and David were within shouting distance. Jim was about 150 feet out from shore, and David was about 150 feet beyond that. David's distance from shore made Jim a little nervous. They weren't close enough for any sort of discussion about the risk posed by an offshore wind, so Jim signaled to David, yelling and waving a number of times, to encourage him to come closer to where he was. He could see that he'd attracted David's attention, but David didn't come closer. Jim had seen less experienced paddlers who often were afraid of being too close to shore, afraid of waves pushing them into the rocks. He thought David might be concerned about that.

Jim knew David was out too far and already slipping out of the protection offered by the lee of the land.

"It was getting windier and the waves were bigger. He was working a lot harder to paddle than I was. In hindsight, I hadn't established enough authority that he should do what I requested of him."

It was about noon now, an hour after they'd left camp.

"David called to me and said, 'I'm going back.' He turned around and I turned around, and very quickly I noticed he'd gone over.

"When the waves are at your back, you don't know what's happening. They're pushing you and you never know quite how they'll hit you. It's as if someone comes up behind you and shoves you."

Jim paddled over to David, grabbed the bow of his kayak, flipped it upright, brought it alongside, and steadied it while David climbed in and reattached his spray skirt.

"He was in the water maybe a minute and a half. We were very fast."

In his two decades of kayaking Jim had never had anybody go over in open water before. He was pleased that the T-rescue went almost flawlessly. A few of David's belongings had fallen out of his kayak, and Jim paddled away to gather what he could: a hat, water bottle, pump. By now, both of them were farther from shore.

"The waves and the wind were pushing us out, and by the time I got to his things, David was over again. The waves had hit him and he couldn't balance."

David was in the water for a second time, and Jim did a second rescue.

"I asked, 'Are you OK?' I gave him a few instructions. I said, 'We don't want you in again.' I told him all he had to do was stay upright. Riding the waves was easily doable," he said, but David had trouble keeping his balance and soon capsized a third time.

Again, "It was like someone had pushed him from behind," Jim recalled. "He fell right over. So I went back to get him in again."

Getting David back in the boat was more of a struggle the third time. Jim had to pull him in. David was weakened by three immersions in cold water in big waves and wind. Jim noticed a gash on David's head.

"I focused on getting him back in the kayak. I saw his gear floating away, including his pump. But I couldn't get to it because I had to steady his kayak. I couldn't leave him alone."

Jim's own pump, too, had disappeared, likely during one of the rescue attempts.

"I realized neither of us could go over again. I couldn't let go of his kayak. I was holding it to keep it steady. The waves were coming at us, and we were rolling with the waves." With the kayaks in constant motion, neither David nor Jim could get his spray skirt back on his cockpit coaming, so when waves crashed over him, water filled the cockpit.

The waves were 4 to 6 feet high at this point, and the men were about a half mile from shore. David was silent, rarely talking.

"I told David, 'We're just gonna ride with this, instead of trying to paddle.' The one thing we couldn't do is tip over. We couldn't let go of each other."

Jim kept one hand on David's kayak and used his other hand to take out the SPOT Satellite Messenger from his yellow pack on deck. He had purchased the GPS-equipped device the year before, for their first trip together. It had an "OK" button to push to alert family back home they were safe, a "HELP" button for assistance, and a "911" button for a true emergency. Jim pushed the 911 button and kept his eye on it because he had a sinking feeling it wouldn't work.

The night before, when they had used the device at the campsite to send the routine OK signal to family, the light was supposed to flash green. Instead it was red, a signal that indicated it needed new batteries. They hadn't checked that before they left home. Jim had opened the SPOT device up then and saw the tag in the battery compartment that said to use AAA lithium batteries. They didn't have any. They figured they would pick some up when they returned to Coachman's Cove and their car. With their situation worsening as they drifted farther offshore, there was no reassuring green light that told him his emergency signal had been sent. Jim glumly took bearings around them.

"We were headed straight for an island way out in the distance, and I said to David, 'We're being blown to an island,' but David didn't say anything. I said, 'We're so lucky we're being blown to this island. And it's a full moon. We'll be able to see even when it gets dark.' "

Jim didn't know it then, but the island he saw in the distance was the nearest of the Horse Islands. It lay 9.25 nautical miles off the Newfoundland coast. For the next 6 hours they drifted, the island in distant view.

"My focus was entirely on staying afloat and upright. Not tipping over or taking waves over the edge." Jim watched how each wave was rolling and decided which way to lean to keep from tipping over and to prevent water from pouring into David's open cockpit. The waves had grown to 8 feet and were pushing the kayaks fast. By 6 P.M. the men were 6 to 7 miles from shore.

Jim kept holding on to David's kayak and twice talked him through bailing his kayak out with a water bottle. David never spoke and kept his eyes closed. Jim kept talking, keeping David informed about the size of the waves, the distance to the island.

"I was chattering pretty often. I don't know if I was talking for me or for him."

Jim felt strong and was confident he could get himself to the island, but he was deeply worried about his friend's condition.

Jim and David stayed rafted up until early evening, their kayaks tied together with Jim's 20-foot towline. Then the wind and waves died down, and Jim realized he might be able to paddle to try to get them to land. He asked David to hang on to his kayak to keep the two kayaks side by side now. Jim paddled on one side and used his rudder to keep on a straight course toward the island. It was slow going. Paddling on just one side and pulling David along on the other side was exhausting work. Jim started counting strokes and would do 100 strokes and then take a rest.

The pair were getting close to the island, but David was having trouble keeping his kayak steady. Jim stopped paddling and held the kayaks together as they drifted. The moon had set and it grew dark. Jim could make out the silhouette of the island and knew they were getting closer but couldn't gauge how far they still had to go to reach land.

David was unsteady, often allowing the coaming to dip low enough for water to pour into the cockpit.

"I told him, 'David, you have to sit straight. If you go over, there's nothing I can do.' " But David didn't have the strength or the balance to keep fully upright.

Jim could think of nothing but that moment. He didn't think of the island or rescue. Only of holding on to David's kayak and keeping it steady.

But each unsteady tip put more water in David's kayak. Both pumps were gone, and Jim had his hands full just keeping the kayaks together. By 2 A.M. David's cockpit was filled with water and unstable. It was harder and harder for Jim to keep it steady. David couldn't sit up straight. Water kept coming over the edge. Gradually, the kayak filled with water until it rolled over, pulling out of Jim's grasp and spilling David into the dark, 50°F sea.

It was pitch black. Jim couldn't see his friend. David's kayak was between them. Jim's mind was racing. He called to David to try to grab on but heard no response. David had been unresponsive for hours, so Jim had little hope his friend could hear him. "He didn't call to me. I couldn't see him. I couldn't hear him."

David's kayak was now about 12 feet away, and David must have been out beyond that, Jim thought. Even if he could get to him, he thought, what could he do?

"If I go in," he thought, "we're both goners."

That moment still haunts him. "What bothered me is that I should have looked for him more," he said. "But I still can't think of how I could have helped him. I went into 'I have to save myself' mode. I couldn't think of anything that I could possibly do. It's what haunts me the most."

With David now gone, Jim took a sip of water but threw up. Then he paddled toward the island, David's kayak still tied to his with the 20-foot towline. He reached the shore at 2:15 A.M.

Jim hadn't realized the island was that close. He got out of his kayak and pulled it up onto the boulder beach, clear of the water, and left it on the rocky shore, still tied to David's.

He gathered some driftwood logs, poured a can of cook-stove fuel on them, and lit a match. Cold and shivering, he collapsed next to the roaring fire. He was confused over what had just happened and filled with overwhelming grief at the loss of his friend. He had no hope that David was still alive. He finally fell asleep, shivering in the cold.

The sun woke him at 5 or 6 A.M. Jim went through the contents of both kayaks and found the GPS in the hold of David's boat. He had no real hope that the alkaline batteries in it would work in the satellite signaling device, since the label in the device's battery compartment specified "lithium batteries only," but decided to try anyway, even if it meant damaging the device. The light flashed green. It worked.

Jim didn't know how to feel. Rescue would come, but it would be too late, he knew, for David.

Neither David, an engineer, nor he had thought to try a different kind of battery. [Editor's note: On the SPOT website, www.findmespot.com, a customer's question about batteries was answered by a manufacturer representative: "SPOT highly recommends that you use only non-rechargeable Energizer Ultimate 8x AAA Lithium Batteries to achieve reliable performance. If you are in an emergency situation and you have alkaline or a different type of non-rechargeable AAA lithium battery with you, SPOT may be able to intermittently transmit messages but you may experience the low battery light and sharply degraded performance and battery life. Always carry extra Energizer Ultimate 8x AAA Lithium batteries with you."]

About 45 minutes later, a Canadian Coast Guard helicopter, having received the position coordinates sent out with the SPOT distress signal, flew to Jim's location. A Coast Guard rescue specialist was lowered by winch to assess the situation, then a basket was lowered to hoist Jim up.

Jim told the rescuers about David and how he had slipped into the water in the middle of the night. Jim didn't think his friend was still alive, but said the rescuers responded as if they would be looking to rescue a person, not recover a body. They asked Jim if he felt stable enough for them to begin a search immediately. He did. The chopper searched the water for an hour before heading to a small airfield to refuel. They had radioed ahead for a police officer to meet them there and take Jim to the police station for debriefing.

The chopper quickly departed to resume the search for David. Meanwhile, Jim was interviewed by the police and then taken to the home of the police dispatcher in Baie Verte, where her family fed him, consoled him, and put him up for the night. By late Saturday night, rescue personnel reported they had not found David's body.

On Sunday morning Jim asked the dispatcher if he could join the search. While the chopper continued its search, Jim went out on a local fisherman's boat with the boat's captain, two deck hands, and the husband of the police dispatcher who'd housed him. A large Coast Guard boat now joined the search, too, and the two boats covered the area in a systematic pattern. David's body was found and recovered early Sunday afternoon. The coroner's report would later list the cause of death as drowning.

Jim's brother-in-law flew to Newfoundland and drove back with him to Michigan. Back home, the tragedy consumed Jim. He played the details over and over in his mind, always trying to think of something he could have done differently. He wanted to talk about it with friends and family, but while his wife listened patiently and helped him work through it, everyone else seemed uncomfortable.

"People didn't know what to say. They were obviously uncomfortable. It didn't help me or them to talk about it."

Many nights he couldn't sleep. "It wasn't good at all." He would get up to read a book to try to calm his thoughts.

It did help to talk to professionals, and he consulted with two or three different psychologists. He could talk freely with them. They listened patiently, asked questions, and helped him work through it.

About eight weeks after the incident, he went out in his kayak again with several friends. It was difficult. He relived parts of the tragedy but discovered that he could still get into a kayak.

Jim believed he survived because something in his nature maintained his ability to focus and to make decisions quickly. David had not been as fortunate; the chaos of that night along with the shock and despair of the situation may have affected him in a way that sapped his strength and will. Jim discovered that you don't know how you'll act in such a life-threatening situation until you're faced with one.

In retrospect, Jim wished he had given more thought to the experience and temperament of his friend before deciding to make the trip together. He regretted that he hadn't made it more clear that he, the more experienced kayaker, was in charge, so that when he first signaled David to come in closer to shore, David would have known to comply immediately.

"I didn't clearly lay out 'I'm in charge, you have to do what I say.' That's tricky territory between friends. Until this, I had mostly gone out with young people who always did what I said. The question I think you should ask of partners is, do they add or subtract from your safety? If you realize a partner subtracts, then you'll have to do things that make up for it, to compensate. I would have kept David closer to me. He didn't have the skills to react in that situation."

He called the SPOT Messenger company to tell them what happened. He suggested they change the instructions so it didn't appear the device would work only with lithium batteries.

"In hindsight, we should have tested the equipment at home." Had they discovered the low battery charge, they would have purchased another set of lithium batteries.

Jim remained in touch with David's grown daughter, and the two of them met occasionally. It helped them both to talk about David. She, like everyone, told Jim he did everything he could, but the incident still haunted him.

"I did all I could. I've been able to put it into perspective with the knowledge that I couldn't have done any more. I think we took reasonable precautions. There was nothing daredevilish about it. Riding my bike on country roads is much more dangerous. Know who you're kayaking with. Where you see shortfalls, be aware of them. It was the human element that played out. I believe I did everything I could, I'm 99 percent sure of that. But there's that part that still wonders if there's something else I could have done. I'll always live with that."

LESSONS LEARNED
Roger Schumann

With the near misses in this book it's easy to see how lucky the paddlers involved had been, and how easily things could have turned out much worse. In this account, however, we're left instead to imagine the actual horror of a long night as the situation, and eventually David's swamped kayak, slipped slowly, slowly out of hand—until one paddler was left facing what I can only imagine must have been the toughest decision of his life.

Jim did more things right and was more prepared and better trained than many, but he was just not as lucky. And so, he was the one left haunted by sleepless nights and struggles to find peace in wondering if he did everything he could.

The most important lesson to be learned from this incident, in my mind, is a reminder of the number-one rule taught in all rescue training courses. From professional firefighters and search-and-rescue teams to basic first-aid trainees or introductory kayaking students, it is the golden rule. I first learned it as a young, rather inept EMT trainee fresh out of high school before changing career paths and getting off the ambulance before doing any real harm. I hear that golden rule echo loud and clear on the morning of the first day every time I take my required biannual update for my Wilderness First Responder certification. If it ever gets right down to it, the rule is this: Save yourself first. In this story it is one of the many decisions Jim got right. Absolutely no purpose is served by doubling down and becoming a victim yourself.

It is my belief that when friends go paddling together, outside the context of a professionally guided excursion, responsibility for personal safety ultimately falls on each individual paddler. It was David's responsibility, not Jim's, to choose to leave shore dressed and equipped as he was and without stronger rough-water paddling skills. Jim was only responsible, ultimately, for his own safety. But he was also responsible for whatever nightmares he might later have from choosing to paddle with the resources he had in those conditions and a partner who was not better prepared, and for whatever self-doubts he may carry to his grave about whether he did everything that he could to save his friend.

In my mind, Jim did do everything he was capable of doing. In addition to hauling along a bunch of safety gear, he also brought years of experience to the table. He'd taken skills courses from professionals, and he had practiced rescue skills at least annually. Because of this, he was able to rescue his friend once, twice, three times and then to struggle heroically for endless hours, deep into the night, to hang on to his buddy. He was not only more skilled and more prepared than those in some of the near misses in other chapters of this book, but also more so than many typical recreational paddlers I've met. And yet . . .

While I do believe that Jim did everything he was capable of doing given his relatively extensive amount of training and experience, he just didn't have the background necessary to be able to do some of it quite soon enough in this situation. Note that I'm making a subtle distinction here between someone doing everything he can do and someone doing everything that might be done.

My job here is to imagine what else might have been done or what might have been done differently. To do this, I draw on my levels of experience, beyond what typical recreational paddlers might think of. My perspective is not what recreational paddlers and friends typically do, but rather, as a trainer of professional guides and instructors, I think about what those paddlers do who are required to assume ultimate responsibility for others in their groups. And I hope I can offer some ideas that recreational paddlers might take from the pros when paddling with friends.

It is tempting to focus on the obvious: the low batteries in the rescue beacon or the fact that neither of the two was dressed for hours on end of immersion in 50°F water. It is not hard to imagine how a dry suit and fresh batteries in the SPOT might well have saved David's life. End of story.

But not everyone can afford dry suits and emergency beacons, and many kayakers manage to stay out of trouble without them. When I first started kayaking, and for most of the long history of the sport, such technologies didn't even exist. I think it is more interesting and ultimately more informative, then, to focus instead on the less obvious aspects of the accident. There is still something to be learned from them.

It is not hard to imagine Jim and David paddling without coming to grief, even in offshore wind conditions without dry suits and a functioning rescue beacon. Many, many kayakers do so all the time without incident. In addition, Jim's regularly practiced rescue skills—for which I most applaud him—put him well ahead of the curve of many recreational paddlers.

Often the link that breaks the chain in these sorts of mishaps involves a lack of rescue skills. But after the first capsize, Jim was quickly able to get his partner back into his boat, just as he'd practiced so many times—though, unlike in typical practice situations, his partner fell right back into the chilly water less than a minute later. Again, Jim pulled off a second, near flawless rescue, but David dumped back in the drink shortly afterward. This third time was not the charm, and in the brief time that they were doing the rescues they were being driven out into rougher water and stronger wind. Given David's inability to fend for himself in that situation and Jim not fully grasping that fact a little sooner, the pair were set adrift on a long, slow, grisly journey.

Jim showed great, big-picture awareness at the beginning of their paddle when he took the time to paddle back into the wind to make sure they could actually return in the direction they'd come. But he did miss a few subtle clues.

Let's rewind a few hours to when the pair set off from shore. A couple of small details were overlooked, the main one being what Jim himself realized in retrospect: that he had not been more emphatic when explaining the dangers of offshore winds to David. As Jim noted, it can be tricky territory between friends to try to say, "I'm in charge, you have to do what I say." But imagine that he had explained he was deeply concerned about the offshore conditions and insisted that if they were going to paddle in such conditions, they had to stay not only close to shore but close to each other. Then imagine he defined exactly what he meant by "close" in both situations. Professional guides often specify things like, "We need to stay within 100 feet of shore and within two to three boat lengths of each other." Guides typically like to position themselves between their group and any potential danger, so another specific instruction Jim might have given to David is, "And you need to stay to the shoreward side of me." If David was unwilling or unable to do this at any point, the outbound journey would have been over and they would have turned around and headed back immediately.

In lieu of this, Jim would have needed to act more quickly when he said he first "felt nervous" about how far offshore David was getting. When David chose to ignore Jim's signaling and yelling, Jim would have needed to paddle out to David immediately to insist that he paddle closer to shore or they would turn around and head back.

Another small but potentially important thing Jim might have missed was the fact that after spending a day getting used to paddling a kayak fully loaded with expedition gear, his inexperienced partner was now paddling a nearly empty kayak with relatively much less stability. Even as an experienced paddler, I've sometimes felt tippy during an expedition when first using an empty kayak for a day trip after having gotten used to the stability of a fully loaded boat.

When David capsized the first time, Jim did everything that his prior training and practice had prepared him to do, and he did it well. Mostly. More on that a little later.

But he was slow to realize his partner's lack of stability. Whether from cold water in the ears possibly causing vertigo (see "An Analysis" in Chapter 4 and "Vertigo and the Missed Roll," *SK*, Winter 1990), cold, fear, water in the boat, or whatever, once a paddling partner has capsized once, that person's stability is not likely to improve. The first time could be bad luck, but a second time in quick succession is a problem that needs immediate attention. It is important to keep your eye out for loss of balance after a partner capsizes, and give support if not after the first, then certainly after the second capsize. Waiting for a third time might not matter in many situations—unless you happen to be drifting out of the lee of shore into open water with an offshore wind and a partner who is not well dressed for extended immersion.

Digging deep into my professional rescuer's kit, there are two lesser-known rescue techniques Jim might have been able to use to get David back into the protection of shore. Imagine that Jim had been able to stabilize David immediately after the second rescue and had initiated a contact tow: where the rescued but still unstable paddler hangs on to the rescuer's kayak for support while the rescuer paddles their rafted-together kayaks. This technique was actually employed by Jim hours later in his last-ditch attempt to reach the island. Had the two men thought to use it quickly after the first or second rescue, ignoring the water bottle and David's other loose gear that was floating away, they might have been able to regain the protection of the shore, which at that point was still a mere half mile away.

While contact tows can be awkward, especially into the wind, with one paddler trying to propel two kayaks, an even lesser-known option existed. Digging deeper into the pro's toolkit, I offer the paddle-float tow. Jim had a towrope and both men had paddle floats, but they did not think to employ them beyond the usual context of a self-rescue. Jim couldn't use his towline to tow David back to shore because David would have quickly tipped over again. However, when towing an otherwise able paddler who needs stabilization, putting a paddle float on one or both of David's blades might well have allowed him to stabilize himself while Jim towed him the short distance back toward shore.

Had neither of these instructor tricks worked, the two would still have found themselves out on the water, drifting toward a distant island and cursing the dead batteries in the SPOT. But at this point, let's turn our attention to lesser gear and a seemingly inconsequential but potentially fatal mistake: In the wake of three nearly flawless rescues, they both lost their pumps.

In the glare of focusing on big-ticket items like dry suits and locator beacons, the importance of a cheap, plastic bilge pump is easy to overlook. Stowing a pump where it is easy to get to but won't float away in a capsize (such as securely under your front-deck bungees) can be crucial.

When teaching rescue classes I often see students in the heat of the moment losing hold of things like their paddles, pumps, or other gear that drifts away in a "yard sale" around the scene of a rescue. In calm-water practice sessions it is often a challenge to get people to realize how important it can be to keep hold of such things. "Hey, can you grab that for me?" they ask. Sometimes I decline to fetch their

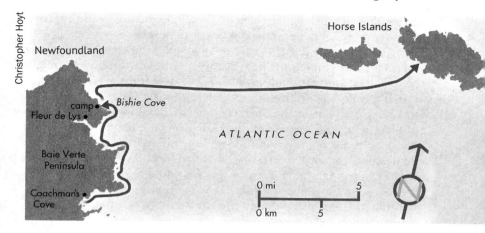

lost gear for them in hopes of driving home a teachable moment, but many typically shrug and roll their eyes—"Whatever!" In their minds I think many are pleased that they've just pulled off a successful re-entry. So what if a little gear floated away? They're back in their boats, right? Success!

So it is not hard for me to imagine, in all Jim's rescue practice sessions in relatively tame conditions, that this might not have been the first time he ever had a pump float away during a rescue. And if so, like many, he might well not have realized that in certain situations, such a seemingly unimportant oversight could end up being the difference between life and death. Somewhere during that long night, however, as David's kayak kept filling with water and getting more and more difficult to hold on to, I'm betting that (if their minds had not still been stuck on dead batteries) Jim and David would have given their kingdoms for one of the lost bilge pumps.

That, or having David's skirt in place to keep the water out. Jim doesn't recall if it had been lost or tangled up or if it had been so difficult to put back on the coaming that they gave up trying to reattach it. Some spray skirts may be inadequate for any real-life rescue scenario. If a spray skirt is too loose around the waist, or has no suspenders or improperly adjusted suspenders, it can slip off in rough conditions or during reentry. A common practice for flatwater paddlers is to wear a spray skirt over a PFD instead of under it, but a skirt worn underneath a life vest is less likely to wash off during a rescue. Having a spray skirt that fits both paddler and kayak is essential for keeping a kayak seaworthy in challenging conditions. Had David's spray skirt been in place, it would have helped keep water out of the cockpit and would in turn have kept David warmer and his boat more stable, giving them a much better chance of reaching the nearer of the Horse Islands, shortening their ordeal by critical minutes.

A contact-tow device—a footlong length of line with a carabiner on each end to attach the kayaks together by the deck lines—might have helped Jim. It could have made it easier for him to paddle the rafted kayaks toward the island. But without a spray skirt attached to keep water out of the open cockpit, this would likely have been of little help. And aside from the clear benefit a dry suit would have provided to David, had Jim followed the safety maxim to "dress for immersion" rather than dressing as he had for the air temperature, his mental state might have been clearer for a longer period of time. He was becoming hypothermic himself by the time he reached the island. But that also might have had little effect on the eventual outcome of this particular incident.

Did Jim really do everything he could with the resources he had? Most emphatically, yes.

With all the preparation, all the experience, all the precautions taken, and all the things done right, a few small errors in judgment quickly compounded into a situation beyond his control. For his part, faced with a situation that had gotten out of his control, Jim did everything he could—including risking his own life in an attempt to save his friend's. In the end, he was left with little choice except to go into "I have to save myself" mode. As callous as it may sound, this final decision, given the situation at the time he was forced to make it, was the best one he could have made. And I like to imagine, particularly for the sake of my family and loved ones, that I would have been able to muster the strength to do the same if I had been in Jim's boat.

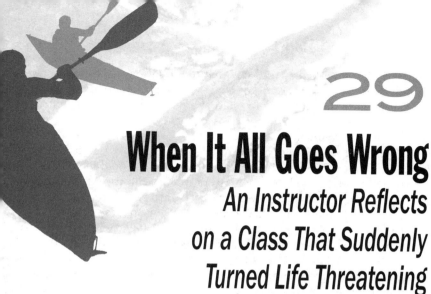

29

When It All Goes Wrong

An Instructor Reflects on a Class That Suddenly Turned Life Threatening

Sean Morley

Having to call the Coast Guard for help is perhaps every sea kayaker's worst nightmare. During more than thirty-five years and several thousands of miles of traveling on the sea, I have only once had to make that call. I knew it had all gone horribly wrong long before I found myself separated from my kayak, swimming desperately through the 6-foot surf for my paddle, which I could see just 30 yards away.

I was teaching a sea-kayak surfing class on the Oregon coast. It was day one of the 2011 Lumpy Waters Symposium, and this debacle was definitely not what I'd had in mind when I suggested launching from Happy Camp and surfing the waves in the entrance to Netarts Bay. But now we were dealing with a life-threatening scenario that could have, and should have, been avoided.

It began with a basic error of judgment, so obvious and significant that in hindsight it seems ridiculous. The decision to launch two large groups of eight students each with two instructors and attempt to surf the narrow entrance to Netarts Bay during an ebbing tide was not mine alone, but it was quickly followed and compounded by a series of bad decisions and poor leadership that was all mine. I didn't explain my plan clearly enough to my assistant instructor, Jamie, which left him unclear about his role. I helped everyone in my group get afloat, which immediately put me at the back of the group instead of up front where I needed to be. I stopped to assist one of my students who had an issue with a foot peg. By the time I finished dealing with that, I looked up and saw that the situation was already well out of hand. Students had forgotten or were ignoring my instructions and were paddling directly into the surf break without waiting for me to join the group and make a final assessment of the conditions from the deepwater channel.

The rapid domino effect of bad decisions paired with ineffective leadership immediately led to multiple capsizes. I should have blown my whistle and directed those who were still in their kayaks to paddle back to shore, but instead I went directly into rescue mode. I tried to reunite swimmers with their own kayaks, or any kayak that was nearby. I attempted to put Donna into Shay's kayak, which was obviously too small for her, while a set of waves logrolled us multiple times. Within seconds, Shay's kayak and mine were gone, swept toward shore along with my spare paddle. I reached my paddle and then chased down Shay's kayak, which had (continued page 313)

A LAPSE OF ATTENTION

Christopher Cunningham

If there had to be just one lesson to learn from this book, it would be this: To err is human. Skill, knowledge, and experience go a long way toward making safer paddlers, but even those of us who have extensive backgrounds in sea kayaking can make mistakes. Sometimes, just an off day can lead to trouble. I had one of those days a few years ago.

The wind was up. It was a nice, stiff southwesterly, a warmish wind that can kick up a good crop of waves against a beach on the south side of West Point. I had taken a new kayak—a boat that I hadn't paddled in rough water before—out to see how it performed. I paddled in the lee along the north side of the point, but the wind was strong enough that it was wrapping over the land and rippling the water even right up against the shore.

Before rounding the point, I stopped to make sure all my gear was in order and secured. I'd lost my pencil on the way out because I hadn't bothered to tether it to the waterproof notebook I carry on deck. I had a spare pencil in the cockpit behind the seat, so I paddled to within a boat length of the beach and pulled the skirt back to get the pencil. I had a hard time getting my hand past the back strap, and when I did, my neoprene gloves made it impossible to know if I'd touched the pencil. I set my paddle behind me with one blade in the water and sat on its shaft to steady the kayak as I slipped out of the cockpit and onto the aft deck. I got the pencil, but in the half minute it took to do that the breeze pushed me away from the beach another couple of boat lengths.

I thought I could slip back into the seat, butt first and then feet, but the cockpit was about an inch too short for me to get my legs tucked in. I lifted myself out of the cockpit again and sat on the aft deck. With my paddle out to the side again to stabilize the kayak, I slipped my feet into the cockpit and started to slide in, but something stopped me before I could drop down into the seat. I pulled the forward end of my spray skirt out from under me, thinking it had snagged on deck, but I was still hung up on something. I was frustrated that such simple tasks were becoming so difficult. I hadn't been in a great mood when I'd started this outing, and I was getting annoyed. I slipped into the water to check the deck. As I settled in the water, the kayak rolled toward me and came to rest on edge. I was dismayed to see the cockpit take on water, and I tried in vain to right the kayak. I realized my weight must be hanging on the boat somehow, and I found that the knot on the end of my PFD's drawstring had slipped under a deck line and jammed up against a deck fitting. I got that untangled. My spare pencil had floated out of the cockpit and I put it between my teeth before I righted the boat.

I climbed up on the aft deck again and started another reentry. I had the paddle extended on the downwind side. The drift of the kayak helped drive the blade down, but I didn't think at the time to switch the paddle to the upwind side where it would provide more support; I just felt that my reentry was oddly unstable. As I slid forward, both halves of the spare paddle I had stowed on the aft deck came with me and blocked my way into the cockpit. I drifted farther from shore and out of the lee and I could feel the wind gain strength. I was quickly heading toward rougher water. I moved back onto the aft deck again and hurried to secure the loose gear.

The cockpit was pretty well swamped. It had a lot of volume behind the seat and ahead of the foot rests—at the expense of the flotation in the end compartments—and now the kayak was weighed down with water. The cockpit coaming was awash when I sat on deck. To dump some of the water, I scooted back to the stern and twisted the kayak on edge. The bow rose, but there was not enough flotation in the stern to lift the cockpit clear of the water to drain. The bow kited downwind and pointed out over the whitecaps off shore.

I was about to drift by a motorboat anchored about 25 yards offshore. I dropped into the water, grabbed the kayak by the stern toggle, swam over to the motorboat, and took hold of its anchor line. Pausing in the water, I had a chance to regain the focus I had lost in my impatience to get on the water and my myopic search for my spare pencil. Although I still had several *(continued next page)* options for getting back in the boat and back to shore, the strange things that had happened with the PFD cord and the paddle slipping into the cockpit made me wonder if I could count on other self-rescue routines going as I would normally have expected them. I was not going to take the chance that one more fluke would make matters worse. I was wearing a wetsuit, so I was not cold and my neoprene gloves kept my hands warm. I noticed that half of my spare paddle had drifted away.

I believed that I could swim to shore if necessary, but I wasn't going to allow myself to drift beyond the motorboat into more wind and rougher water. Downwind of the motorboat, it was about a mile and a half to the next point of land.

I looked back at the beach. If people were watching me, I didn't want them to rush to my rescue. I had finally given up on the pencil, but I was still hoping to preserve my pride. I set the kayak on edge and slipped my legs into the cockpit. Using the motorboat's anchor line, I pulled myself upright. The combination of the water in the cockpit and my 200-plus pounds nearly overwhelmed the flotation provided by the bulkhead compartments, and the kayak was almost submerged. I was, however, stable enough to paddle and make headway, so I turned the bow toward the beach and paddled to shore, a mere 25 yards away. When I reached the beach, I drained the kayak and, for a moment, considered going on around the point. But I was out of pencils, short half of my spare paddle, and shockingly low on confidence.

When I got home, I called the Coast Guard about the drifting paddle half. It had my name on it, but I didn't care about getting it back—I just didn't want the Coast Guard to launch a search if a boater came across that bit of flotsam.

I think of myself as a cautious paddler—as a representative of *Sea Kayaker* it is important that I practice what the magazine preaches—and I am especially careful to keep the risks I take well within my abilities. I often paddle solo, but I always wear a wetsuit or a dry suit and don't stray far from land. It alarmed me how little space and time—25 yards and 2 to 3 minutes—it took to throw me back on my defenses. What surprised me most about the experience was not how a few quirky things had happened but how long it took me to broaden my focus from my search for a pencil to an awareness of the conditions around me. That lapse of attention may have lasted less than 2 minutes, but in that time I lost a significant part of my margin of safety. I realized that no matter how much I practice my paddling and self-rescue techniques, I cannot afford to paddle without presence of mind.

miraculously lingered nearby. I cowboy-scrambled into it only to realize it was badly damaged and sinking fast. Never mind—it would have to do. I tried to tow Donna toward the spit of sand now exposed on the southern shore. She gamely held on to my stern toggle, still cheerful but clearly anxious without her kayak.

At this point, Donna was relatively safe as we were pushed by the soup zone into the beach, but I had no idea where Shay or the rest of the students were. Richard, one of my co-instructors, appeared and took over towing Donna to shore. This allowed me to paddle back across the entrance to the lagoon that was now ebbing at an alarming rate and get reunited with my own kayak, which Mark, another co-instructor, had in tow. Scrambling out of Shay's kayak and into my own, I let go of her boat, and it was never seen again. Relieved to be back in my own boat and now able to contribute to resolving the ongoing incident, it was apparent that the situation was still deteriorating with several folks swimming and getting beaten down by the unrelenting surf. I might well have called the Coast Guard at that point if I'd had a marine radio in my possession; yet another bad decision prior to launching meant that my radio was located, useless, in my truck onshore.

For perhaps another 10 minutes I worked with Mark, Richard, and Jamie to try to resolve the situation. We directed those who were still in their boats to paddle to shore, and we performed numerous rescues and then shepherded those other kayakers toward the beach.

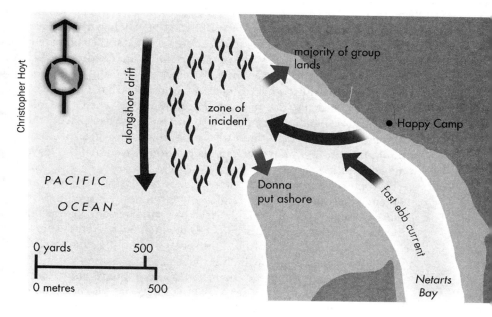

Jamie had been carrying Shay on his back deck for what must have seemed like a lifetime to both of them. Jamie was unable to reach shore because of the strong ebb. I had been told that the alongshore drift would likely be northward, so despite evidence to the contrary I continued to give Jamie bad advice on which direction he should paddle. Shay was becoming hypothermic and was clearly struggling to hang on, making Jamie's job even more challenging.

Fred, a professional photographer and superb boater, was supposed to have been shooting fun pictures of us surfing but was instead helping everyone get to safety. In a moment of clarity I asked him to paddle to shore and make a 911 emergency call. I knew we needed outside help, and I told Fred to request Jet Skis as I doubted a regular Coast Guard motor lifeboat could operate effectively in the shallow bay entrance. He didn't need to be told twice and used his prodigious paddling skills to race to shore.

In what seemed like no time at all, there were flashing lights on the beach shortly followed by Jet Skis in the surf, lifeboats offshore, and a helicopter overhead. They were all such a welcome sight despite my deep embarrassment and anger at myself for allowing things to go so wrong. I was grateful that after a truly exhausting 2 hours, everyone was safe, no one was seriously injured, and the only casualties were my ego and Shay's kayak, which remained lost at sea.

LESSONS LEARNED

Being involved in this incident certainly gave me cause to take a long, hard look at myself, my attitude to risk, and the way I go about making decisions. It also forced me to take another look at the equipment I carry and how I carry it, and to practice skills that I thought I had either mastered or had written off as gimmicks.

The incident caused me to focus my mind on what I needed to know, what I needed to do, and what I needed to have when it all goes wrong. Clearly, avoiding an emergency incident in the first place is the best approach, and without a doubt, good judgment is the most important attribute a sea kayaker can have. I don't ever intend to leave home without it again!

However, we must accept that while it is possible to avoid an emergency incident during a lifetime of paddling, the more time we spend exposed to the undeniable risks of venturing out to sea, the more likely it is that something unforeseen will happen. And the more we seek to push the limits of both ourselves and our equipment, the more likely that something will go wrong.

There are a handful of excellent books and, more recently, some great DVDs on the subject of sea kayaking safety and rescues. These add to our knowledge of what we need to know when it all goes wrong, and we support this knowledge by cultivating skills and gaining experience with professional coaching through a club, kayak school, or symposium. This chapter does not seek to replace any of the above but rather addresses a perceived gap in the training that I've received in respect to the worst-case scenario, specifically when to *make that call*. Knowing when to request outside help from the Coast Guard and what is likely to happen when you do receive help could be critical for keeping an unfortunate incident from escalating into a tragedy.

In Michael Pardy and Doug Alderson's *Handbook of Safety and Rescue* (Ragged Mountain Press, 2003), they describe our four lines of defense in sea kayak safety as:

1. Planning
2. Physical and mental skills
3. Self-rescue and assisted rescue
4. Outside rescue

With proper training, the first three can be adequately addressed and thus can significantly reduce the likelihood that we will ever need outside help. But things can, and do, go wrong. Errors of judgment can be made and medical emergencies can occur that compromise the most watertight plans and the most skillful paddlers. So we need to know when to make that call and what to do when circumstances arise that overwhelm the resources we have. Some key principles can be applied in every situation. Gordon Brown, in his most excellent *Sea Kayak: A Manual for Intermediate and Advanced Sea Kayakers* (Pesda Press, 2006), gives us a useful mnemonic, CAMERA, to guide us through an incident:

C Collect your thoughts.
A Assess the complete situation and formulate a plan.
M Manage yourself first, then the rest of the group, then any casualty who requires assistance.
E Execute plan A.
R Review the effectiveness of plan A.
A Assess plan A and modify (go to plan B) as necessary given the evolving situation.

Following this process will likely help speed up your decision making and dissuade you from leaping in before having considered all the risks. Remember, it is better to do something rather than nothing. By doing something, you will gain more information upon which to make future decisions. Sometimes doing something might mean making the decision to remain *in situ* because you need to wait for the tide, weather, or your own energy level to become more favorable.

You may cycle through the CAMERA mnemonic several times before the situation is resolved. But the key point is that before making the decision to request outside help, it is necessary not to have attempted every other avenue but merely to have considered and precluded them. Speed may be of the essence, and a decision to call for help should not be delayed by inaction or indecision. Too often individuals involved in incidents are slow to request outside help through embarrassment, ego, ignorance, or sheer panic.

Reflecting on the Netarts Bay incident, I believe there was very little panic on my part, but without a doubt I was deeply frustrated and embarrassed. My ego and belief that my own skills and those of my fellow instructors would allow us to resolve the situation almost certainly caused me to delay making that call for outside help.

A timely request will make any rescue much more likely to succeed and easier to execute, ultimately saving time, resources, and possibly lives while reducing the risk to kayakers and rescuers. An early call to the Coast Guard asking them to stand by while you deal with the situation may provide them the opportunity to locate appropriate resources and gives them a heads-up. Then you follow up this early call with either a stand-down or Mayday call as appropriate.

The challenge is to recognize the point at which we need to make the call for help. For me, it was seeing the rapid deterioration in Shay's condition and her demeanor: Grim determination had transitioned to mild panic, then to a quiet whimper. We needed to get her out of the cold water fast, and we weren't able to accomplish that without help. My concern for Shay's well-being is what overrode protecting my ego. When sea kayaking, it is not always obvious when we have lost control to the point of needing outside help. Or the point of recognition might be obvious, the way a sailor whose yacht is sinking has a clear indication of that point. All I can say is that if you are asking yourself the question, the best moment at which you should have called for help might well have already passed.

Required Equipment

The fact that at some point in our future we may have to request outside help brings us to what we need to have with us when it all goes wrong. Boating laws vary from state to state (for a list of state requirements, see www.uscgboating.org/state_boating_laws.aspx), but here in California any sea kayaker venturing onto coastal waters is required to have the following:

Life Jacket. Types III and V are best suited to paddling. Spend time swimming in your life jacket. Does it ride up, hindering your mobility and vision? Does it shift you onto your back to keep your face out of the water or do you feel unbalanced? If you become separated from your kayak, do you have what you need in your life jacket to summon help and survive? Do you have so much stuff on you that it makes it difficult or impossible to do a self-rescue in realistic conditions?

Whistle. The louder, the better. As with all distress signals, practicing the use of a whistle can be mistaken for an actual distress call. If you can find a place where you are quite sure that you won't inadvertently trigger a rescue operation, you'll find that in rough water, blowing a whistle as hard as you can takes work and can be quite exhausting. California doesn't specify what kind of audible signaling device must be carried, but a whistle is the most compact, easiest to carry, and perhaps least susceptible to malfunction. Three blasts of the whistle is commonly understood as a distress signal.

Flashlight. (For use between sunset and sunrise.) A chemical lightstick does not satisfy the regulations and can barely be seen in low visibility. It may be helpful for keeping track of others in your group, but it shouldn't be considered the equivalent of a running light such as is carried by a larger vessel. A headlamp may be useful ashore, but on open water there's not much to see and the white light will interfere with your night vision. A powerful LED (50+ lumens) handheld flashlight that can be pointed directly at an approaching vessel is most effective. Regulations state that a vessel under oars (the category closest to paddled craft) must show a white light "in sufficient time to avoid a collision." Most of the time it is best to navigate without lights, lest they impair your night vision, and to keep well clear of other vessels so you don't have to use your flashlight.

Visual Distress Signals. I carry mini rocket flares in my life jacket, plus parachute flares and red handheld flares in my day hatch. When I was separated from my kayak, only the flares I had in my PFD were available to me. To meet legal requirements, the signals must be U.S. Coast Guard–approved, readily accessible, present in the required number, and not expired. Know how to use them without having to read the instructions!

Just imagine being in need of help and not having the required equipment with you. Not only are your chances of being rescued significantly reduced, but the potential for embarrassment afterward is greatly increased. In the Netarts Bay incident, our rescuers recognized that we were appropriately equipped (except for marine radios), an indication, I think, that we appreciate the nature of the work they do.

Recommended Equipment

While not required equipment, orange smoke signals are extremely effective for daytime use.

Conditions of reduced visibility or darkness certainly make it more difficult for rescue personnel to see us. A strobe light fitted to the shoulder of your life jacket may not impede your night vision but will surely affect that of others in your group. It should not be used routinely to mark your position but be activated only if you are in need of rescue. Reflective tape on your PFD and on the blades of your paddle is a remarkably effective way to stand out if a searchlight beam sweeps over you.

Helicopters and lifeboats are fitted with radio direction finder (RDF) receivers that will lock on to your signal when you transmit using your VHF radio or pick up the signal transmitted by an emergency position-indicating radio beacon (EPIRB) or personal locator beacon (PLB). (See the sidebar "EPIRB and PLB Recommendations" in Chapter 17.)

There is no requirement for a handheld VHF marine radio, but depending on the location, a VHF might be the most effective way to call for help and is a highly recommended piece of equipment. The best place for a VHF is attached to your PFD, so get a submersible model that will still function after a capsize. For general guidance on the use of a VHF marine radio in an emergency, consult the website www.boatsafe.com/nauticalknowhow/radio.htm#emergency.

Some high-end handheld marine radios have a Digital Selective Calling (DSC) function. This allows the user to send a digital help message identifying you and including your GPS coordinates to the Coast Guard and any vessels nearby equipped with a DSC radio.

U.S. law does not require a license for you to own and operate a handheld VHF marine radio, and that is a good thing. But something for us sea kayakers to consider is that as a result, we do not, as a matter of course, have a designated call sign or registered boat name. (VHFs with digital selective calling [DCS] can send distress signals and with a nine-digit maritime mobile service identity [MMSI] number identify the VHF user.) Therefore, in an emergency, how should we clearly and succinctly explain who and what we are? I asked Paul Newman, Recreational Boating Safety Program manager for the Eleventh Coast Guard District based in Alameda, California, for his thoughts on radio protocol. Following is what he advised:

> *The best practice is to help rescuers identify you and your kayak should you lose communication during the search. You could use your name and then describe your kayak: "This is Sean Morley, last name spelled M-O-R-L-E-Y, in an 18-foot kayak with a red deck and white hull off Fort Point."*
>
> *That way, if your radio fails, we know we're looking for a red kayak with the characteristics you gave us. If we find you, we know we've found the Sean Morley we were search-*

ing for. With your position we'll calculate the set and drift so we can plot an accurate search plan.

Once we have radio communication with you we'll ask for a few more pieces of info. The rescuers will be pulling people out of the water over the gunwales of a boat and/ or hoisting them in a small basket to a helicopter. Both can be stressful situations, so we need to know about any medical issues that would affect a rescue (heart condition, excessive weight or size, seizures, limb prosthetics, etc.), whether anyone is carrying medications for an acute medical condition, and where the medication is (top left pocket of the PFD, etc.). We might need to get to these medications if the person exhibits symptoms of their medical condition.

You may be asked for a land-based point of contact—a spouse or relative—we can contact to get further info and to keep them informed. Whether or not we can recover your kayak will depend on the conditions and method of recovery. If you're picked up by a boat in calm conditions and there's enough room onboard, then maybe the kayak will be picked up too. If the seas are rough and it would hazard the rescue crew to retrieve the kayak, then we will try to mark it and leave it for the owner to arrange salvage. If you're picked up by a helicopter, the kayak will be left behind. It's always up to the owner to arrange commercial or private salvage of the vessel.

A group of kayakers in need of help can facilitate a rescue by staying together and making sure everyone has their life jacket on and snapped/zipped up. Once you can see the rescue craft, wave your paddles or arms to attract attention. They might not have seen you yet. When the rescuers approach, listen to them for directions. They are now the ones in charge, so do as they say. They'll want to handle any injuries and life-threatening situations first. Sometimes you might think you're being helpful by being proactive, but you could be complicating matters for the rescuers.

Don't just race over and clamber onto the rescue boat. Sit back and allow rescuers time to maneuver their boat into the best position for the seas and wind. If a helicopter arrives, tie down any loose gear, hats, etc., so they won't fly up in the rotor wash and hit the helicopter. The downdraft from a typical rescue helicopter can be as much as 80 mph and can create very choppy water, blow kayaks around, and frighten people in the water. The spray will make it hard to see and the noise will make it almost impossible to communicate.

Anyone not needing to be rescued should paddle away from the rotor wash and choppy water and stay together in a group, looking on from a distance. This will simplify the rescue and allow the pilot and crew to focus on the people in need of rescue. The rescuers can also keep a head count more easily if the rest of the group stays together, off to the side. In a Coast Guard helicopter rescue we will most likely have a rescue swimmer jump into the water to organize the rescue. He or she will tell you or motion to you what you need to do. You will need to get out of your kayak and into the water to be hoisted. If the rescue basket comes down, don't touch it or any trailing line until it has touched the water. It carries a strong charge of static electricity. The charge gets released when the basket or the line hits the water.

Those kayakers who do not need to be evacuated may resume their journey unless the conditions are especially hazardous. In that case they'll be asked to go ashore. You should comply quickly and land as soon as you can safely do so.

My 911 call brought a quick response from Tillamook County Sheriff's Office deputies, two ambulances from Tillamook Fire Department and Netarts-Oceanside Fire Department (who also provided the indispensable Jet Skis), as well as two Coast Guard motor lifeboats and a helicopter. I wouldn't begin to guess at the cost involved, and I wouldn't want to have to bring the expense of a rescue into the decision to call for one. Fortunately, the U.S. Coast Guard and local agencies are paid for by federal, state, and local taxes.

For kayakers, the "What-if?" game helps us prepare for unexpected emergencies. If you play the game to its extreme, the worst of the worst-case scenarios that you might imagine will involve making that call for outside help. Your practice of "What-if?" should include making mock Mayday or 911 calls so that you can more quickly and accurately identify the tipping point that puts you beyond the scope of your own resources and better prepare yourself for the rescue that you require.

Acknowledgment

The author wishes to thank Paul Newman, Recreational Boating Safety Program Manager, Eleventh Coast Guard District, and Ed Schiller, Chair, ACA Coastal Kayak Committee, for their contributions to this article.

ABOUT THE EDITOR

Christopher Cunningham has been the editor of *Sea Kayaker* magazine since 1989 and was the editor of the first *Deep Trouble* book. His
travels in small sailing, rowing, and paddling craft have covered over
7,000 miles of North American waterways. His longest paddling trip
covered 2,500 miles in four months. His accounts of his boat travels
and articles on boat building have been published in *Sea Kayaker*,
WoodenBoat, Nor'westing, and *Small Boat Journal* as well as in two
anthologies, *Oyo* and *Seekers of the Horizon.* He is the author of
*Building the Greenland Kayak: A Manual for Its Construction and
Use.* He has taught traditional kayak construction in the United States
and France. A Washington native, he makes his home in Seattle.

ABOUT THE CONTRIBUTORS

Perry Abedor has been in Baja California Sur for two years. He com-
peted with the United States Surf Team in Venezuela during the 2002–
03 season, and he currently gives surf lessons and repairs surfboards.
He enjoyed whale watching from his double kayak until it broke in
the breaching incident described in Chapter 27.

   Doug Alderson taught sea kayaking for many years. He has written four books and numerous magazine articles. While still a sea kayaking enthusiast, he is now a coxswain and training officer with the
Royal Canadian Marine Search and Rescue.

   John Andrew lives in Saint Paul, Minnesota, where he directs a
paddling school. He is an American Canoe Association Instructor
Trainer and a British Canoe Union Coach 3, Advanced Senior Instructor and Assessor. He is also a Wilderness First Responder and an
American Red Cross CPR and Community First Aid instructor.

   Robert F. Beltran, a biologist and geographer, retired in 2007. He
worked for the U.S. Environmental Protection Agency's Great Lakes
National Program Office, where he coauthored *The Great Lakes: An
Environmental Atlas and Resource Book*, a joint effort of the EPA

and Environment Canada. He and his late wife, Ronna, kayaked Lake Superior annually from 1986 until she developed cancer in 1997. Bob resumed kayaking with his new partner, Judy, in 2005. While they have found themselves to be considerably less intrepid at sea following the mishap described in Chapter 25, it seemed to clarify their priorities and has bonded them much more closely together.

Gregg Berman is an ER nurse living and playing near San Francisco. He spends time as a tide pool naturalist as well as teaching kayaking and has been an expedition leader around the United States, from the Florida Everglades to the Alaskan glaciers. Gregg is always refining his knowledge of getting into and out of "deep trouble" while playing on the California coast as a member of Neptune's Rangers: www.neptunesrangers.com.

David Boyle lives in Bath, Maine, where he has retired from his job as a civilian naval architect with the U.S. Navy. Since the incident described in Chapter 4 he no longer paddles alone. In 2003 he paddled the coast of Maine with two friends on an 18-day trip, and he has subsequently done sea kayaking trips with various friends to Croatia, Alaska, Mexico, Tasmania, Newfoundland, and Belize. He continues to enjoy exploring the Maine coast, preferably in calm conditions.

Rob Casey is a photographer and kayaker based in Seattle, Washington. He is the author of two paddling guides published by Mountaineers Books and teaches stand-up paddling through his business, Salmon Bay Paddle. Rob can often be found surfing freighter and tug waves on Puget Sound near his home.

Derek Crook has lived in Nanaimo, British Columbia, for 35 years. An avid paddler who has traveled all over the world, he has circumnavigated Vancouver Island, raced down the Yukon River, and just two days later, paddled solo from Skagway, Alaska, to Port Hardy, British Columbia, in thirty days.

Brian Day has been an avid sea kayaker since discovering the sport in the early 1990s. He has paddled extensively on Lake Michigan and Lake Superior, and his travels have included a number of crossings, the longest of which was 47 miles.

James Michael Dorsey is an explorer, award-winning author, and photographer who has traveled extensively in forty-four countries. His journeys are usually far off the beaten path to document vanishing cultures. He is also a certified marine naturalist who has kayaked, canoed, or sailed the Rim of Fire from Southern Alaska to the tip of Baja plus the California Channel Islands and Hawaii. He works annually as resident naturalist in the nursery lagoon of San Ignacio, Mexico. He is also a frequent contributor to the *Christian Science Monitor*, *Los Angeles Times*, *Wend*, *Sea Kayaker*, *Natural History*, and *Collier's*. His website is www.jamesdorsey.com.

Andrew Emlen started kayak guiding in 1998. He is currently an owner of and guide for Columbia River Kayaking (www. columbiariverkayaking.com) with partners Ginni Callahan, Mark Whitaker, Josh Phelps, Katie Vegvary, and Levi Helms. He leads kayak-based Road Scholar programs on the natural and cultural history of the lower Columbia River, which lets him pursue his passions for wildlife, history, and music in addition to paddling. Andrew lives on a small farm in Skamokawa, Washington, with his wife, two sons, two dogs, lots of chickens, and a flock of black Welsh mountain sheep.

Leif Erickson loves the outdoors and spends his spare time kayaking and mountain biking with his wife, Sherri. He participates in amateur marathon kayak races in upstate New York and has paddled Saguenay Fjord in Quebec. Presently working as an electronics technician, he hopes to start a retirement kayak-touring business. Since the rescue described in Chapter 15, he has taken kayaking courses including Paddle Canada Level 2 and has built a couple of Greenland skin-on-frame kayaks.

Ciaran Eustace, a native of Dublin, Ireland, moved to the San Francisco Bay Area in 1987 at the age of 22. He is a building contractor, married with two children, living in Sonoma County, California. He started kayaking six years ago after his wife bought him lessons as a Christmas gift, a decision she has regretted only occasionally.

Sara Francis was a U.S. Coast Guard Petty Officer 1st Class when she wrote this Coast Guard Report.

Christian Gaggia is a Puget Sound native and enjoys anything that keeps him outdoors and traveling. He is currently on land somewhere in Italy.

Gadi Goldfarb was born in Moscow, Russia, and lives in Israel, working as a software engineer. He takes full advantage of the Mediterranean for sea paddling all year-round. Prior to the Alaskan expedition, he paddled in Israel, Greece, and England, and took part in a circumnavigation of Ireland, completing 500 miles from Dublin, Ireland, to Carna. Gadi can be reached at gadi.goldfarb@gmail.com.

Gail Green and **Grant Herman** are the founders of Living Adventure, Inc., an outdoor adventure company that specializes in sea kayaking experiences on Lake Superior and the Apostle Islands National Lakeshore. Both Grant and Gail have been longtime instructor-trainer educators for the ACA, and they have paddled, guided, and taught in the Lake Superior watershed for over 30 years. They can be reached via their website: www.livingadventure.com.

George Gronseth has been a frequent contributor to *Sea Kayaker* and was the coeditor of *Deep Trouble*. He is the founder of a Seattle, Washington–based kayak instruction school and may be reached via email at kayak@kayakacademy.com.

Tim Hamilton is a fitness consultant and personal trainer living in Corpus Christi, Texas, with his wife and three children. He has paddled extensively in and around Corpus Christi Bay, the Laguna Madre, and the Gulf of Mexico, as well as several Texas rivers. He enjoys practicing rolls and surfing wind waves in his kayak.

Terri Finch Hamilton is a freelance writer and a former newspaper reporter and feature writer. She lives in Grand Rapids, Michigan, with her husband and two sons.

Susan Jewell is a wildlife biologist and environmental writer. She is the author of two Florida nature guidebooks and a book about her fieldwork experiences. She lives in Springfield, Virginia. Her website is http://naturewriter.us.

Ken Johnson first started kayaking in Chicago, Illinois, in 1987 at age 55. In 1992 he retired to Corpus Christi, Texas, to kayak full-time. He paddles almost daily and has done extended kayak trips in Florida, South Carolina, Georgia, Mississippi, Michigan, California, Washington, Canada, and Mexico. Photo albums of his many kayak trips can be viewed at http://tinyurl.com/c4hg2jd.

Aras Kriauciunas is an ACA Coastal Kayaking instructor who has been kayaking for 12 years. He enjoys paddling on Lake Superior and lists his favorite destinations as the Apostle Islands, Isle Royale, and pretty much anywhere on the Canadian side of the lake. Aras suggests that bringing along a good book and beverage will help to ensure that a high opportunity cost is maintained at all times. He can be reached at akriauciunas@yahoo.com.

Doug Lloyd is an avid paddler who lives in Victoria, British Columbia. He is a medical assessor for the provincial government and enjoys research, fact-finding, and contributing to the greater awareness and understanding of paddling safety.

Paul McMullen is a 1996 Olympian (1500-meter run) and married 41-year-old father of two living in Grand Haven, Michigan. Paul served four years with the U.S. Coast Guard as a surface swimmer and boarding officer. He started kayaking in 1997 and can be found on the water most days of the week. He is the CEO of an antibullying mobile phone app company called TruthLocker and can be reached through his website: www.truthlocker.com.

Randy Morgart works for the Federal Aviation Administration and has been kayaking since 1997 and canoeing since 1972. He is the proud grandpa of a new generation of kayakers and is vice president of the St. Louis Canoe and Kayak Club, found at http://stlcanoekayak.com.

Sean Morley is an ACA Level 5 Advanced Open Water Instructor who works for California Canoe & Kayak and lives in the San Francisco Bay Area with his young family. He is the director of the

Golden Gate Sea Kayak Symposium, supported by P&H Sea Kayaks, Kokatat Watersports Wear, and Werner Paddles. He can be contacted at sean@calkayak.com.

Colin Mullen and his longtime girlfriend, Dara, are avid kayakers who belong to three kayak clubs, one of which is a Greenland organization. They live in Hampton Bays, New York, with their four dogs. They have traveled as far as Washington State to kayak. Before the rescue described in Chapter 26, Colin was a paratrooper, advanced open water scuba diver, ACA trip leader, and coastal kayaker. The rescue encouraged him to become an ACA-certified coastal kayaking instructor and the training director of North Atlantic Canoe & Kayak, which allows him to emphasize the importance of rescue skills to both kayak students and kayak club members.

Birgit Piskor is an award-winning sculptor and landscape consultant whose evocative works add beauty and value to homes and gardens around the world. Her compelling sensuous forms explore the process of transformation and embrace the timeless beauty inherent in the constancy of impermanence. Her experience with the whales left her with an intensely visceral appreciation for the ephemeral nature of life. Her powerful new works are alive with cetaceous curves and probe the liminal space between life and death, between what was and what is yet to be—a space that is expansive and teeming with the possibility of everything. Her website is www.birgitpiskor.com.

Melesa (Hamer) Rennak, after paddling more than 5,000 miles all over North and South America, is currently just trying to keep her head above water raising two small children. The Rennak family plans to continue their water adventures when the kids are a bit more drown resistant, and they are currently on the lookout for a pair of good tandem kayaks, preferably with seat buckles.

Roger Schumann is the author of *Sea Kayak Rescue* and *Guide to Sea Kayaking Central & Northern California*, which won a National Outdoor Book Award. As the owner of Eskape Sea Kayaking school in Santa Cruz, California, he's been helping his students refine their paddling skills for over 20 years. An ACA Level 5 Instructor Trainer for Advanced Open Water, he specializes in training and certifying instructors. He leads classes, tours, and instructor workshops across the Americas from California to the Carolinas and from Baja to Brazil. He can be reached through his website at EskapeKayak.com or via email at info@eskapekayak.com.

Tore Sivertsen lives in Sisimiut, West Greenland, and for ten years worked as a helicopter pilot for a Greenland aviation service. In the winter, Tore spends his free time dog sledding, skiing, and hunting with his Greenlandic huskies. In the summer he sails, backpacks, canoes, and kayaks, which he combines with hunting and fishing. Tore, 40, is Norwegian, born in Mo i Rana in northern Norway.

Charles A. Sutherland is a medical writer, biochemist, and coastal kayaker living in Green Lane, Pennsylvania. He is an expert in respiratory and cardiovascular physiology and has been studying cold-water boating accidents since 1983. His reports have been published in several boating journals. He received a grant from the National Safe Boating Council in January 2007 to publish a cold-water boating brochure for coastal kayakers. Some 120,000 brochures were printed and distributed in the United States and Canada (www.enter.net/~skimmer/coldwater.html). A brochure pdf is available at the website free for anyone interested. He can be contacted via email at skimmer@enter.net.

Paul Thomas makes his home in Seattle, Washington, and enjoys paddling local waters and taking wilderness trips in British Columbia. He runs a commercial real estate auction company to support his paddling habit.

David Workman was raised in a small village in Mexico. He has been both a whitewater and flatwater kayaker since 1980. He plays in a classic rock band, and his spare-time activities include sailing, canoeing, hiking, motor biking, photography, adventure travel, and mountain and road biking. He works as an IT administrative assistant at Hotel Dieu Hospital in Kingston, Ontario. His website is http://davidworkman.150m.com.